THE PHILOSOPHICAL WORKS

OF

DESCARTES

RENDERED INTO ENGLISH BY

ELIZABETH S. HALDANE, C.H., LL.D.

AND

G. R. T. ROSS, M.A., D.PHIL.

IN TWO VOLUMES

VOLUME I

DOVER PUBLICATIONS, INC.

This new Dover edition first published in
1955 is an unabridged republication of the last
corrected edition of 1931. It is published through
special arrangement with Cambridge University Press

First Edition 1911
Reprinted, with corrections 1931

PREFACE

THE aim of this edition is to present to English readers all the philosophical works of Descartes which were originally intended for publication. More than one valuable translation of the treatises which give a general view of Descartes' system has already appeared. But certain others which are quite indispensable for a thorough comprehension of his views have not yet been made accessible to English readers. The chief of these are probably the "Rules for the Direction of the Understanding" and the "Passions of the Soul." As a matter of fact the "Passions of the Soul" was actually translated into English by an anonymous writer in the year 1650, but this translation is now exceedingly rare, and no other has appeared until the present time. In the "Passions" we find the full exposition of Descartes' theory that mental and physiological phenomena may be explained by simple mechanical processes. It was a completely new departure to state that such matters were capable of being interpreted thus, and one that has had a fundamental influence on the psychology and physiology of the present time.

It is also most important to mark the result of Descartes' speculations on contemporary thought; and the complete translation now presented of the "Objections" directed against the "Meditations," published together with Descartes' replies thereto, in the second volume, will enable the English reader to realize the novelty of the Cartesian doctrine, and the enormous effect it had upon European thought at the time. He will further be able to judge better of the success of Descartes' attempts to extricate himself from the difficulties which his philosophy undoubtedly contains.

The works translated here are the "Rules," the "Method," the "Meditations," with the "Objections and Replies," part of the "Principles," the "Search after Truth," the "Passions," and the "Notes." Unfortunately it has been found impossible to include Descartes' philosophical correspondence and his more specially physiological treatises, but perhaps in the not too distant future the work of the present translators will be supplemented in this direction.

The translators have used the new and complete edition of Descartes' Works which has been prepared by M. Adam and the late M. Tannery (Paris, Léopold Cerf). The translator of the "Rules for the Direction of the Understanding" has also had recourse to an edition published by Dr Artur Buchenau (Leipzig, Dürr'schen Buchhandlung 1907). Moreover his especial thanks are due to Mr W. R. Boyce Gibson, who already had a translation of the work in manuscript, for kindly permitting him to use, as he did with great profit, this previous version.

E. S. HALDANE
G. R. T. ROSS

March 1911

CONTENTS

CONTENTS

RULES FOR THE DIRECTION
OF THE MIND

"RULES FOR THE DIRECTION OF OUR INTELLIGENCE."

PREFATORY NOTE.

This seems to be the earliest of Descartes' philosophical works. The editors of the latest French edition of his works assign it to the year 1628 (*Œuvres*, edit. Adam et Tannery, Vol. x. pp. 486 sqq.), just before his removal to Holland and nine years after the idea of a new Method in philosophy first occurred to him.

The work was to have been complete in thirty-six rules falling into three parts containing twelve rules each. The first part gives the general nature of Descartes' new Method; while in the second a transition is made to its application in the field of Mathematics. Unfortunately the treatise, which was never completed, breaks off after Rule XXI, and indeed the explanation of the last three rules is also omitted. The third part was to have shown the application of the Method to the general problems of Philosophy.

The treatise was not published during the author's lifetime and appeared first in print in the *Opuscula Posthuma* published at Amsterdam in 1701. The original MS. had passed to Clerselier and was employed by Arnauld and Nicole, the authors of the Port Royal Logic, in their second edition of that work, which appeared in 1664. It appears now to be irrevocably lost. The Amsterdam edition seems to have been made from a copy left in Holland, and M. Adam has been able to collate the text with another copy (not in Descartes' handwriting) which Leibniz secured in Holland in 1670 and which still remains in the Royal Public Library of Hanover.

Much of the doctrine contained in this work will be afterwards met with in the "Method," "Meditations," etc., but there are important points in which there is a discrepancy between the earlier and later writings. More noteworthy still is the fact that there are several speculative suggestions (*e.g.* certain of those about 'simple natures') which never received further development in Descartes' philosophy.

For further information about our author's mathematical doctrine the reader is referred to his *Géometrie*, etc.

G. R. T. R.

RULES FOR THE DIRECTION OF
THE MIND[1].

RULE I.

The end of study should be to direct the mind towards the enunciation of sound and correct judgments on all matters that come before it.

Whenever men notice some similarity between two things, they are wont to ascribe to each, even in those respects in which the two differ, what they have found to be true of the other. Thus they erroneously compare the sciences, which entirely consist in the cognitive exercise of the mind, with the arts, which depend upon an exercise and disposition of the body. They see that not all the arts can be acquired by the same man, but that he who restricts himself to one, most readily becomes the best executant, since it is not so easy for the same hand to adapt itself both to agricultural operations and to harp-playing, or to the performance of several such tasks as to one alone. Hence they have held the same to be true of the sciences also, and distinguishing them from one another according to their subject matter, they have imagined that they ought to be studied separately, each in isolation from all the rest. But this is certainly wrong. For since the sciences taken all together are identical with human wisdom, which always remains one and the same, however applied to different subjects, and suffers no more differentiation proceeding from them than the light of the sun experiences from the variety of the things which it illumines, there is no need for minds to be confined at all within limits; for neither does the knowing of one truth have an effect like that of the acquisition of one art and prevent us from finding out another, it rather aids us to do so. Certainly it appears to me strange that so many people should investigate human customs with such care, the virtues of plants, the motions of the stars, the transmutations of metals, and the objects of similar sciences, while at the same time practically none bethink themselves about good understanding, or universal Wisdom, though nevertheless all other studies are to be esteemed not so much for their own value as because they contribute something to this. Consequently we are justified in bringing forward this as the first rule of all, since there is nothing more prone to turn us aside from the correct way of seeking out truth than this directing of our inquiries, not towards their general end, but towards certain special investigations. I do not here refer to perverse and censurable pursuits like empty glory or base gain; obviously counterfeit reasonings and quibbles suited to vulgar understanding open up a much more direct route to such a goal than does a sound apprehension of the truth. But I have in view even honourable and laudable pursuits, because these mislead us in a more subtle fashion. For example take our investigations of those sciences conducive to the conveniences of life or which yield that pleasure which is found in the contemplation of truth, practically the only joy in life that is complete and untroubled with any pain. There we may indeed expect to receive the legitimate fruits of scientific inquiry; but if, in the course of our study, we think of them, they frequently cause us to omit many facts which are necessary to the understanding of other matters, because they seem to be either of slight value or of little interest. Hence we must believe that all the sciences are so inter-connected, that it is much easier to study them all together than to isolate one from all the others. If, therefore, anyone wishes to search out the truth of things in serious earnest, he ought not to select one special science; for all the sciences are conjoined with each other and interdependent: he ought rather to think how to increase the natural light of reason, not for the purpose of resolving this or that difficulty of scholastic type[1], but in order that his understanding may light his will to its proper choice in all the contingencies of life. In a short time he will see with amazement that he has made much more progress than those who are eager about particular ends, and that he has not only obtained all that they desire, but even higher results than fall within his expectation.

[1] scholae.

RULE II.

Only those objects should engage our attention, to the sure and indubitable knowledge of which our mental powers[1] seem to be adequate.

Science in its entirety is true and evident cognition. He is no more learned who has doubts on many matters than the man who has never thought of them ; nay he appears to be less learned if he has formed wrong opinions on any particulars. Hence it were better not to study at all than to occupy one's self with objects of such difficulty, that, owing to our inability to distinguish true from false, we are forced to regard the doubtful as certain ; for in those matters any hope of augmenting our knowledge is exceeded by the risk of diminishing it. Thus in accordance with the above maxim we reject all such merely probable knowledge and make it a rule to trust only what is completely known and incapable of being doubted. No doubt men of education may persuade themselves that there is but little of such certain knowledge, because, forsooth, a common failing of human nature has made them deem it too easy and open to everyone, and so led them to neglect to think upon such truths ; but I nevertheless announce that there are more of these than they think—truths which suffice to give a rigorous demonstration of innumerable propositions, the discussion of which they have hitherto been unable to free from the element of probability. Further, because they have believed that it was unbecoming for a man of education to confess ignorance on any point, they have so accustomed themselves to trick out their fabricated explanations, that they have ended by gradually imposing on themselves and thus have issued them to the public as genuine.

But if we adhere closely to this rule we shall find left but few objects of legitimate study. For there is scarce any question occurring in the sciences about which talented men have not disagreed. But whenever two men come to opposite decisions about the same matter one of them at least must certainly be in the wrong, and apparently there is not even one of them who knows ; for if the reasoning of the second was sound and clear he would be able so to lay it before the other as finally to succeed in convincing *his* understanding also. Hence apparently we cannot attain to a perfect knowledge in any such case of probable opinion, for it would be rashness to hope for more than others have attained to. Con-

[1] ingenia.

sequently if we reckon correctly, of the sciences already discovered, Arithmetic and Geometry alone are left, to which the observance of this rule reduces us.

Yet we do not therefore condemn that method of philosophizing which others have already discovered and those weapons of the schoolmen, probable syllogisms, which are so well suited for polemics. They indeed give practice to the wits of youths and, producing emulation among them, act as a stimulus; and it is much better for their minds to be moulded by opinions of this sort, uncertain though they appear, as being objects of controversy among the learned, than to be left entirely to their own devices. For thus through lack of guidance they might stray into some abyss; but as long as they follow in their masters' footsteps, though they may diverge at times from the truth, they will yet certainly find a path which is at least in this respect safer, that it has been approved of by more prudent people. We ourselves rejoice that we in earlier years experienced this scholastic training; but now, being released from that oath of allegiance which bound us to our old masters, and since, as becomes our riper years, we are no longer subject to the ferule, if we wish in earnest to establish for ourselves those rules which shall aid us in scaling the heights of human knowledge, we must admit assuredly among the primary members of our catalogue that maxim which forbids us to abuse our leisure as many do, who neglect all easy quests and take up their time only with difficult matters; for they, though certainly making all sorts of subtle conjectures and elaborating most plausible arguments with great ingenuity, frequently find too late that after all their labours they have only increased the multitude of their doubts, without acquiring any knowledge whatsoever.

But now let us proceed to explain more carefully our reasons for saying, as we did a little while ago, that of all the sciences known as yet, Arithmetic and Geometry alone are free from any taint of falsity or uncertainty. We must note then that there are two ways by which we arrive at the knowledge of facts, viz. by experience and by deduction. We must further observe that while our inferences from experience[1] are frequently fallacious, deduction, or the pure illation of one thing from another, though it may be passed over, if it is not seen through[2], cannot be erroneous when performed by an

---

[1] experientias. This is a technical term used (like experimentum) for inductive arguments.

[2] si non videatur. Leibniz's ms. adds in brackets 'ea opus esse.' Tr. 'if it is not seen to be necessary.'

understanding that is in the least degree rational. And it seems to me that the operation is profited but little by those constraining bonds by means of which the Dialecticians claim to control human reason, though I do not deny that that discipline may be serviceable for other purposes. My reason for saying so is that none of the mistakes which men can make (men, I say, not beasts) are due to faulty inference ; they are caused merely by the fact that we found upon a basis of poorly comprehended experiences, or that propositions are posited which are hasty and groundless.

This furnishes us with an evident explanation of the great superiority in certitude of Arithmetic and Geometry to other sciences. The former alone deal with an object so pure and uncomplicated, that they need make no assumptions at all which experience renders uncertain, but wholly consist in the rational deduction of consequences. They are on that account much the easiest and clearest of all, and possess an object such as we require, for in them it is scarce humanly possible for anyone to err except by inadvertence. And yet we should not be surprised to find that plenty of people of their own accord prefer to apply their intelligence to other studies, or to Philosophy. The reason for this is that every person permits himself the liberty of making guesses in the matter of an obscure subject with more confidence than in one which is clear, and that it is much easier to have some vague notion about any subject, no matter what, than to arrive at the real truth about a single question however simple[1] that may be.

But one conclusion now emerges out of these considerations, viz. not, indeed, that Arithmetic and Geometry are the sole sciences to be studied, but only that in our search for the direct road towards truth we should busy ourselves with no object about which we cannot attain a certitude equal to that of the demonstrations of Arithmetic and Geometry.

Rule III.

In the subjects we propose to investigate, our inquiries should be directed, not to what others have thought[2], nor to what we ourselves conjecture, but to what we can clearly and perspicuously behold and with certainty deduce ; for knowledge is not won in any other way.

To study the writings of the ancients is right, because it is a great boon for us to be able to make use of the labours of so many

---

[1] facili.　　　　　　[2] senserint.

men; and we should do so, both in order to discover what they have correctly made out in previous ages, and also that we may inform ourselves as to what in the various sciences is still left for investigation. But yet there is a great danger lest in a too absorbed study of these works we should become infected with their errors, guard against them as we may. For it is the way of writers, whenever they have allowed themselves rashly and credulously to take up a position in any controverted matter, to try with the subtlest of arguments to compel us to go along with them. But when, on the contrary, they have happily come upon something certain and evident, in displaying it they never fail to surround it with ambiguities, fearing, it would seem, lest the simplicity of their explanation should make us respect their discovery less, or because they grudge us an open vision of the truth.

Further, supposing now that all were wholly open and candid, and never thrust upon us doubtful opinions as true, but expounded every matter in good faith, yet since scarce anything has been asserted by any one man the contrary of which has not been alleged by another, we should be eternally uncertain which of the two to believe. It would be no use to total up the testimonies in favour of each, meaning to follow that opinion which was supported by the greater number of authors; for if it is a question of difficulty that is in dispute, it is more likely that the truth would have been discovered by few than by many. But even though all these men agreed among themselves, what they teach us would not suffice for us. For we shall not, e.g. all turn out to be mathematicians though we know by heart all the proofs that others have elaborated, unless we have an intellectual talent that fits us to resolve difficulties of any kind. Neither, though we have mastered all the arguments of Plato and Aristotle, if yet we have not the capacity for passing a solid judgment on these matters, shall we become Philosophers; we should have acquired the knowledge not of a science, but of history.

I lay down the rule also, that we must wholly refrain from ever mixing up conjectures with our pronouncements on the truth of things. This warning is of no little importance. There is no stronger reason for our finding nothing in the current[1] Philosophy which is so evident and certain as not to be capable of being controverted, than the tact that the learned, not content with the recognition of what is clear and certain, in the first instance hazard the assertion of obscure and ill-comprehended theories, at which

[1] vulgari.

they have arrived merely by probable conjecture. Then afterwards they gradually attach complete credence to them, and mingling them promiscuously with what is true and evident, they finish by being unable to deduce any conclusion which does not appear to depend upon some proposition of the doubtful sort, and hence is not uncertain.

But lest we in turn should slip into the same error, we shall here take note of all those mental operations by which we are able, wholly without fear of illusion, to arrive at the knowledge of things. Now I admit only two, viz. intuition and induction.

By *intuition* I understand, not the fluctuating testimony of the senses, nor the misleading judgment that proceeds from the blundering constructions of imagination, but the conception which an unclouded and attentive mind gives us so readily and distinctly that we are wholly freed from doubt about that which we understand. Or, what comes to the same thing, *intuition* is the undoubting conception of an unclouded[1] and attentive mind, and springs from the light of reason alone; it is more certain than deduction itself, in that it is simpler, though deduction, as we have noted above, cannot by us be erroneously conducted. Thus each individual can mentally have intuition of the fact that he exists, and that he thinks; that the triangle is bounded by three lines only, the sphere by a single superficies, and so on. Facts of such a kind are far more numerous than many people think, disdaining as they do to direct their attention upon such simple matters.

But in case anyone may be put out by this new use of the term intuition[2] and of other terms which in the following pages I am similarly compelled to dissever from their current meaning, I here make the general announcement that I pay no attention to the way in which particular terms have of late been employed in the schools, because it would have been difficult to employ the same terminology while my theory was wholly different. All that I take note of is the meaning of the Latin of each word, when, in cases where an appropriate term is lacking, I wish to transfer to the vocabulary that expresses my own meaning those that I deem most suitable.

This evidence and certitude, however, which belongs to intuition, is required not only in the enunciation of propositions, but also in discursive reasoning of whatever sort. For example consider this consequence: 2 and 2 amount to the same as 3 and 1. Now we

[1] purae.
[2] 'Intuitus' is but sparingly used in Descartes' later writings.

need to see intuitively not only that 2 and 2 make **4**, and that likewise 3 and 1 make 4, but further that the third of the above statements is a necessary conclusion from these two.

Hence now we are in a position to raise the question as to why we have, besides intuition, given this supplementary method of knowing, viz. knowing by *deduction*, by which we understand all necessary inference from other facts that are known with certainty. This, however, we could not avoid, because many things are known with certainty, though not by themselves evident, but only deduced from true and known principles by the continuous and uninterrupted action of a mind[1] that has a clear vision of each step in the process. It is in a similar way that we know that the last link in a long chain is connected with the first, even though we do not take in by means of one and the same act of vision all the intermediate links on which that connection depends, but only remember that we have taken them successively under review and that each single one is united to its neighbour, from the first even to the last. Hence we distinguish this mental intuition from deduction by the fact that into the conception of the latter there enters a certain movement or succession, into that of the former there does not. Further deduction does not require an immediately presented evidence such as intuition possesses; its certitude is rather conferred upon it in some way by memory. The upshot of the matter is that it is possible to say that those propositions indeed which are immediately deduced from first principles are known now by intuition, now by deduction, i.e. in a way that differs according to our point of view. But the first principles themselves are given by intuition alone, while, on the contrary, the remote conclusions are furnished only by deduction.

These two methods are the most certain routes to knowledge, and the mind should admit no others. All the rest should be rejected as suspect of error and dangerous. But this does not prevent us from believing matters that have been divinely revealed as being more certain than our surest knowledge, since belief in these things[2], as[3] all faith in obscure matters, is an action not of our intelligence[4], but of our will. They should be heeded also since, if they have any basis in our understanding, they can and ought to be, more than all things else, discovered by one or other of the ways above-mentioned, as we hope perhaps to show at greater length on some future opportunity.

---

[1] cogitationis.   [2] 'that faith of ours,' Leibniz's MS.
[3] <ut> quaecunque est de obscuris.   [4] ingenii.

RULE IV.

There is need of a method for finding out the truth.

So blind is the curiosity by which mortals are possessed, that they often conduct their minds along unexplored routes, having no reason to hope for success, but merely being willing to risk the experiment of finding whether the truth they seek lies there. As well might a man burning with an unintelligent desire to find treasure, continuously roam the streets, seeking to find something that a passer by might have chanced to drop. This is the way in which most Chemists, many Geometricians, and Philosophers not a few prosecute their studies. I do not deny that sometimes in these wanderings they are lucky enough to find something true. But I do not allow that this argues greater industry on their part, but only better luck. But however that may be, it were far better never to think of investigating truth at all, than to do so without a method. For it is very certain that unregulated inquiries and confused reflections of this kind only confound the natural light and blind our mental powers. Those who so become accustomed to walk in darkness weaken their eye-sight so much that afterwards they cannot bear the light of day. This is confirmed by experience ; for how often do we not see that those who have never taken to letters, give a sounder and clearer decision about obvious matters than those who have spent all their time in the schools ? Moreover by a method I mean certain and simple rules, such that, if a man observe them accurately, he shall never assume what is false as true, and will never spend his mental efforts to no purpose, but will always gradually increase his knowledge and so arrive at a true understanding of all that does not surpass his powers.

These two points must be carefully noted, viz. never to assume what is false as true, and to arrive at a knowledge which takes in all things. For, if we are without the knowledge of any of the things which we are capable of understanding, that is only because we have never perceived any way to bring us to this knowledge, or because we have fallen into the contrary error. But if our method rightly explains how our mental vision should be used, so as not to fall into the contrary error, and how deduction should be discovered in order that we may arrive at the knowledge of all things, I do not see what else is needed to make it complete ; for I have already said that no science is acquired except by mental intuition or deduction. There is besides no question of extending it further in order to show how these said operations ought to be effected, because they are the most simple and primary of all. Consequently, unless our understanding were already able to employ them, it could comprehend none of the precepts of that very method, not even the simplest. But as for the other mental operations, which Dialectic does its best to direct by making use of these prior ones, they are quite useless here ; rather they are to be accounted impediments, because nothing can be added to the pure light of reason which does not in some way obscure it.

Since then the usefulness of this method is so great that without it study seems to be harmful rather than profitable, I am quite ready to believe that the greater minds of former ages had some knowledge of it, nature even conducting them to it. For the human mind has in it something that we may call divine, wherein are scattered the first germs of useful modes of thought. Consequently it often happens that however much neglected and choked by interfering studies they bear fruit of their own accord. Arithmetic and Geometry, the simplest sciences, give us an instance of this ; for we have sufficient evidence that the ancient Geometricians made use of a certain analysis which they extended to the resolution of all problems, though they grudged the secret to posterity. At the present day also there flourishes a certain kind of Arithmetic, called Algebra, which designs to effect, when dealing with numbers, what the ancients achieved in the matter of figures. These two methods are nothing else than the spontaneous fruit sprung from the inborn principles of the discipline here in question ; and I do not wonder that these sciences with their very simple subject matter[1] should have yielded results so much more satisfactory than others in which greater obstructions choke all growth. But even in the latter case, if only we take care to cultivate them assiduously, fruits will certainly be able to come to full maturity.

This is the chief result which I have had in view in writing this treatise. For I should not think much of these rules, if they had no utility save for the solution of the empty problems with which Logicians and Geometers have been wont to beguile their leisure ; my only achievement thus would have seemed to be an ability to argue about trifles more subtly than others. Further, though much

[1] objecta.

mention is here made of numbers and figures, because no other sciences furnish us with illustrations of such self-evidence and certainty, the reader who follows my drift with sufficient attention will easily see that nothing is less in my mind than ordinary Mathematics, and that I am expounding quite another science, of which these illustrations are rather the outer husk than the constituents. Such a science should contain the primary rudiments of human reason, and its province ought to extend to the eliciting of true results in every subject. To speak freely, I am convinced that it is a more powerful instrument of knowledge than any other that has been bequeathed to us by human agency, as being the source of all others. But as for the outer covering I mentioned, I mean not to employ it to cover up and conceal my method for the purpose of warding off the vulgar; rather I hope so to clothe and embellish it that I may make it more suitable for presentation to the human mind.

When first I applied my mind to Mathematics I read straight away most of what is usually given by the mathematical writers, and I paid special attention to Arithmetic and Geometry, because they were said to be the simplest and so to speak the way to all the rest. But in neither case did I then meet with authors who fully satisfied me. I did indeed learn in their works many propositions about numbers which I found on calculation to be true. As to figures, they in a sense exhibited to my eyes a great number of truths and drew conclusions from certain consequences. But they did not seem to make it sufficiently plain to the mind itself why those things are so, and how they discovered them. Consequently I was not surprised that many people, even of talent and scholarship, should, after glancing at these sciences, have either given them up as being empty and childish or, taking them to be very difficult and intricate, been deterred at the very outset from learning them. For really there is nothing more futile than to busy one's self with bare numbers and imaginary figures in such a way as to appear to rest content with such trifles, and so to resort to those superficial demonstrations, which are discovered more frequently by chance than by skill, and are a matter more of the eyes and the imagination than of the understanding, that in a sense one ceases to make use of one's reason. I might add that there is no more intricate task than that of solving by this method of proof new difficulties that arise, involved as they are with numerical confusions. But when I afterwards bethought myself how it could be that the earliest pioneers of Philosophy in bygone ages refused to admit to the study of wisdom any one who was not versed in Mathematics, evidently believing that this was the easiest and most indispensable mental exercise and preparation for laying hold of other more important sciences, I was confirmed in my suspicion that they had knowledge of a species of Mathematics very different from that which passes current in our time. I do not indeed imagine that they had a perfect knowledge of it, for they plainly show how little advanced they were by the insensate rejoicings they display and the pompous thanksgivings[1] they offer for the most trifling discoveries. I am not shaken in my opinion by the fact that historians make a great deal of certain machines of theirs. Possibly these machines were quite simple, and yet the ignorant and wonder-loving multitude might easily have lauded them as miraculous. But I am convinced that certain primary germs of truth implanted by nature in human minds—though in our case the daily reading and hearing of innumerable diverse errors stifle them —had a very great vitality in that rude and unsophisticated age of the ancient world. Thus the same mental illumination which let them see that virtue was to be preferred to pleasure, and honour to utility, although they knew not why this was so, made them recognize true notions in Philosophy and Mathematics, although they were not yet able thoroughly to grasp these sciences. Indeed I seem to recognize certain traces of this true Mathematics in Pappus and Diophantus, who though not belonging to the earliest age, yet lived many centuries before our own times. But my opinion is that these writers then with a sort of low cunning, deplorable indeed, suppressed this knowledge. Possibly they acted just as many inventors are known to have done in the case of their discoveries, i.e. they feared that their method being so easy and simple would become cheapened on being divulged, and they preferred to exhibit in its place certain barren truths, deductively demonstrated with show enough of ingenuity, as the results of their art, in order to win from us our admiration for these achievements, rather than to disclose to us that method itself which would have wholly annulled the admiration accorded. Finally there have been certain men of talent who in the present age have tried to revive this same art. For it seems to be precisely that science known by the barbarous name Algebra, if only we could extricate it from that vast array of numbers and inexplicable figures by which it is overwhelmed, so that it might display the clearness and simplicity which, we

---

[1] *sacrificia.*

imagine, ought to exist in a genuine Mathematics. It was these reflections that recalled me from the particular studies of Arithmetic and Geometry to a general investigation of Mathematics, and thereupon I sought to determine what precisely was universally meant by that term, and why not only the above mentioned sciences, but also Astronomy, Music, Optics, Mechanics and several others are styled parts of Mathematics. Here indeed it is not enough to look to the origin of the word ; for since the name 'Mathematics' means exactly the same thing as 'scientific study[1],' these other branches could, with as much right as Geometry itself, be called Mathematics. Yet we see that almost anyone who has had the slightest schooling, can easily distinguish what relates to Mathematics in any question from that which belongs to the other sciences. But as I considered the matter carefully it gradually came to light that all those matters only were referred to Mathematics in which order and measurement are investigated, and that it makes no difference whether it be in numbers, figures, stars, sounds or any other object that the question of measurement arises. I saw consequently that there must be some general science to explain that element as a whole which gives rise to problems about order and measurement, restricted as these are to no special subject matter. This, I perceived, was called 'Universal Mathematics,' not a far fetched designation, but one of long standing which has passed into current use, because in this science is contained everything on account of which the others are called parts of Mathematics. We can see how much it excels in utility and simplicity the sciences subordinate to it, by the fact that it can deal with all the objects of which they have cognizance and many more besides, and that any difficulties it contains are found in them as well, added to the fact that in them fresh difficulties arise due to their special subject matter which in it do not exist. But now how comes it that though everyone knows the name of this science and understands what is its province even without studying it attentively, so many people laboriously pursue the other dependent sciences, and no one cares to master this one ? I should marvel indeed were I not aware that everyone thinks it to be so very easy, and had I not long since observed that the human mind passes over what it thinks it can easily accomplish, and hastens straight away to new and more imposing occupations.

I, however, conscious as I am of my inadequacy, have resolved

---

[1] disciplina.

that in my investigation into truth I shall follow obstinately such an order as will require me first to start with what is simplest and easiest, and never permit me to proceed farther until in the first sphere there seems to be nothing further to be done.   This is why up to the present time to the best of my ability I have made a study of this universal Mathematics ; consequently I believe that when I go on to deal in their turn with more profound sciences, as I hope to do soon, my efforts will not be premature.   But before I make this transition I shall try to bring together and arrange in an orderly manner, the facts which in my previous studies I have noted as being more worthy of attention.   Thus I hope both that at a future date, when through advancing years my memory is enfeebled, I shall, if need be, conveniently be able to recall them by looking in this little book, and that having now disburdened my memory of them I may be free to concentrate my mind on my future studies.

RULE V

Method consists entirely in the order and disposition of the objects towards which our mental vision must be directed if we would find out any truth.   We shall comply with it exactly if we reduce involved and obscure propositions step by step to those that are simpler, and then starting with the intuitive apprehension of all those that are absolutely simple, attempt to ascend to the knowledge of all others by precisely similar steps.

In this alone lies the sum of all human endeavour, and he who would approach the investigation of truth must hold to this rule as closely as he who enters the labyrinth must follow the thread which guided Theseus.   But many people either do not reflect on the precept at all, or ignore it altogether, or presume not to need it. Consequently they often investigate the most difficult questions with so little regard to order, that, to my mind, they act like a man who should attempt to leap with one bound from the base to the summit of a house, either making no account of the ladders provided for his ascent or not noticing them.   It is thus that all Astrologers behave, who, though in ignorance of the nature of the heavens, and even without having made proper observations of the movements of the heavenly bodies, expect to be able to indicate their effects.   This is also what many do who study Mechanics apart from Physics, and rashly set about devising new instruments for producing motion.

Along with them go also those Philosophers who, neglecting experience, imagine that truth will spring from their brain like Pallas[1] from the head of Zeus[2].

Now it is obvious that all such people violate the present rule. But since the order here required is often so obscure and intricate that not everyone can make it out, they can scarcely avoid error unless they diligently observe what is laid down in the following proposition.

RULE VI.

In order to separate out what is quite simple from what is complex, and to arrange these matters methodically, we ought, in the case of every series in which we have deduced certain facts the one from the other, to notice which fact is simple, and to mark the interval, greater, less, or equal, which separates all the others from this.

Although this proposition seems to teach nothing very new, it contains, nevertheless, the chief secret of method, and none in the whole of this treatise is of greater utility. For it tells us that all facts can be arranged in certain series, not indeed in the sense of being referred to some ontological genus such as the categories employed by Philosophers in their classification, but in so far as certain truths can be known from others; and thus, whenever a difficulty occurs we are able at once to perceive whether it will be profitable to examine certain others first, and which, and in what order.

Further, in order to do that correctly, we must note first that for the purpose of our procedure, which does not regard things as isolated realities[3], but compares them with one another in order to discover the dependence in knowledge of one upon the other, all things can be said to be either absolute or relative.

I call that absolute which contains within itself the pure and simple essence of which we are in quest. Thus the term will be applicable to whatever is considered as being independent, or a cause, or simple, universal, one, equal, like, straight, and so forth; and the absolute I call the simplest and the easiest of all, so that we can make use of it in the solution of questions.

But the relative is that which, while participating in the same nature, or at least sharing in it to some degree which enables us to relate it to the absolute and to deduce it from that by a chain of

[1] Minerva.   [2] Jovis.   [3] naturas.

operations, involves in addition something else in its concept which I call relativity[1]. Examples of this are found in whatever is said to be dependent, or an effect, composite, particular, many, unequal, unlike, oblique, etc. These relatives are the further removed from the absolute, in proportion as they contain more elements of relativity subordinate the one to the other. We state in this rule that these should all be distinguished and their correlative connection and natural order so observed, that we may be able by traversing all the intermediate steps to proceed from the ·most remote to that which is in the highest degree absolute.

Herein lies the secret of this whole method, that in all things we should diligently mark that which is most absolute. For some things are from one point of view more absolute than others, but from a different standpoint are more relative. Thus though the universal is more absolute than the particular because its essence is simpler, yet it can be held to be more relative than the latter, because it depends upon individuals for its existence, and so on. Certain things likewise are truly more absolute than others, but yet are not the most absolute of all. Thus relatively to individuals, species is something absolute, but contrasted with genus it is relative. So too, among things that can be measured, extension is something absolute, but among the various aspects of extension[2] it is length that is absolute, and so on. Finally also, in order to bring out more clearly that we are considering here not the nature of each thing taken in isolation, but the series involved in knowing them, we have purposely enumerated cause and equality among our absolutes, though the nature of these terms is really relative. For though Philosophers make cause and effect correlative, we find that here even, if we ask what the effect is, we must first know the cause and not conversely. Equals too mutually imply one another, but we can know unequals only by comparing them with equals and not *per contra*.

Secondly we must note that there are but few pure and simple essences[3], which either our experiences or some sort of light innate in us enable us to behold as primary and existing *per se*, not as depending on any others. These we say should be carefully noticed, for they are just those facts which we have called the simplest in any single series. All the others can only be perceived as deductions from these, either immediate and proximate, or not to be

---

[1] respectus.   [2] extensiones.   [3] naturas.

attained save by two or three or more acts of inference. The number of these acts should be noted in order that we may perceive whether the facts are separated from the primary and simplest proposition by a greater or smaller number of steps. And so pronounced is everywhere the inter-connection of ground and consequence, which gives rise, in the objects to be examined, to those series to which every inquiry must be reduced, that it can be investigated by a sure method. But because it is not easy to make a review of them all, and besides, since they have not so much to be kept in the memory as to be detected by a sort of mental penetration, we must seek for something which will so mould our intelligence as to let it perceive these connected sequences immediately whenever it needs to do so. For this purpose I have found nothing so effectual as to accustom ourselves to turn our attention with a sort of penetrative insight[1] on the very minutest of the facts which we have already discovered.

Finally we must in the third place note that our inquiry ought not to start with the investigation of difficult matters. Rather, before setting out to attack any definite problem, it behoves us first, without making any selection, to assemble those truths that are obvious as they present themselves to us, and afterwards, proceeding step by step, to inquire whether any others can be deduced from these, and again any others from these conclusions and so on, in order. This done, we should attentively think over the truths we have discovered and mark with diligence the reasons why we have been able to detect some more easily than others, and which these are. Thus, when we come to attack some definite problem we shall be able to judge what previous questions it were best to settle first. For example, if it comes into my thought that the number 6 is twice 3, I may then ask what is twice 6, viz. 12; again, perhaps I seek for the double of this, viz. 24, and again of this, viz. 48. Thus I may easily deduce that there is the same proportion between 3 and 6, as between 6 and 12, and likewise 12 and 24, and so on, and hence that the numbers 3, 6, 12, 24, 48, etc. are in continued proportion. But though these facts are all so clear as to seem almost childish, I am now able by attentive reflection to understand what is the form involved by all questions that can be propounded about the proportions or relations[2] of things, and the order in which they should be investigated; and this discovery embraces the sum of the entire science of Pure Mathematics.

[1] cum quadam sagacitate.   [2] habitudines.

For first I perceive that it was not more difficult to discover the double of six than that of three; and that equally in all cases, when we have found a proportion between any two magnitudes, we can find innumerable others which have the same proportion between them. So too there is no increase of difficulty, if three, or four, or more of such magnitudes are sought for, because each has to be found separately and without any relation to the others. But next I notice that though, when the magnitudes 3 and 6 are given, one can easily find a third in continued proportion, viz. 12, it is yet not equally easy, when the two extremes, 3 and 12, are given, to find the mean proportional, viz. 6. When we look into the reason for this, it is clear that here we have a type of difficulty quite different from the former; for, in order to find the mean proportional, we must at the same time attend to the two extremes and to the proportion which exists between these two in order to discover a new ratio by dividing the previous one; and this is a very different thing from finding a third term in continued proportion with two given numbers. I go forward likewise and examine whether, when the numbers 3 and 24 were given, it would have been equally easy to determine one of the two intermediate proportionals, viz. 6 and 12. But here still another sort of difficulty arises more involved than the previous ones, for on this occasion we have to attend not to one or two things only but to three, in order to discover the fourth. We may go still further and inquire whether if only 3 and 48 had been given it would have been still more difficult to discover one of the three mean proportionals, viz. 6, 12, and 24. At the first blush this indeed appears to be so; but immediately afterwards it comes to mind that this difficulty can be split up and lessened, if first of all we ask only for the mean proportional between 3 and 48, viz. 12, and then seek for the other mean proportional between 3 and 12, viz. 6, and the other between 12 and 48, viz. 24. Thus we have reduced the problem to the difficulty of the second type shown above.

These illustrations further lead me to note that the quest for knowledge about the same thing can traverse different routes, the one much more difficult and obscure than the other. Thus to find these four continued proportionals, 3, 6, 12, and 24, if two consecutive numbers be assumed, e.g. 3 and 6, or 6 and 12, or 12 and 24, in order that we may discover the others, our task will be easy. In this case we shall say that the proposition to be discovered is directly examined. But if the two numbers given are alternates, like 3 and 12, or 6 and 24, which are to lead us to the discovery of the others, then we shall call this an indirect investigation of the first mode. Likewise if we are given two extremes like 3 and 24, in order to find out from these the intermediates 6 and 12, the investigation will be indirect and of the second mode. Thus I should be able to proceed further and deduce many other results from this example ; but these will be sufficient, if the reader follows my meaning when I say that a proposition is directly deduced, or indirectly, and will reflect that from a knowledge of each of these matters that are simplest and primary, much may be discovered in other sciences by those who bring to them attentive thought and a power of sagacious analysis.

RULE VII.

If we wish our science to be complete, those matters which promote the end we have in view must one and all be scrutinized by a movement of thought which is continuous and nowhere interrupted ; they must also be included in an enumeration which is both adequate and methodical.

It is necessary to obey the injunctions of this rule if we hope to gain admission among the certain truths for those which, we have declared above, are not immediate deductions from primary and self-evident principles. For this deduction frequently involves such a long series of transitions from ground to consequent that when we come to the conclusion we have difficulty in recalling the whole of the route by which we have arrived at it. This is why I say that there must be a continuous movement of thought to make good this weakness of the memory. Thus, e.g. if I have first found out by separate mental operations what the relation is between the magnitudes A and B, then what between B and C, between C and D, and finally between D and E, that does not entail my seeing what the relation is between A and E, nor can the truths previously learnt give me a precise knowledge of it unless I recall them all. To remedy this I would run them over from time to time, keeping the imagination moving continuously in such a way that while it is intuitively perceiving each fact it simultaneously passes on to the next ; and this I would do until I had learned to pass from the first to the last so quickly, that no stage in the process was left to the care of the memory, but I seemed to have the whole in intuition before me at the same time. This method will both relieve the memory, diminish the sluggishness of our thinking, and definitely enlarge our mental capacity.

But we must add that this movement should nowhere be interrupted. Often people who attempt to deduce a conclusion too quickly and from remote principles do not trace the whole chain of intermediate conclusions with sufficient accuracy to prevent them from passing over many steps without due consideration. But it is certain that wherever the smallest link is left out the chain is broken and the whole of the certainty of the conclusion falls to the ground.

Here we maintain that an enumeration [of the steps in a proof] **is** required as well, if we wish to make our science complete. For resolving most problems other precepts are profitable, but enumeration alone will secure our always passing a true and certain judgment on whatsoever engages our attention ; by means of it nothing at all will escape us, but we shall evidently have some knowledge of every step.

This enumeration or induction is thus a review or inventory of all those matters that have a bearing on the problem raised, which is so thorough and accurate that by its means we can clearly and with confidence conclude that we have omitted nothing by mistake. Consequently as often as we have employed it, if the problem defies us, we shall at least be wiser in this respect, viz. that we are quite certain that we know of no way of resolving it. If it chance, as often it does, that we have been able to scan all the routes leading to it which lie open to the human intelligence, we shall be entitled boldly to assert that the solution of the problem lies outside the reach of human knowledge.

Furthermore we must note that by adequate enumeration or induction is only meant that method by which we may attain surer conclusions than by any other type of proof, with the exception of simple intuition. But when the knowledge of some matter cannot be reduced to this, we must cast aside all syllogistic fetters and employ induction, the only method left us, but one in which all confidence should be reposed. For whenever single facts have been immediately deduced the one from the other, they have been already reduced, if the inference was evident, to a true intuition. But if we infer any single thing from various and disconnected facts, often our intellectual capacity is not so great as to be able to embrace them all in a single intuition ; in which case our mind should be content with the certitude attaching to this operation. It is in precisely similar fashion that though we cannot with one single gaze distinguish all the links of a lengthy chain, yet if we have seen the connection of each with its neighbour, we shall be entitled to say that we have seen how the first is connected with the last.

I have declared that this operation ought to be adequate, because it is often in danger of being defective and consequently exposed to error. For sometimes, even though in our enumeration we scrutinize many facts which are highly evident, yet if we omit the smallest step the chain is broken and the whole of the certitude of the conclusion falls to the ground. Sometimes also, even though all the facts are included in an accurate enumeration, the single steps are not distinguished from one another, and our knowledge of them all is thus only confused.

Further, while now the enumeration ought to be complete, now distinct, there are times when it need have neither of these characters ; it was for this reason that I said only that it should be adequate. For if I want to prove by enumeration how many genera there are of corporeal things, or of those that in any way fall under the senses, I shall not assert that they are just so many and no more, unless I previously have become aware that I have included them all in my enumeration, and have distinguished them each separately from all the others. But if in the same way I wish to prove that the rational soul is not corporeal, I do not need a complete enumeration ; it will be sufficient to include all bodies in certain collections in such a way as to be able to demonstrate that the rational soul has nothing to do with any of these. If, finally, I wish to show by enumeration that the area of a circle is greater than the area of all other figures whose perimeter is equal, there is no need for me to call in review all other figures ; it is enough to demonstrate this of certain others in particular, in order to get thence by induction[1] the same conclusion about all the others.

I added also that the enumeration ought to be methodical. This is both because we have no more serviceable remedy for the defects already instanced, than to scan all things in an orderly manner ; and also because it often happens that if each single matter which concerns the quest in hand were to be investigated separately, no man's life would be long enough for the purpose, whether because they are far too many, or because it would chance that the same things had to be repeated too often. But if all these facts are arranged in the best order, they will for the most part be reduced to

[1] This seems to be a different sense of the word 'inductio' from that above.

determinate classes, out of which it will be sufficient to take one example for exact inspection, or some one feature in a single case, or certain things rather than others, or at least we shall never have to waste our time in traversing the same ground twice. The advantage of this course is so great that often many particulars can, owing to a well devised arrangement, be gone over in a short space of time and with little trouble, though at first view the matter looked immense.

But this order which we employ in our enumerations can for the most part be varied and depends upon each man's judgment. For this reason, if we would elaborate it in our thought with greater penetration, we must remember what was said in our fifth proposition[1]. There are also many of the trivial things of man's devising, in the discovery of which the whole method lies in the disposal of this order. Thus if you wish to construct a perfect anagram by the transposition of the letters of a name, there is no need to pass from the easy to the difficult, nor to distinguish absolute from relative. Here there is no place for these operations; it will be sufficient to adopt an order to be followed in the transpositions of the letters which we are to examine, such that the same arrangements are never handled twice over. The total number of transpositions should, e.g. be split up into definite classes, so that it may immediately appear in which there is the best hope of finding what is sought. In this way the task is often not tedious but merely child's play.

However, these three propositions should not be separated, because for the most part we have to think of them together, and all equally tend towards the perfecting of our method. There was no great reason for treating one before the other, and we have expounded them but briefly here. The reason for this is that in the rest of the treatise we have practically nothing else left for consideration. Therefore we shall then exhibit in detail what here we have brought together in a general way.

Rule VIII.

If in the matters to be examined we come to a step in the series of which our understanding is not sufficiently well able to have an intuitive cognition, we must stop short there. We must make no attempt to examine what follows; thus we shall spare ourselves superfluous labour.

[1] Cf. p. 14

The three preceding rules prescribe and explain the order to be followed. The present rule, on the other hand, shows when it is wholly necessary and when it is merely useful. Thus it is necessary to examine whatever constitutes a single step in that series, by which we pass from relative to absolute, or conversely, before discussing what follows from it. But if, as often happens, many things pertain to the same step, though it is indeed always profitable to review them in order, in this case we are not forced to apply our method of observation so strictly and rigidly. Frequently it is permissible to proceed farther, even though we have not clear knowledge of all the facts it involves, but know only a few or a single one of them.

This rule is a necessary consequence of the reasons brought forward in support of the second. But it must not be thought that the present rule contributes nothing fresh towards the advancement of learning, though it seems only to bid us refrain from further discussion, and apparently does not unfold any truth. For beginners, indeed, it has no further value than to teach them how not to waste time, and it employs nearly the same arguments in doing so as Rule II. But it shows those who have perfectly mastered the seven preceding maxims, how in the pursuit of any science so to satisfy themselves as not to desire anything further. For the man who faithfully complies with the former rules in the solution of any difficulty, and yet by the present rule is bidden desist at a certain point, will then know for certainty that no amount of application will enable him to attain to the knowledge desired, and that not owing to a defect in his intelligence, but because the nature of the problem itself, or the fact that he is human, prevents him. But this knowledge is not the less science than that which reveals the nature of the thing itself; in fact he would seem to have some mental defect who should extend his curiosity farther.

But what we have been saying must be illustrated by one or two examples. If, for example, one who studies only Mathematics were to seek to find that curve which in dioptrics is called the anaclastic, that from which parallel rays are so refracted that after the refraction they all meet in one point,—it will be easy to see, by applying Rules V and VI, that the determination of this line depends upon the relation which the angles of refraction bear to the angles of incidence. But because he is unable to discover this, since it is a matter not of Mathematics but of Physics, he is here forced to pause at the threshold. Nor will it avail him to try and learn this from the Philosophers or to gather it from experience; for this would be to break Rule III. Furthermore this proposition is both composite and relative; but in the proper place we shall show that experience is unambiguous only when dealing with the wholly simple and absolute. Again, it will be vain for him to assume some relation or other as being that which prevails between such angles, and conjecture that this is the truest to fact; for in that case he would be on the track not of the anaclastic, but merely of that curve which could be deduced from his assumption.

If, however, a man who does not confine his studies to Mathematics, but, in accordance with the first rule, tries to discover the truth on all points, meets with the same difficulty, he will find in addition that this ratio between the angles of incidence and of refraction depends upon changes in their relation produced by varying the medium. Again these changes depend upon the manner in which the ray of light traverses the whole transparent body; while the knowledge of the way in which the light thus passes through presupposes a knowledge of the nature of the action of light, to understand which finally we must know what a natural potency is in general, this last being the most absolute term in the whole series in question. When, therefore, by a mental intuition he has clearly comprehended the nature of this, he will, in compliance with Rule V, proceed backwards by the same steps. And if when he comes to the second step he is unable straightway to determine the nature of light, he will, in accordance with the seventh rule, enumerate all the other natural potencies, in order that the knowledge of some other of them may help him, at least by analogy (of which more anon), to understand this. This done, he will ask how the ray traverses the whole of the transparent body, and will so follow out the other points methodically, that at last he will arrive at the anaclastic itself. Though this has long defied the efforts of many inquirers, I see no reason why a man who fully carried out our method should fail to arrive at a convincing knowledge of the matter.

But let us give the most splendid example of all. If a man proposes to himself the problem of examining all the truths for the knowledge of which human reason suffices—and I think that this is a task which should be undertaken once at least in his life by every person who seriously endeavours to attain equilibrium[1] of thought—, he will, by the rules given above, certainly discover that nothing can be known prior to the understanding, since the knowledge of all

---

[1] bonam mentem.

things else depends upon this and not conversely. Then, when he has clearly grasped all those things which follow proximately on the knowledge of the naked understanding, he will enumerate among other things whatever instruments of thought we have other than the understanding ; and these are only two, viz. imagination and sense. He will therefore devote all his energies to the distinguishing and examining of these three modes of cognition, and seeing that in the strict sense truth and falsity can be a matter of the understanding alone, though often it derives its origin from the other two faculties, he will attend carefully to every source of deception in order that he may be on his guard. He will also enumerate exactly all the ways leading to truth which lie open to us, in order that he may follow the right way. They are not so many that they cannot all be easily discovered and embraced in an adequate enumeration. And though this will seem marvellous and incredible to the inexpert, as soon as in each matter he has distinguished those cognitions which only fill and embellish the memory, from those which cause one to be deemed really more instructed, which it will be easy for him to do ......[1] ; he will feel assured that any absence of further knowledge is not due to lack of intelligence or of skill, and that nothing at all can be known by anyone else which he is not capable of knowing, provided only that he gives to it his utmost mental application. And though many problems may present themselves, from the solution of which this rule prohibits him, yet because he will clearly perceive that they pass the limits of human intelligence, he will deem that he is not the more ignorant on that account; rather, if he is reasonable, this very knowledge, that the solution can be discovered by no one, will abundantly satisfy his curiosity.

But lest we should always be uncertain as to the powers of the mind, and in order that we may not labour wrongly and at random before we set ourselves to think out things in detail, we ought once in our life to inquire diligently what the thoughts are of which the human mind is capable. In order the better to attain this end we ought, when two sets of inquiries are equally simple, to choose the more useful.

This method of ours resembles indeed those devices employed by the mechanical crafts, which do not need the aid of anything outside of them, but themselves supply the directions for making their own instruments. Thus if a man wished to practise any one of them,

---

[1] The Amsterdam ed. of 1701 indicates an omission here.

e.g. the craft of a smith, and were destitute of all instruments, he would be forced to use at first a hard stone or a rough lump of iron as an anvil, take a piece of rock in place of a hammer, make pieces of wood serve as tongs, and provide himself with other such tools as necessity required. Thus equipped, he would not then at once attempt to forge swords or helmets or any manufactured article of iron for others to use. He would first of all fashion hammer, anvil, tongs, and the other tools useful for himself. This example teaches us that, since thus at the outset we have been able to discover only some rough precepts, apparently the innate possession of our mind, rather than the product of technical skill, we should not forthwith attempt to settle the controversies of Philosophers, or solve the puzzles of the Mathematicians, by their help. We must first employ them for searching out with our utmost attention all the other things that are more urgently required in the investigation of truth. And this since there is no reason why it should appear more difficult to discover these than any of the answers which the problems propounded by Geometry or Physics or the other sciences are wont to demand.

Now no more useful inquiry can be proposed than that which seeks to determine the nature and the scope of human knowledge. This is why we state this very problem succinctly in the single question, which we deem should be answered at the very outset with the aid of the rules which we have already laid down. This investigation should be undertaken once at least in his life by anyone who has the slightest regard for truth, since in pursuing it the true instruments of knowledge and the whole method of inquiry come to light. But nothing seems to me more futile than the conduct of those who boldly dispute about the secrets of nature, the influence of the heavens on these lower regions, the predicting of future events and similar matters, as many do, without yet having ever asked even whether human reason is adequate to the solution of these problems. Neither ought it to seem such a toilsome and difficult matter to define the limits of that understanding[1] of which we are directly aware[2] as being within us, when we often have no hesitation in passing judgment even on things that are without us and quite foreign to us. Neither is it such an immense task to attempt to grasp in thought all the objects comprised within this whole of things, in order to discover how they singly fall under our

---

[1] ingenii. [2] sentimus.

mental scrutiny. For nothing can prove to be so complex or so vague as to defeat the efforts of the method of enumeration above described, directed towards restraining it within certain limits or arranging it under certain categories[1]. But to put this to the test in the matter of the question above propounded, we first of all divide the whole problem relative to it into two parts ; for it ought either to relate to us who are capable of knowledge, or to the things themselves which can be known : and these two factors we discuss separately.

In ourselves we notice that while it is the understanding alone which is capable of knowing, it yet is either helped or hindered by three other faculties, namely imagination, sense, and memory. We must therefore examine these faculties in order, with a view to finding out where each may prove to be an impediment, so that we may be on our guard ; or where it may profit us, so that we may use to the full the resources of these powers. This first part of our problem will accordingly be discussed with the aid of a sufficient enumeration, as will be shown in the succeeding proposition.

We come secondly to the things themselves which must be considered only in so far as they are the objects of the understanding. From this point of view we divide them into the class (1) of those whose nature is of the extremest simplicity and (2) of the complex and composite. Simple natures must be either spiritual or corporeal or at once spiritual and corporeal. Finally among the composites there are some which the understanding realises to be complex before it judges that it can determine anything about them ; but there are also others which it itself puts together. All these matters will be expounded at greater length in the twelfth proposition, where it will be shown that there can be no falsity save in the last class—that of the compounds made by the understanding itself. This is why we further subdivide these into the class of those which are deducible from natures which are of the maximum simplicity and are known *per se*, of which we shall treat in the whole of the succeeding book[2]; and into those which presuppose the existence of others which the facts themselves show us to be composite. To the exposition of these we destine the whole of the third[3] book.

But we shall indeed attempt in the whole of this treatise to follow so accurately the paths which conduct men to the knowledge

[1] capita.
[2] This begins at Prop. XIII. Of the later propositions we have the titles only in the case of XIX—XXI, while the last three are entirely lacking.
[3] Apparently not even begun.

of the truth and to make them so easy, that anyone who has perfectly learned the whole of this method, however moderate may be his talent, may see that no avenue to the truth is closed to him from which everyone else is not also excluded, and that his ignorance is due neither to a deficiency in his capacity nor to his method of procedure. But as often as he applies his mind to the understanding of some matter, he will either be entirely successful, or he will realise that success depends upon a certain experiment which he is unable to perform, and in that case he will not blame his mental capacity although he is compelled to stop short there. Or finally he may show that the knowledge desired wholly exceeds the limits of the human intelligence ; and consequently he will believe that he is none the more ignorant on that account. For to have discovered this is knowledge in no less degree than the knowledge of anything else.

Rule IX.

We ought to give the whole of our attention to the most insignificant and most easily mastered facts, and remain a long time in contemplation of them until we are accustomed to behold the truth clearly and distinctly.

We have now indicated the two operations of our understanding, intuition and deduction, on which alone we have said we must rely in the acquisition of knowledge. Let us therefore in this and in the following proposition proceed to explain how we can render ourselves more skilful in employing them, and at the same time cultivate the two principal faculties of the mind, to wit perspicacity, by viewing single objects distinctly, and sagacity, by the skilful deduction of certain facts from others.

Truly we shall learn how to employ our mental intuition from comparing it with the way in which we employ our eyes. For he who attempts to view a multitude of objects with one and the same glance, sees none of them distinctly ; and similarly the man who is wont to attend to many things at the same time by means of a single act of thought is confused in mind. But just as workmen, who are employed in very fine and delicate operations and are accustomed to direct their eyesight attentively to separate points, by practice have acquired a capacity for distinguishing objects of extreme minuteness and subtlety ; so likewise do people who do not allow their thought to be distracted by various objects at the same time, but always concentrate it in attending to the simplest and easiest particulars, are clear-headed.

But it is a common failing of mortals to deem the more difficult the fairer; and they often think that they have learned nothing when they see a very clear and simple cause for a fact, while at the same time they are lost in admiration of certain sublime and profound philosophical explanations, even though these for the most part are based upon foundations which no one has adequately surveyed—a mental disorder which prizes the darkness higher than the light. But it is notable that those who have real knowledge discern the truth with equal facility whether they evolve it from matter that is simple or that is obscure; they grasp each fact by an act of thought that is similar, single, and distinct, after they have once arrived at the point in question. The whole of the difference between the apprehension of the simple and of the obscure lies in the route taken, which certainly ought to be longer if it conducts us from our initial and most absolute principles to a truth that is somewhat remote.

Everyone ought therefore to accustom himself to grasp in his thought at the same time facts that are at once so few and so simple, that he shall never believe that he has knowledge of anything which he does not mentally behold with a distinctness equal to that of the objects which he knows most distinctly of all. It is true that some men are born with a much greater aptitude for such discernment than others, but the mind can be made much more expert at such work by art and exercise. But there is one fact which I should here emphasize above all others; and that is that everyone should firmly persuade himself that none of the sciences, however abstruse, is to be deduced from lofty and obscure matters, but that they all proceed only from what is easy and more readily understood.

For example if I wish to examine whether it is possible for a natural force to pass at one and the same moment to a spot at a distance and yet to traverse the whole space in between, I shall not begin to study the force of magnetism or the influence of the stars, not even the speed of light, in order to discover whether actions such as these occur instantaneously; for the solution of this question would be more difficult than the problem proposed. I should rather bethink myself of the spatial motions of bodies, because nothing in the sphere of motion can be found more obvious to sense than this. I shall observe that while a stone cannot pass to another place in one and the same moment, because it is a body, yet a force similar to that which moves the stone is communicated exactly instantaneously if it passes unencumbered[1] from one object to another. For instance, if I move one end of a stick of whatever length, I easily understand that the power by which that part of the stick is moved necessarily moves also all its other parts at the same moment, because then the force passes unencumbered and is not imprisoned in any body, e.g. a stone, which bears it along.

In the same way if I wish to understand how one and the same simple cause can produce contrary effects at the same time, I shall not cite the drugs of the doctors which expel certain humours and retain others; nor shall I romance about the moon's power of warming with its light and chilling by means of some occult power. I shall rather cast my eyes upon the balance in which the same weight raises one arm at the same time as it depresses the other, or take some other familiar instance.

Rule X.

In order that it may acquire sagacity the mind should be exercised in pursuing just those inquiries of which the solution has already been found by others; and it ought to traverse in a systematic way even the most trifling of men's inventions, though those ought to be preferred in which order is explained or implied.

I confess that my natural disposition is such that I have always found, not the following of the arguments of others, but the discovery of reasons by my own proper efforts, to yield me the highest intellectual satisfaction. It was this alone that attracted me, when I was still a young man, to the study of science. And whenever any book by its title promised some new discovery, before I read further, I tried whether I could achieve something similar by means of some inborn faculty of invention[2], and I was careful lest a premature perusal of the book might deprive me of this harmless pleasure. So often was I successful that at length I perceived that I no longer came upon the truth by proceeding as others commonly do, viz. by pursuing vague and blind inquiries and relying more on good fortune than on skill. I saw that by long experience I had discovered certain rules which are of no little help in this inquiry, and which I used afterwards in devising further rules. Thus it was that I diligently elaborated the whole of this method and came to

---

[1] nuda. [2] sagacitatem.

the conclusion that I had followed that plan of study which was the most fruitful of all.

But because not all minds are so much inclined to puzzle things out unaided, this proposition announces that we ought not immediately to occupy ourselves with the more difficult and arduous problems, but first should discuss those disciplines[1] which are easiest and simplest, and those above all in which order most prevails. Such are the arts of the craftsmen who weave webs and tapestry, or of women who embroider or use in the same work threads with infinite modification of texture. With these are ranked all play with numbers and everything that belongs to Arithmetic, and the like. It is wonderful how all these studies discipline our mental powers, provided that we do not know the solutions from others, but invent them ourselves. For since nothing in these arts remains hidden, and they are wholly adjusted to the capacity of human cognition, they reveal to us with the greatest distinctness innumerable orderly systems, all different from each other, but none the less conforming to rule, in the proper observance of which systems of order consists the whole of human sagacity.

It was for this reason that we insisted that method must be employed in studying those matters ; and this in those arts of less importance consists wholly in the close observation of the order which is found in the object studied, whether that be an order existing in the thing itself, or due to subtle human devising. Thus if we wish to make out some writing in which the meaning is disguised by the use of a cypher, though the order here fails to present itself, we yet make up an imaginary one, for the purpose both of testing all the conjectures we may make about single letters, words or sentences, and in order to arrange them so that when we sum them up we shall be able to tell all the inferences that we can deduce from them. We must principally beware of wasting our time in such cases by proceeding at random and unmethodically ; for even though the solution can often be found without method, and by lucky people sometimes quicker, yet such procedure is likely to enfeeble the faculties and to make people accustomed to the trifling and the childish, so that for the future their minds will stick on the surface of things, incapable of penetrating beyond it. But meanwhile we must not fall into the error of those who, having devoted themselves solely to what is lofty and serious, find that after many years of

---

[1] artes.

toil they have acquired, not the profound knowledge they hoped for, but only mental confusion.   Hence we must give ourselves practice first in those easier disciplines, but methodically, so that by open and familiar ways we may ceaselessly accustom ourselves to penetrate as easily as though we were at play into the very heart of these subjects.   For by this means we shall afterwards gradually feel (and in a space of time shorter than we could at all hope for) that we are in a position with equal facility to deduce from evident first principles many propositions which at first sight are highly intricate and difficult.

It may perhaps strike some with surprise that here, where we are discussing how to improve our power of deducing one truth from another, we have omitted all the precepts of the dialecticians, by which they think to control the human reason.   They prescribe certain formulae of argument, which lead to a conclusion with such necessity that, if the reason commits itself to their trust, even though it slackens its interest and no longer pays a heedful and close attention to the very proposition inferred, it can nevertheless at the same time come to a sure conclusion by virtue of the form of the argument alone.   Exactly so ; the fact is that frequently we notice that often the truth escapes away out of these imprisoning bonds, while the people themselves who have used them in order to capture it remain entangled in them.   Other people are not so frequently entrapped ; and it is a matter of experience that the most ingenious sophisms hardly ever impose on anyone who uses his unaided reason, while they are wont to deceive the sophists themselves.

Wherefore as we wish here to be particularly careful lest our reason should go on holiday while we are examining the truth of any matter, we reject those formulae as being opposed to our project, and look out rather for all the aids by which our thought may be kept attentive, as will be shown in the sequel.   But, to say a few words more, that it may appear still more evident that this style of argument contributes nothing at all to the discovery of the truth, we must note that the Dialecticians are unable to devise any syllogism which has a true conclusion, unless they have first secured the material out of which to construct it, i.e. unless they have already ascertained the very truth which is deduced in that syllogism. Whence it is clear that from a formula of this kind they can gather nothing that is new, and hence the ordinary Dialectic is quite value-less for those who desire to investigate the truth of things.   Its only possible use is to serve to explain at times more easily to others the truths we have already ascertained; hence it should be transferred from Philosophy to Rhetoric.

Rule XI.

If, after we have recognized intuitively a number of simple truths, we wish to draw any inference from them, it is useful to run them over in a continuous and uninterrupted act of thought, to reflect upon their relations to one another, and to grasp together distinctly a number of these propositions so far as is possible at the same time. For this is a way of making our knowledge much more certain, and of greatly increasing the power of the mind.

Here we have an opportunity of expounding more clearly what has been already said of mental intuition in the third and seventh rules[1]. In one passage[2] we opposed it to deduction, while in the other we distinguished it from enumeration only, which we defined as an inference drawn from many and diverse things[3]. But the simple deduction of one thing from another, we said in the same passage[4], was effected by intuition.

It was necessary to do this, because two things are requisite for mental intuition. Firstly the proposition intuited must be clear and distinct; secondly it must be grasped in its totality at the same time and not successively. As for deduction, if we are thinking of how the process works, as we were in Rule III, it appears not to occur all at the same time, but involves a sort of movement on the part of our mind when it infers one thing from another. We were justified therefore in distinguishing deduction in that rule from intuition. But if we wish to consider deduction as an accomplished fact, as we did in what we said relatively to the seventh rule, then it no longer designates a movement, but rather the completion of a movement, and therefore we suppose that it is presented to us by intuition when it is simple and clear, but not when it is complex and involved. When this is the case we give it the name of enumeration or induction, because it cannot then be grasped as a whole at the same time by the mind, and its certainty depends to some extent on the memory, in which our judgments about the various matters enumerated must be retained, if from their assemblage a single fact is to be inferred.

[1] Cf. pp. 5, 19.   [2] Cf. p. 8.   [3] Cf. p. 20.   [4] Cf. p. 7.

All these distinctions had to be made if we were to elucidate this rule. We treated of mental intuition solely in Rule IX; the tenth dealt with enumeration alone; but now the present rule explains how these two operations aid and complete each other. In doing so they seem to grow into a single process by virtue of a sort of motion of thought which has an attentive and vision-like knowledge of one fact and yet can pass at the very same moment to another.

Now to this co-operation we assign a two-fold advantage. Firstly it promotes a more certain knowledge of the conclusion with which we are concerned, and secondly it makes the mind readier to discover fresh truths. In fact the memory, on which we have said depends the certainty of the conclusions which embrace more than we can grasp in a single act of intuition, though weak and liable to fail us, can be renewed and made stronger by this continuous and constantly repeated process of thought. Thus if diverse mental acts have led me to know what is the relation between a first and a second magnitude, next between the second and a third, then between the third and a fourth, and finally the fourth and a fifth, that need not lead me to see what is the relation between the first and the fifth, nor can I deduce it from what I already know, unless I remember all the other relations. Hence what I have to do is to run over them all repeatedly in my mind, until I pass so quickly from the first to the last that practically no step is left to the memory, and I seem to view the whole all at the same time.

Everyone must see that this plan does much to counteract the slowness of the mind and to enlarge its capacity. But in addition we must note that the greatest advantage of this rule consists in the fact that, by reflecting on the mutual dependence of two propositions, we acquire the habit of distinguishing at a glance what is more or less relative, and what the steps are by which a relative fact is related to something absolute. For example, if I run over a number of magnitudes that are in continued proportion, I shall reflect upon all the following facts: viz. that the mental act is entirely similar—and not easier in the one case, more difficult in another—by which I grasp the relation between the first and the second, the second and third, third and fourth, and so on; while yet it is more difficult for me to conceive what the relation of the second is to the first and to the third at the same time, and much more difficult still to tell its relation to the first and fourth, and so on. These considerations then lead me to see why, if the first and second alone are given, I can easily find the third and fourth, and all the others; the reason being that this process requires only single and distinct acts of thought. But if only the first and the third are given, it is not so easy to recognize the mean, because this can only be accomplished by means of a mental operation in which two of the previous acts are involved. If the first and the fourth magnitudes alone are given, it is still more difficult to present to ourselves the two means, because here three acts of thought come in simultaneously. It would seem likely as a consequence that it would be even more difficult to discover the three means between the first and the fifth. The reason why this is not so is due to a fresh fact; viz. even though here four mental acts come together they can yet be disjoined, since four can be divided by another number. Thus I can discover the third by itself from the first and fifth, then the second from the first and third, and so on. If one accustoms one's self to reflect on these and similar problems, as often as a new question arises, at once one recognizes what produces its special difficulty, and what is the simplest method of dealing with all cases; and to be able to do so is a valuable aid to the discovery of the truth.

Rule XII.

Finally we ought to employ all the aids of understanding, imagination, sense and memory, first for the purpose of having a distinct intuition of simple propositions; partly also in order to compare the propositions to be proved with those we know already, so that we may be able to recognize their truth; partly also in order to discover the truths, which should be compared with each other so that nothing may be left lacking on which human industry may exercise itself.

This rule states the conclusion of all that we said before, and shows in general outline what had to be explained in detail, in this wise.

In the matter of the cognition of facts two things alone have to be considered, ourselves who know and the objects themselves which are to be known. Within us there are four faculties only which we can use for this purpose, viz. understanding, imagination, sense and memory. The understanding is indeed alone capable of perceiving the truth, but yet it ought to be aided by imagination, sense and memory, lest perchance we omit any expedient that lies within our power. On the side of the facts to be known it is enough to examine three things; first that which presents itself spontaneously, secondly how we learn one thing by means of another, and thirdly what (truths) are deduced from what. This enumeration appears to me to be complete, and to omit nothing to which our human powers can apply.

I should have liked therefore to have turned to the first point and to have explained in this passage, what the human mind is, what body, and how it is 'informed' by mind ; what the faculties in the complex whole are which serve the attainment of knowledge, and what the agency of each is. But this place[1] seems hardly to give me sufficient room to take in all the matters which must be premised before the truth in this subject can become clear to all. For my desire is in all that I write to assert nothing controversial unless I have already stated the very reasons which have brought me to that conclusion, and by which I think that others also may be convinced.

But because at present I am prevented from doing this, it will suffice me to explain as briefly as possible that mode of viewing everything within us which is directed towards the discovery of truth, which most promotes my purpose. You need not believe that the facts are so unless you like. But what prevents us following these suppositions, if it appears that they do no harm to the truth, but only render it all much clearer ? In Geometry you do precisely the same thing when you make certain assumptions about a quantity which do not in any way weaken the force of your arguments, though often our experience of its nature in Physics makes us judge of it quite otherwise.

Let us then conceive of the matter as follows :—all our external senses, in so far as they are part of the body, and despite the fact that we direct them towards objects, so manifesting activity, viz. a movement in space, nevertheless properly speaking perceive in virtue of passivity alone, just in the way that wax receives an impression[2] from a seal. And it should not be thought that all we mean to assert is an analogy between the two. We ought to believe that the way is entirely the same in which the exterior figure of the sentient body is really modified by the object, as that in which the shape of the surface of the wax is altered by the seal. This has to be admitted not only in the case of the figure, hardness, roughness, etc. of a body which we perceive by touch, but even when we are aware

---

[1] <locus> is added in another hand in the Hanover MS.
[2] figuram.

of heat, cold, and the like qualities. It is likewise with the other senses. The first opaque structure in the eye receives the figure impressed upon it by the light with its various colours; and the first membrane[1] in the ears, the nose, and the tongue that resists the further passage of the object, thus also acquires a new figure from the sound, the odour, and the savour, as the case may be.

It is exceedingly helpful to conceive all those matters thus, for nothing falls more readily under sense than figure, which can be touched and seen. Moreover that nothing false issues from this supposition more than from any other, is proved by the fact that the concept of figure is so common and simple that it is involved in every object of sense. Thus whatever you suppose colour to be, you cannot deny that it is extended and in consequence possessed of figure. Is there then any disadvantage, if, while taking care not to admit any new entity uselessly, or rashly to imagine that it exists, and not denying indeed the beliefs of others concerning colour, but merely abstracting from every other feature except that it possesses the nature of figure, we conceive the diversity existing between white, blue, and red, etc., as being like the difference between the following similar figures? The same argument applies to all cases;

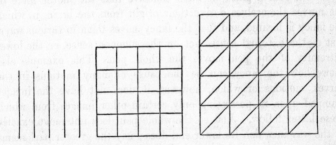

for it is certain that the infinitude of figures suffices to express all the differences in sensible things.

Secondly we must believe that while the external sense is stimulated[2] by the object, the figure which is conveyed to it is carried off to some other part of the body, that part called the common sense[3], in the very same instant and without the passage

---

[1] cutem.
[2] movetur.
[3] sensus communis. This theory is indistinguishable from one interpretation of the Aristotelian doctrine of a central sense with a central organ in the body.

of any real entity from one to the other. It is in exactly the same manner that now when I write I recognize that at the very moment when the separate characters are being written down on the paper, not only is the lower end of the pen moved, but every motion in that part is simultaneously shared by the whole pen. All these diverse motions are traced by the upper end of the pen likewise in the air, although I do not conceive of anything real passing from the one extremity to the other. Now who imagines that the connection between the different parts of the human body is slighter than that between the ends of a pen, and what simpler way of expressing this could be found?

Thirdly we must believe that the common sense has a function like that of a seal, and impresses on the fancy or imagination, as though on wax, those very figures and ideas which come uncontaminated and without bodily admixture from the external senses. But this fancy is a genuine part of the body, of sufficient size to allow its different parts to assume various figures in distinctness from each other and to let those parts acquire the practice of retaining the impressions for some time. In the latter case we give the faculty the name of memory.

In the fourth place we must conceive that the motor force or the nerves themselves derive their origin from the brain, in which the fancy is located, and that the fancy moves them in various ways, just as the external senses act on the common sense, or the lower extremity of the pen moves the whole pen. This example also shows how the fancy can be the cause of many motions in the nerves, motions of which, however, it does not have the images stamped upon it, possessing only certain other images from which these latter follow. Just so the whole pen does not move exactly in the way in which its lower end does; nay the greater part seems to have a motion that is quite different from and contrary to that of the other. This lets us understand how all the motions of the other animals can come about, though we can ascribe to them no knowledge at all, but only fancy of a purely corporeal kind. We can explain also how in ourselves all those operations occur which we perform without any aid from the reason.

Finally and in the fifth place, we must think that that power by which we are properly said to know things, is purely spiritual, and not less distinct from every part of the body than blood from bone, or hand from eye. It is a single agency, whether it receives impressions from the common sense simultaneously with the fancy, or applies itself to those that are preserved in the memory, or forms new ones. Often the imagination is so beset by these impressions that it is unable at the same time to receive ideas from the common sense, or to transfer them to the motor mechanism in the way befitting its purely corporeal character. In all these operations this cognitive power is at one time passive, at another active, and resembles now the seal and now the wax. But the resemblance on this occasion is only one of analogy, for among corporeal things there is nothing wholly similar to this faculty. It is one and the same agency which, when applying itself along with the imagination to the common sense, is said to see, touch, etc.; if applying itself to the imagination alone in so far as that is endowed with diverse impressions, it is said to remember; if it turn to the imagination in order to create fresh impressions, it is said to imagine or conceive; finally if it act alone it is said to understand. How this latter function takes place I shall explain at greater length in the proper place. Now it is the same faculty that in correspondence with those various functions is called either pure understanding, or imagination, or memory, or sense. It is properly called mind[1] when it either forms new ideas in the fancy, or attends to those already formed. We consider it as capable of the above various operations, and this distinction between those terms must in the sequel be borne in mind. But after having grasped these facts the attentive reader will gather what help is to be expected from each particular faculty, and discover how far human effort can avail to supplement the deficiencies of our mental powers.

For, since the understanding can be stimulated by the imagination, or on the contrary act on it; and seeing that the imagination can act on the senses by means of the motor power applying them to objects, while they on the contrary can act on it, depicting on it the images of bodies; considering on the other hand that the memory, at least that which is corporeal and similar to that of the brutes, is in no respect distinct from the imagination; we come to the sure conclusion that, if the understanding deal with matters in which there is nothing corporeal or similar to the corporeal, it cannot be helped by those faculties, but that, on the contrary, to prevent their hampering it, the senses must be banished and the imagination as far as possible divested of every distinct impression. But if the understanding proposes to examine something that can

[1] ingenium.

be referred to the body, we must form the idea of that thing as distinctly as possible in the imagination ; and in order to effect this with greater ease, the thing itself which this idea is to represent must be exhibited to the external senses. Now when the understanding wishes to have a distinct intuition of particular facts a multitude of objects is of no use to it. But if it wishes to deduce one thing from a number of objects, as often has to be done, we must banish from the ideas of the objects presented whatsoever does not require present attention, in order that the remainder may be the more readily retained in memory. In the same way it is not on those occasions that the objects themselves ought to be presented to the external senses, but rather certain compendious abbreviations which, provided they guard the memory against lapse, are the handier the shorter they are. Whosoever observes all these recommendations, will, in my opinion, omit nothing that relates to the first part of our rule.

Now we must approach the second part of our task. That was to distinguish accurately the notions of simple things from those which are built up out of them ; to see in both cases where falsity might come in, so that we might be on our guard and give our attention to those matters only in which certainty was possible. But here, as before, we must make certain assumptions which probably are not agreed on by all. It matters little, however, though they are not believed to be more real than those imaginary circles by means of which Astronomers describe their phenomena, provided that you employ them to aid you in discerning in each particular case what sort of knowledge is true and what false.

Finally, then, we assert that relatively to our knowledge single things should be taken in an order different from that in which we should regard them when considered in their more real nature. Thus, for example, if we consider a body as having extension and figure, we shall indeed admit that from the point of view of the thing itself it is one and simple. For we cannot from that point of view regard it as compounded of corporeal nature, extension and figure, since these elements have never existed in isolation from each other. But relatively to our understanding we call it a compound constructed out of these three natures, because we have thought of them separately before we were able to judge that all three were found in one and the same subject. Hence here we shall treat of things only in relation to our understanding's awareness of them, and shall call those only simple, the cognition of which is so clear and so distinct that they cannot be analysed by the mind into others more distinctly known. Such are figure, extension, motion, etc.; all others we conceive to be in some way compounded out of these. This principle must be taken so universally as not even to leave out those objects which we sometimes obtain by abstraction from the simple natures themselves. This we do, for example, when we say that figure is the limit of an extended thing, conceiving by the term limit something more universal than by the term figure, since we can talk of a limit of duration, a limit of motion, and so on. But our contention is right, for then, even though we find the meaning of limit by abstracting it from figure, nevertheless it should not for that reason seem simpler than figure. Rather, since it is predicated of other things, as for example of the extreme bounds of a space of time or of a motion, etc., things which are wholly different from figure, it must be abstracted from those natures also; consequently it is something compounded out of a number of natures wholly diverse, of which it can be only ambiguously predicated.

Our second assertion is that those things which relatively to our understanding[1] are called simple, are either purely intellectual[2] or purely material, or else common both to intellect and to matter. Those are purely intellectual which our understanding[1] apprehends by means of a certain inborn light, and without the aid of any corporeal image. That a number of such things exist is certain; and it is impossible to construct any corporeal idea which shall represent to us what the act of knowing is, what doubt is, what ignorance, and likewise what the action of the will is which it is possible to term volition, and so with other things. Yet we have a genuine knowledge of all these things, and know them so easily that in order to recognize them it is enough to be endowed with reason. Those things are purely material which we discern only in bodies; e.g. figure, extension, motion, etc. Finally those must be styled common which are ascribed now to corporeal things, now to spirits, without distinction. Such are existence, unity, duration and the like. To this group also we must ascribe those common notions which are, as it were, bonds for connecting together the other simple natures, and on whose evidence all the inferences which we obtain by reasoning depend. The following are examples:—things that are the same as a third thing are the same as one another. So too:—things which do not bear the same relation to a third thing, have some diversity

---

[1] intellectus. [2] intellectuales.

from each other, etc. As a matter of fact these common notions can be discerned by the understanding either unaided[1] or when it is aware of the images of material things.

But among these simple natures we must rank the privative and negative terms corresponding to them in so far as our intelligence grasps them. For it is quite as genuinely an act of knowledge by which I am intuitively aware of what nothing is, or an instant, or rest, as that by which I know what existence is, or lapse of time, or motion. This way of viewing the matter will be helpful in enabling us henceforth to say that all the rest of what we know is formed by composition out of these simple natures. Thus, for example, if I pronounce the judgment that some figure is not moving, I shall say that in a certain sense my idea[2] is a complex of figure and rest; and so in other cases.

Thirdly we assert that all these simple natures are known *per se* and are wholly free from falsity. It will be easy to show this, provided we distinguish that faculty of our understanding by which it has intuitive awareness of things and knows them, from that by which it judges, making use of affirmation and denial. For we may imagine ourselves to be ignorant of things which we really know, for example on such occasions as when we believe that in such things, over and above what we have present to us or attain to by thinking, there is something else hidden from us, and when this belief of ours is false. Whence it is evident that we are in error if we judge that any one of these simple natures is not completely known by us. For if our mind attains to the least acquaintance with it, as must be the case, since we are assumed to pass some judgment on it, this fact alone makes us infer that we know it completely. For otherwise it could not be said to be simple, but must be complex—a compound of that which is present in our perception of it, and that of which we think we are ignorant.

In the fourth place we point out that the union of these things one with another is either necessary or contingent. It is necessary when one is so implied in the concept of another in a confused sort of way that we cannot conceive either distinctly, if our thought assigns to them separateness from each other. Thus figure is conjoined with extension, motion with duration or time, and so on, because it is impossible to conceive of a figure that has no extension, nor of a motion that has no duration. Thus likewise if I say

---

[1] puro.   [2] cogitatio.

'four and three are seven,' this union is necessary. For we do not conceive the number seven distinctly unless we include in it the numbers three and four in some confused way. In the same way whatever is demonstrated of figures or numbers is necessarily united with that of which it is affirmed. Further, this necessity is not restricted to the field of sensible matters alone. The conclusion is necessary also in such a case—If Socrates says he doubts everything, it follows necessarily that he knows this at least—that he doubts. Likewise he knows that something can be either true or false, and so on, for all those consequences necessarily attach to the nature of doubt. The union, however, is contingent in those cases where the things are conjoined by no inseparable bond. Thus when we say a body is animate, a man is clothed, etc. Likewise many things are often necessarily united with one another, though most people, not noticing what their true relation is, reckons them among those that are contingently connected. As example, I give the following propositions:—'I exist, therefore God exists': also 'I know, therefore I have a mind distinct from my body,' etc. Finally we must note that very many necessary propositions become contingent when converted. Thus though from the fact that I exist I may infallibly conclude that God exists, it is not for that reason allowable to affirm that because God exists I also exist.

Fifthly we remark that no knowledge is at any time possible of anything beyond those simple natures and what may be called their intermixture or combination with each other. Indeed it is often easier to be aware of several of them in union with each other, than to separate one of them from the others. For, to illustrate, I am able to know what a triangle is, though I have never thought that in that knowledge was contained the knowledge of an angle, a line, the number three, figure, extension, etc. But that does not prevent me from saying that the nature of the triangle is composed of all these natures, and that they are better known than the triangle since they are the elements which we comprehend in it. It is possible also that in the triangle many other features are involved which escape our notice, such as the magnitude of the angles, which are equal to two right angles, and the innumerable relations which exist between the sides and the angles, or the size of the area, etc.

Sixthly, we say that those natures which we call composite are known by us, either because experience shows us what they are, or because we ourselves are responsible for their composition. Matter of experience consists of what we perceive by sense, what we hear

from the lips of others, and generally whatever reaches our understanding either from external sources or from that contemplation
which our mind directs backwards on itself. Here it must be noted
that no direct experience can ever deceive the understanding if it
restrict its attention accurately to the object presented to it, just as
it is given to it either at firsthand[1] or by means of an image; and
if it moreover refrain from judging that the imagination faithfully
reports the objects of the senses, or that the senses take on the true
forms of things, or in fine that external things always are as they
appear to be; for in all these judgments we are exposed to error.
This happens, for example, when we believe as fact what is merely a
story that someone has told us; or when one who is ill with jaundice
judges everything to be yellow because his eye is tinged with yellow.
So finally, too, when the imagination is diseased, as in cases of
melancholia, and a man thinks that his own disorderly fancies
represent real things. But the understanding of a wise man will not
be deceived by these fancies, since he will judge that whatever
comes to him from his imagination is really depicted in it, but yet
will never assert that the object has passed complete and without
any alteration from the external world to his senses, and from his
senses to his imagination, unless he has some previous ground for
believing this. Moreover we ourselves are responsible for the composition of the things present to our understanding when we believe
that there is something in them which our mind never experiences
when exercising direct perception[2]. Thus if a man suffering
from jaundice persuades himself that the things he sees are yellow,
this thought of his will be composite, consisting partly of what his
imagination represents to him, and partly of what he assumes on his
own account, namely that the colour looks yellow not owing to the
defect in his eye, but because the things he sees really are yellow.
Whence the conclusion comes that we can go wrong only when the
things we believe are in some way compounded by ourselves.

Seventhly, this compounding can come about in other ways,
namely by impulse, by conjecture, or by deduction. Impulse sways
the formation of judgments about things on the part of those whom
their own initiative constrains to believe something, though they can
assign no reason for their belief, but are merely determined either by
some higher Power, or by their own free will, or by their fanciful

---

[1] prout illam habet vel in se ipso.
[2] This translation is doubtful. The Latin might at least equally well mean
'which our mind perceives immediately without any experience.'

disposition. The first cause is never a source of error, the second rarely, the third almost always. But a consideration of the first does not concern us here because it does not fall within the province of human skill[1]. The working of conjecture is shown, for example, in this: water which is at a greater distance from the centre of the globe than earth, is likewise less dense substance, and likewise the air which is above the water, is still rarer; hence we hazard the guess that above the air nothing exists but a very pure aether, which is much rarer than air itself. Moreover nothing that we construct in this way really deceives us, if we merely judge it to be probable and never affirm it to be true; in fact it makes us better instructed.

Deduction is thus left to us as the only means of putting things together so as to be sure of their truth. Yet in it too there may be many defects. Thus if, in this space which is full of air, there is nothing to be perceived either by sight, touch, or any other sense, we conclude that the space is empty, we are in error, and our synthesis of the nature of a vacuum with that of this space is wrong. This is the result as often as we judge that we can deduce anything universal and necessary from a particular or contingent fact. But it is within our power to avoid this error, if, for example, we never interconnect any objects unless we are directly aware that the conjunction of the one with the other is wholly necessary. Thus we are justified if we deduce that nothing can have figure which has not extension, from the fact that figure and extension are necessarily conjoined.

From all these considerations we conclude firstly—that we have shown distinctly and, as we judge, by an adequate enumeration, what we were originally able to express only confusedly and in a rough and ready way. This was that mankind has no road towards certain knowledge open to it, save those of self-evident intuition and necessary deduction; further, that we have shown what those simple natures are of which we spoke in the eighth proposition. It is also quite clear that this mental vision extends both to all those simple natures, and to the knowledge of the necessary connections between them, and finally to everything else which the understanding accurately experiences either at first hand[2] or in the imagination. Deduction, however, will be further treated in what follows.

Our second conclusion is that in order to know these simple

---

[1] artem.   [2] in se ipso.

natures no pains need be taken, because they are of themselves sufficiently well known. Application comes in only in isolating them from each other and scrutinizing them separately with steadfast mental gaze. There is no one whose intelligence is so dull as not to perceive that when he is seated he in some way differs from what he is when standing. But not everyone separates with equal distinctness the nature of position[1] from the other elements contained in the cognition in question, or is able to assert that in this case nothing alters save the position. Now it is not without reason that we call attention to the above doctrine; for the learned have a way of being so clever as to contrive to render themselves blind to things that are in their own nature evident, and known by the simplest peasant. This happens when they try to explain by something more evident those things that are self-evident. For what they do is either to explain something else, or nothing at all. Who, for instance, does not perfectly see what that is, whatsoever it may be, in respect of which alteration occurs when we change position[2]? But is there anyone who would grasp that very thing when he was told that *place[2] is the surface of the body surrounding us*?[3] This would be strange seeing that that surface can change though I stay still and do not change my place, or that, on the contrary, it can so move along with me that, although it continues to surround me, I am nevertheless no longer in the same place. Do not these people really seem to use magic words which have a hidden force that eludes the grasp of human apprehension? They define *motion*, a fact with which everyone is quite familiar, as *the actualisation of what exists in potentiality, in so far as it is potential!* Now who understands these words? And who at the same time does not know what motion is? Will not everyone admit that those philosophers have been trying to find a knot in a bulrush? We must therefore maintain that no definitions are to be used in explaining things of this kind lest we should take what is complex in place of what is simple. We must be content to isolate them from each other, and to give them, each of us, our individual attention, studying them with that degree of mental illumination which each of us possesses.

Our third conclusion is that the whole of human knowledge consists in a distinct perception of the way in which those simple natures combine in order to build up other objects. It is important to note this; because whenever some difficulty is brought forward

---

[1] situs.   [2] locum.   [3] Cf. reply to VI. Obj. (7).

for examination, almost everyone is brought to a standstill at the very outset, being in doubt as to the nature of the notions he ought to call to mind, and believing that he has to search for some new kind of fact previously unknown to him. Thus, if the question is, ' what is the nature of the magnet?' people like that at once prognosticate difficulty and toil in the inquiry, and dismissing from mind every well-known fact, fasten on whatsoever is most difficult, vaguely hoping that by ranging over the fruitless field where multifarious causes lie, they will find something fresh. But he who reflects that there can be nothing to know in the magnet which does not consist of certain simple natures evident in themselves, will have no doubt how to proceed. He will first collect all the observations with which experience can supply him about this stone, and from these he will next try to deduce the character of that inter-mixture of simple natures which is necessary to produce all those effects which he has seen to take place in connection with the magnet. This achieved, he can boldly assert that he has discovered the real nature of the magnet in so far as human intelligence and the given experimental observations can supply him with this knowledge.

Finally, it follows fourthly from what has been said that we must not fancy that one kind of knowledge is more obscure than another, since all knowledge is of the same nature throughout, and consists solely in combining what is self-evident. This is a fact recognized by very few. People have their minds already occupied by the contrary opinion, and the more bold among them, indeed, allow themselves to uphold their private conjectures as though they were sound demonstrations, and in matters of which they are wholly ignorant feel premonitions of the vision of truths which seem to present themselves through a cloud. These they have no hesitation in propounding, attaching to their concepts certain words by means of which they are wont to carry on long and reasoned out discussions, but which in reality neither they nor their audience understand. On the other hand more diffident people often refrain from many investigations that are quite easy and are in the first degree necessary to life, merely because they think themselves unequal to the task. They believe that these matters can be discovered by others who are endowed with better mental faculties, and embrace the opinion of those in whose authority they have most confidence.

We assert fifthly[1] that by deduction we can get only things from

---

[1] So Leibniz's ms. The Amsterdam edition has *eighthly* which carries on the previous list of assertions.

words, cause from effect, or effect from cause, like from like, or parts or the whole itself from the parts......[1].

For the rest, in order that there may be no want of coherence in our series of precepts, we divide the whole matter of knowledge into simple propositions and 'questions[2].' In connection with simple propositions the only precepts we give are those which prepare our cognitive faculties for fixing distinctly before them any objects, whatsoever they are, and scrutinizing them with keen intelligence, since propositions of this type do not arise as the result of inquiry, but present themselves to us spontaneously. This part of our task we have undertaken in the first twelve rules, in which, we believe, we have displayed everything which, in our opinion, can facilitate the exercise of our reason. But as to 'questions' some of them can be perfectly well comprehended, even though we are ignorant of their solution; these we shall treat by themselves in the next twelve rules. Finally there are others, whose meaning is not quite clear, and these we reserve for the last twelve. This division has been made advisedly, both in order to avoid mentioning anything which presupposes an acquaintance with what follows, and also for the purpose of unfolding first what we feel to be most important first to inculcate in cultivating the mental powers. Among the 'questions' whose meaning is quite plain, we must to begin with note that we place those only in which we perceive three things distinctly; to wit, the marks by which we can identify what we are looking for when it occurs; what precisely the fact is from which our answer ought to be deduced; and how it is to be proved that these (the ground and its consequence) so depend one on another that it is impossible for either to change while the other remains unchanged. In this way we shall have all the premisses we require, and the only thing remaining to be shown will be how to discover the conclusion. This will not be a matter of deducing some one fact from a single simple matter (we have already said that we can do this without the help of rules), but of disentangling so skilfully some one fact that is conditioned by a number of others which all involve one another, that in recognizing it there shall be no need to call upon a higher degree of mental power than in making the simplest inference. 'Questions' of this kind, being highly abstract and occurring almost exclusively in Arithmetic and Geometry, seem to the inexperienced

[1] There seems to be a break here. For a continuation of the doctrine cf. p. 51.

[2] Quaestiones. Inverted commas have been employed wherever it is important to remember Descartes' special technical of this term.

of little value. But I warn them that people ought to busy and exercise themselves a long time in learning this art, who desire to master the subsequent portions of this method, in which all the other types of 'question' are treated.

RULE XIII.

Once a 'question' is perfectly understood, we must free it of every conception superfluous to its meaning, state it in its simplest terms, and, having recourse to an enumeration, split it up into the various sections beyond which analysis cannot go in minuteness.

This is the only respect in which we imitate the Dialecticians; just as they, in teaching their doctrine of the forms of syllogism, assume that the terms or matter of their syllogisms are already known, so also we on this occasion lay it down as a prerequisite that the question to be solved should be perfectly understood. But we do not, as they, distinguish two extremes and a middle term. The following is the way in which we look at the whole matter. Firstly, in every 'question' there must be something of which we are ignorant; otherwise there is no use asking the question. Secondly, this very matter must be designated in some way or other; otherwise there would be nothing to determine us to investigate it rather than anything else. Thirdly, it can only be so designated by the aid of something else which is already known. All three conditions are realised even in questions that are not fully understood. Thus if the problem be the nature of the magnet, we already know what is meant by the two words 'magnet' and 'nature,' and this knowledge determines us to seek one sort of answer rather than another, and so on. But over and above this, if the question is to be perfectly stated, we require that it should be wholly determinate, so that we shall have nothing more to seek for than what can be inferred from the data. For example some one might set me the question, what is to be inferred about the nature of the magnet from that set of experiments precisely which Gilbert[1] asserts he has performed, be they trustworthy or not. So again the question may be, what my conclusion is as to the nature of sound, founding my judgment merely on the precise fact that the three strings A, B, and C give out an identical[2] sound, when by hypothesis B, though twice as thick as A, but not longer, is kept in tension by a weight that is

[1] *Gilbertus*, presumably the English physicist W. Gilbert 1540-1603 author of *De Magneto* (1600).
[2] aequalem.

twice as heavy; while C, though no thicker than A, but merely twice as long, is nevertheless kept in tension by a weight four times as heavy. Other illustrations might be given; but they all make it quite clear how all imperfectly expressed 'questions' may be reduced to others whose meaning is quite clear, as I shall show at greater length in the proper place. We see also how it is possible to follow this rule in divesting any difficulty, where the problem is properly realised, of every superfluous conception, and in reducing it to a form in which we no longer deem that we are treating of this or that special matter, but are dealing only in a general way with certain magnitudes which have to be fitted together[1]. Thus, to illustrate, after we have limited ourselves to the consideration of this or that set of experiments merely relative to the magnet, there is no difficulty in dismissing from view all other aspects of the case.

We add also that the problem[2] ought to be reduced to its simplest statement in accordance with Rules V and VI, and resolved into parts in accordance with Rule VII. Thus if I employ a number of experiments in investigating the magnet, I shall run them over successively, taking each by itself. Again if my inquiry is about sound, as in the case above, I shall separately consider the relation between strings A and B, then that between A and C, and so on, so that afterwards my enumeration of results may be sufficient, and may embrace every case. These three rules are the only ones which the pure understanding need observe in dealing with the terms of any proposition before approaching its ultimate solution, though that requires us to employ the following eleven rules. The third part of this Treatise will show us more clearly how to apply them. Further by a 'question' we understand everything in which either truth or falsity is found; and we must enumerate the different types of 'question' in order to determine what we are able to accomplish in each case.

We have already said that there can be no falsity in the mere intuition of things, whether they are simple or united together. So conceived these are not called 'questions,' but they acquire that designation so soon as we prepare to pass some determinate judgment about them. Neither do we limit the title to those questions which are set us by other people. His own ignorance, or more correctly his own doubt, presented a subject of inquiry to Socrates when first he began to study it and to inquire whether it

---

[1] 'componendas,' Amsterdam edit.; 'compared with one another,' Leibniz's MS.
[2] difficultatem.

was true that he doubted everything, and maintained that such was indeed the case.

Moreover in our 'questions' we seek to derive either things from words, or causes from effects, or effects from causes, or the whole or other parts from parts, or to infer several of these simultaneously.

We are said to seek to derive things from words when the difficulty consists merely in the obscurity of the language employed. To this class we refer firstly all riddles, like that of the Sphinx about the animal which to begin with is four-footed, then two-footed, and finally three-footed. A similar instance is that of the fishers who, standing on the bank with rods and hooks ready for the capture of fish, said that they no longer possessed those creatures which they had caught, but on the other hand had those which they had not yet been able to catch. So in other cases; but besides these, in the majority of matters on which the learned dispute, the question is almost always one of names. We ought not to judge so ill of our great thinkers as to imagine that they conceive the objects themselves wrongly, in cases where they do not employ fit words in explaining them. Thus when people call *place* the *surface of the surrounding body*, there is no real error in their conception; they merely employ wrongly the word *place*, which by common use signifies that simple and self-evident nature in virtue of which a thing is said to be here or there. This consists wholly in a certain relation of the thing said to be in the place towards the parts of the space external to it, and is a feature which certain writers, seeing that the name place was reserved for the surface of the surrounding body, have improperly called the thing's *intrinsic position*[1]. So it is in other cases; indeed these verbal questions are of such frequent occurrence, that almost all controversy would be removed from among Philosophers, if they were always to agree as to the meaning of words.

We seek to derive causes from effects when we ask concerning anything, whether it exists or what it is[2]....

Since, however, when a 'question' is propounded for solution we are frequently unable at once to discern its type, or to determine whether the problem is to derive things from words, or causes from effects, etc., for this reason it seems to be superfluous to say more here in detail about these matters. It will occupy less space and

---

[1] ubi intrinsecum.
[2] There is obviously a lacuna here. The lost MS. seems to have contained matter which is partly reproduced in a passage by Arnauld in the 2nd edition of the Port-Royal Logic. Cf. A. and T. x. pp. 470 sqq.

will be more convenient, if at the same time we go over in order all the steps which must be followed if we are to solve a problem of any sort. After that, when any 'question' is set, we must strive to understand distinctly what the inquiry is about.

For frequently people are in such a hurry in their investigations, that they bring only a blank understanding to their solution, without having settled what the marks are by which they are to recognize the fact of which they are in search, if it chance to occur. This is a proceeding as foolish as that of a boy, who, sent on an errand by his master, should be so eager to obey as to run off without having received his orders or knowing where to go.

However, though in every 'question' something must be unknown, otherwise there is no need to raise it, we should nevertheless so define this unknown element by means of specific conditions that we shall be determined towards the investigation of one thing rather than another. These are conditions to which, we maintain, attention must be paid at the very outset. We shall succeed in this if we so direct our mental vision as to have a distinct and intuitive presentation of each by itself, and inquire diligently how far the unknown fact for which we are in search is limited by each. For the human mind is wont to fall into error in two ways here; it either assumes more than is really given in determining the question, or, on the other hand, leaves something out.

We must take care to assume neither more nor less than our data furnish us. This applies chiefly to riddles and other problems where the object of the skill employed is to try to puzzle people's wits. But frequently also we must bear it in mind in other 'questions,' when it appears as though we could assume as true for the purpose of their solution a certain matter which we have accepted, not because we had a good reason for doing so, but merely because we had always believed it. Thus, for example, in the riddle put by the Sphinx, it is not necessary to believe that the word 'foot' refers merely to the real foot of an animal; we must inquire also whether the term cannot be transferred to other things, as it may be, as it happens, to the hands of an infant, or an old man's staff, because in either case these accessories are employed as feet are in walking. So too, in the fishermen's conundrum, we must beware of letting the thought of fish occupy our minds to the exclusion of those creatures which the poor so often carry about with them unwillingly, and fling away from them when caught. So again, we must be on our guard when inquiring into the construction of a vessel, such as we once saw, in the midst of which stood a column and upon that a figure of Tantalus in the attitude of a man who wants to drink. Water when poured into the vessel remained within without leaking as long as it was not high enough to enter the mouth of Tantalus; but as soon as it touched the unhappy man's lips the whole of it at once flowed out and escaped. Now at the first blush it seems as if the whole of the ingenuity consisted in the construction of this figure of Tantalus, whereas in reality this is a mere accompaniment of the fact requiring explanation, and in no way conditions it. For the whole difficulty consists solely in the problem of how the vessel was constructed so as to let out the whole of the water when that arrived at a certain height, whereas before none escaped. Finally, likewise, if we seek to extract from the recorded observations of the stars an answer to the question as to what we can assert about their motions, it is not to be gratuitously assumed that the earth is immoveable and established in the midst of the universe, as the Ancients would have it, because from our earliest years it appears to be so. We ought to regard this as dubious, in order afterwards to examine what certainty there is in this matter to which we are able to attain. So in other cases.

On the other hand we sin by omission when there is some condition requisite to the determination of the question either expressed in it or in some way to be understood, which we do not bear in mind. This may happen in an inquiry into the subject of perpetual motion, not as we meet with it in nature in the movements of the stars and the flowing of springs, but as a motion contrived by human industry. Numbers of people have believed this to be possible, their idea being that the earth is in perpetual motion in a circle round its own axis, while again the magnet retains all the properties of the earth. A man might then believe that he would discover a perpetual motion if he so contrived it that a magnet should revolve in a circle, or at least that it communicated its own motion along with its other properties to a piece of iron. Now although he were to succeed in this, it would not be a perpetual motion artificially contrived; all he did would be to utilize a natural motion, just as if he were to station a wheel in the current of a river so as to secure an unceasing motion on its part. Thus in his procedure he would have omitted a condition requisite for the resolution of his problem.

When we have once adequately grasped the meaning of a 'question,' we ought to try and see exactly wherein the difficulty consists, in order that, by separating it out from all complicating circumstances, we may solve it the more easily. But over and above this we must attend to the various separate problems involved in it, in order that if there are any which are easy to resolve we may omit them; when these are removed, only that will remain of which we are still in ignorance. Thus in that instance of the vessel which was described a short time ago, it is indeed quite easy to see how the vessel should be made; a column must be fixed in its centre, a bird[1] must be painted on it. But all these things will be set aside as not touching the essential point; thus we are left with the difficulty by itself, consisting in the fact that the whole of the water, which had previously remained in the vessel, after reaching a certain height, flows out. It is for this that we have to seek a reason.

Here therefore we maintain that what is worth while doing is simply this—to explore in an orderly way all the data furnished by the proposition, to set aside everything which we see is clearly immaterial, to retain what is necessarily bound up with the problem, and to reserve what is doubtful for a more careful examination.

Rule XIV.

The same rule is to be applied also to the real extension of bodies. It must be set before the imagination by means of mere figures, for this is the best way to make it clear to the understanding.

But[2] in proposing to make use of the imagination as an aid to our thinking, we must note that whenever one unknown fact is deduced from another that is already known, that does not show that we discover any new kind of entity, but merely that this whole mass of knowledge is extended in such a way that we perceive that the matter sought for participates in one way or another in the nature of the data given in the proposition. For example if a man has been blind from his birth it is not to be expected that we shall be able by any train of reasoning to make him perceive the true ideas of the colours which we have derived from our senses. But if a man has indeed once perceived the primary colours, though he has never seen the intermediate or mixed tints, it is possible for

---

[1] Leibniz's MS. has 'axis' and Garnier conjectures 'fingenda' Translate 'a valve must be fitted in it.'

[2] Clearly the sense is continuous with that of the last paragraph in the exposition of the previous rule. The formulated rule has in this case at least been inserted later.

him to construct the images of those which he has not seen from their likeness to the others, by a sort of deduction. Similarly if in the magnet there be any sort of nature[1] the like of which our mind has never yet known, it is hopeless to expect that reasoning will ever make us grasp it; we should have to be furnished either with some new sense or with a divine intellect[2]. But we shall believe ourselves to have attained whatever in this matter can be achieved by our human faculties, if we discern with all possible distinctness that mixture of entities or natures already known which produces just those effects which we notice in the magnet.

Indeed all these previously known entities, viz. extension, figure, motion and the like, the enumeration of which does not belong to this place, are recognized by means of an idea which is one and the same in the various subject matters. The figure of a silver crown which we imagine, is just the same as that of one that is golden. Further this common idea is transferred from one subject to another, merely by means of the simple comparison by which we affirm that the object sought for is in this or that respect like, or identical with, or equal to a particular datum. Consequently in every train of reasoning it is by comparison merely that we attain to a precise knowledge of the truth. Here is an example:—all *A* is *B*, all *B* is *C*, therefore all *A* is *C*. Here we compare with one another a *quaesitum* and a *datum*, viz. *A* and *C*, in respect of the fact that each is *B*, and so on. But because, as we have often announced, the syllogistic forms are of no aid in perceiving the truth about objects, it will be for the reader's profit to reject them altogether and to conceive that all knowledge whatsoever, other than that which consists in the simple and naked intuition of single independent objects, is a matter of the comparison of two things or more, with each other. In fact practically the whole of the task set the human reason consists in preparing for this operation; for when it is open and simple, we need no aid from art, but are bound to rely upon the light of nature alone, in beholding the truth which comparison gives us.

We must further mark that comparison should be simple and open, only as often as *quaesitum* and *datum* participate equally in a certain nature. Note that the only reason why preparation is required for comparison that is not of this nature is the fact that the common nature we spoke of does not exist equally in both, but

---

[1] entis.   [2] mente.

is complicated with certain other relations or ratios. The chief part of our human industry consists merely in so transmuting these ratios as to show clearly a uniformity[1] between the matter sought for and something else already known.

Next we must mark that nothing can be reduced to this uniformity[1], save that which admits of a greater and a less, and that all such matter is included under the term magnitude. Consequently when, in conformity with the previous rule, we have freed the terms of the problem from any reference to a particular subject, we shall discover that all we have left to deal with consists of magnitudes in general.

We shall, however, even in this case make use of our imagination, employing not the naked understanding but the intellect as aided by images of particulars[2] depicted on the fancy. Finally we must note that nothing can be asserted of magnitudes in general that cannot also be ascribed to any particular instance[3].

This lets us easily conclude that there will be no slight profit in transferring whatsoever we find asserted of magnitudes in general to that particular species of magnitude which is most easily and distinctly depicted in our imagination. But it follows from what we stated about the twelfth rule that this must be the real extension of body abstracted from everything else except the fact that it has figure ; for in that place we represented the imagination itself along with the ideas it contains as nothing more than a really material body possessing extension and figure. This is also itself evident ; for no other subject displays more distinctly differences in ratio of whatsoever kind. Though one thing can be said to be more or less white than another, or a sound sharper or flatter, and so on, it is yet impossible to determine exactly whether the greater exceeds the less in the proportion two to one, or three to one, etc., unless we treat the quantity as being in a certain way analogous to the extension of a body possessing figure. Let us then take it as fixed and certain that perfectly definite 'questions' are almost free from difficulty other than that of transmuting ratios so that they may be stated as equations[4]. Let us agree too that everything in which we discover precisely this difficulty, can be easily, and ought to be,

---

[1] aequalitas.   [2] speciebus.

[3] An alternative way of translating this paragraph would be to make the previous sentence follow the present one. We should then have to begin it differently, viz. 'This will teach us even then to make use of our imagination etc.'

[4] 'in proportionibus in aequalitates evolvendis,' conj. A. and T. ; 'in aequalitatibus,' Leibniz's MS.; 'inaequalitatis,' Amsterdam ed.

disengaged from reference to every other subject, and immediately stated in terms of extension and figure. It is about these alone that we shall for this reason henceforth treat, up to and as far as the twenty-fifth rule, omitting the consideration of everything else.

My desire is that here I may find a reader who is an eager student of Arithmetic and Geometry, though indeed I should prefer him to have had no practice in these arts, rather than to be an adept after the ordinary standard. For the employment of the rules which I here unfold is much easier in the study of Arithmetic and Geometry (and it is all that is needed in learning them) than in inquiries of any other kind. Further its usefulness as a means towards the attainment of a profounder knowledge is so great, that I have no hesitation in saying that it was not the case that this part of our method was invented for the purpose of dealing with mathematical problems, but rather that mathematics should be studied almost solely for the purpose of training us in this method. I shall presume no knowledge of anything in mathematics except perhaps such facts as are self-evident and obvious to everyone. But the way in which people ordinarily think about them, even though not vitiated by any glaring errors, yet obscures our knowledge with many ambiguous and ill-conceived principles, which we shall try incidentally to correct in the following pages.

By extension we understand whatever has length, breadth, and depth, not inquiring whether it be a real body or merely space; nor does it appear to require further explanation, since there is nothing more easily perceived by our imagination. Yet the learned frequently employ distinctions so subtle that the light of nature is dissipated in attending to them, and even those matters of which no peasant is ever in doubt become invested in obscurity. Hence we announce that by extension we do not here mean anything distinct and separate from the extended object itself; and we make it a rule not to recognize those metaphysical[1] entities which really cannot be presented to the imagination. For even though someone could persuade himself, for example, that supposing every extended object in the universe were annihilated, that would not prevent extension in itself alone existing, this conception of his would not involve the use of any corporeal image[2], but would be based on a false judgment of the intellect working by itself. He will admit this himself, if he reflect attentively on this very image of extension when, as will then

---

[1] philosophica.　　　　[2] idea.

happen, he tries to construct it in his imagination. For he will notice that, as he perceives it, it is not divested of a reference to every object, but that his imagination of it is quite different from his judgment about it. Consequently, whatever our understanding may believe as to the truth of the matter, those abstract entities are never given to our imagination as separate from the objects in which they inhere.

But since henceforth we are to attempt nothing without the aid of the imagination, it will be worth our while to distinguish carefully the ideas which in each separate case are to convey to the understanding the meaning of the words we employ. To this end we submit for consideration these three forms of expression :—*extension occupies place, body possesses extension*, and *extension is not body.*

The first statement shows how extension may be substituted for that which is extended. My conception is entirely the same if I say *extension occupies place*, as when I say *that which is extended occupies place*. Yet that is no reason why, in order to avoid ambiguity, it should be better to use the term *that which is extended;* for that does not indicate so distinctly our precise meaning, which is, that a subject occupies place owing to the fact that it is extended. Someone might interpret the expression to mean merely *that which is extended is an object occupying place*, just in the same way as if I had said *that which is animate occupies place*. This explains why we announced that here we would treat of extension[1], preferring that to ' the extended[2],' although we believe that there is no difference in the conception of the two.

Let us now take up these words : *body possesses extension*. Here the meaning of *extension* is not identical with that of body, yet we do not construct two distinct ideas in our imagination, one of body, the other of extension, but merely a single image of extended body; and from the point of view of the thing it is exactly as if I had said : *body is extended*, or better, *the extended is extended*. This is a peculiarity of those entities which have their being merely in something else, and can never be conceived without the subject in which they exist. How different is it with those matters which are really distinct from the subjects of which they are predicated. If, for example, I say *Peter has wealth*, my idea of Peter is quite different from that of wealth. So if I say *Paul is wealthy*, my image is quite different from that which I should have if I said *the*

[1] extensio.   [2] extensum.

wealthy man is wealthy. Failure to distinguish the diversity between these two cases is the cause of the error of those numerous people who believe that extension contains something distinct from that which is extended, in the same way as Paul's wealth is something different from Paul himself.

Finally, take the expression : *extension is not body.* Here the term extension is taken quite otherwise than as above. When we give it this meaning there is no special idea corresponding to it in the imagination. In fact this entire assertion is the work of the naked understanding, which alone has the power of separating out abstract entities of this type. But this is a stumbling-block for many, who, not perceiving that extension so taken, cannot be grasped by the imagination, represent it to themselves by means of a genuine image. Now such an idea necessarily involves the concept of body, and if they say that extension so conceived is not body, their heedlessness involves them in the contradiction of saying that *the same thing is at the same time body and not body.* It is likewise of great moment to distinguish the meaning of the enunciations in which such names as *extension, figure, number, superficies, line, point, unity,* etc. are used in so restricted a way as to exclude matters from which they are not really distinct. Thus when we say : *extension* or *figure is not body ; number is not the thing that is counted ; a super ficies is the boundary of a body, the line the limit of a surface, the point of a line ; unity is not a quantity,* etc.; all these and similar propositions must be taken altogether outside the bounds of the imagination, if they are to be true. Consequently we shall not discuss them in the sequel.

But we should carefully note that in all other propositions in which these terms, though retaining the same signification and employed in abstraction from their subject matter, do not exclude or deny anything from which they are not really distinct, it is both possible and necessary to use the imagination as an aid. The reason is that even though the understanding in the strict sense attends merely to what is signified by the name, the imagination nevertheless ought to fashion a correct image[1] of the object, in order that the very understanding itself may be able to fix upon other features belonging to it that are not expressed by the name in question, whenever there is occasion to do so, and may never imprudently believe that they have been excluded. Thus, if number be the

---

[1] ideam.

question, we imagine an object which we can measure by summing a plurality of units. Now though it is allowable for the understanding to confine its attention for the present solely to the multiplicity displayed by the object, we must be on our guard nevertheless not on that account afterwards to come to any conclusion which implies that the object which we have described numerically has been excluded from our concept. But this is what those people do who ascribe mysterious properties to number, empty inanities in which they certainly would not believe so strongly, unless they conceived that number was something distinct from the things we number. In the same way, if we are dealing with figure, let us remember that we are concerned with an extended subject, though we restrict ourselves to conceiving it merely as possessing figure. When body is the object let us reflect that we are dealing with the very same thing, taken as possessing length, breadth and depth. Where superficies comes in, our object will still be the same[1] though we conceive it as having length and breadth, and we shall leave out the element of depth, without denying it. The line will be considered as having length merely, while in the case of the point the object, though still the same, will be divested in our thought of every characteristic save that of being something existent.

In spite of the way in which I have dwelt on this topic, I fear that men's minds are so dominated by prejudice that very few are free from the danger of losing their way here, and that, notwithstanding the length of my discourse, I shall be found to have explained myself too briefly. Those very disciplines Arithmetic and Geometry, though the most certain of all the sciences, nevertheless lead us astray here. For is there a single Arithmetician who does not believe that the numbers with which he deals are not merely held in abstraction from any subject matter by the understanding, but are really distinct objects of the imagination? Does not your Geometrician obscure the clearness of his subject by employing irreconcileable principles? He tells you that lines have no breadth, surfaces no depth; yet he subsequently wishes to generate the one out of the other, not noticing that a line, the movement of which is conceived to create a surface, is really a body; or that, on the other hand, the line which has no breadth, is merely a mode of body. But, not to take more time in going over these matters, it will be more expeditious for us to expound the way in which we assume our

---

[1] Adopting A. and T.'s conjecture of 'idem' for 'item.'

object should be taken, in order that we may most easily give a proof of whatsoever is true in Arithmetic and Geometry.

Here therefore we deal with an extended object, considering nothing at all involved in it save extension, and purposely refraining from using the word quantity, because there are certain Philosophers so subtle as to distinguish it also from extension. We assume such a simplification of our problems as to leave nothing else to be inquired about except the determination of a certain extension by comparing it with a certain other extension that is already determinately known. For here we do not look to discover any new sort of fact; we merely wish to make a simplification of ratios, be they ever so involved, such that we may discover some equation[1] between what is unknown and something known. Since this is so, it is certain that whatsoever differences in ratio exist in these subjects can be found to prevail also between two or more extensions. Hence our purpose is sufficiently served if in extension itself we consider everything that can aid us in setting out differences in ratio ; but there are only three such features, viz. dimension, unity and figure.

By dimension I understand nothing but the mode and aspect according to which a subject is considered to be measurable. Thus it is not merely the case that length, breadth and depth are dimensions; but weight also is a dimension in terms of which the heaviness of objects is estimated. So, too, speed is a dimension of motion, and there are an infinite number of similar instances. For that very division of the whole into a number of parts of identical nature, whether it exist in the real order of things or be merely the work of the understanding, gives us exactly that dimension in terms of which we apply number to objects. Again that mode which constitutes number is properly said to be a species of dimension, though there is not an absolute identity between the meaning of the two terms. For if we proceed by taking part after part until we reach the whole, the operation is then said to be counting, whereas if conversely we look upon the whole as something split up into parts, it is an object which we measure. Thus we measure centuries by years, days, hours and moments, while if we count up moments, hours, days and years, we shall finish with a total of centuries.

It clearly follows that there may be an infinite number of dimensions in the same subject, which make no addition at all to the

---

[1] ut illud, quod est ignotum, aequale cuidam cognito reperiatur.

objects which possess them, but have the same meaning whether they are based on anything real in the objects themselves, or are the arbitrary inventions of our own mind. Weight is indeed something real existing in a body, and the speed of motion is a reality, and so with the division of a century into years and days. But it is otherwise with the division of the day into hours and moments, etc. Yet all these subdivisions are exactly similar if considered merely from the point of view of dimension, as we ought to regard them both here and in the science of Mathematics. It falls rather to Physics to inquire whether they are founded on anything real.

Recognition of this fact throws much light on Geometry, since in that science almost everyone goes wrong in conceiving that quantity has three species, the line, the superficies, and the solid. But we have already stated that the line and the superficies are not conceived as being really distinct from solid body, or from one another. Moreover if they are taken in their bare essence as abstractions of the understanding, they are no more diverse species of quantity than the 'animal' and 'living creature' in man are diverse species of substance. Incidentally also we have to note that the three dimensions of body, length, breadth and depth, are only in name distinct from one another. For there is nothing to prevent us, in any solid body with which we are dealing, from taking any of the extensions it presents as the length, or any other as its depth, and so on. And though these three dimensions have a real basis in every extended object quâ extended, we have nevertheless no special concern in this science with them more than with countless others, which are either mental creations or have some other ground in objects. For example in the case of the triangle, if we wish to measure it exactly, we must acquaint ourselves with three features of its existence, viz. either its three sides, or two sides and an angle, or two angles and its area, and so forth. Now these can all be styled dimensions. Similarly in a trapezium five facts have to be noted, in a tetrahedron six, and so on. But if we wish to choose here those dimensions which shall give most aid to our imagination, we shall never attend at the same time to more than one or two of those depicted in our imagination, even though we know that in the matter set before us with which we are dealing several others are involved. For the art of our method consists in distinguishing as many elements as possible, so that though we attend to only a few simultaneously, we shall yet cover them all in time, taking one after the other.

The unit is that common element in which, as above remarked, all the things compared with each other should equally participate. If this be not already settled in our problems, we can represent it by one of the magnitudes already presented to us, or by any other magnitude we like, and it will be the common measure of all the others. We shall understand that in it there exists every dimension found in those very widely sundered facts which are to be compared with each other, and we shall conceive it either (1) merely as something extended, omitting every other more precise determination—and then it will be identical with the point of Geometry, considered as generating a line by its movement; or (2) we shall conceive it as a line, or (3) as a square.

To come to figures, we have already shown above how it is they alone that give us a means of constructing the images of all objects whatsoever. It remains to give notice in this place, that of the innumerable diverse species of figure, we shall employ only those which most readily express differences of relation or proportion. Moreover there are two sorts of objects only which are compared with each other, viz. numerical assemblages[1] and magnitudes. Now there are also two sorts of figures by means of which these may be presented to our conception. For example we have the points

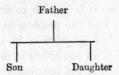

which represent a triangular[2] number, or again the 'tree which illustrates genealogical relation as in such a case—

Father

Son   Daughter

So in similar instances. Now these are figures designed to express

---

[1] multitudines.

[2] 'triangularis,' conjecture, A. and T. Previous versions give 'triangulorum.' 'Triangular' numbers are the sums of the natural numbers, viz. 1, 3, 6, 10, etc., and thus can be constructed from any number n according to the formula $\dfrac{n\,(n+1)}{2}$.

numerical assemblages; but those which are continuous and undivided like the triangle, the square, etc.,

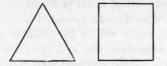

explain the nature of magnitudes.

But in order that we may point out which of all these figures we
are going to use, it ought to be known that all the relations which
can exist between things of this kind, must be referred to two heads,
viz. either to order or to measurement.

We must further realise that while the discovery of an order is
no light task, as may be seen throughout this treatise, which makes
this practically its sole subject, yet once the order has been discovered there is no difficulty at all in knowing it. The seventh rule
shows us how we may easily review in sequence mentally the
separate elements which have been arranged in order, for the reason
that in this class of relation the bond between the terms is a direct
one involving nothing but the terms themselves, and not requiring
mediation by means of a third term, as is the case in measurement.
The unfolding of relations of measurement will therefore be all that
we shall treat of here. For I recognize the order in which *A* and *B*
stand, without considering anything except these two—the extreme
terms of the relation. But I can recognize the ratio of the
magnitude of two to that of three, only by considering some third
thing, namely unity, which is the common measure of both.

We must likewise bear in mind that, by the help of the unit we
have assumed, continuous magnitudes can sometimes be reduced in
their entirety to numerical expressions, and that this can always be
partly realised. Further it is possible to arrange our assemblage of
units in such an order that the problem which previously[1] was one
requiring the solution of a question in measurement, is now a
matter merely involving an inspection of order. Now our method
helps us greatly in making the progress which this transformation
effects.

Finally remember that of the dimensions of continuous magnitude none are more distinctly conceived than length and breadth,
and that we ought not to attend to more than these two simultaneously in the same figure, if we are to compare two diverse things

---

[1] 'pertinebat,' conj. A. and T.; edd. and MS. 'pertineat.'

with each other. The reason is, that when we have more than two diverse things to compare with each other, our method consists in reviewing them successively and attending only to two of them at the same time.

Observation of these facts leads us easily to our conclusion. This is that there is no less reason for abstracting our propositions from those figures of which Geometry treats, if the inquiry is one involving them, than from any other subject matter. Further, in doing so we need retain nothing but rectilinear and rectangular superficies, or else straight lines, which we also call figures, because they serve quite as well as surfaces in aiding us to imagine an object which actually has extension, as we have already said. Finally those same figures have to represent for us now continuous magnitudes, again a plurality of units or number also. Human ingenuity can devise nothing simpler for the complete expression of differences of relation.

Rule XV.

It is likewise very often helpful to draw these figures and display them to the external senses, in order thus to facilitate the continued fixation of our attention.

The way in which these figures should be depicted so that, in being displayed before our eyes, the images may be the more distinctly formed in our imagination is quite self-evident. To begin with we represent unity in three ways, viz. by a square, $\square$, if we consider our unit as having length and breadth, or secondly by a line, ——, if we take it merely as having length, or lastly by a point, •, if we think only of the fact that it is that by aid of which we construct a numerical assemblage. But however it is depicted and conceived, we shall always remember that the unit is an object extended in every direction, and admitting of countless dimensions. So also the terms of our proposition, in cases where we have to attend at the same time to two different magnitudes belonging to them, will be represented by a rectangle whose two sides will be the two magnitudes in question. Where they are incommensurable[1] with our unit we shall employ the following figure,

---

[1] A correction first made by Garnier. The Amsterdam ed. and Leibniz's MS. have 'commensurabiles.'

but where they are commensurable[1] we shall use this

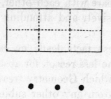

or this

and nothing more is needed save where it is a question of a numerical assemblage of units. Finally if we attend only to one of the magnitudes of the terms employed, we shall portray that either as a rectangle, of which one side is the magnitude considered and the other is unity, thus [   ]—and this will happen whenever the magnitude has to be compared with some surface. Or we shall employ a line alone, in this fashion, ——, if we take it as an incommensurable[2] length; or thus, • • • • •, if it be a number.

RULE XVI.

When we come across matters which do not require our present attention, it is better, even though they are necessary to our conclusion, to represent them by highly abbreviated symbols, rather than by complete figures. This guards against error due to defect of memory on the one hand, and, on the other, prevents that distraction of thought which an effort to keep those matters in mind while attending to other inferences would cause.

But[3] because our maxim is that not more than two different dimensions out of the countless number that can be depicted in our imagination ought to be the object either of our bodily or of our mental vision, it is of importance so to retain all those outside the range of present attention that they may easily come up to mind as often as need requires. Now memory seems to be a faculty created by nature for this very purpose. But since it is liable to fail us, and in order to obviate the need of expending any part of our attention

---

[1] If we adopt a different punctuation of the text, the sentence will continue 'and it is only a question of a numerical assemblage of units,' omitting what follows the figures.

[2] It is not clear whether this means 'incommensurable with the standard unit of length' or 'incommensurable with a surface.'

[3] Cf. note on Rule XIV. ad init.

in refreshing it, while we are engaged with other thoughts, art has most opportunely invented the device of writing. Relying on the help this gives us, we leave nothing whatsoever to memory, but keep our imagination wholly free to receive the ideas which are immediately occupying us, and set down on paper whatever ought to be preserved. In doing so we employ the very briefest symbols, in order that, after distinctly examining each point in accordance with Rule IX, we may be able, as Rule XI bids us do, to traverse them all with an extremely rapid motion of our thought and include as many as possible in a single intuitive glance.

Everything, therefore, which is to be looked upon as single from the point of view of the solution of our problem, will be represented by a single symbol which can be constructed in any way we please. But to make things easier we shall employ the characters a, b, c, etc. for expressing magnitudes already known, and A, B, C, etc. for symbolising those that are unknown. To these we shall often prefix the numerical symbols, 1, 2, 3, 4, etc., for the purpose of making clear their number, and again we shall append those symbols to the former when we want to indicate the number of the relations which are to be remarked in them. Thus if I employ the formula $2a^3$ that will be the equivalent of the words 'the double of the magnitude which is symbolised by the letter a, and which contains three relations.' By this device not only shall we economize our words, but, which is the chief thing, display the terms of our problem in such a detached and unencumbered way that, even though it is so full as to omit nothing, there will nevertheless be nothing superfluous to be discovered in our symbols, or anything to exercise our mental powers to no purpose, by requiring the mind to grasp a number of things at the same time.

In order that all this may be more clearly understood, we must note first, that while Arithmeticians have been wont to designate undivided magnitudes by groups of units, or else by some number, we on the other hand abstract at this point from numbers themselves no less than from Geometrical figures or anything else, as we did a little time ago. Our reason for doing this is partly to avoid the tedium of a long and superfluous calculation, but chiefly that those portions of the matter considered which are relevant to the problem may always remain distinct, and may not be entangled with numbers that are of no help to us at all. Thus if we are trying to find the hypotenuse of the right-angled triangle whose sides are 9 and 12, the Arithmetician will tell us that it is $\sqrt{225}$, i.e. 15. But we shall write a and b in place of 9 and 12, and shall find the hypotenuse to be $\sqrt{a^2 + b^2}$; and the two members of the expression a^2 and b^2 will remain distinct, whereas the number confuses them altogether.

Note further that by the number of relations attaching to a quantity I mean a sequence of ratios in continued proportion, such as the Algebra now in vogue attempts to express by sundry dimensions and figures. It calls the first of these the radix, the second the square, the third the cube, the fourth the biquadratic, and so on. I confess that for a long time I myself was imposed upon by these names. For, after the straight line and the square there was nothing which seemed to be capable of being placed more clearly before my imagination than the cube and the other figures of the same type; and with their aid I succeeded in solving not a few difficulties. But at last, after testing the matter well, I discovered that I had never found out anything by their means which I could not have recognized more easily and distinctly without employing their aid. I saw that this whole nomenclature must be abandoned, if our conceptions are not to become confused; for that very magnitude which goes by the name of the cube or the biquadratic, is nevertheless never to be presented to the imagination otherwise than as a line or a surface, in accordance with the previous rule. We must therefore be very clear about the fact that the radix, the square, the cube, etc., are merely magnitudes in continued proportion, which always imply the previous assumption of that arbitrarily chosen unit of which we spoke above. Now the first proportional is related to this unit directly and by a single ratio. But the second proportional requires the mediation of the first, and consequently is related to the unit by a pair of ratios. The third, being mediated by the first and second, has a triple relation to the standard unit, and so on. Therefore we shall henceforth call that magnitude, which in Algebra is styled the radix, the first proportional; that called the square we shall term the second proportional, and so in other cases.

Finally it must be noticed that even though here, in order to examine the nature of a difficulty, we abstract the terms involved from certain numerical complications, it yet often happens that a simpler solution will be found by employing the given numbers than if we abstract from them. This is due to the double function of numbers, already pointed out, which use the same symbols to express now order, and now measure. Hence, after seeking a solution in general terms for our problem, we ought to transform its terms by substituting for them the given numbers, in order to see whether these supply us with any simpler solution. Thus, to illustrate, after seeing that the hypotenuse of the right-angled triangle whose sides are a and b is $\sqrt{a^2 + b^2}$, we should substitute 81 for a^2, and 144 for b^2. These added together give 225, the root of which, or mean proportional between unity and 225, is 15. This will let us see that a hypotenuse whose length is 15 is commensurable with sides whose lengths are 9 and 12, quite apart from the general law that it is the hypotenuse of a right-angled triangle whose sides are as 3 to 4. We, whose object is to discover a knowledge of things which shall be evident and distinct, insist on all those distinctions. It is quite otherwise with Arithmeticians, who, if the result required turns up, are quite content even though they do not perceive how it depends upon the data, though it is really in knowledge of this kind alone that science properly consists.

Moreover, it must be observed that, as a general rule, nothing that does not require to be continuously borne in mind ought to be committed to memory, if we can set it down on paper. This is to prevent that waste of our powers which occurs if some part of our attention is taken up with the presence of an object in our thought which it is superfluous to bear in mind. What we ought to do is to make a reference-table and set down in it the terms of the problem as they are first stated. Then we should state the way in which the abstract formulation is to be made and the symbols to be employed, in order that, when the solution has been obtained in terms of these symbols, we may easily apply it, without calling in the aid of memory at all, to the particular case we are considering : for it is only in passing from a lesser to a greater degree of generality that abstraction has any *raison d'être*. What I should write therefore would be something like this:—

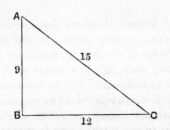

In the right-angled triangle ABC to find the hypotenuse AC (stating the problem abstractly, in order that the derivation of the length of the hypotenuse from the lengths of the sides may be quite

general).   Then for *AB*, which is equal to 9, I shall substitute *a*;
for *BC*, equal to 12, I put *b*, and similarly in other cases.

To conclude, we draw attention to the fact that these four rules
will be further employed in the third part of this Treatise, though
we shall conceive them somewhat more generally than we have been
doing.   But all this will be explained in its proper place.

RULE XVII.

*When a problem is proposed for discussion we should run it over,
taking a direct course, and for this reason neglecting the fact that
some of its terms are known, others unknown.   To follow the true
connection, when presenting to mind the dependence of separate items
on one another, will also aid us to do this.*

The four previous rules showed us how, when the problems are
determinate and fully comprehended, we may abstract them from
their subject matter and so transform them that nothing remains to
be investigated save how to discover certain magnitudes, from the
fact that they bear such and such a relation to certain other magnitudes already given.   But in the five following rules we shall now
explain how these same problems are to be treated in such a way
that though a single proposition contains ever so many unknown
magnitudes they may all be subordinated to one another ; the second
will stand to the first, as the first to unity, and so too the third to
the second, and the fourth to the third, and so in succession, making,
however numerous, a total magnitude equal to a certain known
magnitude.   In doing this our method will be so sure that we may
safely affirm that it passes the wit of man to reduce our terms to
anything simpler.

For the present, however, I remark that in every inquiry that is
to be solved by deduction there is one way that is plain and direct,
by which we may more easily than by any other pass from one set
of terms to another, while all other routes are more difficult and
indirect.   In order to understand this we must remember what was
said relative to the eleventh rule, where we expounded the nature of
that chain of propositions, a comparison of the neighbouring members
of which enables us to see how the first is related to the last, even
though it is not so easy to deduce the intermediate terms from the
extremes.   Now therefore if we fix our attention on the interdepend-

ence of the various links, without ever interrupting the order, so that we may thence infer how the last depends upon the first, we review the problem in a direct manner. But, on the other hand, if, from the fact that we know the first and the last to be connected with each other in a certain way, we should want to deduce the nature of the middle terms which connect them, we should then be following an order that was wholly indirect and upside down. But because here we are considering only involved inquiries, in which the problem is, given certain extremes, to find certain intermediates by the inverse process of reasoning, the whole of the device here disclosed will consist in treating the unknown as though they were known, and thus being able to adopt the easy and direct method of investigation even in problems involving any amount of intricacy. There is nothing to prevent us always achieving this result, since we have assumed from the commencement of this section of our work that we recognize the dependence of the unknown terms in the inquiry on those that are known to be such that the former are determined by the latter. This determination also is such that if, recognizing it, we consider the terms which first present themselves and reckon them even though unknown among the known, and thus deduce from them step by step and by a true connection all the other terms, even those which are known, treating them as though they were unknown, we shall fully realise the purpose of this rule. Illustrations of this doctrine, as of the most of what is immediately to follow, will be reserved until the twenty-fourth rule[1], since it will be more convenient to expound them there.

Rule XVIII.

To this end only four operations are required, addition, subtraction, multiplication and division. Of these the two latter are often to be dispensed with here, both in order to avoid any unforeseen complication, and because it will be easier to deal with them at a later stage.

It is often from lack of experience on the part of the teacher that the multiplicity of rules proceeds; and matters that might have been reduced to one general rule are less clear if distributed among many particular statements. Wherefore we propose to reduce the whole of the operations which it is advisable to employ in going through our inquiry, i.e. in deducing certain magnitudes

---

[1] No such rule has been found among Descartes' papers.

from others, to as few as four heads. It will become clear when we come to explain these how it is that they suffice for the purpose.

This is how we proceed. If we arrive at the knowledge of one magnitude owing to the fact that we already know the parts of which it is composed, the process is one of addition. If we discover the part because we already know the whole and the excess of the whole over this part, it is division. Further it is impossible to derive a magnitude from others that are determinately fixed, and in which it is in any way contained, by any other methods. But if we have to derive a magnitude from others from which it is wholly diverse and in which it is in nowise contained, we must find some other way of relating it to them. Now if we trace out this connection or relation directly we must employ multiplication; if indirectly, division.

In explaining clearly these latter two operations the fact must be grasped that the unit of which we spoke before is here the basis and foundation of all the relations, and has the first place in the series of magnitudes in continued proportion. Further, remember that the given magnitudes occupy the second position, while those to be discovered stand at the third, the fourth and the remaining points in the series, if the proportion[1] be direct. If, however, the proportion be indirect, the magnitude to be discovered occupies the second position or the other intermediate points, and that which is given, the last.

Thus if it is stated that as unity is to a, say to 5, which is given, so is b, i.e. 7, to the magnitude to be found[2], which is ab, i.e. 35, then a and b are at the second position, and ab, their product, at the third. So too if we are further told that as 1 is to c, say 9, so is ab, say 35, to the magnitude we are seeking, i.e. 315, then abc is in the fourth position, and is the product of two multiplications among the terms a, b and c, which are at the second position; so it is in other cases. Likewise as 1 is to a, say 5, so a, i.e. 5, is to a^2, i.e. 25. Again, as unity is to a, i.e. 5, so is a^2, i.e. 25, to a^3, i.e. 125; and finally as unity is to a, i.e. 5, so is a^3, i.e. 125, to a^4, i.e. 625, and so on. For the multiplication is performed in precisely the same way, whether the magnitude is multiplied by itself or by some other quite different number.

But if we now are told that, as unity is to a, say 5, the given

---

[1] A correction first made by Cousin—'proportio' instead of 'propositio.'

[2] Note that here Descartes does not, and could not conveniently, adhere to his scheme of employing capital letters for the unknown quantities.

divisor, so is *B*, say 7, *the quaesitum*, to *ab*, i.e. 35, the given dividend, we have on this occasion an example of the indirect or inverted order. For the only way to discover *B*, the *quaesitum*, is to divide the given *ab* by *a*, which is also given. The case is the same if the proposition is, 'as unity is to *A*, say 5, the *quaesitum*, so is this *A* to *a²*, i.e. 25, which is given'; or again, 'as unity is to *A*, i.e. 5, the *quaesitum*, so is *A²*, i.e. 25, which we also have to discover, to *a³*, i.e. 125, which is given'; similarly in other cases. All these processes fall under the title 'division,' although we must note that these latter specimens of the process contain more difficulty than the former, because the magnitude to be found comes in a greater number of times in them, and consequently it involves a greater number of relations in such problems. For on such occasions the meaning is the same as if the enunciation were, 'extract the square root of *a²*, i.e. 25,' or 'extract the cube root of *a³*, i.e. 125,' and so in other cases. This then is the way in which Arithmeticians commonly put the matter. But alternatively we may explain the problems in the terms employed by Geometricians: it comes to the same thing if we say, 'find a mean proportional between that assumed magnitude, which we call unity, and that indicated by *a²*,' or 'find two mean proportionals between unity and *a³*,' and so in other cases.

From these considerations it is easy to infer how these two operations suffice for the discovery of any magnitudes whatsoever which are to be deduced from others in virtue of some relation. And now that we have grasped them, the next thing to do is to show how these operations are to be brought before the scrutiny of the imagination and how presented to our actual vision, in order that we may explain how they may be used or practised.

In addition or subtraction we conceive our object under the aspect of a line, or of some extended magnitude in which length is alone to be considered. For if we are to add line *a* to line *b*,

we add the one to the other in the following way *ab*,

and get as a result *c*.

But if the smaller has to be taken from the larger, viz. *b* from *a*,

we place the one above the other thus,

and this will give us that part of the larger which the smaller cannot cover, viz. ——— .

In multiplication we also conceive the given magnitudes as lines. But we imagine a rectangle to be constructed out of them; for, if we multiply *a* by *b*,

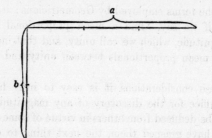

we fit them together at right angles in the following way,

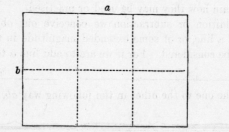

and so make the rectangle

Again, if we wish to multiply *ab* by *c*,

we ought to conceive *ab* as a line, viz. *ab*,

in order that to represent *abc* we may obtain the following figure:

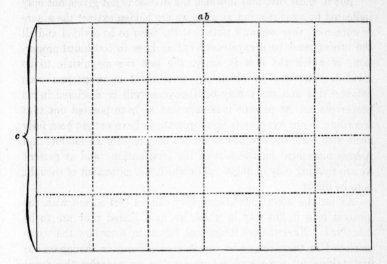

Finally in a division in which the divisor is given, we imagine the magnitude to be divided to be a rectangle, one side of which is the divisor and the other the quotient. Thus if the rectangle *ab* is to be divided by *a*,

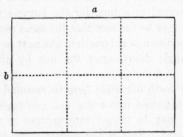

we take away from it the breadth *a* and are left with *b* for quotient:

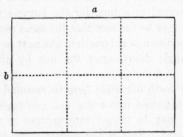

On the contrary if this rectangle is divided by b, we take away the height b, and the quotient will be a,

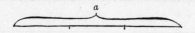

But in those divisions in which the divisor is not given, but only indicated by some relation, as when we are bidden extract the square or cube root, then we must note that the term to be divided and all the others must be always conceived as lines in continued proportion, of which the first is unity, the last the magnitude to be divided. The way in which any number of mean proportionals between this and unity may be discovered will be disclosed in its proper place. At present it is sufficient to have pointed out that according to our hypothesis those operations have not yet been fully dealt with here, since to be carried out they require an indirect and reverse movement on the part of the imagination; and at present we are treating only of questions in which the movement of thought is to be direct.

As for the other[1] operations, they can be carried out with the greatest ease in the way in which we have stated they are to be conceived. Nevertheless it remains for us to show how the terms employed in them are to be constructed. For even though on our first taking up some problem we are free to conceive the terms involved as lines or as rectangles, without introducing any other figures, as was said in reference to the fourteenth rule, nevertheless it is frequently the case that, in the course of the solution, what was a rectangle, constructed by the multiplication of two lines, must presently be conceived as a line, for the purpose of some further operation. Or it may be the case that the same rectangle, or a line formed by some addition or subtraction, has next to be conceived as some other rectangle drawn upon the line by which it is to be divided.

It is therefore worth our while here to expound how every rectangle may be transformed into a line, and conversely how a line or even a rectangle may be turned into another rectangle of which the side is indicated. This is the easiest thing in the world for Geometricians to do, provided they recognize that whenever we compare lines with some rectangle, as here, we always conceive those lines as rectangles, one side of which is the length that we took to

---

[1] i.e. the direct operations.

represent our unit. For if we do so the whole matter resolves itself into the following proposition : Given a rectangle, to construct another rectangle equal to it upon a given side.

Now though this problem is one familiar to a mere beginner in Geometry, I wish to explain it, lest I should seem to have omitted something[1].

RULE XIX.

Employing this method of reasoning we have to find out as many magnitudes as we have unknown terms, treated as though they were known, for the purpose of handling the problem in the direct way ; and these must be expressed in the two different ways. For this will give us as many equations as there are unknowns.

RULE XX.

Having got our equations, we must proceed to carry out such operations as we have neglected, taking care never to multiply where we can divide.

RULE XXI.

If there are several equations of this kind, we should reduce them all to a single one, viz. that the terms of which do not occupy so many places in the series of magnitudes that are in continued proportion. The terms of the equation should then be themselves arranged in the order which this series follows.

THE END[2].

[1] 'The rest is wanting' is added here both in the Amsterdam ed. and in Leibniz's MS.

[2] This appears both in the Amsterdam ed. and in Leibniz's MS.

DISCOURSE ON METHOD

PREFATORY NOTE TO THE METHOD.

The *Discourse on the Method and Essays* was originally published anonymously in 1637 by Jan Maire of Leiden, in somewhat shabby form. It was Descartes' first published work, the much talked of 'World' or 'Cosmos' having been suppressed or destroyed on his hearing of the condemnation of Galileo in 1632. In 1636, however, when forty years of age, he felt that it was time to bring his views before the public and publish them abroad. The Elzevirs naturally suggested themselves as the publishers to be selected, especially as they had once before made advances and as the original member of the firm resided in Leiden, where Descartes probably was at the time. They, however, had become less friendly, evidently doubting the success of an anonymous book of the kind, and consequently the author went elsewhere. Descartes endeavoured to preserve the anonymity of his work with scrupulous care, and was annoyed by his zealous but fussy friend Mersenne showing the work to others, and announcing the author's name, with the ostensible object of obtaining from the King of France permission for its publication. In the end he found himself compelled to avow his authorship.

The book was written in French 'the language of my country,' as Descartes says, 'in the hope that those who avail themselves of their natural reason alone, may be better judges of my opinions than those who give heed only to the writings of the ancients.' Four hundred copies were given him for distribution to his friends and this was probably all the remuneration that he expected; none other seems in any case to have come to him.

The Latin version is the work of Étienne de Courcelles, a protestant minister at Amsterdam, and was published in 1644 by Louis Elzevir at the same time as the 'Principles.' The Essays (the Dioptric, the Meteors and the Geometry) which are termed 'Essays on this Method' have not been translated here.

E. S. H.

DISCOURSE ON THE METHOD OF RIGHTLY CONDUCTING THE REASON AND SEEKING FOR TRUTH IN THE SCIENCES.

If this Discourse appears too long to be read all at once, it may be separated into six portions. And in the first there will be found various considerations respecting the sciences; in the second, the principal rules regarding the Method which the author has sought out; while in the third are some of the rules of morality which he has derived from this Method. In the fourth are the reasons by which he proves the existence of God and of the human soul, which form the foundation of his Metaphysic. In the fifth, the order of the questions regarding physics which he has investigated, and particularly the explanation of the movement of the heart, and of some other difficulties which pertain to medicine, as also the difference between the soul of man and that of the brutes. And in the last part the questions raised relate to those matters which the author believes to be requisite in order to advance further in the investigation of nature, in addition to the reasons that caused him to write.

PART I.

Good sense is of all things in the world the most equally distributed, for everybody thinks himself so abundantly provided with it, that even those most difficult to please in all other matters do not commonly desire more of it than they already possess. It is unlikely that this is an error on their part; it seems rather to be evidence in support of the view that the power of forming a good judgment and of distinguishing the true from the false, which is properly speaking what is called Good sense or Reason, is by nature equal in all men. Hence too it will show that the diversity of our opinions does not proceed from some men being more rational than others, but solely from the fact that our thoughts pass through diverse channels and the same objects are not considered by all. For to be possessed of good mental powers is not sufficient; the principal matter is to apply them well. The greatest minds are capable of the greatest vices as well as of the greatest virtues, and those who proceed very slowly may, provided they always follow the straight road, really advance much faster than those who, though they run, forsake it.

For myself I have never ventured to presume that my mind was in any way more perfect than that of the ordinary man; I have even longed to possess thought as quick, or an imagination as accurate and distinct, or a memory as comprehensive or ready, as some others. And besides these I do not know any other qualities that make for the perfection of the human mind. For as to reason or sense, inasmuch as it is the only thing that constitutes us men and distinguishes us from the brutes, I would fain believe that it is to be found complete in each individual, and in this I follow the common opinion of the philosophers, who say that the question of more or less occurs only in the sphere of the *accidents* and does not affect the *forms* or natures of the *individuals* in the same *species*.

But I shall not hesitate to say that I have had great good fortune from my youth up, in lighting upon and pursuing certain paths which have conducted me to considerations and maxims from which I have formed a Method, by whose assistance it appears to me I have the means of gradually increasing my knowledge and of little by little raising it to the highest possible point which the mediocrity of my talents and the brief duration of my life can permit me to reach. For I have already reaped from it fruits of such a nature that, even though I always try in the judgments I make on myself to lean to the side of self-depreciation rather than to that of arrogance, and though, looking with the eye of a philosopher on the diverse actions and enterprises of all mankind, I find scarcely any which do not seem to me vain and useless, I do not cease to receive extreme satisfaction in the progress which I seem to have already made in the search after truth, and to form such hopes for the future as to venture to believe that, if amongst the occupations of men, simply as men, there is some one in particular that is excellent and important, that is the one which I have selected.

It must always be recollected, however, that possibly I deceive myself, and that what I take to be gold and diamonds is perhaps no more than copper and glass. I know how subject we are to delusion in whatever touches ourselves, and also how much the judgments of our friends ought to be suspected when they are in our favour. But in this Discourse I shall be very happy to show the paths I have followed, and to set forth my life as in a picture, so that everyone may judge of it for himself; and thus in learning from the common talk what are the opinions which are held of it, a new means of obtaining self-instruction will be reached, which I shall add to those which I have been in the habit of using.

Thus my design is not here to teach the Method which everyone should follow in order to promote the good conduct of his Reason, but only to show in what manner I have endeavoured to conduct my own. Those who set about giving precepts must esteem themselves more skilful than those to whom they advance them, and if they fall short in the smallest matter they must of course take the blame for it. But regarding this Treatise simply as a history, or, if you prefer it, a fable in which, amongst certain things which may be imitated, there are possibly others also which it would not be right to follow, I hope that it will be of use to some without being hurtful to any, and that all will thank me for my frankness.

I have been nourished on letters since my childhood, and since I was given to believe that by their means a clear and certain knowledge could be obtained of all that is useful in life, I had an extreme desire to acquire instruction. But so soon as I had achieved the entire course of study at the close of which one is usually received into the ranks of the learned, I entirely changed my opinion. For I found myself embarrassed with so many doubts and errors that it seemed to me that the effort to instruct myself had no effect other than the increasing discovery of my own ignorance. And yet I was studying at one of the most celebrated Schools in Europe, where I thought that there must be men of learning if they were to be found anywhere in the world. I learned there all that others learned; and not being satisfied with the sciences that we were taught, I even read through all the books which fell into my hands, treating of what is considered most curious and rare. Along with this I knew the judgments that others had formed of me, and I did not feel that I was esteemed inferior to my fellow-students, although there were amongst them some destined to fill the places of our masters. And finally our century seemed to me as flourishing, and as fertile in great minds, as any which had preceded. And this made me take the liberty of judging all others by myself and of coming to the conclusion that there was no learning in the world such as I was formerly led to believe it to be.

I did not omit, however, always to hold in esteem those exercises which are the occupation of the Schools. I knew that the Languages which one learns there are essential for the understanding of all ancient literature; that fables with their charm stimulate the mind and histories of memorable deeds exalt it; and that, when read with discretion, these books assist in forming a sound judgment. I was aware that the reading of all good books is indeed like a conversation with the noblest men of past centuries who were the authors of them, nay a carefully studied conversation, in which they reveal to us none but the best of their thoughts. I deemed Eloquence to have a power and beauty beyond compare; that Poesy has most ravishing delicacy and sweetness; that in Mathematics there are the subtlest discoveries and inventions which may accomplish much, both in satisfying the curious, and in furthering all the arts, and in diminishing man's labour; that those writings that deal with Morals contain much that is instructive, and many exhortations to virtue which are most useful; that Theology points out the way to Heaven; that Philosophy teaches us to speak with an appearance of truth on all things, and causes us to be admired by the less learned; that Jurisprudence, Medicine and all other sciences bring honour and riches to those who cultivate them; and finally that it is good to have examined all things, even those most full of superstition and falsehood, in order that we may know their just value, and avoid being deceived by them.

But I considered that I had already given sufficient time to languages and likewise even to the reading of the literature of the ancients, both their histories and their fables. For to converse with those of other centuries is almost the same thing as to travel. It is good to know something of the customs of different peoples in order to judge more sanely of our own, and not to think that everything of a fashion not ours is absurd and contrary to reason, as do those who have seen nothing. But when one employs too much time in travelling, one becomes a stranger in one's own country, and when one is too curious about things which were practised in past centuries, one is usually very ignorant about those which are practised in our own time. Besides, fables make one imagine many events possible which in reality are not so, and even the most accurate of histories, if they do not exactly misrepresent or exaggerate the value of things in order to render them more worthy of being read, at least omit in them all the circumstances which are basest and least notable; and from this fact it follows that what is retained is not portrayed as it really is, and that those who regulate their conduct by examples which they derive from such a source, are liable to fall into the extravagances of the knights-errant of Romance, and form projects beyond their power of performance.

I esteemed Eloquence most highly and I was enamoured of Poesy, but I thought that both were gifts of the mind rather than fruits of study. Those who have the strongest power of reasoning, and who most skilfully arrange their thoughts in order to render them clear and intelligible, have the best power of persuasion even if they can but speak the language of Lower Brittany and have never learned Rhetoric. And those who have the most delightful original ideas and who know how to express them with the maximum of style and suavity, would not fail to be the best poets even if the art of Poetry were unknown to them.

Most of all was I delighted with Mathematics because of the certainty of its demonstrations and the evidence of its reasoning; but I did not yet understand its true use, and, believing that it was of service only in the mechanical arts, I was astonished that, seeing how firm and solid was its basis, no loftier edifice had been reared thereupon. On the other hand I compared the works of the ancient pagans which deal with Morals to palaces most superb and magnificent, which are yet built on sand and mud alone. They praise the virtues most highly and show them to be more worthy of being prized than anything else in the world, but they do not sufficiently teach us to become acquainted with them, and often that which is called by a fine name is nothing but insensibility, or pride, or despair, or parricide.

I honoured our Theology and aspired as much as anyone to reach to heaven, but having learned to regard it as a most highly assured fact that the road is not less open to the most ignorant than to the most learned, and that the revealed truths which conduct thither are quite above our intelligence, I should not have dared to submit them to the feebleness of my reasonings; and I thought that, in order to undertake to examine them and succeed in so doing, it was necessary to have some extraordinary assistance from above and to be more than a mere man.

I shall not say anything about Philosophy, but that, seeing that it has been cultivated for many centuries by the best minds that have ever lived, and that nevertheless no single thing is to be found in it which is not subject of dispute, and in consequence which is not dubious, I had not enough presumption to hope to fare better there than other men had done. And also, considering how many conflicting opinions there may be regarding the self-same matter, all supported by learned people, while there can never be more than one which is true, I esteemed as well-nigh false all that only went as far as being probable.

Then as to the other sciences, inasmuch as they derive their principles from Philosophy, I judged that one could have built nothing solid on foundations so far from firm. And neither the honour nor the promised gain was sufficient to persuade me to cultivate them, for, thanks be to God, I did not find myself in a condition which obliged me to make a merchandise of science for the improvement of my fortune; and, although I did not pretend to scorn all glory like the Cynics, I yet had very small esteem for what I could not hope to acquire, excepting through fictitious titles. And, finally, as to false doctrines, I thought that I already knew well enough what they were worth to be subject to deception neither by the promises of an alchemist, the predictions of an astrologer, the impostures of a magician, the artifices or the empty boastings of any of those who make a profession of knowing that of which they are ignorant.

This is why, as soon as age permitted me to emerge from the control of my tutors, I entirely quitted the study of letters. And resolving to seek no other science than that which could be found in myself, or at least in the great book of the world, I employed the rest of my youth in travel, in seeing courts and armies, in intercourse with men of diverse temperaments and conditions, in collecting varied experiences, in proving myself in the various predicaments in which I was placed by fortune, and under all circumstances bringing my mind to bear on the things which came before it, so that I might derive some profit from my experience. For it seemed to me that I might meet with much more truth in the reasonings that each man makes on the matters that specially concern him, and the issue of which would very soon punish him if he made a wrong judgment, than in the case of those made by a man of letters in his study touching speculations which lead to no result, and which bring about no other consequences to himself excepting that he will be all the more vain the more they are removed from common sense, since in this case it proves him to have employed so much the more ingenuity and skill in trying to make them seem probable. And I always had an excessive desire to learn to distinguish the true from the false, in order to see clearly in my actions and to walk with confidence in this life.

It is true that while I only considered the manners of other men I found in them nothing to give me settled convictions; and I remarked in them almost as much diversity as I had formerly seen in the opinions of philosophers. So much was this the case that the greatest profit which I derived from their study was that, in seeing many things which, although they seem to us very extravagant and ridiculous, were yet commonly received and approved by other great nations, I learned to believe nothing too certainly of which I had only been convinced by example and custom. Thus little by little I was delivered from many errors which might have obscured our natural vision and rendered us less capable of listening to Reason. But after I had employed several years in thus studying the book of the world and trying to acquire some experience, I one day formed the resolution of also making myself an object of study and of employing all the strength of my mind in choosing the road I should follow. This succeeded much better, it appeared to me, than if I had never departed either from my country or my books.

Part II.

I was then in Germany, to which country I had been attracted by the wars which are not yet at an end. And as I was returning from the coronation of the Emperor to join the army, the setting in of winter detained me in a quarter where, since I found no society to divert me, while fortunately I had also no cares or passions to trouble me, I remained the whole day shut up alone in a stove-heated room, where I had complete leisure to occupy myself with my own thoughts. One of the first of the considerations that occurred to me was that there is very often less perfection in works composed of several portions, and carried out by the hands of various masters, than in those on which one individual alone has worked. Thus we see that buildings planned and carried out by one architect alone are usually more beautiful and better proportioned than those which many have tried to put in order and improve, making use of old walls which were built with other ends in view. In the same way also, those ancient cities which, originally mere villages, have become in the process of time great towns, are usually badly constructed in comparison with those which are regularly laid out on a plain by a surveyor who is free to follow his own ideas. Even though, considering their buildings each one apart, there is often as much or more display of skill in the one case than in the other, the former have large buildings and small buildings indiscriminately placed together, thus rendering the streets crooked and irregular, so that it might be said that it was chance rather than the will of men guided by reason that led to such an arrangement. And if we consider that this happens despite the fact that from all time there have been certain officials who have had the special duty of looking after the buildings of private individuals in order that they may be public ornaments, we shall understand how difficult it is to bring about much that is satisfactory in operating only upon the works of others. Thus I imagined that those people who were once half-savage, and who have become civilized only by slow degrees, merely forming their laws as the disagreeable necessities of their crimes and quarrels constrained them, could not succeed in establishing so good a system of government as those who, from the time they first came together as communities, carried into effect the constitution laid down by some prudent legislator. Thus it is quite certain that the constitution of the true Religion whose ordinances are of God alone is incomparably better regulated than any other. And, to come down to human affairs, I believe that if Sparta was very flourishing in former times, this was not because of the excellence of each and every one of its laws, seeing that many were very strange and even contrary to good morals, but because, being drawn up by one individual, they all tended towards the same end. And similarly I thought that the sciences found in books—in those at least whose reasonings are only probable and which have no demonstrations, composed as they are of the gradually accumulated opinions of many different individuals—do not approach so near to the truth as the simple reasoning which a man of common sense can quite naturally carry out respecting the things which come immediately before him. Again I thought that since we have all been children before being men, and since it has for long fallen to us to be governed by our appetites and by our teachers (who often enough contradicted one another, and none of whom perhaps counselled us always for the best), it is almost impossible that our judgments should be so excellent or solid as they should have been had we had complete use of our reason since our birth, and had we been guided by its means alone.

It is true that we do not find that all the houses in a town are rased to the ground for the sole reason that the town is to be rebuilt in another fashion, with streets made more beautiful; but at the same time we see that many people cause their own houses to be knocked down in order to rebuild them, and that sometimes they are forced so to do where there is danger of the houses falling of themselves, and when the foundations are not secure. From such examples I argued to myself that there was no plausibility in the claim of any private individual to reform a state by altering every-thing, and by overturning it throughout, in order to set it right again. Nor is it likewise probable that the whole body of the Sciences, or the order of teaching established by the Schools, should be reformed. But as regards all the opinions which up to this time I had embraced, I thought I could not do better than endeavour once for all to sweep them completely away, so that they might later on be replaced, either by others which were better, or by the same, when I had made them conform to the uniformity of a rational scheme. And I firmly believed that by this means I should succeed in directing my life much better than if I had only built on old found-ations, and relied on principles of which I allowed myself to be in youth persuaded without having inquired into their truth. For although in so doing I recognised various difficulties, these were at the same time not unsurmountable, nor comparable to those which are found in reformation of the most insignificant kind in matters which concern the public. In the case of great bodies it is too difficult a task to raise them again when they are once thrown down, or even to keep them in their places when once thoroughly shaken; and their fall cannot be otherwise than very violent. Then as to any imperfections that they may possess (and the very diversity that is found between them is sufficient to tell us that these in many cases exist) custom has doubtless greatly mitigated them, while it has also helped us to avoid, or insensibly corrected a number against which mere foresight would have found it difficult to guard. And finally the imperfections are almost always more supportable than would be the process of removing them, just as the great roads which wind about amongst the mountains become, because of being frequented, little by little so well-beaten and easy that it is much better to follow them than to try to go more directly by climbing over rocks and descending to the foot of precipices.

This is the reason why I cannot in any way approve of those turbulent and unrestful spirits who, being called neither by birth nor fortune to the management of public affairs, never fail to have always in their minds some new reforms. And if I thought that in this treatise there was contained the smallest justification for this folly, I should be very sorry to allow it to be published. My design has never extended beyond trying to reform my own opinion and to build on a foundation which is entirely my own. If my work has given me a certain satisfaction, so that I here present to you a draft of it, I do not so do because I wish to advise anybody to imitate it. Those to whom God has been most beneficent in the bestowal of His graces will perhaps form designs which are more elevated; but I fear much that this particular one will seem too venturesome for many. The simple resolve to strip oneself of all opinions and beliefs formerly received is not to be regarded as an example that each man should follow, and the world may be said to be mainly composed of two classes of minds neither of which could prudently adopt it. There are those who, believing themselves to be cleverer than they are, cannot restrain themselves from being precipitate in judgment and have not sufficient patience to arrange their thoughts in proper order; hence, once a man of this description had taken the liberty of doubting the principles he formerly accepted, and had deviated from the beaten track, he would never be able to maintain the path which must be followed to reach the appointed end more quickly, and he would hence remain wandering astray all through his life. Secondly, there are those who having reason or modesty enough to judge that they are less capable of distinguishing truth from falsehood than some others from whom instruction might be obtained, are right in contenting themselves with following the opinions of these others rather than in searching better ones for themselves.

For myself I should doubtless have been of these last if I had never had more than a single master, or had I never known the diversities which have from all time existed between the opinions of men of the greatest learning. But I had been taught, even in my College days, that there is nothing imaginable so strange or so little credible that it has not been maintained by one philosopher or other, and I further recognised in the course of my travels that all those whose sentiments are very contrary to ours are yet not necessarily barbarians or savages, but may be possessed of reason in as great or even a greater degree than ourselves. I also considered how very different the self-same man, identical in mind and spirit, may become, according as he is brought up from childhood amongst the French or Germans, or has passed his whole life amongst Chinese or cannibals. I likewise noticed how even in the fashions of one's clothing the same thing that pleased us ten years ago, and which will perhaps please us once again before ten years are passed, seems at the present time extravagant and ridiculous. I thus concluded that it is much more custom and example that persuade us than any certain knowledge, and yet in spite of this the voice of the majority does not afford a proof of any value in truths a little difficult to discover, because such truths are much more likely to have been discovered by one man than by a nation. I could not, however, put my finger on a single person whose opinions seemed preferable to those of others, and I found that I was, so to speak, constrained myself to undertake the direction of my procedure.

But like one who walks alone and in the twilight I resolved to go so slowly, and to use so much circumspection in all things, that if my advance was but very small, at least I guarded myself well from falling. I did not wish to set about the final rejection of any single opinion which might formerly have crept into my beliefs without having been introduced there by means of Reason, until I had first of all employed sufficient time in planning out the task which I had undertaken, and in seeking the true Method of arriving at a knowledge of all the things of which my mind was capable.

Among the different branches of Philosophy, I had in my younger days to a certain extent studied Logic; and in those of Mathematics, Geometrical Analysis and Algebra—three arts or sciences which seemed as though they ought to contribute something to the design I had in view. But in examining them I observed in respect to Logic that the syllogisms and the greater part of the other teaching served better in explaining to others those things that one knows (or like the art of Lully, in enabling one to speak without judgment of those things of which one is ignorant) than in learning what is new. And although in reality Logic contains many precepts which are very true and very good, there are at the same time mingled with them so many others which are hurtful or superfluous, that it is almost as difficult to separate the two as to draw a Diana or a Minerva out of a block of marble which is not yet roughly hewn. And as to the Analysis of the ancients and the Algebra of the moderns, besides the fact that they embrace only matters the most abstract, such as appear to have no actual use, the former is always so restricted to the consideration of symbols that it cannot exercise the Understanding without greatly fatiguing the Imagination; and in the latter one is so subjected to certain rules and formulas that the result is the construction of an art which is confused and obscure, and which embarrasses the mind, instead of a science which contributes to its cultivation. This made me feel that some other Method must be found, which, comprising the advantages of the three, is yet exempt from their faults. And as a multiplicity of laws often furnishes excuses for evil-doing, and as a State is hence much better ruled when, having but very few laws, these are most strictly observed; so, instead of the great number of precepts of which Logic is composed, I believed that I should find the four which I shall state quite sufficient, provided that I adhered to a firm and constant resolve never on any single occasion to fail in their observance.

The first of these was to accept nothing as true which I did not clearly recognise to be so : that is to say, carefully to avoid precipitation and prejudice in judgments, and to accept in them nothing more than what was presented to my mind so clearly and distinctly that I could have no occasion to doubt it.

The second was to divide up each of the difficulties which I examined into as many parts as possible, and as seemed requisite in order that it might be resolved in the best manner possible.

The third was to carry on my reflections in due order, commencing with objects that were the most simple and easy to understand, in order to rise little by little, or by degrees, to knowledge of the most complex, assuming an order, even if a fictitious one, among those which do not follow a natural sequence relatively to one another.

The last was in all cases to make enumerations so complete and reviews so general that I should be certain of having omitted nothing.

Those long chains of reasoning, simple and easy as they are, of which geometricians make use in order to arrive at the most difficult demonstrations, had caused me to imagine that all those things which fall under the cognizance of man might very likely be mutually related in the same fashion ; and that, provided only that we abstain from receiving anything as true which is not so, and always retain the order which is necessary in order to deduce the one conclusion from the other, there can be nothing so remote that we cannot reach to it, nor so recondite that we cannot discover it. And I had not much trouble in discovering which objects it was necessary to begin with, for I already knew that it was with the most simple and those most easy to apprehend. Considering also that of all those who have hitherto sought for the truth in the

Sciences, it has been the mathematicians alone who have been able to succeed in making any demonstrations, that is to say producing reasons which are evident and certain, I did not doubt that it had been by means of a similar kind that they carried on their investigations. I did not at the same time hope for any practical result in so doing, except that my mind would become accustomed to the nourishment of truth and would not content itself with false reasoning. But for all that I had no intention of trying to master all those particular sciences that receive in common the name of Mathematics; but observing that, although their objects are different, they do not fail to agree in this, that they take nothing under consideration but the various relationships or proportions which are present in these objects, I thought that it would be better if I only examined these proportions in their general aspect, and without viewing them otherwise than in the objects which would serve most to facilitate a knowledge of them. Not that I should in any way restrict them to these objects, for I might later on all the more easily apply them to all other objects to which they were applicable. Then, having carefully noted that in order to comprehend the proportions I should sometimes require to consider each one in particular, and sometimes merely keep them in mind, or take them in groups, I thought that, in order the better to consider them in detail, I should picture them in the form of lines, because I could find no method more simple nor more capable of being distinctly represented to my imagination and senses. I considered, however, that in order to keep them in my memory or to embrace several at once, it would be essential that I should explain them by means of certain formulas, the shorter the better. And for this purpose it was requisite that I should borrow all that is best in Geometrical Analysis and Algebra, and correct the errors of the one by the other.

As a matter of fact, I can venture to say that the exact observation of the few precepts which I had chosen gave me so much facility in sifting out all the questions embraced in these two sciences, that in the two or three months which I employed in examining them—commencing with the most simple and general, and making each truth that I discovered a rule for helping me to find others—not only did I arrive at the solution of many questions which I had hitherto regarded as most difficult, but, towards the end, it seemed to me that I was able to determine in the case of those of which I was still ignorant, by what means, and in how far, it was possible to solve them. In this I might perhaps appear to you to be very vain if you did not remember that having but one truth to discover in respect to each matter, whoever succeeds in finding it knows in its regard as much as can be known. It is the same as with a child, for instance, who has been instructed in Arithmetic and has made an addition according to the rule prescribed; he may be sure of having found as regards the sum of figures given to him all that the human mind can know. For, in conclusion, the Method which teaches us to follow the true order and enumerate exactly every term in the matter under investigation contains everything which gives certainty to the rules of Arithmetic.

But what pleased me most in this Method was that I was certain by its means of exercising my reason in all things, if not perfectly, at least as well as was in my power. And besides this, I felt in making use of it that my mind gradually accustomed itself to conceive of its objects more accurately and distinctly; and not having restricted this Method to any particular matter, I promised myself to apply it as usefully to the difficulties of other sciences as I had done to those of Algebra. Not that on this account I dared undertake to examine just at once all those that might present themselves; for that would itself have been contrary to the order which the Method prescribes. But having noticed that the knowledge of these difficulties must be dependent on principles derived from Philosophy in which I yet found nothing to be certain, I thought that it was requisite above all to try to establish certainty in it. I considered also that since this endeavour is the most important in all the world, and that in which precipitation and prejudice were most to be feared, I should not try to grapple with it till I had attained to a much riper age than that of three and twenty, which was the age I had reached. I thought, too, that I should first of all employ much time in preparing myself for the work by eradicating from my mind all the wrong opinions which I had up to this time accepted, and accumulating a variety of experiences fitted later on to afford matter for my reasonings, and by ever exercising myself in the Method which I had prescribed, in order more and more to fortify myself in the power of using it.

PART III.

And finally, as it is not sufficient, before commencing to rebuild the house which we inhabit, to pull it down and provide materials and an architect (or to act in this capacity ourselves, and make a careful drawing of its design), unless we have also provided ourselves with some other house where we can be comfortably lodged during the time of rebuilding, so in order that I should not remain irresolute in my actions while reason obliged me to be so in my judgments, and that I might not omit to carry on my life as happily as I could, I formed for myself a code of morals for the time being which did not consist of more than three or four maxims, which maxims I should like to enumerate to you.

The first was to obey the laws and customs of my country, adhering constantly to the religion in which by God's grace I had been instructed since my childhood, and in all other things directing my conduct by opinions the most moderate in nature, and the farthest removed from excess in all those which are commonly received and acted on by the most judicious of those with whom I might come in contact. For since I began to count my own opinions as nought, because I desired to place all under examination, I was convinced that I could not do better than follow those held by people on whose judgment reliance could be placed. And although such persons may possibly exist amongst the Persians and Chinese as well as amongst ourselves, it seemed to me that it was most expedient to bring my conduct into harmony with the ideas of those with whom I should have to live; and that, in order to ascertain that these were their real opinions, I should observe what they did rather than what they said, not only because in the corrupt state of our manners there are few people who desire to say all that they believe, but also because many are themselves ignorant of their beliefs. For since the act of thought by which we believe a thing is different from that by which we know that we believe it, the one often exists without the other. And amongst many opinions all equally received, I chose only the most moderate, both because these are always most suited for putting into practice, and probably the best (for all excess has a tendency to be bad), and also because I should have in a less degree turned aside from the right path, supposing that I was wrong, than if, having chosen an extreme course, I found that I had chosen amiss. I also made a point of counting as excess all the engagements by means of which we limit in some degree our liberty. Not that I hold in low esteem those laws which, in order to remedy the inconstancy of feeble souls, permit, when we have a good object in our view, that certain vows be taken, or contracts made, which oblige us to carry out that object. This sanction is even given for security in commerce where designs are wholly indifferent. But because I saw nothing in all the world remaining constant, and because for my own part I promised myself gradually to get my judgments to grow better and never to grow worse, I should have thought that I had committed a serious sin against commonsense if, because I approved of something at one time, I was obliged to regard it similarly at a later time, after it had possibly ceased to meet my approval, or after I had ceased to regard it in a favourable light.

My second maxim was that of being as firm and resolute in my actions as I could be, and not to follow less faithfully opinions the most dubious, when my mind was once made up regarding them, than if these had been beyond doubt. In this I should be following the example of travellers, who, finding themselves lost in a forest, know that they ought not to wander first to one side and then to the other, nor, still less, to stop in one place, but understand that they should continue to walk as straight as they can in one direction, not diverging for any slight reason, even though it was possibly chance alone that first determined them in their choice. By this means if they do not go exactly where they wish, they will at least arrive somewhere at the end, where probably they will be better off than in the middle of a forest. And thus since often enough in the actions of life no delay is permissible, it is very certain that, when it is beyond our power to discern the opinions which carry most truth, we should follow the most probable ; and even although we notice no greater probability in the one opinion than in the other, we at least should make up our minds to follow a particular one and afterwards consider it as no longer doubtful in its relationship to practice, but as very true and very certain, inasmuch as the reason which caused us to determine upon it is known to be so. And henceforward this principle was sufficient to deliver me from all the penitence and remorse which usually affect the mind and agitate the conscience of those weak and vacillating creatures who allow themselves to keep changing their procedure, and practise as good, things which they afterwards judge to be evil.

My third maxim was to try always to conquer myself rather than fortune, and to alter my desires rather than change the order of the world, and generally to accustom myself to believe that there is nothing entirely within our power but our own thoughts : so that after we have done our best in regard to the things that are without us, our ill-success cannot possibly be failure on our part[1]. And this alone seemed to me sufficient to prevent my desiring anything in the future beyond what I could actually obtain, hence rendering me content ; for since our will does not naturally induce us to desire anything but what our understanding represents to it as in some way possible of attainment, it is certain that if we consider all good things which are outside of us as equally outside of our power, we should not have more regret in resigning those goods which appear to pertain to our birth, when we are deprived of them for no fault of our own, than we have in not possessing the kingdoms of China or Mexico. In the same way, making what is called a virtue out of a necessity, we should no more desire to be well if ill, or free, if in prison, than we now do to have our bodies formed of a substance as little corruptible as diamonds, or to have wings to fly with like birds. I allow, however, that to accustom oneself to regard all things from this point of view requires long exercise and meditation often repeated ; and I believe that it is principally in this that is to be found the secret of those philosophers who, in ancient times, were able to free themselves from the empire of fortune, or, despite suffering or poverty, to rival their gods in their happiness. For, ceaselessly occupying themselves in considering the limits which were prescribed to them by nature, they persuaded themselves so completely that nothing was within their own power but their thoughts, that this conviction alone was sufficient to prevent their having any longing for other things. And they had so absolute a mastery over their thoughts that they had some reason for esteeming themselves as more rich and more powerful, and more free and more happy than other men, who, however favoured by nature or fortune they might be, if devoid of this philosophy, never could arrive at all at which they aim.

And last of all, to conclude this moral code, I felt it incumbent on me to make a review of the various occupations of men in this life in order to try to choose out the best ; and without wishing to say anything of the employment of others I thought that I could

---

[1] "So that whatever does not eventuate after we have done all in our power that it should happen is to be accounted by us as among the things which evidently cannot be done and which in philosophical phrase are called impossible." Latin Version.

not do better than continue in the one in which I found myself engaged, that is to say, in occupying my whole life in cultivating my Reason, and in advancing myself as much as possible in the knowledge of the truth in accordance with the method which I had prescribed myself. I had experienced so much satisfaction since beginning to use this method, that I did not believe that any sweeter or more innocent could in this life be found,—every day discovering by its means some truths which seemed to me sufficiently important, although commonly ignored by other men. The satisfaction which I had so filled my mind that all else· seemed of no account. And, besides, the three preceding maxims were founded solely on the plan which I had formed of continuing to instruct myself. For since God has given to each of us some light with which to distinguish truth from error, I could not believe that I ought for a single moment to content myself with accepting the opinions held by others unless I had in view the employment of my own judgment in examining them at the proper time ; and I could not have held myself free of scruple in following such opinions, if nevertheless I had not intended to lose no occasion of finding superior opinions, supposing them to exist; and finally, I should not have been able to restrain my desires nor to remain content, if I had not followed a road by which, thinking that I should be certain to be able to acquire all the knowledge of which I was capable, I also thought I should likewise be certain of obtaining all the best things which could ever come within my power. And inasmuch as our will impels us neither to follow after nor to flee from anything, excepting as our understanding represents it as good or evil, it is sufficient to judge wisely in order to act well, and the best judgment brings the best action—that is to say, the acquisition of all the virtues and all the other good things that it is possible to obtain. When one is certain that this point is reached, one cannot fail to be contented.

Having thus assured myself of these maxims, and having set them on one side along with the truths of religion which have always taken the first place in my creed, I judged that as far as the rest of my opinions were concerned, I could safely undertake to rid myself of them. And inasmuch as I hoped to be able to reach my end more successfully in converse with man than in living longer shut up in the warm room where these reflections had come to me, I hardly awaited the end of winter before I once more set myself to travel. And in all the nine following years I did nought but roam hither and thither, trying to be a spectator rather than an actor in all the comedies the world displays. More especially did I reflect in each matter that came before me as to anything which could make it subject to suspicion or doubt, and give occasion for mistake, and I rooted out of my mind all the errors which might have formerly crept in. Not that indeed I imitated the sceptics, who only doubt for the sake of doubting, and pretend to be always uncertain; for, on the contrary, my design was only to provide myself with good ground for assurance, and to reject the quicksand and mud in order to find the rock or clay. In this task it seems to me, I succeeded pretty well, since in trying to discover the error or uncertainty of the propositions which I examined, not by feeble conjectures, but by clear and assured reasonings, I encountered nothing so dubious that I could not draw from it some conclusion that was tolerably secure, if this were no more than the inference that it contained in it nothing that was certain. And just as in pulling down an old house we usually preserve the debris to serve in building up another, so in destroying all those opinions which I considered to be ill-founded, I made various observations and acquired many experiences, which have since been of use to me in establishing those which are more certain. And more than this, I continued to exercise myself in the method which I had laid down for my use; for besides the fact that I was careful as a rule to conduct all my thoughts according to its maxims, I set aside some hours from time to time which I more especially employed in practising myself in the solution of mathematical problems according to the Method, or in the solution of other problems which though pertaining to other sciences, I was able to make almost similar to those of mathematics, by detaching them from all principles of other sciences which I found to be not sufficiently secure. You will see the result in many examples which are expounded in this volume[1]. And hence, without living to all appearance in any way differently from those who, having no occupation beyond spending their lives in ease and innocence, study to separate pleasure from vice, and who, in order to enjoy their leisure without weariness, make use of all distractions that are innocent and good, I did not cease to prosecute my design, and to profit perhaps even more in my study of Truth than if I had done nothing but read books or associate with literary people.

[1] The Dioptrics, Meteors and Geometry were published originally in the same volume.

These nine years thus passed away before I had taken any definite part in regard to the difficulties as to which the learned are in the habit of disputing, or had commenced to seek the foundation of any philosophy more certain than the vulgar. And the example of many excellent men who had tried to do the same before me, but, as it appears to me, without success, made me imagine it to be so hard that possibly I should not have dared to undertake the task, had I not discovered that someone had spread abroad the report that I had already reached its conclusion. I cannot tell on what they based this opinion; if my conversation has contributed anything to it, this must have arisen from my confessing my ignorance more ingenuously than those who have studied a little usually do. And perhaps it was also due to my having shown forth my reasons for doubting many things which were held by others to be certain, rather than from having boasted of any special philosophic system. But being at heart honest enough not to desire to be esteemed as different from what I am, I thought that I must try by every means in my power to render myself worthy of the reputation which I had gained. And it is just eight years ago that this desire made me resolve to remove myself from all places where any acquaintances were possible, and to retire to a country such as this[1], where the long-continued war has caused such order to be established that the armies which are maintained seem only to be of use in allowing the inhabitants to enjoy the fruits of peace with so much the more security; and where, in the crowded throng of a great and very active nation, which is more concerned with its own affairs than curious about those of others, without missing any of the conveniences of the most populous towns, I can live as solitary and retired as in deserts the most remote.

Part IV.

I do not know that I ought to tell you of the first meditations there made by me, for they are so metaphysical and so unusual that they may perhaps not be acceptable to everyone. And yet at the same time, in order that one may judge whether the foundations which I have laid are sufficiently secure, I find myself constrained in some measure to refer to them. For a long time I had remarked that it is sometimes requisite in common life to follow opinions which one knows to be most uncertain, exactly as though they were indisputable, as has been said above. But because in this case

[1] i.e. Holland, where Descartes settled in 1629.

I wished to give myself entirely to the search after Truth, I thought that it was necessary for me to take an apparently opposite course, and to reject as absolutely false everything as to which I could imagine the least ground of doubt, in order to see if afterwards there remained anything in my belief that was entirely certain. Thus, because our senses sometimes deceive us, I wished to suppose that nothing is just as they cause us to imagine it to be; and because there are men who deceive themselves in their reasoning and fall into paralogisms, even concerning the simplest matters of geometry, and judging that I was as subject to error as was any other, I rejected as false all the reasons formerly accepted by me as demonstrations. And since all the same thoughts and conceptions which we have while awake may also come to us in sleep, without any of them being at that time true, I resolved to assume that everything that ever entered into my mind was no more true than the illusions of my dreams. But immediately afterwards I noticed that whilst I thus wished to think all things false, it was absolutely essential that the 'I' who thought this should be somewhat, and remarking that this truth '*I think, therefore I am*' was so certain and so assured that all the most extravagant suppositions brought forward by the sceptics were incapable of shaking it, I came to the conclusion that I could receive it without scruple as the first principle of the Philosophy for which I was seeking.

And then, examining attentively that which I was, I saw that I could conceive that I had no body, and that there was no world nor place where I might be; but yet that I could not for all that conceive that I was not. On the contrary, I saw from the very fact that I thought of doubting the truth of other things, it very evidently and certainly followed that I was; on the other hand if I had only ceased from thinking, even if all the rest of what I had ever imagined had really existed, I should have no reason for thinking that I had existed. From that I knew that I was a substance the whole essence or nature of which is to think, and that for its existence there is no need of any place, nor does it depend on any material thing; so that this 'me,' that is to say, the soul by which I am what I am, is entirely distinct from body, and is even more easy to know than is the latter; and even if body were not, the soul would not cease to be what it is.

After this I considered generally what in a proposition is requisite in order to be true and certain; for since I had just discovered one which I knew to be such, I thought that I ought also to know in what this certainty consisted. And having remarked that there was nothing at all in the statement ' *I think, therefore I am* ' which assures me of having thereby made a true assertion, excepting that I see very clearly that to think it is necessary to be, I came to the conclusion that I might assume, as a general rule, that the things which we conceive very clearly and distinctly are all true—remembering, however, that there is some difficulty in ascertaining which are those that we distinctly conceive.

Following upon this, and reflecting on the fact that I doubted, and that consequently my existence was not quite perfect (for I saw clearly that it was a greater perfection to know than to doubt), I resolved to inquire whence I had learnt to think of anything more perfect than I myself was ; and I recognised very clearly that this conception must proceed from some nature which was really more perfect. As to the thoughts which I had of many other things outside of me, like the heavens, the earth, light, heat, and a thousand others, I had not so much difficulty in knowing whence they came, because, remarking nothing in them which seemed to render them superior to me, I could believe that, if they were true, they were dependencies upon my nature, in so far as it possessed some perfection ; and if they were not true, that I held them from nought, that is to say, that they were in me because I had something lacking in my nature. But this could not apply to the idea of a Being more perfect than my own, for to hold it from nought would be manifestly impossible ; and because it is no less contradictory to say of the more perfect that it is what results from and depends on the less perfect, than to say that there is something which proceeds from nothing, it was equally impossible that I should hold it from myself. In this way it could but follow that it had been placed in me by a Nature which was really more perfect than mine could be, and which even had within itself all the perfections of which I could form any idea—that is to say, to put it in a word, which was God. To which I added that since I knew some perfections which I did not possess, I was not the only being in existence (I shall here use freely, if you will allow, the terms of the School) ; but that there was necessarily some other more perfect Being on which I depended, or from which I acquired all that I had. For if I had existed alone and independent of any others, so that I should have had from myself all that perfection of being in which I participated to however small an extent, I should have been able for the same reason to have had all the remainder which

I knew that I lacked; and thus I myself should have been infinite, eternal, immutable, omniscient, all-powerful, and, finally, I should have all the perfections which I could discern in God. For, in pursuance of the reasonings which I have just carried on, in order to know the nature of God as far as my nature is capable of knowing it, I had only to consider in reference to all these things of which I found some idea in myself, whether it was a perfection to possess them or not. And I was assured that none of those which indicated some imperfection were in Him, but that all else was present; and I saw that doubt, inconstancy, sadness, and such things, could not be in Him considering that I myself should have been glad to be without them. In addition to this, I had ideas of many things which are sensible and corporeal, for, although I might suppose that I was dreaming, and that all that I saw or imagined was false, I could not at the same time deny that the ideas were really in my thoughts. But because I had already recognised very clearly in myself that the nature of the intelligence is distinct from that of the body, and observing that all composition gives evidence of dependency, and that dependency is manifestly an imperfection, I came to the conclusion that it could not be a perfection in God to be composed of these two natures, and that consequently He was not so composed. I judged, however, that if there were any bodies in the world, or even any intelligences or other natures which were not wholly perfect, their existence must depend on His power in such a way that they could not subsist without Him for a single moment.

After that I desired to seek for other truths, and having put before myself the object of the geometricians, which I conceived to be a continuous body, or a space indefinitely extended in length, breadth, height or depth, which was divisible into various parts, and which might have various figures and sizes, and might be moved or transposed in all sorts of ways (for all this the geometricians suppose to be in the object of their contemplation), I went through some of their simplest demonstrations, and having noticed that this great certainty which everyone attributes to these demonstrations is founded solely on the fact that they are conceived of with clearness, in accordance with the rule which I have just laid down, I also noticed that there was nothing at all in them to assure me of the existence of their object. For, to take an example, I saw very well that if we suppose a triangle to be given, the three angles must certainly be equal to two right angles; but for all that I saw no reason to be assured that there was any such triangle in existence, while on the contrary, on reverting to the examination of the idea which I had of a Perfect Being, I found that in this case existence was implied in it in the same manner in which the equality of its three angles to two right angles is implied in the idea of a triangle; or in the idea of a sphere, that all the points on its surface are equidistant from its centre, or even more evidently still. Consequently it is at least as certain that God, who is a Being so perfect, is, or exists, as any demonstration of geometry can possibly be.

What causes many, however, to persuade themselves that there is difficulty in knowing this truth, and even in knowing the nature of their soul, is the fact that they never raise their minds above the things of sense, or that they are so accustomed to consider nothing excepting by imagining it, which is a mode of thought specially adapted to material objects, that all that is not capable of being imagined appears to them not to be intelligible at all. This is manifest enough from the fact that even the philosophers in the Schools hold it as a maxim that there is nothing in the understanding which has not first of all been in the senses, in which there is certainly no doubt that the ideas of God and of the soul have never been. And it seems to me that those who desire to make use of their imagination in order to understand these ideas, act in the same way as if, to hear sounds or smell odours, they should wish to make use of their eyes: excepting that there is indeed this difference, that the sense of sight does not give us less assurance of the truth of its objects, than do those of scent or of hearing, while neither our imagination nor our senses can ever assure us of anything, if our understanding does not intervene.

If there are finally any persons who are not sufficiently persuaded of the existence of God and of their soul by the reasons which I have brought forward, I wish that they should know that all other things of which they perhaps think themselves more assured (such as possessing a body, and that there are stars and an earth and so on) are less certain. For, although we have a moral assurance of these things which is such that it seems that it would be extravagant in us to doubt them, at the same time no one, unless he is devoid of reason, can deny, when a metaphysical certainty is in question, that there is sufficient cause for our not having complete assurance, by observing the fact that when asleep we may similarly imagine that we have another body, and that we see other stars and another earth, without there being anything of the kind.

For how do we know that the thoughts that come in dreams are more false than those that we have when we are awake, seeing that often enough the former are not less lively and vivid than the latter? And though the wisest minds may study the matter as much as they will, I do not believe that they will be able to give any sufficient reason for removing this doubt, unless they presuppose the existence of God. For to begin with, that which I have just taken as a rule, that is to say, that all the things that we very clearly and very distinctly conceive of are true, is certain only because God is or exists, and that He is a Perfect Being, and that all that is in us issues from Him. From this it follows that our ideas or notions, which to the extent of their being clear or distinct are ideas of real things issuing from God, cannot but to that extent be true. So that though we often enough have ideas which have an element of falsity, this can only be the case in regard to those which have in them somewhat that is confused or obscure, because in so far as they have this character they participate in negation —that is, they exist in us as confused only because we are not quite perfect. And it is evident that there is no less repugnance in the idea that error or imperfection, inasmuch as it is imperfection, proceeds from God, than there is in the idea of truth or perfection proceeding from nought. But if we did not know that all that is in us of reality and truth proceeds from a perfect and infinite Being, however clear and distinct were our ideas, we should not have any reason to assure ourselves that they had the perfection of being true.

But after the knowledge of God and of the soul has thus rendered us certain of this rule, it is very easy to understand that the dreams which we imagine in our sleep should not make us in any way doubt the truth of the thoughts which we have when awake. For even if in sleep we had some very distinct idea such as a geometrician might have who discovered some new demonstration, the fact of being asleep would not militate against its truth. And as to the most ordinary error in our dreams, which consists in their representing to us various objects in the same way as do our external senses, it does not matter that this should give us occasion to suspect the truth of such ideas, because we may be likewise often enough deceived in them without our sleeping at all, just as when those who have the jaundice see everything as yellow, or when stars or other bodies which are very remote appear much smaller than they really are. For, finally, whether we are awake or asleep, we should never allow ourselves to be persuaded excepting by the evidence of our Reason. And it must be remarked that I speak of our Reason and not of our imagination nor of our senses; just as though we see the sun very clearly, we should not for that reason judge that it is of the size of which it appears to be; likewise we could quite well distinctly imagine the head of a lion on the body of a goat, without necessarily concluding that a chimera exists. For Reason does not insist that whatever we see or imagine thus is a truth, but it tells us clearly that all our ideas or notions must have some foundation of truth. For otherwise it could not be possible that God, who is all perfection and truth, should have placed them within us. And because our reasonings are never so evident nor so complete during sleep as during wakefulness, although sometimes our imaginations are then just as lively and acute, or even more so, Reason tells us that since our thoughts cannot possibly be all true, because we are not altogether perfect, that which they have of truth must infallibly be met with in our waking experience rather than in that of our dreams.

Part V.

I should be very glad to proceed to show forth the complete chain of truths which I have deduced from these first, but because to do this it would have been necessary now to speak of many matters of dispute among the learned, with whom I have no desire to embroil myself, I think that it will be better to abstain. I shall only state generally what these truths are, so that it may be left to the decision of those best able to judge whether it would be of use for the public to be more particularly informed of them or not. I always remained firm in the resolution which I had made, not to assume any other principle than that of which I have just made use, in order to demonstrate the existence of God and of the Soul, and to accept nothing as true which did not appear to be more clear and more certain than the demonstrations of the geometricians had formerly seemed. And nevertheless I venture to say that not only have I found the means of satisfying myself in a short time as to the more important of those difficulties usually dealt with in philosophy, but I have also observed certain laws which God has so established in Nature, and of which He has imprinted such ideas on our minds, that, after having reflected sufficiently upon the matter, we cannot doubt their being accurately observed in all that exists or is done in the world. Further, in considering the sequence of these laws, it seems to me that I have discovered many truths more useful and more important than all that I had formerly learned or even hoped to learn.

But because I tried to explain the most important of these in a Treatise[1] which certain considerations prevented me from publishing, I cannot do better, in making them known, than here summarise briefly what that Treatise contains. I had planned to comprise in it all that I believed myself to know regarding the nature of material objects, before I set myself to write. However, just as the painters who cannot represent equally well on a plain surface all the various sides of a solid body, make selection of one of the most important, which alone is set in the light, while the others are put in shadow and made to appear only as they may be seen in looking at the former, so, fearing that I could not put in my Treatise all that I had in my mind, I undertook only to show very fully my conceptions of light. Later on, when occasion occurred, I resolved to add something about the sun and fixed stars, because light proceeds almost entirely from them ; the heavens would be dealt with because they transmit light, the planets, the comets and the earth because they reflect it, and more particularly would all bodies which are on the earth, because they are either coloured or transparent, or else luminous ; and finally I should deal with man because he is the spectator of all. For the very purpose of putting all these topics somewhat in shadow, and being able to express myself freely about them, without being obliged to adopt or to refute the opinions which are accepted by the learned, I resolved to leave all this world to their disputes, and to speak only of what would happen in a new world if God now created, somewhere in an imaginary space, matter sufficient where-with to form it, and if He agitated in diverse ways, and without any order, the diverse portions of this matter, so that there resulted a chaos as confused as the poets ever feigned, and concluded His work by merely lending His concurrence to Nature in the usual way, leaving her to act in accordance with the laws which He had established. So, to begin with, I described this matter and tried to represent it in such a way, that it seems to me that nothing in the world could be more clear or intelligible, excepting what has just been said of God and the Soul. For I even went so far as expressly to assume that there was in it none of these forms or qualities which are so debated in the Schools, nor anything at all the

---

[1] i.e. 'Le Monde,' suppressed on hearing of Galileo's condemnation.

knowledge of which is not so natural to our minds that none could even pretend to be ignorant of it. Further I pointed out what are the laws of Nature, and, without resting my reasons on any other principle than the infinite perfections of God, I tried to demonstrate all those of which one could have any doubt, and to show that they are of such a nature that even if God had created other worlds, He could not have created any in which these laws would fail to be observed. After that, I showed how the greatest part of the matter of which this chaos is constituted, must, in accordance with these laws, dispose and arrange itself in such a fashion as to render it similar to our heavens; and how meantime some of its parts must form an earth, some planets and comets, and some others a sun and fixed stars. And, enlarging on the subject of light, I here explained at length the nature of the light which would be found in the sun and stars, and how from these it crossed in an instant the immense space of the heavens, and how it was reflected from the planets and comets to the earth. To this I also added many things touching the substance, situation, movements, and all the different qualities of these heavens and stars, so that I thought I had said enough to make it clear that there is nothing to be seen in the heavens and stars pertaining to our system which must not, or at least may not, appear exactly the same in those of the system which I described. From this point I came to speak more particularly of the earth, showing how, though I had expressly presupposed that God had not placed any weight in the matter of which it is composed, its parts did not fail all to gravitate exactly to its centre; and how, having water and air on its surface, the disposition of the heavens and of the stars, more particularly of the moon, must cause a flux or reflux, which in all its circumstances is similar to that which is observed in our seas, and besides that, a certain current both of water and air from east to west, such as may also be observed in the tropics. I also showed how the mountains, seas, fountains and rivers, could naturally be formed in it, how the metals came to be in the mines and the plants to grow in the fields; and generally how all bodies, called mixed or composite, might arise. And because I knew nothing but fire which could produce light, excepting the stars, I studied amongst other things to make very clear all that pertains to its nature, how it is formed, how nourished, how there is sometimes only heat without light, and sometimes light without heat; I showed, too, how different colours might by it be induced upon different bodies and qualities of diverse kinds, how some of these were liquefied and others solidified, how nearly all can be consumed or converted into ashes and smoke by its means, and finally how of these ashes, by the intensity of its action alone, it forms glass. Since this transformation of ashes into glass seemed to me as wonderful as any other process in nature, I took particular pleasure in describing it.

I did not at the same time wish to infer from all these facts that this world has been created in the manner which I described; for it is much more probable that at the beginning God made it such as it was to be. But it is certain, and it is an opinion commonly received by the theologians, that the action by which He now preserves it is just the same as that by which He at first created it. In this way, although He had not, to begin with, given this world any other form than that of chaos, provided that the laws of nature had once been established and that He had lent His aid in order that its action should be according to its wont, we may well believe, without doing outrage to the miracle of creation, that by this means alone all things which are purely material might in course of time have become such as we observe them to be at present; and their nature is much easier to understand when we see them coming to pass little by little in this manner, than were we to consider them as all complete to begin with.

From a description of inanimate bodies and plants I passed on to that of animals, and particularly to that of men. But since I had not yet sufficient knowledge to speak of them in the same style as of the rest, that is to say, demonstrating the effects from the causes, and showing from what beginnings and in what fashion Nature must produce them, I contented myself with supposing that God formed the body of man altogether like one of ours, in the outward figure of its members as well as in the interior conformation of its organs, without making use of any matter other than that which I had described, and without at the first placing in it a rational soul, or any other thing which might serve as a vegetative or as a sensitive soul; excepting that He kindled in the heart one of these fires without light, which I have already described, and which I did not conceive of as in any way different from that which makes the hay heat when shut up before it is dry, and which makes new wine grow frothy when it is left to ferment over the fruit. For, examining the functions which might in accordance with this supposition exist in this body, I found precisely all those which might exist in us without our having the power of thought, and con-

sequently without our soul—that is to say, this part of us, distinct
from the body, of which it has just been said that its nature is to
think—contributing to it, functions which are identically the same
as those in which animals lacking reason may be said to resemble
us. For all that, I could not find in these functions any which,
being dependent on thought, pertain to us alone, inasmuch as we
are men; while I found all of them afterwards, when I assumed
that God had created a rational soul and that He had united it
to this body in a particular manner which I described.

But in order to show how I there treated of this matter, I wish here
to set forth the explanation of the movement of heart and arteries
which, being the first and most general movement that is observed
in animals, will give us the means of easily judging as to what we
ought to think about all the rest. And so that there may be less
difficulty in understanding what I shall say on this matter, I should
like that those not versed in anatomy should take the trouble, before
reading this, of having cut up before their eyes the heart of some
large animal which has lungs (for it is in all respects sufficiently
similar to the heart of a man), and cause that there be demonstrated
to them the two chambers or cavities which are within it. There is
first of all that which is on the right side, with which two very large
tubes or channels correspond, viz. the *vena cava*, which is the
principal receptacle of the blood, and so to speak the trunk of a
tree of which all the other veins of the body are the branches; and
there is the arterial vein which has been badly named because it
is nothing but an artery which, taking its origin from the heart,
divides, after having issued from it, into many branches which
proceed to disperse themselves all through the lungs. Then there
is secondly the cavity on the left side with which there again
correspond two tubes which are as large or larger than the preceding, viz. the venous artery, which has also been badly named,
because it is nothing but a vein which comes from the lungs, where
it is divided into many branches, interlaced with those of the
arterial vein, and with those of the tube which is called the windpipe,
through which enters the air which we breathe; and the great
artery which, issuing from the heart, sends its branches throughout
the body. I should also wish that the eleven little membranes,
which, like so many doors, open and shut the four entrances which
are in these two cavities, should be carefully shown. There are of
these three at the entrance of the *vena cava*, where they are so
arranged that they can in nowise prevent the blood which it contains

from flowing into the right cavity of the heart and yet exactly prevent its issuing out ; there are three at the entrance to the arterial vein, which, being arranged quite the other way, easily allow the blood which is in this cavity to pass into the lungs, but not that which is already in the lungs to return to this cavity. There are also two others at the entrance of the venous artery, which allow the blood in the lungs to flow towards the left cavity of the heart, but do not permit its return ; and three at the entrance of the great artery, which allow the blood to flow from the heart, but prevent its return. There is then no cause to seek for any other reason for the number of these membranes, except that the opening of the venous artery being oval, because of the situation where it is met with, may be conveniently closed with two membranes, while the others, being round, can be better closed with three. Further, I should have my readers consider that the grand artery and the arterial vein are much harder and firmer than are the venous artery and the *vena cava* ; and that these two last expand before entering the heart, and there form so to speak two pockets called the auricles of the heart, which are composed of a tissue similar to its own ; and also that there is always more heat in the heart than in any other part of the body ; and finally that this heat is capable of causing any drop of blood that enters into its cavities promptly to expand and dilate, as liquids usually do when they are allowed to fall drop by drop into some very hot vessel.

After this I do not need to say anything with a view to explaining the movement of the heart, except that when its cavities are not full of blood there necessarily flows from the *vena cava* into the right cavity, and from the venous artery into the left, enough blood to keep these two vessels always full, and being full, that their orifices, which are turned towards the heart, cannot then be closed. But as soon as two drops of blood have thus entered, one into each of the cavities, these drops, which cannot be otherwise than very large, because the openings by which they enter are very wide and the vessels from whence they come are very full of blood, rarefy and dilate because of the heat which they find there. By this means, causing the whole heart to expand, they force home and close the five little doors which are at the entrances of the two vessels whence they flow, thus preventing any more blood from coming down into the heart ; and becoming more and more rarefied, they push open the six doors which are in the entrances of the two other vessels through which they make their exit, by this means causing all the branches of the arterial vein and of the great artery to expand almost at the same instant as the heart. This last immediately afterward contracts as do also the arteries, because the blood which has entered them has cooled ; and the six little doors close up again, and the five doors of the *vena cava* and of the venous artery re-open and make a way for two other drops of blood which cause the heart and the arteries once more to expand, just as we saw before. And because the blood which then enters the heart passes through these two pouches which are called auricles, it comes to pass that their movement is contrary to the movement of the heart, and that they contract when it expands. For the rest, in order that those who do not know the force of mathematical demonstration and are unaccustomed to distinguish true reasons from merely probable reasons, should not venture to deny what has been said without examination, I wish to acquaint them with the fact that this movement which I have just explained follows as necessarily from the very disposition of the organs, as can be seen by looking at the heart, and from the heat which can be felt with the fingers, and from the nature of the blood of which we can learn by experience, as does that of a clock from the power, the situation, and the form, of its counterpoise and of its wheels.

But if we ask how the blood in the veins does not exhaust itself in thus flowing continually into the heart, and how the arteries do not become too full of blood, since all that passes through the heart flows into them, I need only reply by stating what has already been written by an English physician[1], to whom the credit of having broken the ice in this matter must be ascribed, as also of being the first to teach that there are many little tubes at the extremities of the arteries whereby the blood that they receive from the heart enters the little branches of the veins, whence it returns once more to the heart; in this way its course is just a perpetual circulation. He proves this very clearly by the common experience of surgeons, who, by binding the arm moderately firmly above the place where they open the vein, cause the blood to issue more abundantly than it would have done if they had not bound it at all ; while quite a contrary result would occur if they bound it below, between the hand and the opening, or if they bound it very firmly above. For it is clear that when the bandage is moderately tight, though it may prevent the blood already in the arm from

[1] Harvey (Latin Tr.).

returning to the heart by the veins, it cannot for all that prevent more blood from coming anew by the arteries, because these are situated below the veins, and their walls, being stronger, are less easy to compress; and also that the blood which comes from the heart tends to pass by means of the arteries to the hand with greater force than it does to return from the hand to the heart by the veins. And because this blood escapes from the arm by the opening which is made in one of the veins, there must necessarily be some passages below the ligature, that is to say, towards the extremities of the arm, through which it can come thither from the arteries. This physician likewise proves very clearly the truth of that which he says of the course of the blood, by the existence of certain little membranes or valves which are so arranged in different places along the course of the veins, that they do not permit the blood to pass from the middle of the body towards the extremities, but only to return from the extremities to the heart; and further by the experiment which shows that all the blood which is in the body may issue from it in a very short time by means of one single artery that has been cut, and this is so even when it is very tightly bound very near the heart, and cut between it and the ligature, so that there could be no ground for supposing that the blood which flowed out of it could proceed from any other place but the heart.

But there are many other things which demonstrate that the true cause of this motion of the blood is that which I have stated. To begin with, the difference which is seen between the blood which issues from the veins, and that which issues from the arteries, can only proceed from the fact, that, being rarefied, and so to speak distilled by passing through the heart, it is more subtle and lively and warmer immediately after leaving the heart (that is to say, when in the arteries) than it is a little while before entering it (that is, when in the veins). And if attention be paid, we shall find that this difference does not appear clearly, excepting in the vicinity of the heart, and is not so clear in those parts which are further removed from it. Further, the consistency of the coverings of which the arterial vein and the great artery are composed, shows clearly enough that the blood beats against them with more force than it does in the case of the veins. And why should the left cavity of the heart and the great artery be larger and wider than the right cavity and the arterial vein, if it is not that the blood of the venous artery having only been in the lungs since it had passed through the heart, is more subtle and rarefies more effectively and

easily than that which proceeds immediately from the *vena cava*?
And what is it that the physicians can discover in feeling the pulse,
unless they know that, according as the blood changes its nature, it
may be rarefied by the warmth of the heart in a greater or less
degree, and more or less quickly than before? And if we inquire
how this heat is communicated to the other members, must it not
be allowed that it is by means of the blood which, passing through
the heart, is heated once again and thence is spread throughout
all the body? From this it happens that if we take away the blood
from any particular part, by that same means we take away from it
the heat; even if the heart were as ardent as a red hot iron it
would not suffice to heat up the feet and hands as it actually does,
unless it continually sent out to them new blood. We further
understand from this that the true use of respiration is to carry
sufficient fresh air into the lungs to cause the blood, which comes
there from the right cavity of the heart, where it has been rarefied
and so to speak transformed into vapours, to thicken, and become
anew converted into blood before falling into the left cavity, without
which process it would not be fit to serve as fuel for the fire which
there exists. We are confirmed in this statement by seeing that
the animals which have no lungs have also but one cavity in their
hearts, and that in children, who cannot use them while still within
their mother's wombs, there is an opening by which the blood flows
from the *vena cava* into the left cavity of the heart, and a conduit
through which it passes from the arterial vein into the great artery
without passing through the lung. Again, how could digestion be
carried on in the stomach if the heart did not send heat there by
the arteries, and along with this some of the more fluid parts of
the blood which aid in dissolving the foods which have been there
placed? And is not the action which converts the juice of foods
into blood easy to understand if we consider that it is distilled by
passing and repassing through the heart possibly more than one or
two hundred times in a day? What further need is there to explain
the process of nutrition and the production of the different humours
which are in the body, if we can say that the force with which
the blood, in being rarefied, passes from the heart towards the
extremities of the arteries, causes some of its parts to remain among
those of the members where they are found and there to take the
place of others which they oust; and that according to the situation
or form or smallness of the little pores which they encounter,
certain ones proceed to certain parts rather than others, just as

a number of different sieves variously perforated, as everyone has probably seen, are capable of separating different species of grain? And finally what in all this is most remarkable of all, is the generation of the animal spirits, which resemble a very subtle wind, or rather a flame which is very pure and very vivid, and which, continually rising up in great abundance from the heart to the brain, thence proceeds through the nerves to the muscles, thereby giving the power of motion to all the members. And it is not necessary to suppose any other cause to explain how the particles of blood, which, being most agitated and most penetrating, are the most proper to constitute these spirits, proceed towards the brain rather than elsewhere, than that the arteries which carry them thither are those which proceed from the heart in the most direct lines, and that according to the laws of Mechanics, which are identical with those of Nature, when many objects tend to move together to the same point, where there is not room for all (as is the case with the particles of blood which issue from the left cavity of the heart and tend to go towards the brain), the weakest and least agitated parts must necessarily be turned aside by those that are stronger, which by this means are the only ones to reach it.

I had explained all these matters in some detail in the Treatise which I formerly intended to publish. And afterwards I had shown there, what must be the fabric of the nerves and muscles of the human body in order that the animal spirits therein contained should have the power to move the members, just as the heads of animals, a little while after decapitation, are still observed to move and bite the earth, notwithstanding that they are no longer animate; what changes are necessary in the brain to cause wakefulness, sleep and dreams; how light, sounds, smells, tastes, heat and all other qualities pertaining to external objects are able to imprint on it various ideas by the intervention of the senses; how hunger, thirst and other internal affections can also convey their impressions upon it; what should be regarded as the 'common sense' by which these ideas are received, and what is meant by the memory which retains them, by the fancy which can change them in diverse ways and out of them constitute new ideas, and which, by the same means, distributing the animal spirits through the muscles, can cause the members of such a body to move in as many diverse ways, and in a manner as suitable to the objects which present themselves to its senses and to its internal passions, as can happen in our own case apart from the direction of our free will. And this will not seem strange to those, who, knowing how many different *automata* or moving machines can be made by the industry of man, without employing in so doing more than a very few parts in comparison with the great multitude of bones, muscles, nerves, arteries, veins, or other parts that are found in the body of each animal. From this aspect the body is regarded as a machine which, having been made by the hands of God, is incomparably better arranged, and possesses in itself movements which are much more admirable, than any of those which can be invented by man. Here I specially stopped to show that if there had been such machines, possessing the organs and outward form of a monkey or some other animal without reason, we should not have had any means of ascertaining that they were not of the same nature as those animals. On the other hand, if there were machines which bore a resemblance to our body and imitated our actions as far as it was morally possible to do so, we should always have two very certain tests by which to recognise that, for all that, they were not real men. The first is, that they could never use speech or other signs as we do when placing our thoughts on record for the benefit of others. For we can easily understand a machine's being constituted so that it can utter words, and even emit some responses to action on it of a corporeal kind, which brings about a change in its organs ; for instance, if it is touched in a particular part it may ask what we wish to say to it; if in another part it may exclaim that it is being hurt, and so on. But it never happens that it arranges its speech in various ways, in order to reply appropriately to everything that may be said in its presence, as even the lowest type of man can do. And the second difference is, that although machines can perform certain things as well as or perhaps better than any of us can do, they infallibly fall short in others, by the which means we may discover that they did not act from knowledge, but only from the disposition of their organs. For while reason is a universal instrument which can serve for all contingencies, these organs have need of some special adaptation for every particular action. From this it follows that it is morally impossible that there should be sufficient diversity in any machine to allow it to act in all the events of life in the same way as our reason causes us to act.

By these two methods we may also recognise the difference that exists between men and brutes. For it is a very remarkable fact that there are none so depraved and stupid, without even excepting idiots, that they cannot arrange different words together, forming of them a statement by which they make known their thoughts ; while, on the other hand, there is no other animal, however perfect and fortunately circumstanced it may be, which can do the same. It is not the want of organs that brings this to pass, for it is evident that magpies and parrots are able to utter words just like ourselves, and yet they cannot speak as we do, that is, so as to give evidence that they think of what they say. On the other hand, men who, being born deaf and dumb, are in the same degree, or even more than the brutes, destitute of the organs which serve the others for talking, are in the habit of themselves inventing certain signs by which they make themselves understood by those who, being usually in their company, have leisure to learn their language. And this does not merely show that the brutes have less reason than men, but that they have none at all, since it is clear that very little is required in order to be able to talk. And when we notice the inequality that exists between animals of the same species, as well as between men, and observe that some are more capable of receiving instruction than others, it is not credible that a monkey or a parrot, selected as the most perfect of its species, should not in these matters equal the stupidest child to be found, or at least a child whose mind is clouded, unless in the case of the brute the soul were of an entirely different nature from ours. And we ought not to confound speech with natural movements which betray passions and may be imitated by machines as well as be manifested by animals ; nor must we think, as did some of the ancients, that brutes talk, although we do not understand their language. For if this were true, since they have many organs which are allied to our own, they could communicate their thoughts to us just as easily as to those of their own race. It is also a very remarkable fact that although there are many animals which exhibit more dexterity than we do in some of their actions, we at the same time observe that they do not manifest any dexterity at all in many others. Hence the fact that they do better than we do, does not prove that they are endowed with mind, for in this case they would have more reason than any of us, and would surpass us in all other things. It rather shows that they have no reason at all, and that it is nature which acts in them according to the disposition of their organs, just as a clock, which is only composed of wheels and weights is able to tell the hours and measure the time more correctly than we can do with all our wisdom.

I had described after this the rational soul and shown that it could not be in any way derived from the power of matter, like the other things of which I had spoken, but that it must be expressly created. I showed, too, that it is not sufficie; that it should be lodged in the human body like a pilot in his ship, unless perhaps for the moving of its members, but that it is necessary that it should also be joined and united more closely to the body in order to have sensations and appetites similar to our own, and thus to form a true man. In conclusion, I have here enlarged a little on the subject of the soul, because it is one of the greatest importance. For next to the error of those who deny God, which I think I have already sufficiently refuted, there is none which is more effectual in leading feeble spirits from the straight path of virtue, than to imagine that the soul of the brute is of the same nature as our own, and that in consequence, after this life we have nothing to fear or to hope for, any more than the flies and ants. As a matter of fact, when one comes to know how greatly they differ, we understand much better the reasons which go to prove that our soul is in its nature entirely independent of body, and in consequence that it is not liable to die with it. And then, inasmuch as we observe no other causes capable of destroying it, we are naturally inclined to judge that it is immortal.

Part VI.

It is three years since I arrived at the end of the Treatise which contained all these things; and I was commencing to revise it in order to place it in the hands of a printer, when I learned that certain persons, to whose opinions I defer, and whose authority cannot have less weight with my actions than my own reason has over my thoughts, had disapproved of a physical theory published a little while before by another person[1]. I will not say that I agreed with this opinion, but only that before their censure I observed in it nothing which I could possibly imagine to be prejudicial either to Religion or the State, or consequently which could have prevented me from giving expression to it in writing, if my reason had persuaded me to do so: and this made me fear that among my own opinions one might be found which should be misunderstood, notwithstanding the great care which I have always taken not to accept any new beliefs unless I had very certain proof of their truth, and not to give expression to what could tend to the dis-

---

[1] i.e. Galileo.

advantage of any person. This sufficed to cause me to alter the resolution which I had made to publish. For, although the reasons for my former resolution were very strong, my inclination, which always made me hate the profession of writing books, caused me immediately to find plenty of other reasons for excusing myself from doing so. And these reasons, on the one side and on the other, are of such a nature that not only have I here some interest in giving expression to them, but possibly the public may also have some interest in knowing them.

I have never made much of those things which proceed from my own mind, and so long as I culled no other fruits from the Method which I use, beyond that of satisfying myself respecting certain difficulties which pertain to the speculative sciences, or trying to regulate my conduct by the reasons which it has taught me, I never believed myself to be obliged to write anything about it. For as regards that which concerns conduct, everyone is so confident of his own common sense, that there might be found as many reformers as heads, if it were permitted that others than those whom God has established as the sovereigns of his people, or at least to whom He has given sufficient grace and zeal to be prophets, should be allowed to make any changes in that. And, although my speculations give me the greatest pleasure, I believed that others also had speculations which possibly pleased them even more. But so soon as I had acquired some general notions concerning Physics, and as, beginning to make use of them in various special difficulties, I observed to what point they might lead us, and how much they differ from the principles of which we have made use up to the present time, I believed that I could not keep them concealed without greatly sinning against the law which obliges us to procure, as much as in us lies, the general good of all mankind. For they caused me to see that it is possible to attain knowledge which is very useful in life, and that, instead of that speculative philosophy which is taught in the Schools, we may find a practical philosophy by means of which, knowing the force and the action of fire, water, air, the stars, heavens and all other bodies that environ us, as distinctly as we know the different crafts of our artisans, we can in the same way employ them in all those uses to which they are adapted, and thus render ourselves the masters and possessors of nature. This is not merely to be desired with a view to the invention of an infinity of arts and crafts which enable us to enjoy without any trouble the fruits of the earth and all the good things which are to be found there, but also principally because it brings about the preservation of health, which is without doubt the chief blessing and the foundation of all other blessings in this life. For the mind depends so much on the temperament and disposition of the bodily organs that, if it is possible to find a means of rendering men wiser and cleverer than they have hitherto been, I believe that it is in medicine that it must be sought. It is true that the medicine which is now in vogue contains little of which the utility is remarkable; but, without having any intention of decrying it, I am sure that there is no one, even among those who make its study a profession, who does not confess that all that men know is almost nothing in comparison with what remains to be known; and that we could be free of an infinitude of maladies both of body and mind, and even also possibly of the infirmities of age, if we had sufficient knowledge of their causes, and of all the remedies with which nature has provided us. But, having the intention of devoting all my life to the investigation of a knowledge which is so essential, and having discovered a path which appears to me to be of such a nature that we must by its means infallibly reach our end if we pursue it, unless, indeed, we are prevented by the shortness of life or by lack of experience, I judged that there was no better provision against these two impediments than faithfully to communicate to the public the little which I should myself have discovered, and to beg all well-inclined persons to proceed further by contributing, each one according to his own inclination and ability, to the experiments which must be made, and then to communicate to the public all the things which they might discover, in order that the last should commence where the preceding had left off; and thus, by joining together the lives and labours of many, we should collectively proceed much further than any one in particular could succeed in doing.

I remarked also respecting experiments, that they become so much the more necessary the more one is advanced in knowledge, for to begin with it is better to make use simply of those which present themselves spontaneously to our senses, and of which we could not be ignorant provided that we reflected ever so little, rather than to seek out those which are more rare and recondite; the reason of this is that those which are more rare often mislead us so long as we do not know the causes of the more common, and the fact that the circumstances on which they depend are almost always so particular and so minute that it is very difficult to observe them. But in this the order which I have followed is as follows : I have first tried to discover generally the principles or first causes of everything that is or that can be in the world, without considering anything that might accomplish this end but God Himself who has created the world, or deriving them from any source excepting from certain germs of truths which are naturally existent in our souls. After that I considered which were the primary and most ordinary effects which might be deduced from these causes, and it seems to me that in this way I discovered the heavens, the stars, an earth, and even on the earth, water, air, fire, the minerals and some other such things, which are the most common and simple of any that exist, and consequently the easiest to know. Then, when I wished to descend to those which were more particular, so many objects of various kinds presented themselves to me, that I did not think it was possible for the human mind to distinguish the forms or species of bodies which are on the earth from an infinitude of others which might have been so if it had been the will of God to place them there, or consequently to apply them to our use, if it were not that we arrive at the causes by the effects, and avail ourselves of many particular experiments. In subsequently passing over in my mind all the objects which have ever been presented to my senses, I can truly venture to say that I have not there observed anything which I could not easily explain by the principles which I had discovered. But I must also confess that the power of nature is so ample and so vast, and these principles are so simple and general, that I observed hardly any particular effect as to which I could not at once recognise that it might be deduced from the principles in many different ways; and my greatest difficulty is usually to discover in which of these ways the effect does depend upon them. As to that, I do not know any other plan but again to try to find experiments of such a nature that their result is not the same if it has to be explained by one of the methods, as it would be if explained by the other. For the rest, I have now reached a position in which I discern, as it seems to me, sufficiently clearly what course must be adopted in order to make the majority of the experiments which may conduce to carry out this end. But I also perceive that they are of such a nature, and of so great a number, that neither my hands nor my income, though the latter were a thousand times larger than it is, could suffice for the whole ; so that just in proportion as henceforth I shall have the power of carrying out more of them or less, shall I make more or less progress in arriving at a knowledge of nature. This is what I had promised myself to make known by the Treatise which I had written, and to demonstrate in it so clearly the advantage which the public might receive from it, that I should induce all those who have the good of mankind at heart—that is to say, all those who are really virtuous in fact, and not only by a false semblance or by opinion—both to communicate to me those experiments that they have already carried out, and to help me in the investigation of those that still remain to be accomplished.

But I have since that time found other reasons which caused me to change my opinion, and consider that I should indeed continue to put in writing all the things which I judged to be of importance whenever I discovered them to be true, and that I should bestow on them the same care as I should have done had I wished to have them printed. I did this because it would give me so much the more occasion to examine them carefully (for there is no doubt that we always scrutinize more closely what we think will be seen by many, than what is done simply for ourselves, and often the things which have seemed true to me when I began to think about them, seemed false when I tried to place them on paper); and because I did not desire to lose any opportunity of benefiting the public if I were able to do so, and in order that if my works have any value, those into whose hands they will fall after my death, might have the power of making use of them as seems best to them. I, however, resolved that I should not consent to their being published during my lifetime, so that neither the contradictions and controversies to which they might possibly give rise, nor even the reputation, such as it might be, which they would bring to me, should give me any occasion to lose the time which I meant to set apart for my own instruction. For although it is true that each man is obliged to procure, as much as in him lies, the good of others, and that to be useful to nobody is popularly speaking to be worthless, it is at the same time true that our cares should extend further than the present time, and that it is good to set aside those things which may possibly be adapted to bring profit to the living, when we have in view the accomplishment of other ends which will bring much more advantage to our descendants. In the same way I should much like that men should know that the little which I have learned hitherto is almost nothing in comparison with that of which I am ignorant, and with the knowledge of which I do not despair of being able to attain. For it is much the same with those who little by little discover the truth in the Sciences, as with those who, commencing to become rich, have less trouble in obtaining great acquisitions than they formerly experienced, when poorer, in arriving at those much smaller in amount. Or we might compare them to the Generals of our armies, whose forces usually grow in proportion to their victories, and who require more leadership in order to hold together their troops after the loss of a battle, than is needed to take towns and provinces after having obtained a success. For he really gives battle who attempts to conquer all the difficulties and errors which prevent him from arriving at a knowledge of the truth, and it is to lose a battle to admit a false opinion touching a matter of any generality and importance. Much more skill is required in order to recover the position that one beforehand held, than is necessary to make great progress when one already possesses principles which are assured. For myself, if I have succeeded in discovering certain truths in the Sciences (and I hope that the matters contained in this volume will show that I have discovered some), I may say that they are resultant from, and dependent on, five or six principal difficulties which I have surmounted, and my encounter with these I look upon as so many battles in which I have had fortune on my side. I will not even hesitate to say that I think I shall have no need to win more than two or three other victories similar in kind in order to reach the accomplishment of my plans. And my age is not so advanced but that, in the ordinary course of nature, I may still have sufficient leisure for this end. But I believe myself to be so much the more bound to make the most of the time which remains, as I have the greater hope of being able to employ it well. And without doubt I should have many chances of being robbed of it, were I to publish the foundations of my Physics ; for though these are nearly all so evident that it is only necessary to understand them in order to accept them, and although there are none of them as to which I do not believe myself capable of giving demonstration, yet because it is impossible that they should accord with all the various opinions of other men, I foresee that I should often be diverted from my main design by the opposition which they would bring to birth.

We may say that these contradictions might be useful both in making me aware of my errors, and, supposing that I had reached some satisfactory conclusion, in bringing others to a fuller understanding of my speculations ; and, as many can see more than can a single man, they might help in leading others who from the present time may begin to avail themselves of my system, to assist me likewise with their discoveries. But though I recognise that I am extremely liable to err, and though I almost never trust the first reflections that I arrive at, the experience which I have had of the objections which may be made to my system prevents my having any hope of deriving profit from them. For I have often had experience of the judgments both of those whom I have esteemed as my friends, and of some others to whom I believed myself to be indifferent, and even, too, of some whose ill-feeling and envy would, I felt sure, make them endeavour to reveal what affection concealed from the eyes of my friends. But rarely has it happened that any objection has been made which I did not in some sort foresee, unless where it was something very far removed from my subject. In this way hardly ever have I encountered any censor of my opinions who did not appear to me to be either less rigorous or less judicial than myself. And I certainly never remarked that by means of disputations employed by the Schools any truth has been discovered of which we were formerly ignorant. And so long as each side attempts to vanquish his opponent, there is a much more serious attempt to establish probability than to weigh the reasons on either side ; and those who have for long been excellent pleaders are not for that reason the best judges.

As to the advantage which others may receive from the communication of my reflections, it could not be very great, inasmuch as I have not yet carried them so far as that it is not necessary to add many things before they can be brought into practice. And I think I can without vanity say that if anyone is capable of doing this, it should be myself rather than another—not indeed that there may not be in the world many minds incomparably superior to my own, but because no one can so well understand a thing and make it his own when learnt from another as when it is discovered for himself. As regards the matter in hand there is so much truth in this, that although I have often explained some of my opinions to persons of very good intelligence, who, while I talked to them appeared to understand them very clearly, yet when they recounted them I remarked that they had almost always altered them in such a manner that I could no longer acknowledge them as mine. On this account I am very glad to have the opportunity here of begging my descendants never to believe that what is told to them proceeded from myself unless I have myself divulged it. And I do not in the least wonder at the extravagances attributed to all the ancient philosophers whose writings we do not possess, nor do I judge from these that their thoughts were very unreasonable, considering that theirs were the best minds of the time they lived in, but only that they have been imperfectly represented to us. We see, too, that it hardly ever happens that any of their disciples surpassed them, and I am sure that those who most passionately follow Aristotle now-a-days would think themselves happy if they had as much knowledge of nature as he had, even if this were on the condition that they should never attain to any more. They are like the ivy that never tries to mount above the trees which give it support, and which often even descends again after it has reached their summit; for it appears to me that such men also sink again—that is to say, somehow render themselves more ignorant than they would have been had they abstained from study altogether. For, not content with knowing all that is intelligibly explained in their author, they wish in addition to find in him the solution of many difficulties of which he says nothing, and in regard to which he possibly had no thought at all. At the same time their mode of philosophising is very convenient for those who have abilities of a very mediocre kind, for the obscurity of the distinctions and principles of which they make use, is the reason of their being able to talk of all things as boldly as though they really knew about them, and defend all that they say against the most subtle and acute, without any one having the means of convincing them to the contrary. In this they seem to me like a blind man who, in order to fight on equal terms with one who sees, would have the latter to come into the bottom of a very dark cave. I may say, too, that it is in the interest of such people that I should abstain from publishing the principles of philosophy of which I make use, for, being so simple and evident as they are, I should, in publishing them, do the same as though I threw open the windows and caused daylight to enter the cave into which they have descended in order to fight. But even the best minds have no reason to desire to be acquainted with these principles, for if they wish to be able to talk of everything and acquire a reputation for learning, they will more readily attain their end by contenting themselves with the appearance of truth which may be found in all sorts of things without much trouble, than in seeking for truth which only reveals itself little by little in certain spheres, and which, when others come into question, obliges one to confess one's ignorance. If, however, they prefer the knowledge of some small amount of truth to the vanity of seeming to be ignorant of nothing, which knowledge is doubtless preferable, or if they desire to follow a course similar to my own, it is not necessary that I should say any more than what I have already said in this Discourse. For if they are capable of passing beyond the point I have reached, they will also so much the more be able to find by themselves all that I believe myself to have discovered; since, not having examined anything but in its order, it is certain that what remains for me to discover is in itself more difficult and more recondite than anything that I have hitherto been able to meet with, and they would have much less pleasure in learning from me than from themselves. Besides, the habit which they will acquire of seeking first things that are simple and then little by little and by degrees passing to others more difficult, will be of more use than could be all my instructions. For, as regards myself, I am persuaded that if from my youth up I had been taught all the truths of which I have since sought the demonstrations, or if I had not had any difficulty in learning them, I should perhaps never have known any others, or at least I should never have acquired the habit or facility which I think I have obtained, of ever finding them anew, in proportion as I set myself to seek for them. And, in a word, if there is any work at all which cannot be so well achieved by another as by him who has begun it, it is that at which I labour.

It is true as regards the experiments which may conduce to this end, that one man could not possibly accomplish all of them. But yet he could not, to good advantage, employ other hands than his own, excepting those of artisans or persons of that kind whom he could pay, and whom the hope of gain—which is a very effectual incentive—might cause to perform with exactitude all the things they were directed to accomplish. As to those who, whether by curiosity or desire to learn, might possibly offer him their voluntary assistance, not only are they usually more ready with promises than with performance, planning out fine sounding projects, none of which are ever realised, but they will also infallibly demand payment for their trouble by requesting the explanation of certain difficulties, or at least by empty compliments and useless talk, which could not occupy any of the student's time without causing it to be lost. And as to the experiments already made by others, even if they desired to communicate these to him—which those who term them secrets would never do—they are for the most part accompanied by so many circumstances or superfluous matter, that it would be very difficult for him to disentangle the truth. In addition to this he would find nearly all so badly explained, or even so false (because those who carried them out were forced to make them appear to be in conformity with their principles), that if there had been some which might have been of use to him, they would hardly be worth the time that would be required in making the selection. So true is this, that if there were anywhere in the world a person whom one knew to be assuredly capable of discovering matters of the highest importance and those of the greatest possible utility to the public, and if for this reason all other men were eager by every means in their power to help him in reaching the end which he set before him, I do not see that they could do anything for him beyond contributing to defray the expenses of the experiments which might be requisite, or, for the rest, seeing that he was not deprived of his leisure by the importunities of anyone. But, in addition to the fact that I neither esteem myself so highly as to be willing to promise anything extraordinary, nor give scope to an imagination so vain as to conceive that the public should interest itself greatly in my designs, I do not yet own a soul so base as to be willing to accept from anyone whatever a favour which it might be supposed I did not merit.

All those considerations taken together were, three years ago, the cause of my not desiring to publish the Treatise which I had on hand, and the reason why I even formed the resolution of not bringing to light during my life any other of so general a kind, or one by which the foundations of Physics could be understood. But since then two other reasons came into operation which compelled me to bring forward certain attempts, as I have done here, and to render to the public some account of my actions and designs. The first is that if I failed to do so, many who knew the intention I formerly had of publishing certain writings, might imagine that the causes for which I abstained from so doing were more to my disadvantage than they really were; for although I do not care immoderately for glory, or, if I dare say so, although I even hate it, inasmuch as I judge it to be antagonistic to the repose which I esteem above all other things, at the same time I never tried to conceal my actions as though they were crimes, nor have I used many precautions against being known, partly because I should have thought it damaging to myself, and partly because it would have given me a sort of disquietude which would again have militated against the perfect repose of spirit which I seek. And forasmuch as having in this way always held myself in a condition of indifference as

regards wnether 1 was known or was not known, I have not yet
been able to prevent myself from acquiring some sort of reputation,
I thought that I should do my best at least to prevent myself from
acquiring an evil reputation. The other reason which obliged me
to put this in writing is that I am becoming every day more and
more alive to the delay which is being suffered in the design which
I have of instructing myself, because of the lack of an infinitude of
experiments, which it is impossible that I should perform without
the aid of others : and although I do not flatter myself so much as
to hope that the public should to any large degree participate in my
interest, I yet do not wish to be found wanting, both on my own
account, and as one day giving occasion to those who will survive
me of reproaching me for the fact that I might have left many
matters in a much better condition than I have done, had I not too
much neglected to make them understand in what way they could
have contributed to the accomplishment of my designs.

And I thought that it was easy for me to select certain matters
which would not be the occasion for many controversies, nor yet
oblige me to propound more of my principles than I wish, and
which yet would suffice to allow a pretty clear manifestation of what
I can do and what I cannot do in the sciences. In this I cannot
say whether I have succeeded or have not succeeded, and I do not
wish to anticipate the judgment of any one by myself speaking of
my writings ; but I shall be very glad if they will examine them.
And in order that they may have the better opportunity of so
doing, I beg all those who have any objections to offer to take the
trouble of sending them to my publishers, so that, being made
aware of them, I may try at the same time to subjoin my reply. By
this means, the reader, seeing objections and reply at the same
time, will the more easily judge of the truth ; for I do not promise
in any instance to make lengthy replies, but just to avow my errors
very frankly if I am convinced of them ; or, if I cannot perceive
them, to say simply what I think requisite for the defence of the
matters I have written, without adding the exposition of any new
matter, so that I may not be endlessly engaged in passing from one
side to the other.

If some of the matters of which I spoke in the beginning of the
Dioptrics and *Meteors* should at first sight give offence because
I call them hypotheses and do not appear to care about their proof,
let them have the patience to read these in entirety, and I hope
that they will find themselves satisfied. For it appears to me that

the reasonings are so mutually interwoven, that as the later ones are demonstrated by the earlier, which are their causes, the earlier are reciprocally demonstrated by the later which are their effects. And it must not be imagined that in this I commit the fallacy which logicians name arguing in a circle, for, since experience renders the greater part of these effects very certain, the causes from which I deduce them do not so much serve to prove their existence as to explain them ; on the other hand, the causes are explained by the effects. And I have not named them hypotheses with any other object than that it may be known that while I consider myself able to deduce them from the primary truths which I explained above, yet I particularly desired not to do so, in order that certain persons may not for this reason take occasion to build up some extravagant philosophic system on what they take to be my principles, and thus cause the blame to be put on me. I refer to those who imagine that in one day they may discover all that another has arrived at in twenty years of work, so soon as he has merely spoken to them two or three words on the subject; while they are really all the more subject to err, and less capable of perceiving the truth as they are the more subtle and lively. For as regards the opinions that are truly mine I do not apologise for them as being new, inasmuch as if we consider the reasons of them well, I assure myself that they will be found to be so simple and so conformable to common sense, as to appear less extraordinary and less paradoxical than any others which may be held on similar subjects. And I do not even boast of being the first discoverer of any of them, but only state that I have adopted them, not because they have been held by others, nor because they have not been so held, but only because Reason has persuaded me of their truth.

Even if artisans are not at once able to carry out the invention[1] explained in the *Dioptrics*, I do not for that reason think that it can be said that it is to be condemned ; for, inasmuch as great address and practice is required to make and adjust the mechanism which I have described without omitting any detail, I should not be less astonished at their succeeding at the first effort than I should be supposing some one were in one day to learn to play the guitar with skill, just because a good sheet of musical notation were set up before him. And if I write in French which is the language of my country, rather than in Latin which is that of my teachers, that is

[1] Doubtless the machine for the purpose of cutting lenses which Descartes so minutely describes.

because I hope that those who avail themselves only of their natural reason in its purity may be better judges of my opinions than those who believe only in the writings of the ancients; and as to those who unite good sense with study, whom alone I crave for my judges, they will not, I feel sure, be so partial to Latin as to refuse to follow my reasoning because I expound it in a vulgar tongue.

For the rest, I do not desire to speak here more particularly of the progress which I hope in the future to make in the sciences, nor to bind myself as regards the public with any promise which I shall not with certainty be able to fulfil. But I will just say that I have resolved not to employ the time which remains to me in life in any other matter than in endeavouring to acquire some knowledge of nature, which shall be of such a kind that it will enable us to arrive at rules for Medicine more assured than those which have as yet been attained; and my inclination is so strongly opposed to any other kind of pursuit, more especially to those which can only be useful to some by being harmful to others, that if certain circumstances had constrained me to employ them, I do not think that I should have been capable of succeeding. In so saying I make a declaration that I know very well cannot help me to make myself of consideration in the world, but to this end I have no desire to attain; and I shall always hold myself to be more indebted to those by whose favour I may enjoy my leisure without hindrance, than I shall be to any who may offer me the most honourable position in all the world.

MEDITATIONS
ON FIRST PHILOSOPHY

PREFATORY NOTE TO THE MEDITATIONS.

The first edition of the 'Meditations' was published in Latin by Michael Soly of Paris 'at the Sign of the Phoenix' in 1641 *cum Privilegio et Approbatione Doctorum*. The Royal 'privilege' was indeed given, but the 'approbation' seems to have been of a most indefinite kind. The reason of the book being published in France and not in Holland, where Descartes was living in a charming country house at Endegeest near Leiden, was apparently his fear that the Dutch ministers might in some way lay hold of it. His friend, Père Mersenne, took charge of its publication in Paris and wrote to him about any difficulties that occurred in the course of its progress through the press. The second edition was however published at Amsterdam in 1642 by Louis Elzevir, and this edition was accompanied by the now completed 'Objections and Replies.'[1] The edition from which the present translation is made is the second just mentioned, and is that adopted by MM. Adam and Tannery as the more correct, for reasons that they state in detail in the preface to their edition. The work was translated into French by the Duc de Luynes in 1642 and Descartes considered the translation so excellent that he had it published some years later. Clerselier, to complete matters, had the 'Objections' also published in French with the 'Replies,' and this, like the other, was subject to Descartes' revision and correction. This revision renders the French edition specially valuable. Where it seems desirable an alternative reading from the French is given in square brackets.

E. S. H.

[1] For convenience sake the 'Objections and Replies' are published in the second volume of this edition.

TO THE MOST WISE AND ILLUSTRIOUS THE DEAN AND DOCTORS OF THE SACRED FACULTY OF THEOLOGY IN PARIS.

The motive which induces me to present to you this Treatise is so excellent, and, when you become acquainted with its design, I am convinced that you will also have so excellent a motive for taking it under your protection, that I feel that I cannot do better, in order to render it in some sort acceptable to you, than in a few words to state what I have set myself to do.

I have always considered that the two questions respecting God and the Soul were the chief of those that ought to be demonstrated by philosophical rather than theological argument. For although it is quite enough for us faithful ones to accept by means of faith the fact that the human soul does not perish with the body, and that God exists, it certainly does not seem possible ever to persuade infidels of any religion, indeed, we may almost say, of any moral virtue, unless, to begin with, we prove these two facts by means of the natural reason. And inasmuch as often in this life greater rewards are offered for vice than for virtue, few people would prefer the right to the useful, were they restrained neither by the fear of God nor the expectation of another life; and although it is absolutely true that we must believe that there is a God, because we are so taught in the Holy Scriptures, and, on the other hand, that we must believe the Holy Scriptures because they come from God (the reason of this is, that, faith being a gift of God, He who gives the grace to cause us to believe other things can likewise give it to cause us to believe that He exists), we nevertheless could not place this argument before infidels, who might accuse us of reasoning in a circle. And, in truth, I have noticed that you, along with all the theologians, did not only affirm that the existence of God may be proved by the natural reason, but also that it may be inferred from the Holy Scriptures, that knowledge about Him is much clearer than that which we have of many created things, and, as a matter of fact, is so easy to acquire, that those who have it not are culpable in their ignorance. This indeed appears from the Wisdom of Solomon, chapter xiii., where is is said '*Howbeit they are not to be excused; for if their understanding was so great that they could discern the world and the creatures, why did they not rather find out the Lord thereof?*' and in Romans, chapter i., it is said that they are '*without excuse*'; and again in the same place, by these words '*that which may be known of God is manifest in them,*' it seems as though we were shown that all that which can be known of God may be made manifest by means which are not derived from anywhere but from ourselves, and from the simple consideration of the nature of our minds. Hence I thought it not beside my purpose to inquire how this is so, and how God may be more easily and certainly known than the things of the world.

And as regards the soul, although many have considered that it is not easy to know its nature, and some have even dared to say that human reasons have convinced us that it would perish with the body, and that faith alone could believe the contrary, nevertheless, inasmuch as the Lateran Council held under Leo X (in the eighth session) condemns these tenets, and as Leo expressly ordains Christian philosophers to refute their arguments and to employ all their powers in making known the truth, I have ventured in this treatise to undertake the same task.

More than that, I am aware that the principal reason which causes many impious persons not to desire to believe that there is a God, and that the human soul is distinct from the body, is that they declare that hitherto no one has been able to demonstrate these two facts; and although I am not of their opinion but, on the contrary, hold that the greater part of the reasons which have been brought forward concerning these two questions by so many great men are, when they are rightly understood, equal to so many demonstrations, and that it is almost impossible to invent new ones, it is yet in my opinion the case that nothing more useful can be accomplished in philosophy than once for all to seek with care for the best of these reasons, and to set them forth in so clear and exact a manner, that it will henceforth be evident to everybody that they are veritable demonstrations. And, finally, inasmuch as it was desired that I should undertake this task by many who were aware that I had cultivated a certain Method for the resolution of difficulties of every kind in the Sciences—a method which it is true is not novel, since there is nothing more ancient than the truth, but of which they were aware that I had made use successfully enough in other matters of difficulty—I have thought that it was my duty also to make trial of it in the present matter.

Now all that I could accomplish in the matter is contained in this Treatise. Not that I have here drawn together all the different reasons which might be brought forward to serve as proofs of this subject: for that never seemed to be necessary excepting when there was no one single proof that was certain. But I have treated the first and principal ones in such a manner that I can venture to bring them forward as very evident and very certain demonstrations. And more than that, I will say that these proofs are such that I do not think that there is any way open to the human mind by which it can ever succeed in discovering better. For the importance of the subject, and the glory of God to which all this relates, constrain me to speak here somewhat more freely of myself than is my habit. Nevertheless, whatever certainty and evidence I find in my reasons, I cannot persuade myself that all the world is capable of understanding them. Still, just as in Geometry there are many demonstrations that have been left to us by Archimedes, by Apollonius, by Pappus, and others, which are accepted by everyone as perfectly certain and evident (because they clearly contain nothing which, considered by itself, is not very easy to understand, and as all through that which follows has an exact connection with, and dependence on that which precedes), nevertheless, because they are somewhat lengthy, and demand a mind wholly devoted to their consideration, they are only taken in and understood by a very limited number of persons. Similarly, although I judge that those of which I here make use are equal to, or even surpass in certainty and evidence, the demonstrations of Geometry, I yet apprehend that they cannot be adequately understood by many, both because they are also a little lengthy and dependent the one on the other, and principally because they demand a mind wholly free of prejudices, and one which can be easily detached from the affairs of the senses. And, truth to say, there are not so many in the world who are fitted for metaphysical speculations as there are for those of Geometry. And more than that; there is still this difference, that in Geometry, since each one is persuaded that nothing must be advanced of which there is not a certain demonstration, those who are not entirely adepts more frequently err in approving what is false, in order to give the impression that they understand it, than in refuting the true. But the case is different in philosophy where everyone believes that all is problematical, and few give themselves to the search after truth; and the greater number, in their desire to acquire a reputation for boldness of thought, arrogantly combat the most important of truths[1].

That is why, whatever force there may be in my reasonings, seeing they belong to philosophy, I cannot hope that they will have much effect on the minds of men, unless you extend to them your protection. But the estimation in which your Company is universally held is so great, and the name of SORBONNE carries with it so much authority, that, next to the Sacred Councils, never has such deference been paid to the judgment of any Body, not only in what concerns the faith, but also in what regards human philosophy as well: everyone indeed believes that it is not possible to discover elsewhere more perspicacity and solidity, or more integrity and wisdom in pronouncing judgment. For this reason I have no doubt that if you deign to take the trouble in the first place of correcting this work (for being conscious not only of my infirmity, but also of my ignorance, I should not dare to state that it was free from errors), and then, after adding to it these things that are lacking to it, completing those which are imperfect, and yourselves taking the trouble to give a more ample explanation of those things which have need of it, or at least making me aware of the defects so that I may apply myself to remedy them[1]—when this is done and when finally the reasonings by which I prove that there is a God, and that the human soul differs from the body, shall be carried to that point of perspicuity to which I am sure they can be carried in order that they may be esteemed as perfectly exact demonstrations, if you deign to authorise your approbation and to render public testimony to their truth and certainty, I do not doubt, I say, that henceforward all the errors and false opinions which have ever existed regarding these two questions will soon be effaced from the minds of men. For the truth itself will easily cause all men of mind and learning to subscribe to your judgment; and your authority will cause the atheists, who are usually more arrogant than learned or judicious, to rid themselves of their spirit of contradiction or lead them possibly themselves to defend the reasonings which they find being received as demonstrations by all persons of

---

[1] The French version is followed here.

consideration, lest they appear not to understand them. And, finally, all others will easily yield to such a mass of evidence, and there will be none who dares to doubt the existence of God and the real and true distinction between the human soul and the body. It is for you now in your singular wisdom to judge of the importance of the establishment of such beliefs [you who see the disorders produced by the doubt of them][1]. But it would not become me to say more in consideration of the cause of God and religion to those who have always been the most worthy supports of the Catholic Church.

PREFACE TO THE READER.

I have already slightly touched on these two questions of God and the human soul in the Discourse on the Method of rightly conducting the Reason and seeking truth in the Sciences, published in French in the year 1637. Not that I had the design of treating these with any thoroughness, but only so to speak in passing, and in order to ascertain by the judgment of the readers how I should treat them later on. For these questions have always appeared to me to be of such importance that I judged it suitable to speak of them more than once ; and the road which I follow in the explanation of them is so little trodden, and so far removed from the ordinary path, that I did not judge it to be expedient to set it forth at length in French and in a Discourse which might be read by everyone, in case the feebler minds should believe that it was permitted to them to attempt to follow the same path.

But, having in this Discourse on Method begged all those who have found in my writings somewhat deserving of censure to do me the favour of acquainting me with the grounds of it, nothing worthy of remark has been objected to in them beyond two matters : to these two I wish here to reply in a few words before undertaking their more detailed discussion.

The first objection is that it does not follow from the fact that the human mind reflecting on itself does not perceive itself to be other than a thing that thinks, that its nature or its essence consists only in its being a thing that thinks, in the sense that this word *only* excludes all other things which might also be supposed to pertain to the nature of the soul. To this objection I reply that it was not my intention in that place to exclude these in accordance with the order that looks to the truth of the matter (as to which

---

[1] When it is thought desirable to insert additional readings from the French version this will be indicated by the use of square brackets.

I was not then dealing), but only in accordance with the order of my thought [perception]; thus my meaning was that so far as I was aware, I knew nothing clearly as belonging to my essence, excepting that I was a thing that thinks, or a thing that has in itself the faculty of thinking. But I shall show hereafter how from the fact that I know no other thing which pertains to my essence, it follows that there is no other thing which really does belong to it.

The second objection is that it does not follow from the fact that I have in myself the idea of something more perfect than I am, that this idea is more perfect than I, and much less that what is represented by this idea exists. But I reply that in this term *idea* there is here something equivocal, for it may either be taken materially, as an act of my understanding, and in this sense it cannot be said that it is more perfect than I; or it may be taken objectively, as the thing which is represented by this act, which, although we do not suppose it to exist outside of my understanding, may, none the less, be more perfect than I, because of its essence. And in following out this Treatise I shall show more fully how, from the sole fact that I have in myself the idea of a thing more perfect than myself, it follows that this thing truly exists.

In addition to these two objections I have also seen two fairly lengthy works on this subject, which, however, did not so much impugn my reasonings as my conclusions, and this by arguments drawn from the ordinary atheistic sources. But, because such arguments cannot make any impression on the minds of those who really understand my reasonings, and as the judgments of many are so feeble and irrational that they very often allow themselves to be persuaded by the opinions which they have first formed, however false and far removed from reason they may be, rather than by a true and solid but subsequently received refutation of these opinions, I do not desire to reply here to their criticisms in case of being first of all obliged to state them. I shall only say in general that all that is said by the atheist against the existence of God, always depends either on the fact that we ascribe to God affections which are human, or that we attribute so much strength and wisdom to our minds that we even have the presumption to desire to determine and understand that which God can and ought to do. In this way all that they allege will cause us no difficulty, provided only we remember that we must consider our minds as things which are finite and limited, and God as a Being who is incomprehensible and infinite.

Now that I have once for all recognised and acknowledged the opinions of men, I at once begin to treat of God and the human soul, and at the same time to treat of the whole of the First Philosophy, without however expecting any praise from the vulgar and without the hope that my book will have many readers. On the contrary, I should never advise anyone to read it excepting those who desire to meditate seriously with me, and who can detach their minds from affairs of sense, and deliver themselves entirely from every sort of prejudice. I know too well that such men exist in a very small number. But for those who, without caring to comprehend the order and connections of my reasonings, form their criticisms on detached portions arbitrarily selected, as is the custom with many, these, I say, will not obtain much profit from reading this Treatise. And although they perhaps in several parts find occasion of cavilling, they can for all their pains make no objection which is urgent or deserving of reply.

And inasmuch as I make no promise to others to satisfy them at once, and as I do not presume so much on my own powers as to believe myself capable of foreseeing all that can cause difficulty to anyone, I shall first of all set forth in these Meditations the very considerations by which I persuade myself that I have reached a certain and evident knowledge of the truth, in order to see if, by the same reasons which persuaded me, I can also persuade others. And, after that, I shall reply to the objections which have been made to me by persons of genius and learning to whom I have sent my Meditations for examination, before submitting them to the press. For they have made so many objections and these so different, that I venture to promise that it will be difficult for anyone to bring to mind criticisms of any consequence which have not been already touched upon. This is why I beg those who read these Meditations to form no judgment upon them unless they have given themselves the trouble to read all the objections as well as the replies which I have made to them[1].

---

[1] Between the *Præfatio ad Lectorem* and the *Synopsis*, the Paris Edition (1st Edition) interpolates an *Index* which is not found in the Amsterdam Edition (2nd Edition). Since Descartes did not reproduce it, he was doubtless not its author. Mersenne probably composed it himself, adjusting it to the paging of the first Edition.

(Note in Adam and Tannery's Edition.)

SYNOPSIS OF THE SIX FOLLOWING MEDITATIONS.

In the first Meditation I set forth the reasons for which we may, generally speaking, doubt about all things and especially about material things, at least so long as we have no other foundations for the sciences than those which we have hitherto possessed. But although the utility of a Doubt which is so general does not at first appear, it is at the same time very great, inasmuch as it delivers us from every kind of prejudice, and sets out for us a very simple way by which the mind may detach itself from the senses; and finally it makes it impossible for us ever to doubt those things which we have once discovered to be true.

In the second Meditation, mind, which making use of the liberty which pertains to it, takes for granted that all those things of whose existence it has the least doubt, are non-existent, recognises that it is however absolutely impossible that it does not itself exist. This point is likewise of the greatest moment, inasmuch as by this means a distinction is easily drawn between the things which pertain to mind —that is to say to the intellectual nature—and those which pertain to body.

But because it may be that some expect from me in this place a statement of the reasons establishing the immortality of the soul, I feel that I should here make known to them that having aimed at writing nothing in all this Treatise of which I do not possess very exact demonstrations, I am obliged to follow a similar order to that made use of by the geometers, which is to begin by putting forward as premises all those things upon which the proposition that we seek depends, before coming to any conclusion regarding it. Now the first and principal matter which is requisite for thoroughly understanding the immortality of the soul is to form the clearest possible conception of it, and one which will be entirely distinct from all the conceptions which we may have of body; and in this Meditation this has been done. In addition to this it is requisite that we may be assured that all the things which we conceive clearly and distinctly are true in the very way in which we think them; and this could not be proved previously to the Fourth Meditation. Further we must have a distinct conception of corporeal nature, which is given partly in this Second, and partly in the Fifth and Sixth Meditations. And finally we should conclude from all this, that those things which we conceive clearly and distinctly as being diverse substances, as we regard mind and body to be, are really substances essentially distinct one from the other; and this is the conclusion of the Sixth Meditation. This is further confirmed in this same Meditation by the fact that we cannot conceive of body excepting in so far as it is divisible, while the mind cannot be conceived of excepting as indivisible. For we are not able to conceive of the half of a mind as we can do of the smallest of all bodies; so that we see that not only are their natures different but even in some respects contrary to one another. I have not however dealt further with this matter in this treatise, both because what I have said is sufficient to show clearly enough that the extinction of the mind does not follow from the corruption of the body, and also to give men the hope of another life after death, as also because the premises from which the immortality of the soul may be deduced depend on an elucidation of a complete system of Physics. This would mean to establish in the first place that all substances generally—that is to say all things which cannot exist without being created by God—are in their nature incorruptible, and that they can never cease to exist unless God, in denying to them his concurrence, reduce them to nought; and secondly that body, regarded generally, is a substance, which is the reason why it also cannot perish, but that the human body, inasmuch as it differs from other bodies, is composed only of a certain configuration of members and of other similar accidents, while the human mind is not similarly composed of any accidents, but is a pure substance. For although all the accidents of mind be changed, although, for instance, it think certain things, will others, perceive others, etc., despite all this it does not emerge from these changes another mind: the human body on the other hand becomes a different thing from the sole fact that the figure or form of any of its portions is found to be changed. From this it follows that the human body may indeed easily enough perish, but the mind [or soul of man (I make no distinction between them)] is owing to its nature immortal.

In the third Meditation it seems to me that I have explained at sufficient length the principal argument of which I make use in order to prove the existence of God. But none the less, because I did not wish in that place to make use of any comparisons derived from corporeal things, so as to withdraw as much as I could the minds of readers from the senses, there may perhaps have remained many obscurities which, however, will, I hope, be entirely removed by the Replies which I have made to the Objections which have been set before me. Amongst others there is, for example, this one, 'How the idea in

*us of a being supremely perfect possesses so much objective reality
[that is to say participates by representation in so many degrees of
being and perfection] that it necessarily proceeds from a cause which
is absolutely perfect. This is illustrated in these Replies by the
comparison of a very perfect machine, the idea of which is found in
the mind of some workman. For as the objective contrivance of this
idea must have some cause, i.e. either the science of the workman or
that of some other from whom he has received the idea, it is similarly
impossible that the idea of God which is in us should not have God
himself as its cause.*

*In the fourth Meditation it is shown that all these things which
we very clearly and distinctly perceive are true, and at the same time
it is explained in what the nature of error or falsity consists. This
must of necessity be known both for the confirmation of the preceding truths and for the better comprehension of those that follow.
(But it must meanwhile be remarked that I do not in any way there
treat of sin—that is to say of the error which is committed in the
pursuit of good and evil, but only of that which arises in the deciding
between the true and the false. And I do not intend to speak of
matters pertaining to the Faith or the conduct of life, but only of
those which concern speculative truths, and which may be known by
the sole aid of the light of nature.)*

*In the fifth Meditation corporeal nature generally is explained,
and in addition to this the existence of God is demonstrated by a
new proof in which there may possibly be certain difficulties also, but
the solution of these will be seen in the Replies to the Objections.
And further I show in what sense it is true to say that the certainty
of geometrical demonstrations is itself dependent on the knowledge
of God.*

*Finally in the Sixth I distinguish the action of the under-
standing[1] from that of the imagination[2]; the marks by which this
distinction is made are described. I here show that the mind of man
is really distinct from the body, and at the same time that the two
are so closely joined together that they form, so to speak, a single
thing. All the errors which proceed from the senses are then
surveyed, while the means of avoiding them are demonstrated, and
finally all the reasons from which we may deduce the existence of
material things are set forth. Not that I judge them to be very
useful in establishing that which they prove, to wit, that there is in*

---

[1] *intellectio.* [2] *imaginatio.*

truth a world, that men possess bodies, and other such things which never have been doubted by anyone of sense; but because in considering these closely we come to see that they are neither so strong nor so evident as those arguments which lead us to the knowledge of our mind and of God; so that these last must be the most certain and most evident facts which can fall within the cognizance of the human mind. And this is the whole matter that I have tried to prove in these Meditations, for which reason I here omit to speak of many other questions with which I dealt incidentally in this discussion.

MEDITATIONS ON THE FIRST PHILOSOPHY IN WHICH THE EXISTENCE OF GOD AND THE DISTINCTION BETWEEN MIND AND BODY ARE DEMONSTRATED[1].

MEDITATION I.

Of the things which may be brought within the sphere of the doubtful.

It is now some years since I detected how many were the false beliefs that I had from my earliest youth admitted as true, and how doubtful was everything I had since constructed on this basis; and from that time I was convinced that I must once for all seriously undertake to rid myself of all the opinions which I had formerly accepted, and commence to build anew from the foundation, if I wanted to establish any firm and permanent structure in the sciences. But as this enterprise appeared to be a very great one, I waited until I had attained an age so mature that I could not hope that at any later date I should be better fitted to execute my design. This reason caused me to delay so long that I should feel that I was doing wrong were I to occupy in deliberation the time that yet remains to me for action. To-day, then, since very opportunely for the plan I have in view I have delivered my mind from every care [and am happily agitated by no passions] and since I have procured for myself an assured leisure in a peaceable retirement, I shall at last seriously and freely address myself to the general upheaval of all my former opinions.

---

[1] In place of this long title at the head of the page the first Edition had immediately after the Synopsis, and on the same page 7, simply 'First Meditation.' (Adam's Edition.)

Now for this object it is not necessary that I should show that all of these are false—I shall perhaps never arrive at this end. But inasmuch as reason already persuades me that I ought no less carefully to withhold my assent from matters which are not entirely certain and indubitable than from those which appear to me manifestly to be false, if I am able to find in each one some reason to doubt, this will suffice to justify my rejecting the whole. And for that end it will not be requisite that I should examine each in particular, which would be an endless undertaking; for owing to the fact that the destruction of the foundations of necessity brings with it the downfall of the rest of the edifice, I shall only in the first place attack those principles upon which all my former opinions rested.

All that up to the present time I have accepted as most true and certain I have learned either from the senses or through the senses; but it is sometimes proved to me that these senses are deceptive, and it is wiser not to trust entirely to any thing by which we have once been deceived.

But it may be that although the senses sometimes deceive us concerning things which are hardly perceptible, or very far away, there are yet many others to be met with as to which we cannot reasonably have any doubt, although we recognise them by their means. For example, there is the fact that I am here, seated by the fire, attired in a dressing gown, having this paper in my hands and other similar matters. And how could I deny that these hands and this body are mine, were it not perhaps that I compare myself to certain persons, devoid of sense, whose cerebella are so troubled and clouded by the violent vapours of black bile, that they constantly assure us that they think they are kings when they are really quite poor, or that they are clothed in purple when they are really without covering, or who imagine that they have an earthenware head or are nothing but pumpkins or are made of glass. But they are mad, and I should not be any the less insane were I to follow examples so extravagant.

At the same time I must remember that I am a man, and that consequently I am in the habit of sleeping, and in my dreams representing to myself the same things or sometimes even less probable things, than do those who are insane in their waking moments. How often has it happened to me that in the night I dreamt that I found myself in this particular place, that I was dressed and seated near the fire, whilst in reality I was lying

undressed in bed! At this moment it does indeed seem to me that
it is with eyes awake that I am looking at this paper; that this
head which I move is not asleep, that it is deliberately and of set
purpose that I extend my hand and perceive it; what happens in
sleep does not appear so clear nor so distinct as does all this. But
in thinking over this I remind myself that on many occasions I have
in sleep been deceived by similar illusions, and in dwelling carefully
on this reflection I see so manifestly that there are no certain
indications by which we may clearly distinguish wakefulness from
sleep that I am lost in astonishment. And my astonishment is
such that it is almost capable of persuading me that I now dream.

Now let us assume that we are asleep and that all these
particulars, e.g. that we open our eyes, shake our head, extend our
hands, and so on, are but false delusions; and let us reflect that
possibly neither our hands nor our whole body are such as they
appear to us to be. At the same time we must at least confess that
the things which are represented to us in sleep are like painted
representations which can only have been formed as the counter-
parts of something real and true, and that in this way those general
things at least, i.e. eyes, a head, hands, and a whole body, are not
imaginary things, but things really existent. For, as a matter of
fact, painters, even when they study with the greatest skill to
represent sirens and satyrs by forms the most strange and extraordinary, cannot give them natures which are entirely new, but
merely make a certain medley of the members of different animals;
or if their imagination is extravagant enough to invent something
so novel that nothing similar has ever before been seen, and that
then their work represents a thing purely fictitious and absolutely
false, it is certain all the same that the colours of which this is
composed are necessarily real. And for the same reason, although
these general things, to wit, [a body], eyes, a head, hands, and such
like, may be imaginary, we are bound at the same time to confess
that there are at least some other objects yet more simple and more
universal, which are real and true; and of these just in the same
way as with certain real colours, all these images of things which
dwell in our thoughts, whether true and real or false and fantastic,
are formed.

To such a class of things pertains corporeal nature in general,
and its extension, the figure of extended things, their quantity or
magnitude and number, as also the place in which they are, the
time which measures their duration, and so on.

That is possibly why our reasoning is not unjust when we conclude from this that Physics, Astronomy, Medicine and all other sciences which have as their end the consideration of composite things, are very dubious and uncertain ; but that Arithmetic, Geometry and other sciences of that kind which only treat of things that are very simple and very general, without taking great trouble to ascertain whether they are actually existent or not, contain some measure of certainty and an element of the indubitable. For whether I am awake or asleep, two and three together always form five, and the square can never have more than four sides, and it does not seem possible that truths so clear and apparent can be suspected of any falsity [or uncertainty].

Nevertheless I have long had fixed in my mind the belief that an all-powerful God existed by whom I have been created such as I am. But how do I know that He has not brought it to pass that there is no earth, no heaven, no extended body, no magnitude, no place, and that nevertheless [I possess the perceptions of all these things and that] they seem to me to exist just exactly as I now see them ? And, besides, as I sometimes imagine that others deceive themselves in the things which they think they know best, how do I know that I am not deceived every time that I add two and three, or count the sides of a square, or judge of things yet simpler, if anything simpler can be imagined ? But possibly God has not desired that I should be thus deceived, for He is said to be supremely good. If, however, it is contrary to His goodness to have made me such that I constantly deceive myself, it would also appear to be contrary to His goodness to permit me to be sometimes deceived, and nevertheless I cannot doubt that He does permit this.

There may indeed be those who would prefer to deny the existence of a God so powerful, rather than believe that all other things are uncertain. But let us not oppose them for the present, and grant that all that is here said of a God is a fable ; nevertheless in whatever way they suppose that I have arrived at the state of being that I have reached—whether they attribute it to fate or to accident, or make out that it is by a continual succession of ante-cedents, or by some other method—since to err and deceive oneself is a defect, it is clear that the greater will be the probability of my being so imperfect as to deceive myself ever, as is the Author to whom they assign my origin the less powerful. To these reasons I have certainly nothing to reply, but at the end I feel constrained to confess that there is nothing in all that I formerly believed to be true, of which I cannot in some measure doubt, and that not merely through want of thought or through levity, but for reasons which are very powerful and maturely considered; so that henceforth I ought not the less carefully to refrain from giving credence to these opinions than to that which is manifestly false, if I desire to arrive at any certainty [in the sciences].

But it is not sufficient to have made these remarks, we must also be careful to keep them in mind. For these ancient and commonly held opinions still revert frequently to my mind, long and familiar custom having given them the right to occupy my mind against my inclination and rendered them almost masters of my belief; nor will I ever lose the habit of deferring to them or of placing my confidence in them, so long as I consider them as they really are, i.e. opinions in some measure doubtful, as I have just shown, and at the same time highly probable, so that there is much more reason to believe in than to deny them. That is why I consider that I shall not be acting amiss, if, taking of set purpose a contrary belief, I allow myself to be deceived, and for a certain time pretend that all these opinions are entirely false and imaginary, until at last, having thus balanced my former prejudices with my latter [so that they cannot divert my opinions more to one side than to the other], my judgment will no longer be dominated by bad usage or turned away from the right knowledge of the truth. For I am assured that there can be neither peril nor error in this course, and that I cannot at present yield too much to distrust, since I am not considering the question of action, but only of knowledge.

I shall then suppose, not that God who is supremely good and the fountain of truth, but some evil genius not less powerful than deceitful, has employed his whole energies in deceiving me; I shall consider that the heavens, the earth, colours, figures, sound, and all other external things are nought but the illusions and dreams of which this genius has availed himself in order to lay traps for my credulity; I shall consider myself as having no hands, no eyes, no flesh, no blood, nor any senses, yet falsely believing myself to possess all these things; I shall remain obstinately attached to this idea, and if by this means it is not in my power to arrive at the knowledge of any truth, I may at least do what is in my power [i.e. suspend my judgment], and with firm purpose avoid giving credence to any false thing, or being imposed upon by this arch deceiver, however powerful and deceptive he may be. But this task is a laborious one, and insensibly a certain lassitude leads me into the course of my ordinary life. And just as a captive who in sleep enjoys an imaginary liberty, when he begins to suspect that his liberty is but a dream, fears to awaken, and conspires with these agreeable illusions that the deception may be prolonged, so insensibly of my own accord I fall back into my former opinions, and I dread awakening from this slumber, lest the laborious wakefulness which would follow the tranquillity of this repose should have to be spent not in daylight, but in the excessive darkness of the difficulties which have just been discussed.

MEDITATION II.

Of the Nature of the Human Mind; and that it is more easily known than the Body.

The Meditation of yesterday filled my mind with so many doubts that it is no longer in my power to forget them. And yet I do not see in what manner I can resolve them; and, just as if I had all of a sudden fallen into very deep water, I am so disconcerted that I can neither make certain of setting my feet on the bottom, nor can I swim and so support myself on the surface. I shall nevertheless make an effort and follow anew the same path as that on which I yesterday entered, i.e. I shall proceed by setting aside all that in which the least doubt could be supposed to exist, just as if I had discovered that it was absolutely false; and I shall ever follow in this road until I have met with something which is certain, or at least, if I can do nothing else, until I have learned for certain that there is nothing in the world that is certain. Archimedes, in order that he might draw the terrestrial globe out of its place, and transport it elsewhere, demanded only that one point should be fixed and immoveable; in the same way I shall have the right to conceive high hopes if I am happy enough to discover one thing only which is certain and indubitable.

I suppose, then, that all the things that I see are false; I persuade myself that nothing has ever existed of all that my fallacious memory represents to me. I consider that I possess no senses; I imagine that body, figure, extension, movement and place are but the fictions of my mind. What, then, can be esteemed as true? Perhaps nothing at all, unless that there is nothing in the world that is certain.

But how can I know there is not something different from those things that I have just considered, of which one cannot have the slightest doubt? Is there not some God, or some other being by whatever name we call it, who puts these reflections into my mind? That is not necessary, for is it not possible that I am capable of producing them myself? I myself, am I not at least something? But I have already denied that I had senses and body. Yet I hesitate, for what follows from that? Am I so dependent on body and senses that I cannot exist without these? But I was persuaded that there was nothing in all the world, that there was no heaven, no earth, that there were no minds, nor any bodies : was I not then likewise persuaded that I did not exist? Not at all; of a surety I myself did exist since I persuaded myself of something [or merely because I thought of something]. But there is some deceiver or other, very powerful and very cunning, who ever employs his ingenuity in deceiving me. Then without doubt I exist also if he deceives me, and let him deceive me as much as he will, he can never cause me to be nothing so long as I think that I am something. So that after having reflected well and carefully examined all things, we must come to the definite conclusion that this proposition : I am, I exist, is necessarily true each time that I pronounce it, or that I mentally conceive it.

But I do not yet know clearly enough what I am, I who am certain that I am ; and hence I must be careful to see that I do not imprudently take some other object in place of myself, and thus that I do not go astray in respect of this knowledge that I hold to be the most certain and most evident of all that I have formerly learned. That is why I shall now consider anew what I believed myself to be before I embarked upon these last reflections ; and of my former opinions I shall withdraw all that might even in a small degree be invalidated by the reasons which I have just brought forward, in order that there may be nothing at all left beyond what is absolutely certain and indubitable.

What then did I formerly believe myself to be? Undoubtedly I believed myself to be a man. But what is a man? Shall I say a reasonable animal? Certainly not; for then I should have to inquire what an animal is, and what is reasonable ; and thus from a single question I should insensibly fall into an infinitude of others more difficult ; and I should not wish to waste the little time and leisure remaining to me in trying to unravel subtleties like these. But I shall rather stop here to consider the thoughts which of themselves spring up in my mind, and which were not inspired by anything beyond my own nature alone when I applied myself to the consideration of my being. In the first place, then, I considered myself as having a face, hands, arms, and all that system of members composed of bones and flesh as seen in a corpse which I designated by the name of body. In addition to this I considered that I was nourished, that I walked, that I felt, and that I thought, and I referred all these actions to the soul: but I did not stop to consider what the soul was, or if I did stop, I imagined that it was something extremely rare and subtle like a wind, a flame, or an ether, which was spread throughout my grosser parts. As to body I had no manner of doubt about its nature, but thought I had a very clear knowledge of it; and if I had desired to explain it according to the notions that I had then formed of it, I should have described it thus: By the body I understand all that which can be defined by a certain figure: something which can be confined in a certain place, and which can fill a given space in such a way that every other body will be excluded from it; which can be perceived either by touch, or by sight, or by hearing, or by taste, or by smell: which can be moved in many ways not, in truth, by itself, but by something which is foreign to it, by which it is touched [and from which it receives impressions]: for to have the power of self-movement, as also of feeling or of thinking, I did not consider to appertain to the nature of body: on the contrary, I was rather astonished to find that faculties similar to them existed in some bodies.

But what am I, now that I suppose that there is a certain genius which is extremely powerful, and, if I may say so, malicious, who employs all his powers in deceiving me? Can I affirm that I possess the least of all those things which I have just said pertain to the nature of body? I pause to consider, I revolve all these things in my mind, and I find none of which I can say that it pertains to me. It would be tedious to stop to enumerate them. Let us pass to the attributes of soul and see if there is any one which is in me? What of nutrition or walking [the first mentioned]? But if it is so that I have no body it is also true that I can neither walk nor take nourishment. Another attribute is sensation. But one cannot feel without body, and besides I have thought I perceived many things during sleep that I recognised in my waking moments as not having been experienced at all. What of thinking? I find here that thought is an attribute that belongs to me; it alone cannot be separated from me. I am, I exist, that is certain. But how often? Just when I think; for it might possibly be the case if I ceased entirely to think, that I should likewise cease altogether to exist. I do not now admit anything which is not necessarily true : to speak accurately I am not more than a thing which thinks, that is to say a mind or a soul, or an understanding, or a reason, which are terms whose significance was formerly unknown to me. I am, however, a real thing and really exist; but what thing ? I have answered : a thing which thinks.

And what more ? I shall exercise my imagination [in order to see if I am not something more]. I am not a collection of members which we call the human body : I am not a subtle air distributed through these members, I am not a wind, a fire, a vapour, a breath, nor anything at all which I can imagine or conceive; because I have assumed that all these were nothing. Without changing that supposition I find that I only leave myself certain of the fact that I am somewhat. But perhaps it is true that these same things which I supposed were non-existent because they are unknown to me, are really not different from the self which I know. I am not sure about this, I shall not dispute about it now; I can only give judgment on things that are known to me. I know that I exist, and I inquire what I am, I whom I know to exist. But it is very certain that the knowledge of my existence taken in its precise significance does not depend on things whose existence is not yet known to me; consequently it does not depend on those which I can feign in imagination. And indeed the very term *feign* in imagination[1] proves to me my error, for I really do this if I image myself a something, since to imagine is nothing else than to contemplate the figure or image of a corporeal thing. But I already know for certain that I am, and that it may be that all these images, and, speaking generally, all things that relate to the nature of body are nothing but dreams [and chimeras]. For this reason I see clearly that I have as little reason to say, 'I shall stimulate my imagination in order to know more distinctly what I am,' than if I were to say, 'I am now awake, and I perceive somewhat that is real and true : but because I do not yet perceive it distinctly enough, I shall go to sleep of express purpose, so that my dreams may represent the perception with greatest truth and evidence.' And, thus, I know for certain that nothing of all that I can understand by means of my imagination belongs to this knowledge which I have of myself, and that it is necessary to recall the mind from

[1] Or 'form an image' (effingo).

this mode of thought with the utmost diligence in order that it may be able to know its own nature with perfect distinctness.

But what then am I ?   A thing which thinks.   What is a thing which thinks ?   It is a thing which doubts, understands, [conceives], affirms, denies, wills, refuses, which also imagines and feels.

Certainly it is no small matter if all these things pertain to my nature.   But why should they not so pertain ?   Am I not that being who now doubts nearly everything, who nevertheless understands certain things, who affirms that one only is true, who denies all the others, who desires to know more, is averse from being deceived, who imagines many things, sometimes indeed despite his will, and who perceives many likewise, as by the intervention of the bodily organs ?   Is there nothing in all this which is as true as it is certain that I exist, even though I should always sleep and though he who has given me being employed all his ingenuity in deceiving me ?   Is there likewise any one of these attributes which can be distinguished from my thought, or which might be said to be separated from myself ?   For it is so evident of itself that it is I who doubts, who understands, and who desires, that there is no reason here to add anything to explain it.   And I have certainly the power of imagining likewise ; for although it may happen (as I formerly supposed) that none of the things which I imagine are true, nevertheless this power of imagining does not cease to be really in use, and it forms part of my thought.   Finally, I am the same who feels, that is to say, who perceives certain things, as by the organs of sense, since in truth I see light, I hear noise, I feel heat.   But it will be said that these phenomena are false and that I am dreaming.   Let it be so ; still it is at least quite certain that it seems to me that I see light, that I hear noise and that I feel heat.   That cannot be false ; properly speaking it is what is in me called feeling[1]; and used in this precise sense that is no other thing than thinking.

From this time I begin to know what I am with a little more clearness and distinction than before ; but nevertheless it still seems to me, and I cannot prevent myself from thinking, that corporeal things, whose images are framed by thought, which are tested by the senses, are much more distinctly known than that obscure part of me which does not come under the imagination. Although really it is very strange to say that I know and understand more distinctly these things whose existence seems to me

---

[1] Sentire.

dubious, which are unknown to me, and which do not belong to me, than others of the truth of which I am convinced, which are known to me and which pertain to my real nature, in a word, than myself. But I see clearly how the case stands : my mind loves to wander, and cannot yet suffer itself to be retained within the just limits of truth. Very good, let us once more give it the freest rein, so that, when afterwards we seize the proper occasion for pulling up, it may the more easily be regulated and controlled.

Let us begin by considering the commonest matters, those which we believe to be the most distinctly comprehended, to wit, the bodies which we touch and see; not indeed bodies in general, for these general ideas are usually a little more confused, but let us consider one body in particular. Let us take, for example, this piece of wax : it has been taken quite freshly from the hive, and it has not yet lost the sweetness of the honey which it contains; it still retains somewhat of the odour of the flowers from which it has been culled; its colour, its figure, its size are apparent; it is hard, cold, easily handled, and if you strike it with the finger, it will emit a sound. Finally all the things which are requisite to cause us distinctly to recognise a body, are met with in it. But notice that while I speak and approach the fire what remained of the taste is exhaled, the smell evaporates, the colour alters, the figure is destroyed, the size increases, it becomes liquid, it heats, scarcely can one handle it, and when one strikes it, no sound is emitted. Does the same wax remain after this change ? We must confess that it remains ; none would judge otherwise. What then did I know so distinctly in this piece of wax ? It could certainly be nothing of all that the senses brought to my notice, since all these things which fall under taste, smell, sight, touch, and hearing, are found to be changed, and yet the same wax remains.

Perhaps it was what I now think, viz. that this wax was not that sweetness of honey, nor that agreeable scent of flowers, nor that particular whiteness, nor that figure, nor that sound, but simply a body which a little while before appeared to me as perceptible under these forms, and which is now perceptible under others. But what, precisely, is it that I imagine when I form such conceptions ? Let us attentively consider this, and, abstracting from all that does not belong to the wax, let us see what remains. Certainly nothing remains excepting a certain extended thing which is flexible and movable. But what is the meaning of flexible and movable ? Is it not that I imagine that this piece of wax being round is capable of becoming square and of passing from a square to a triangular figure? No, certainly it is not that, since I imagine it admits of an infinitude of similar changes, and I nevertheless do not know how to compass the infinitude by my imagination, and consequently this conception which I have of the wax is not brought about by the faculty of imagination. What now is this extension? Is it not also unknown? For it becomes greater when the wax is melted, greater when it is boiled, and greater still when the heat increases; and I should not conceive [clearly] according to truth what wax is, if I did not think that even this piece that we are considering is capable of receiving more variations in extension than I have ever imagined. We must then grant that I could not even understand through the imagination what this piece of wax is, and that it is my mind[1] alone which perceives it. I say this piece of wax in particular, for as to wax in general it is yet clearer. But what is this piece of wax which cannot be understood excepting by the [understanding or] mind? It is certainly the same that I see, touch, imagine, and finally it is the same which I have always believed it to be from the beginning. But what must particularly be observed is that its perception is neither an act of vision, nor of touch, nor of imagination, and has never been such although it may have appeared formerly to be so, but only an intuition[2] of the mind, which may be imperfect and confused as it was formerly, or clear and distinct as it is at present, according as my attention is more or less directed to the elements which are found in it, and of which it is composed.

Yet in the meantime I am greatly astonished when I consider [the great feebleness of mind] and its proneness to fall [insensibly] into error; for although without giving expression to my thoughts I consider all this in my own mind, words often impede me and I am almost deceived by the terms of ordinary language. For we say that we see the same wax, if it is present, and not that we simply judge that it is the same from its having the same colour and figure. From this I should conclude that I knew the wax by means of vision and not simply by the intuition of the mind; unless by chance I remember that, when looking from a window and saying I see men who pass in the street, I really do not see them, but infer that what I see is men, just as I say that I see wax. And yet what do I see from the window but hats and coats which may cover automatic machines? Yet I judge these to be men. And similarly

---

[1] entendement F., mens L.　　　　　　[2] inspectio.

solely by the faculty of judgment which rests in my mind, I comprehend that which I believed I saw with my eyes.

A man who makes it his aim to raise his knowledge above the common should be ashamed to derive the occasion for doubting from the forms of speech invented by the vulgar; I prefer to pass on and consider whether I had a more evident and perfect conception of what the wax was when I first perceived it, and when I believed I knew it by means of the external senses or at least by the common sense[1] as it is called, that is to say by the imaginative faculty, or whether my present conception is clearer now that I have most carefully examined what it is, and in what way it can be known. It would certainly be absurd to doubt as to this. For what was there in this first perception which was distinct? What was there which might not as well have been perceived by any of the animals? But when I distinguish the wax from its external forms, and when, just as if I had taken from it its vestments, I consider it quite naked, it is certain that although some error may still be found in my judgment, I can nevertheless not perceive it thus without a human mind.

But finally what shall I say of this mind, that is, of myself, for up to this point I do not admit in myself anything but mind? What then, I who seem to perceive this piece of wax so distinctly, do I not know myself, not only with much more truth and certainty, but also with much more distinctness and clearness? For if I judge that the wax is or exists from the fact that I see it, it certainly follows much more clearly that I am or that I exist myself from the fact that I see it. For it may be that what I see is not really wax, it may also be that I do not possess eyes with which to see anything; but it cannot be that when I see, or (for I no longer take account of the distinction) when I think I see, that I myself who think am nought. So if I judge that the wax exists from the fact that I touch it, the same thing will follow, to wit, that I am; and if I judge that my imagination, or some other cause, whatever it is, persuades me that the wax exists, I shall still conclude the same. And what I have here remarked of wax may be applied to all other things which are external to me [and which are met with outside of me]. And further, if the [notion or] perception of wax has seemed to me clearer and more distinct, not only after the sight or the touch, but also after many other causes have rendered it quite manifest to me, with how much more [evidence] and distinctness

[1] *sensus communis.*

must it be said that I now know myself, since all the reasons which contribute to the knowledge of wax, or any other body whatever, are yet better proofs of the nature of my mind! And there are so many other things in the mind itself which may contribute to the elucidation of its nature, that those which depend on body such as these just mentioned, hardly merit being taken into account.

But finally here I am, having insensibly reverted to the point I desired, for, since it is now manifest to me that even bodies are not properly speaking known by the senses or by the faculty of imagination, but by the understanding only, and since they are not known from the fact that they are seen or touched, but only because they are understood, I see clearly that there is nothing which is easier for me to know than my mind. But because it is difficult to rid oneself so promptly of an opinion to which one was accustomed for so long, it will be well that I should halt a little at this point, so that by the length of my meditation I may more deeply imprint on my memory this new knowledge.

MEDITATION III.

Of God: that He exists.

I shall now close my eyes, I shall stop my ears, I shall call away all my senses, I shall efface even from my thoughts all the images of corporeal things, or at least (for that is hardly possible) I shall esteem them as vain and false; and thus holding converse only with myself and considering my own nature, I shall try little by little to reach a better knowledge of and a more familiar acquaintanceship with myself. I am a thing that thinks, that is to say, that doubts, affirms, denies, that knows a few things, that is ignorant of many [that loves, that hates], that wills, that desires, that also imagines and perceives; for as I remarked before, although the things which I perceive and imagine are perhaps nothing at all apart from me and in themselves, I am nevertheless assured that these modes of thought that I call perceptions and imaginations, inasmuch only as they are modes of thought, certainly reside [and are met with] in me.

And in the little that I have just said, I think I have summed up all that I really know, or at least all that hitherto I was aware that I knew. In order to try to extend my knowledge lurther, I shall now look around more carefully and see whether I cannot still discover in myself some other things which I have not hitherto perceived. I am certain that I am a thing which thinks; but do I not then likewise know what is requisite to render me certain of a truth? Certainly in this first knowledge there is nothing that assures me of its truth, excepting the clear and distinct perception of that which I state, which would not indeed suffice to assure me that what I say is true, if it could ever happen that a thing which I conceived so clearly and distinctly could be false; and accordingly it seems to me that already I can establish as a general rule that all things which I perceive[1] very clearly and very distinctly are true.

At the same time I have before received and admitted many things to be very certain and manifest, which yet I afterwards recognised as being dubious. What then were these things? They were the earth, sky, stars and all other objects which I apprehended by means of the senses. But what did I clearly [and distinctly] perceive in them? Nothing more than that the ideas or thoughts of these things were presented to my mind. And not even now do I deny that these ideas are met with in me. But there was yet another thing which I affirmed, and which, owing to the habit which I had formed of believing it, I thought I perceived very clearly, although in truth I did not perceive it at all, to wit, that there were objects outside of me from which these ideas proceeded, and to which they were entirely similar. And it was in this that I erred, or, if perchance my judgment was correct, this was not due to any knowledge arising from my perception.

But when I took anything very simple and easy in the sphere of arithmetic or geometry into consideration, e.g. that two and three together made five, and other things of the sort, were not these present to my mind so clearly as to enable me to affirm that they were true? Certainly if I judged that since such matters could be doubted, this would not have been so for any other reason than that it came into my mind that perhaps a God might have endowed me with such a nature that I may have been deceived even concerning things which seemed to me most manifest. But every time that this preconceived opinion of the sovereign power of a God presents itself to my thought, I am constrained to confess that it is easy to Him, if He wishes it, to cause me to err, even in matters in which I believe myself to have the best evidence. And, on the other hand, always when I direct my attention to things which I believe myself to perceive very clearly, I am so persuaded of their truth that I let myself break out into words such as these: Let

[1] Percipio, F. nous concevons.

who will deceive me, He can never cause me to be nothing while
I think that I am, or some day cause it to be true to say that
I have never been, it being true now to say that I am, or that two
and three make more or less than five, or any such thing in which
I see a manifest contradiction. And, certainly, since I have no
reason to believe that there is a God who is a deceiver, and as
I have not yet satisfied myself that there is a God at all, the reason
for doubt which depends on this opinion alone is very slight, and so
to speak metaphysical. But in order to be able altogether to
remove it, I must inquire whether there is a God as soon as the
occasion presents itself; and if I find that there is a God, I must
also inquire whether He may be a deceiver; for without a knowledge
of these two truths I do not see that I can ever be certain of
anything.

And in order that I may have an opportunity of inquiring into
this in an orderly way [without interrupting the order of meditation
which I have proposed to myself, and which is little by little to
pass from the notions which I find first of all in my mind to those
which I shall later on discover in it] it is requisite that I should
here divide my thoughts into certain kinds, and that I should
consider in which of these kinds there is, properly speaking, truth
or error to be found. Of my thoughts some are, so to speak, images
of the things, and to these alone is the title 'idea' properly applied;
examples are my thought of a man or of a chimera, of heaven, of
an angel, or [even] of God. But other thoughts possess other
forms as well. For example in willing, fearing, approving, denying,
though I always perceive something as the subject of the action
of my mind[1], yet by this action I always add something else to the
idea[2] which I have of that thing; and of the thoughts of this kind
some are called volitions or affections, and others judgments.

Now as to what concerns ideas, if we consider them only in
themselves and do not relate them to anything else beyond
themselves, they cannot properly speaking be false; for whether
I imagine a goat or a chimera, it is not less true that I imagine the
one than the other. We must no fear likewise that falsity can
enter into will and into affections, for although I may desire evil
things, or even things that never existed, it is not the less true that
I desire them. Thus there remains no more than the judgments

---

[1] The French version is followed here as being more explicit. In it 'action
de mon esprit' replaces 'mea cogitatio.'
[2] In the Latin version 'similitudinem.'

which we make, in which I must take the greatest care not to deceive myself. But the principal error and the commonest which we may meet with in them, consists in my judging that the ideas which are in me are similar or conformable to the things which are outside me; for without doubt if I considered the ideas only as certain modes of my thoughts, without trying to relate them to anything beyond, they could scarcely give me material for error.

But among these ideas, some appear to me to be innate, some adventitious, and others to be formed [or invented] by myself; for, as I have the power of understanding what is called a thing, or a truth, or a thought, it appears to me that I hold this power from no other source than my own nature. But if I now hear some sound, if I see the sun, or feel heat, I have hitherto judged that these sensations proceeded from certain things that exist outside of me; and finally it appears to me that sirens, hippogryphs, and the like, are formed out of my own mind. But again I may possibly persuade myself that all these ideas are of the nature of those which I term adventitious, or else that they are all innate, or all fictitious: for I have not yet clearly discovered their true origin.

And my principal task in this place is to consider, in respect to those ideas which appear to me to proceed from certain objects that are outside me, what are the reasons which cause me to think them similar to these objects. It seems indeed in the first place that I am taught this lesson by nature; and, secondly, I experience in myself that these ideas do not depend on my will nor therefore on myself—for they often present themselves to my mind in spite of my will. Just now, for instance, whether I will or whether I do not will, I feel heat, and thus I persuade myself that this feeling, or at least this idea of heat, is produced in me by something which is different from me, i.e. by the heat of the fire near which I sit. And nothing seems to me more obvious than to judge that this object imprints its likeness rather than anything else upon me.

Now I must discover whether these proofs are sufficiently strong and convincing. When I say that I am so instructed by nature, I merely mean a certain spontaneous inclination which impels me to believe in this connection, and not a natural light which makes me recognise that it is true. But these two things are very different; for I cannot doubt that which the natural light causes me to believe to be true, as, for example, it has shown me that I am from the fact that I doubt, or other facts of the same kind. And I possess no other faculty whereby to distinguish truth from falsehood, which can teach me that what this light shows me to be true is not really true, and no other faculty that is equally trustworthy. But as far as [apparently] natural impulses are concerned, I have frequently remarked, when I had to make active choice between virtue and vice, that they often enough led me to the part that was worse ; and this is why I do not see any reason for following them in what regards truth and error.

And as to the other reason, which is that these ideas must proceed from objects outside me, since they do not depend on my will, I do not find it any the more convincing. For just as these impulses of which I have spoken are found in me, notwithstanding that they do not always concur with my will, so perhaps there is in me some faculty fitted to produce these ideas without the assistance of any external things, even though it is not yet known by me ; just as, apparently, they have hitherto always been found in me during sleep without the aid of any external objects.

And finally, though they did proceed from objects different from myself, it is not a necessary consequence that they should resemble these. On the contrary, I have noticed that in many cases there was a great difference between the object and its idea. I find, for example, two completely diverse ideas of the sun in my mind ; the one derives its origin from the senses, and should be placed in the category of adventitious ideas ; according to this idea the sun seems to be extremely small ; but the other is derived from astronomical reasonings, i.e. is elicited from certain notions that are innate in me, or else it is formed by me in some other manner ; in accordance with it the sun appears to be several times greater than the earth. These two ideas cannot, indeed, both resemble the same sun, and reason makes me believe that the one which seems to have originated directly from the sun itself, is the one which is most dissimilar to it.

All this causes me to believe that until the present time it has not been by a judgment that was certain [or premeditated], but only by a sort of blind impulse that I believed that things existed outside of, and different from me, which, by the organs of my senses, or by some other method whatever it might be, conveyed these ideas or images to me [and imprinted on me their similitudes].

But there is yet another method of inquiring whether any of the objects of which I have ideas within me exist outside of me If ideas are only taken as certain modes of thought, I recognise amongst them no difference or inequality, and all appear to proceed from me in the same manner; but when we consider them as images, one representing one thing and the other another, it is clear that they are very different one from the other. There is no doubt that those which represent to me substances are something more, and contain so to speak more objective reality within them [that is to say, by representation participate in a higher degree of being or perfection] than those that simply represent modes or accidents; and that idea again by which I understand a supreme God, eternal, infinite, [immutable], omniscient, omnipotent, and Creator of all things which are outside of Himself, has certainly more objective reality in itself than those ideas by which finite substances are represented.

Now it is manifest by the natural light that there must at least be as much reality in the efficient and total cause as in its effect. For, pray, whence can the effect derive its reality, if not from its cause? And in what way can this cause communicate this reality to it, unless it possessed it in itself? And from this it follows, not only that something cannot proceed from nothing, but likewise that what is more perfect—that is to say, which has more reality within itself—cannot proceed from the less perfect. And this is not only evidently true of those effects which possess actual or formal reality, but also of the ideas in which we consider merely what is termed objective reality. To take an example, the stone which has not yet existed not only cannot now commence to be unless it has been produced by something which possesses within itself, either formally or eminently, all that enters into the composition of the stone [i.e. it must possess the same things or other more excellent things than those which exist in the stone] and heat can only be produced in a subject in which it did not previously exist by a cause that is of an order [degree or kind] at least as perfect as heat, and so in all other cases. But further, the idea of heat, or of a stone, cannot exist in me unless it has been placed within me by some cause which possesses within it at least as much reality as that which I conceive to exist in the heat or the stone. For although this cause does not transmit anything of its actual or formal reality to my idea, we must not for that reason imagine that it is necessarily a less real cause; we must remember that [since every idea is a work of the mind] its nature is such that it demands of itself no other formal reality than that which it borrows from my thought, of which it is only a mode [i.e. a manner or way of thinking]. But in order that an idea should contain some one certain objective reality rather than another, it must without doubt derive it from some cause in which there is at least as much formal reality as this idea contains of objective reality. For if we imagine that something is found in an idea which is not found in the cause, it must then have been derived from nought; but however imperfect may be this mode of being by which a thing is objectively [or by representation] in the understanding by its idea, we cannot certainly say that this mode of being is nothing, nor, consequently, that the idea derives its origin from nothing.

Nor must I imagine that, since the reality that I consider in these ideas is only objective, it is not essential that this reality should be formally in the causes of my ideas, but that it is sufficient that it should be found objectively. For just as this mode of objective existence pertains to ideas by their proper nature, so does the mode of formal existence pertain to the causes of those ideas (this is at least true of the first and principal) by the nature peculiar to them. And although it may be the case that one idea gives birth to another idea, that cannot continue to be so indefinitely; for in the end we must reach an idea whose cause shall be so to speak an archetype, in which the whole reality [or perfection] which is so to speak objectively [or by representation] in these ideas is contained formally [and really]. Thus the light of nature causes me to know clearly that the ideas in me are like [pictures or] images which can, in truth, easily fall short of the perfection of the objects from which they have been derived, but which can never contain anything greater or more perfect.

And the longer and the more carefully that I investigate these matters, the more clearly and distinctly do I recognise their truth. But what am I to conclude from it all in the end? It is this, that if the objective reality of any one of my ideas is of such a nature as clearly to make me recognise that it is not in me either formally or eminently, and that consequently I cannot myself be the cause of it, it follows of necessity that I am not alone in the world, but that there is another being which exists, or which is the cause of this idea. On the other hand, had no such an idea existed in me, I should have had no sufficient argument to convince me of the existence of any being beyond myself; for I have made very careful investigation everywhere and up to the present time have been able to find no other ground.

But of my ideas, beyond that which represents me to myself, as to which there can here be no difficulty, there is another which represents a God, and there are others representing corporeal and inanimate things, others angels, others animals, and others again which represent to me men similar to myself.

As regards the ideas which represent to me other men or animals, or angels, I can however easily conceive that they might be formed by an admixture of the other ideas which I have of myself, of corporeal things, and of God, even although there were apart from me neither men nor animals, nor angels, in all the world.

And in regard to the ideas of corporeal objects, I do not recognise in them anything so great or so excellent that they might not have possibly proceeded from myself; for if I consider them more closely, and examine them individually, as I yesterday examined the idea of wax, I find that there is very little in them which I perceive clearly and distinctly. Magnitude or extension in length, breadth, or depth, I do so perceive; also figure which results from a termination of this extension, the situation which bodies of different figure preserve in relation to one another, and movement or change of situation; to which we may also add substance, duration and number. As to other things such as light, colours, sounds, scents, tastes, heat, cold and the other tactile qualities, they are thought by me with so much obscurity and confusion that I do not even know if they are true or false, i.e. whether the ideas which I form of these qualities are actually the ideas of real objects or not [or whether they only represent chimeras which cannot exist in fact]. For although I have before remarked that it is only in judgments that falsity, properly speaking, or formal falsity, can be met with, a certain material falsity may nevertheless be found in ideas, i.e. when these ideas represent what is nothing as though it were something. For example, the ideas which I have of cold and heat are so far from clear and distinct that by their means I cannot tell whether cold is merely a privation of heat, or heat a privation of cold, or whether both are real qualities, or are not such. And inasmuch as [since ideas resemble images] there cannot be any ideas which do not appear to represent some things, if it is correct to say that cold is merely a privation of heat, the idea which represents it to me as something real and positive will not be improperly termed false, and the same holds good of other similar ideas.

To these it is certainly not necessary that I should attribute any author other than myself. For if they are false, i.e. if they represent things which do not exist, the light of nature shows me that they issue from nought, that is to say, that they are only in me in so far as something is lacking to the perfection of my nature. But if they are true, nevertheless because they exhibit so little reality to me that I cannot even clearly distinguish the thing represented from non-being, I do not see any reason why they should not be produced by myself.

As to the clear and distinct idea which I have of corporeal things, some of them seem as though I might have derived them from the idea which I possess of myself, as those which I have of substance, duration, number, and such like. For [even] when I think that a stone is a substance, or at least a thing capable of existing of itself, and that I am a substance also, although I conceive that I am a thing that thinks and not one that is extended, and that the stone on the other hand is an extended thing which does not think, and that thus there is a notable difference between the two conceptions—they seem, nevertheless, to agree in this, that both represent substances. In the same way, when I perceive that I now exist and further recollect that I have in former times existed, and when I remember that I have various thoughts of which I can recognise the number, I acquire ideas of duration and number which I can afterwards transfer to any object that I please. But as to all the other qualities of which the ideas of corporeal things are composed, to wit, extension, figure, situation and motion, it is true that they are not formally in me, since I am only a thing that thinks; but because they are merely certain modes of substance [and so to speak the vestments under which corporeal substance appears to us] and because I myself am also a substance, it would seem that they might be contained in me eminently.

Hence there remains only the idea of God, concerning which we must consider whether it is something which cannot have proceeded from me myself. By the name God I understand a substance that is infinite [eternal, immutable], independent, all-knowing, all-powerful, and by which I myself and everything else, if anything else does exist, have been created. Now all these characteristics are such that the more diligently I attend to them, the less do they appear capable of proceeding from me alone; hence, from what has been already said, we must conclude that God necessarily exists.

For although the idea of substance is within me owing to the fact that I am substance, nevertheless I should not have the idea of an infinite substance—since I am finite—if it had not proceeded from some substance which was veritably infinite.

Nor should I imagine that I do not perceive the infinite by a true idea, but only by the negation of the finite, just as I perceive repose and darkness by the negation of movement and of light; for, on the contrary, I see that there is manifestly more reality in infinite substance than in finite, and therefore that in some way I have in me the notion of the infinite earlier than the finite—to wit, the notion of God before that of myself. For how would it be possible that I should know that I doubt and desire, that is to say, that something is lacking to me, and that I am not quite perfect, unless I had within me some idea of a Being more perfect than myself, in comparison with which I should recognise the deficiencies of my nature?

And we cannot say that this idea of God is perhaps materially false and that consequently I can derive it from nought [i.e. that possibly it exists in me because I am imperfect], as I have just said is the case with ideas of heat, cold and other such things; for, on the contrary, as this idea is very clear and distinct and contains within it more objective reality than any other, there can be none which is of itself more true, nor any in which there can be less suspicion of falsehood. The idea, I say, of this Being who is absolutely perfect and infinite, is entirely true; for although, perhaps, we can imagine that such a Being does not exist, we cannot nevertheless imagine that His idea represents nothing real to me, as I have said of the idea of cold. This idea is also very clear and distinct; since all that I conceive clearly and distinctly of the real and the true, and of what conveys some perfection, is in its entirety contained in this idea. And this does not cease to be true although I do not comprehend the infinite, or though in God there is an infinitude of things which I cannot comprehend, nor possibly even reach in any way by thought; for it is of the nature of the infinite that my nature, which is finite and limited, should not comprehend it; and it is sufficient that I should understand this, and that I should judge that all things which I clearly perceive and in which I know that there is some perfection, and possibly likewise an infinitude of properties of which I am ignorant, are in God formally or eminently, so that the idea which I have of Him may become the most true, most clear, and most distinct of all the ideas that are in my mind.

But possibly I am something more than I suppose myself to be, and perhaps all those perfections which I attribute to God are in some way potentially in me, although they do not yet disclose themselves, or issue in action. As a matter of fact I am already sensible that my knowledge increases [and perfects itself] little by little, and I see nothing which can prevent it from increasing more and more into infinitude; nor do I see, after it has thus been increased [or perfected], anything to prevent my being able to acquire by its means all the other perfections of the Divine nature; nor finally why the power I have of acquiring these perfections, if it really exists in me, shall not suffice to produce the ideas of them.

At the same time I recognise that this cannot be. For, in the first place, although it were true that every day my knowledge acquired new degrees of perfection, and that there were in my nature many things potentially which are not yet there actually, nevertheless these excellences do not pertain to [or make the smallest approach to] the idea which I have of God in whom there is nothing merely potential [but in whom all is present really and actually]; for it is an infallible token of imperfection in my knowledge that it increases little by little. And further, although my knowledge grows more and more, nevertheless I do not for that reason believe that it can ever be actually infinite, since it can never reach a point so high that it will be unable to attain to any greater increase. But I understand God to be actually infinite, so that He can add nothing to His supreme perfection. And finally I perceive that the objective being of an idea cannot be produced by a being that exists potentially only, which properly speaking is nothing, but only by a being which is formal or actual.

To speak the truth, I see nothing in all that I have just said which by the light of nature is not manifest to anyone who desires to think attentively on the subject; but when I slightly relax my attention, my mind, finding its vision somewhat obscured and so to speak blinded by the images of sensible objects, I do not easily re-collect the reason why the idea that I possess of a being more perfect than I, must necessarily have been placed in me by a being which is really more perfect; and this is why I wish here to go on to inquire whether I, who have this idea, can exist if no such being exists.

And I ask, from whom do I then derive my existence? Perhaps from myself or from my parents, or from some other source less perfect than God; for we can imagine nothing more perfect than God, or even as perfect as He is.

But [were I independent of every other and] were I myself the author of my being, I should doubt nothing and I should desire nothing, and finally no perfection would be lacking to me; for I should have bestowed on myself every perfection of which I possessed any idea and should thus be God. And it must not be imagined that those things that are lacking to me are perhaps more difficult of attainment than those which I already possess; for, on the contrary, it is quite evident that it was a matter of much greater difficulty to bring to pass that I, that is to say, a thing or a substance that thinks, should emerge out of nothing, than it would be to attain to the knowledge of many things of which I am ignorant, and which are only the accidents of this thinking substance. But it is clear that if I had of myself possessed this greater perfection of which I have just spoken [that is to say, if I had been the author of my own existence], I should not at least have denied myself the things which are the more easy to acquire [to wit, many branches of knowledge of which my nature is destitute]; nor should I have deprived myself of any of the things contained in the idea which I form of God, because there are none of them which seem to me specially difficult to acquire: and if there were any that were more difficult to acquire, they would certainly appear to me to be such (supposing I myself were the origin of the other things which I possess) since I should discover in them that my powers were limited.

But though I assume that perhaps I have always existed just as I am at present, neither can I escape the force of this reasoning, and imagine that the conclusion to be drawn from this is, that I need not seek for any author of my existence. For all the course of my life may be divided into an infinite number of parts, none of which is in any way dependent on the other; and thus from the fact that I was in existence a short time ago it does not follow that I must be in existence now, unless some cause at this instant, so to speak, produces me anew, that is to say, conserves me. It is as a matter of fact perfectly clear and evident to all those who consider with attention the nature of time, that, in order to be conserved in each moment in which it endures, a substance has need of the same power and action as would be necessary to produce and create it anew, supposing it did not yet exist, so that the light of nature shows us clearly that the distinction between creation and conservation is solely a distinction of the reason.

All that I thus require here is that I should interrogate myself, if I wish to know whether I possess a power which is capable of bringing it to pass that I who now am shall still be in the future ; for since I am nothing but a thinking thing, or at least since thus far it is only this portion of myself which is precisely in question at present, if such a power did reside in me, I should certainly be conscious of it. But I am conscious of nothing of the kind, and by this I know clearly that I depend on some being different from myself.

Possibly, however, this being on which I depend is not that which I call God, and I am created either by my parents or by some other cause less perfect than God. This cannot be, because, as I have just said, it is perfectly evident that there must be at least as much reality in the cause as in the effect; and thus since I am a thinking thing, and possess an idea of God within me, whatever in the end be the cause assigned to my existence, it must be allowed that it is likewise a thinking thing and that it possesses in itself the idea of all the perfections which I attribute to God. We may again inquire whether this cause derives its origin from itself or from some other thing. For if from itself, it follows by the reasons before brought forward, that this cause must itself be God; for since it possesses the virtue of self-existence, it must also without doubt have the power of actually possessing all the perfections of which it has the idea, that is, all those which I conceive as existing in God. But if it derives its existence from some other cause than itself, we shall again ask, for the same reason, whether this second cause exists by itself or through another, until from one step to another, we finally arrive at an ultimate cause, which will be God.

And it is perfectly manifest that in this there can be no regression into infinity, since what is in question is not so much the cause which formerly created me, as that which conserves me at the present time.

Nor can we suppose that several causes may have concurred in my production, and that from one I have received the idea of one of the perfections which I attribute to God, and from another the idea of some other, so that all these perfections indeed exist somewhere in the universe, but not as complete in one unity which is God. On the contrary, the unity, the simplicity or the inseparability of all things which are in God is one of the principal perfections which I conceive to be in Him. And certainly the idea of this unity of all Divine perfections cannot have been placed in me by any cause from which I have not likewise received the ideas of all the other perfections; for this cause could not make me able to comprehend them as joined together in an inseparable unity without having at the same time caused me in some measure to know what they are [and in some way to recognise each one of them].

Finally, so far as my parents [from whom it appears I have sprung] are concerned, although all that I have ever been able to believe of them were true, that does not make it follow that it is they who conserve me, nor are they even the authors of my being in any sense, in so far as I am a thinking being; since what they did was merely to implant certain dispositions in that matter in which the self—i.e. the mind, which alone I at present identify with myself—is by me deemed to exist. And thus there can be no difficulty in their regard, but we must of necessity conclude from the fact alone that I exist, or that the idea of a Being supremely perfect—that is of God—is in me, that the proof of God's existence is grounded on the highest evidence.

It only remains to me to examine into the manner in which I have acquired this idea from God; for I have not received it through the senses, and it is never presented to me unexpectedly, as is usual with the ideas of sensible things when these things present themselves, or seem to present themselves, to the external organs of my senses; nor is it likewise a fiction of my mind, for it is not in my power to take from or to add anything to it; and consequently the only alternative is that it is innate in me, just as the idea of myself is innate in me.

And one certainly ought not to find it strange that God, in creating me, placed this idea within me to be like the mark of the workman imprinted on his work; and it is likewise not essential that the mark shall be something different from the work itself. For from the sole fact that God created me it is most probable that in some way he has placed his image and similitude upon me, and that I perceive this similitude (in which the idea of God is contained) by means of the same faculty by which I perceive myself—that is to say, when I reflect on myself I not only know that I am something [imperfect], incomplete and dependent on another, which incessantly aspires after something which is better and greater than myself, but I also know that He on whom I depend possesses in Himself all the great things towards which I aspire [and the ideas of which I find within myself], and that not indefinitely or potentially alone, but really, actually and infinitely; and that thus He is God. And the whole strength of the argument which I have here made use of to prove the existence of God consists in this, that I recognise that it is not possible that my nature should be what it is, and indeed that I should have in myself the idea of a God, if God did not veritably exist—a God, I say, whose idea is in me, i.e. who possesses all those supreme perfections of which our mind may indeed have some idea but without understanding them all, who is liable to no errors or defect [and who has none of all those marks which denote imperfection]. From this it is manifest that He cannot be a deceiver, since the light of nature teaches us that fraud and deception necessarily proceed from some defect.

But before I examine this matter with more care, and pass on to the consideration of other truths which may be derived from it, it seems to me right to pause for a while in order to contemplate God Himself, to ponder at leisure His marvellous attributes, to consider, and admire, and adore, the beauty of this light so resplendent, at least as far as the strength of my mind, which is in some measure dazzled by the sight, will allow me to do so. For just as faith teaches us that the supreme felicity of the other life consists only in this contemplation of the Divine Majesty, so we continue to learn by experience that a similar meditation, though incomparably less perfect, causes us to enjoy the greatest satisfaction of which we are capable in this life.

MEDITATION IV.

Of the True and the False.

I have been well accustomed these past days to detach my mind from my senses, and I have accurately observed that there are very few things that one knows with certainty respecting corporeal objects, that there are many more which are known to us respecting the human mind, and yet more still regarding God Himself ; so that I shall now without any difficulty abstract my thoughts from the consideration of [sensible or] imaginable objects, and carry them to those which, being withdrawn from all contact with matter, are purely intelligible. And certainly the idea which I possess of the human mind inasmuch as it is a thinking thing, and not extended in length, width and depth, nor participating in anything pertaining to body, is incomparably more distinct than is the idea of any corporeal thing. And when I consider that I doubt, that is to say, that I am an incomplete and dependent being, the idea of a being that is complete and independent, that is of God, presents itself to my mind with so much distinctness and clearness—and from the fact alone that this idea is found in me, or that I who possess this idea exist, I conclude so certainly that God exists, and that my existence depends entirely on Him in every moment of my life— that I do not think that the human mind is capable of knowing anything with more evidence and certitude. And it seems to me that I now have before me a road which will lead us from the contemplation of the true God (in whom all the treasures of science and wisdom are contained) to the knowledge of the other objects of the universe.

For, first of all, I recognise it to be impossible that He should ever deceive me ; for in all fraud and deception some imperfection is to be found, and although it may appear that the power of deception is a mark of subtilty or power, yet the desire to deceive without doubt testifies to malice or feebleness, and accordingly cannot be found in God.

In the next place I experienced in myself a certain capacity for judging which I have doubtless received from God, like all the other things that I possess ; and as He could not desire to deceive me, it is clear that He has not given me a faculty that will lead me to err if I use it aright.

And no doubt respecting this matter could remain, if it were not that the consequence would seem to follow that I can thus never be deceived ; for if I hold all that I possess from God, and if He has not placed in me the capacity for error, it seems as though I could never fall into error. And it is true that when I think only of God [and direct my mind wholly to Him][1], I discover [in myself] no cause of error, or falsity; yet directly afterwards, when recurring to myself, experience shows me that I am nevertheless subject to an infinitude of errors, as to which, when we come to investigate them more closely, I notice that not only is there a real and positive idea of God or of a Being of supreme perfection present to my mind, but also, so to speak, a certain negative idea of nothing, that is, of that which is infinitely removed from any kind of perfection ; and that I am in a sense something intermediate between God and nought, i.e. placed in such a manner between the supreme Being and non-being, that there is in truth nothing in me that can lead to error in so far as a sovereign Being has formed me ; but that, as I in some degree participate likewise in nought or in non-being, i.e. in so far as I am not myself the supreme Being, and as I find myself subject

[1] Not in the French version.

to an infinitude of imperfections, I ought not to be astonished if I should fall into error. Thus do I recognise that error, in so far as it is such, is not a real thing depending on God, but simply a defect; and therefore, in order to fall into it, that I have no need to possess a special faculty given me by God for this very purpose, but that I fall into error from the fact that the power given me by God for the purpose of distinguishing truth from error is not infinite.

Nevertheless this does not quite satisfy me; for error is not a pure negation [i.e. is not the simple defect or want of some perfection which ought not to be mine], but it is a lack of some knowledge which it seems that I ought to possess. And on considering the nature of God it does not appear to me possible that He should have given me a faculty which is not perfect of its kind, that is, which is wanting in some perfection due to it. For if it is true that the more skilful the artizan, the more perfect is the work of his hands, what can have been produced by this supreme Creator of all things that is not in all its parts perfect? And certainly there is no doubt that God could have created me so that I could never have been subject to error; it is also certain that He ever wills what is best; is it then better that I should be subject to err than that I should not?

In considering this more attentively, it occurs to me in the first place that I should not be astonished if my intelligence is not capable of comprehending why God acts as He does; and that there is thus no reason to doubt of His existence from the fact that I may perhaps find many other things besides this as to which I am able to understand neither for what reason nor how God has produced them. For, in the first place, knowing that my nature is extremely feeble and limited, and that the nature of God is on the contrary immense, incomprehensible, and infinite, I have no further difficulty in recognising that there is an infinitude of matters in His power, the causes of which transcend my knowledge; and this reason suffices to convince me that the species of cause termed final, finds no useful employment in physical [or natural] things; for it does not appear to me that I can without temerity seek to investigate the [inscrutable] ends of God.

It further occurs to me that we should not consider one single creature separately, when we inquire as to whether the works of God are perfect, but should regard all his creations together. For the same thing which might possibly seem very imperfect with some semblance of reason if regarded by itself, is found to be very perfect if regarded as part of the whole universe; and although, since I resolved to doubt all things, I as yet have only known certainly my own existence and that of God, nevertheless since I have recognised the infinite power of God, I cannot deny that He may have produced many other things, or at least that He has the power of producing them, so that I may obtain a place as a part of a great universe.

Whereupon, regarding myself more closely, and considering what are my errors (for they alone testify to there being any imperfection in me), I answer that they depend on a combination of two causes, to wit, on the faculty of knowledge that rests in me, and on the power of choice or of free will—that is to say, of the understanding and at the same time of the will. For by the understanding alone I [neither assert nor deny anything, but] apprehend[1] the ideas of things as to which I can form a judgment. But no error is properly speaking found in it, provided the word error is taken in its proper signification; and though there is possibly an infinitude of things in the world of which I have no idea in my understanding, we cannot for all that say that it is deprived of these ideas [as we might say of something which is required by its nature], but simply it does not possess these; because in truth there is no reason to prove that God should have given me a greater faculty of knowledge than He has given me; and however skilful a workman I represent Him to be, I should not for all that consider that He was bound to have placed in each of His works all the perfections which He may have been able to place in some. I likewise cannot complain that God has not given me a free choice or a will which is sufficient, ample and perfect, since as a matter of fact I am conscious of a will so extended as to be subject to no limits. And what seems to me very remarkable in this regard is that of all the qualities which I possess there is no one so perfect and so comprehensive that I do not very clearly recognise that it might be yet greater and more perfect. For, to take an example, if I consider the faculty of comprehension which I possess, I find that it is of very small extent and extremely limited, and at the same time I find the idea of another faculty much more ample and even infinite, and seeing that I can form the idea of it, I recognise from this very fact that it pertains to the nature of God. If in the same way I examine the memory, the imagination, or some other faculty, I do not find any which is not

[1] percipio.

small and circumscribed, while in God it is immense [or infinite]. It is free-will alone or liberty of choice which I find to be so great in me that I can conceive no other idea to be more great ; it is indeed the case that it is for the most part this will that causes me to know that in some manner I bear the image and similitude of God. For although the power of will is incomparably greater in God than in me, both by reason of the knowledge and the power which, conjoined with it, render it stronger and more efficacious, and by reason of its object, inasmuch as in God it extends to a great many things ; it nevertheless does not seem to me greater if I consider it formally and precisely in itself : for the faculty of will consists alone in our having the power of choosing to do a thing or choosing not to do it (that is, to affirm or deny, to pursue or to shun it), or rather it consists alone in the fact that in order to affirm or deny, pursue or shun those things placed before us by the understanding, we act so that we are unconscious that any outside force constrains us in doing so. For in order that I should be free it is not necessary that I should be indifferent as to the choice of one or the other of two contraries ; but contrariwise the more I lean to the one— whether I recognise clearly that the reasons of the good and true are to be found in it, or whether God so disposes my inward thought—the more freely do I choose and embrace it. And undoubtedly both divine grace and natural knowledge, far from diminishing my liberty, rather increase it and strengthen it. Hence this indifference which I feel, when I am not swayed to one side rather than to the other by lack of reason, is the lowest grade of liberty, and rather evinces a lack or negation in knowledge than a perfection of will : for if I always recognised clearly what was true and good, I should never have trouble in deliberating as to what judgment or choice I should make, and then I should be entirely free without ever being indifferent.

From all this I recognise that the power of will which I have received from God is not of itself the source of my errors—for it is very ample and very perfect of its kind—any more than is the power of understanding ; for since I understand nothing but by the power which God has given me for understanding, there is no doubt that all that I understand, I understand as I ought, and it is not possible that I err in this. Whence then come my errors ? They come from the sole fact that since the will is much wider in its range and compass than the understanding, I do not restrain it within the same bounds, but extend it also to things which I do not understand: and as the will is of itself indifferent to these, it easily falls into error and sin, and chooses the evil for the good, or the false for the true.

For example, when I lately examined whether anything existed in the world, and found that from the very fact that I considered this question it followed very clearly that I myself existed, I could not prevent myself from believing that a thing I so clearly conceived was true: not that I found myself compelled to do so by some external cause, but simply because from great clearness in my mind there followed a great inclination of my will; and I believed this with so much the greater freedom or spontaneity as I possessed the less indifference towards it. Now, on the contrary, I not only know that I exist, inasmuch as I am a thinking thing, but a certain representation of corporeal nature is also presented to my mind; and it comes to pass that I doubt whether this thinking nature which is in me, or rather by which I am what I am, differs from this corporeal nature, or whether both are not simply the same thing; and I here suppose that I do not yet know any reason to persuade me to adopt the one belief rather than the other. From this it follows that I am entirely indifferent as to which of the two I affirm or deny, or even whether I abstain from forming any judgment in the matter.

And this indifference does not only extend to matters as to which the understanding has no knowledge, but also in general to all those which are not apprehended with perfect clearness at the moment when the will is deliberating upon them: for, however probable are the conjectures which render me disposed to form a judgment respecting anything, the simple knowledge that I have that those are conjectures alone and not certain and indubitable reasons, suffices to occasion me to judge the contrary. Of this I have had great experience of late when I set aside as false all that I had formerly held to be absolutely true, for the sole reason that I remarked that it might in some measure be doubted.

But if I abstain from giving my judgment on any thing when I do not perceive it with sufficient clearness and distinctness, it is plain that I act rightly and am not deceived. But if I determine to deny or affirm, I no longer make use as I should of my free will, and if I affirm what is not true, it is evident that I deceive myself; even though I judge according to truth, this comes about only by chance, and I do not escape the blame of misusing my freedom; for the light of nature teaches us that the knowledge of the understanding should always precede the determination of the will.

And it is in the misuse of the free will that the privation which constitutes the characteristic nature of error is met with. Privation, I say, is found in the act, in so far as it proceeds from me, but it is not found in the faculty which I have received from God, nor even in the act in so far as it depends on Him.

For I have certainly no cause to complain that God has not given me an intelligence which is more powerful, or a natural light which is stronger than that which I have received from Him, since it is proper to the finite understanding not to comprehend a multitude of things, and it is proper to a created understanding to be finite; on the contrary, I have every reason to render thanks to God who owes me nothing and who has given me all the perfections I possess, and I should be far from charging Him with injustice, and with having deprived me of, or wrongfully withheld from me, these perfections which He has not bestowed upon me.

I have further no reason to complain that He has given me a will more ample than my understanding, for since the will consists only of one single element, and is so to speak indivisible, it appears that its nature is such that nothing can be abstracted from it [without destroying it]; and certainly the more comprehensive it is found to be, the more reason I have to render gratitude to the giver.

And, finally, I must also not complain that God concurs with me in forming the acts of the will, that is the judgment in which I go astray, because these acts are entirely true and good, inasmuch as they depend on God; and in a certain sense more perfection accrues to my nature from the fact that I can form them, than if I could not do so. As to the privation in which alone the formal reason of error or sin consists, it has no need of any concurrence from God, since it is not a thing [or an existence], and since it is not related to God as to a cause, but should be termed merely a negation [according to the significance given to these words in the Schools]. For in fact it is not an imperfection in God that He has given me the liberty to give or withhold my assent from certain things as to which He has not placed a clear and distinct knowledge in my understanding; but it is without doubt an imperfection in me not to make a good use of my freedom, and to give my judgment readily on matters which I only understand obscurely. I nevertheless perceive that God could easily have created me so that I never should err, although I still remained free, and endowed with a limited knowledge, viz. by giving to my understanding a clear and distinct intelligence of all things as to which I should ever have to deliberate; or simply by His engraving deeply in my memory the resolution never to form a judgment on anything without having a clear and distinct understanding of it, so that I could never forget it. And it is easy for me to understand that, in so far as I consider myself alone, and as if there were only myself in the world, I should have been much more perfect than I am, if God had created me so that I could never err. Nevertheless I cannot deny that in some sense it is a greater perfection in the whole universe that certain parts should not be exempt from error as others are than that all parts should be exactly similar. And I have no right to·complain if God, having placed me in .the world, has not called upon me to play a part that excels all others in distinction and perfection.

And further I have reason to be glad on the ground that if He has not given me the power of never going astray by the first means pointed out above, which depends on a clear and evident knowledge of all the things regarding which I can deliberate, He has at least left within my power the other means, which is firmly to adhere to the resolution never to give judgment on matters whose truth is not clearly known to me; for although I notice a certain weakness in my nature in that I cannot continually concentrate my mind on one single thought, I can yet, by attentive and frequently repeated meditation, impress it so forcibly on my memory that I shall never fail to recollect it whenever I have need of it, and thus acquire the habit of never going astray.

And inasmuch as it is in this that the greatest and principal perfection of man consists, it seems to me that I have not gained little by this day's Meditation, since I have discovered the source of falsity and error. And certainly there can be no other source than that which I have explained; for as often as I so restrain my will within the limits of my knowledge that it forms no judgment except on matters which are clearly and distinctly represented to it by the understanding, I can never be deceived; for every clear and distinct conception[1] is without doubt something, and hence cannot derive its origin from what is nought, but must of necessity have God as its author—God, I say, who being supremely perfect, cannot be the cause of any error; and consequently we must conclude that such a conception [or such a judgment] is true. Nor have I only learned to-day what I should avoid in order that I may not err, but also how I should act in order to arrive at a knowledge of the

---

[1] perceptio.

truth; for without doubt I shall arrive at this end if I devote my attention sufficiently to those things which I perfectly understand; and if I separate from these that which I only understand confusedly and with obscurity. To these I shall henceforth diligently give heed.

MEDITATION V.

Of the essence of material things, and, again, of God, that He exists.

Many other matters respecting the attributes of God and my own nature or mind remain for consideration; but I shall possibly on another occasion resume the investigation of these. Now (after first noting what must be done or avoided, in order to arrive at a knowledge of the truth) my principal task is to endeavour to emerge from the state of doubt into which I have these last days fallen, and to see whether nothing certain can be known regarding material things.

But before examining whether any such objects as I conceive exist outside of me, I must consider the ideas of them in so far as they are in my thought, and see which of them are distinct and which confused.

In the first place, I am able distinctly to imagine that quantity which philosophers commonly call continuous, or the extension in length, breadth, or depth, that is in this quantity, or rather in the object to which it is attributed. Further, I can number in it many different parts, and attribute to each of its parts many sorts of size, figure, situation and local movement, and, finally, I can assign to each of these movements all degrees of duration.

And not only do I know these things with distinctness when I consider them in general, but, likewise [however little I apply my attention to the matter], I discover an infinitude of particulars respecting numbers, figures, movements, and other such things, whose truth is so manifest, and so well accords with my nature, that when I begin to discover them, it seems to me that I learn nothing new, or recollect what I formerly knew—that is to say, that I for the first time perceive things which were already present to my mind, although I had not as yet applied my mind to them.

And what I here find to be most important is that I discover in myself an infinitude of ideas of certain things which cannot be esteemed as pure negations, although they may possibly have no existence outside of my thought, and which are not framed by me, although it is within my power either to think or not to think them, but which possess natures which are true and immutable. For example, when I imagine a triangle, although there may nowhere in the world be such a figure outside my thought, or ever have been, there is nevertheless in this figure a certain determinate nature, form, or essence, which is immutable and eternal, which I have not invented, and which in no wise depends on my mind, as appears from the fact that diverse properties of that triangle can be demonstrated, viz. that its three angles are equal to two right angles, that the greatest side is subtended by the greatest angle, and the like, which now, whether I wish it or do not wish it, I recognise very clearly as pertaining to it, although I never thought of the matter at all when I imagined a triangle for the first time, and which therefore cannot be said to have been invented by me.

Nor does the objection hold good that possibly this idea of a triangle has reached my mind through the medium of my senses, since I have sometimes seen bodies triangular in shape; because I can form in my mind an infinitude of other figures regarding which we cannot have the least conception of their ever having been objects of sense, and I can nevertheless demonstrate various properties pertaining to their nature as well as to that of the triangle, and these must certainly all be true since I conceive them clearly. Hence they are something, and not pure negation; for it is perfectly clear that all that is true is something, and I have already fully demonstrated that all that I know clearly is true. And even although I had not demonstrated this, the nature of my mind is such that I could not prevent myself from holding them to be true so long as I conceive them clearly; and I recollect that even when I was still strongly attached to the objects of sense, I counted as the most certain those truths which I conceived clearly as regards figures, numbers, and the other matters which pertain to arithmetic and geometry, and, in general, to pure and abstract mathematics.

But now, if just because I can draw the idea of something from my thought, it follows that all which I know clearly and distinctly as pertaining to this object does really belong to it, may I not derive from this an argument demonstrating the existence of God? It is certain that I no less find the idea of God, that is to say, the idea of a supremely perfect Being, in me, than that of any figure or number whatever it is; and I do not know any less clearly and distinctly that an [actual and] eternal existence pertains to this nature than I know that all that which I am able to demonstrate of some figure or number truly pertains to the nature of this figure or number, and therefore, although all that I concluded in the preceding Meditations were found to be false, the existence of God would pass with me as at least as certain as I have ever held the truths of mathematics (which concern only numbers and figures) to be.

This indeed is not at first manifest, since it would seem to present some appearance of being a sophism. For being accustomed in all other things to make a distinction between existence and essence, I easily persuade myself that the existence can be separated from the essence of God, and that we can thus conceive God as not actually existing. But, nevertheless, when I think of it with more attention, I clearly see that existence can no more be separated from the essence of God than can its having its three angles equal to two right angles be separated from the essence of a [rectilinear] triangle, or the idea of a mountain from the idea of a valley; and so there is not any less repugnance to our conceiving a God (that is, a Being supremely perfect) to whom existence is lacking (that is to say, to whom a certain perfection is lacking), than to conceive of a mountain which has no valley.

But although I cannot really conceive of a God without existence any more than a mountain without a valley, still from the fact that I conceive of a mountain with a valley, it does not follow that there is such a mountain in the world; similarly although I conceive of God as possessing existence, it would seem that it does not follow that there is a God which exists; for my thought does not impose any necessity upon things, and just as I may imagine a winged horse, although no horse with wings exists, so I could perhaps attribute existence to God, although no God existed.

But a sophism is concealed in this objection; for from the fact that I cannot conceive a mountain without a valley, it does not follow that there is any mountain or any valley in existence, but only that the mountain and the valley, whether they exist or do not exist, cannot in any way be separated one from the other. While from the fact that I cannot conceive God without existence, it follows that existence is inseparable from Him, and hence that He really exists; not that my thought can bring this to pass, or impose any necessity on things, but, on the contrary, because the necessity which lies in the thing itself, i.e. the necessity of the existence of God determines me to think in this way. For it is not within my power to think of God without existence (that is of a supremely perfect Being devoid of a supreme perfection) though it is in my power to imagine a horse either with wings or without wings.

And we must not here object that it is in truth necessary for me to assert that God exists after having presupposed that He possesses every sort of perfection, since existence is one of these, but that as a matter of fact my original supposition was not necessary, just as it is not necessary to consider that all quadrilateral figures can be inscribed in the circle; for supposing I thought this, I should be constrained to admit that the rhombus might be inscribed in the circle since it is a quadrilateral figure, which, however, is manifestly false. [We must not, I say, make any such allegations because] although it is not necessary that I should at any time entertain the notion of God, nevertheless whenever it happens that I think of a first and a sovereign Being, and, so to speak, derive the idea of Him from the storehouse of my mind, it is necessary that I should attribute to Him every sort of perfection, although I do not get so far as to enumerate them all, or to apply my mind to each one in particular. And this necessity suffices to make me conclude (after having recognised that existence is a perfection) that this first and sovereign Being really exists; just as though it is not necessary for me ever to imagine any triangle, yet, whenever I wish to consider a rectilinear figure composed only of three angles, it is absolutely essential that I should attribute to it all those properties which serve to bring about the conclusion that its three angles are not greater than two right angles, even although I may not then be considering this point in particular. But when I consider which figures are capable of being inscribed in the circle, it is in no wise necessary that I should think that all quadrilateral figures are of this number; on the contrary, I cannot even pretend that this is the case, so long as I do not desire to accept anything which I cannot conceive clearly and distinctly. And in consequence there is a great difference between the false suppositions such as this, and the true ideas born within me, the first and principal of which is that of God. For really I discern in many ways that this idea is not something factitious, and depending solely on my thought, but that it is the image of a true and immutable nature; first of all, because I cannot conceive anything but God himself to whose essence existence [necessarily] pertains; in the second place because it is not possible for me to conceive two or more Gods in this same position; and, granted that there is one such God who now exists,

I see clearly that it is necessary that He should have existed from all eternity, and that He must exist eternally; and finally, because I know an infinitude of other properties in God, none of which I can either diminish or change.

For the rest, whatever proof or argument I avail myself of, we must always return to the point that it is only those things which we conceive clearly and distinctly that have the power of persuading me entirely. And although amongst the matters which I conceive of in this way, some indeed are manifestly obvious to all, while others only manifest themselves to those who consider them closely and examine them attentively; still, after they have once been discovered, the latter are not esteemed as any less certain than the former. For example, in the case of every right-angled triangle, although it does not so manifestly appear that the square of the base is equal to the squares of the two other sides as that this base is opposite to the greatest angle; still, when this has once been apprehended, we are just as certain of its truth as of the truth of the other. And as regards God, if my mind were not pre-occupied with prejudices, and if my thought did not find itself on all hands diverted by the continual pressure of sensible things, there would be nothing which I could know more immediately and more easily than Him. For is there anything more manifest than that there is a God, that is to say, a Supreme Being, to whose essence alone existence pertains[1]?

And although for a firm grasp of this truth I have need of a strenuous application of mind, at present I not only feel myself to be as assured of it as of all that I hold as most certain, but I also remark that the certainty of all other things depends on it so absolutely, that without this knowledge it is impossible ever to know anything perfectly.

For although I am of such a nature that as long as[2] I understand anything very clearly and distinctly, I am naturally impelled to believe it to be true, yet because I am also of such a nature that I cannot have my mind constantly fixed on the same object in order to perceive it clearly, and as I often recollect having formed a past judgment without at the same time properly recollecting the reasons that led me to make it, it may happen meanwhile that other reasons present themselves to me, which would easily cause me to change my opinion, if I were ignorant of the facts of the existence

---

[1] 'In the idea of whom alone necessary or eternal existence is comprised.' French version.

[2] 'From the moment that.' French version.

of God, and thus I should have no true and certain knowledge, but
only vague and vacillating opinions. Thus, for example, when I
consider the nature of a [rectilinear] triangle, I who have some
little knowledge of the principles of geometry recognise quite
clearly that the three angles are equal to two right angles, and it
is not possible for me not to believe this so long as I apply my mind
to its demonstration; but so soon as I abstain from attending to
the proof, although I still recollect having clearly comprehended it,
it may easily occur that I come to doubt its truth, if I am
ignorant of there being a God. For I can persuade myself of
having been so constituted by nature that I can easily deceive
myself even in those matters which I believe myself to apprehend
with the greatest evidence and certainty, especially when I recollect
that I have frequently judged matters to be true and certain which
other reasons have afterwards impelled me to judge to be altogether
false.

But after I have recognised that there is a God—because at the
same time I have also recognised that all things depend upon Him,
and that He is not a deceiver, and from that have inferred that
what I perceive clearly and distinctly cannot fail to be true—
although I no longer pay attention to the reasons for which I
have judged this to be true, provided that I recollect having clearly
and distinctly perceived it no contrary reason can be brought
forward which could ever cause me to doubt of its truth; and thus
I have a true and certain knowledge of it. And this same knowledge extends likewise to all other things which I recollect having
formerly demonstrated, such as the truths of geometry and the
like; for what can be alleged against them to cause me to place
them in doubt? Will it be said that my nature is such as to
cause me to be frequently deceived? But I already know that
I cannot be deceived in the judgment whose grounds I know clearly.
Will it be said that I formerly held many things to be true and
certain which I have afterwards recognised to be false? But I had
not had any clear and distinct knowledge of these things, and not
as yet knowing the rule whereby I assure myself of the truth, I had
been impelled to give my assent from reasons which I have since
recognised to be less strong than I had at the time imagined them
to be. What further objection can then be raised? That possibly
I am dreaming (an objection I myself made a little while ago), or
that all the thoughts which I now have are no more true than the
phantasies of my dreams? But even though I slept the case would

be the same, for all that is clearly present to my mind is absolutely true.

And so I very clearly recognise that the certainty and truth of all knowledge depends alone on the knowledge of the true God, in so much that, before I knew Him, I could not have a perfect knowledge of any other thing. And now that I know Him I have the means of acquiring a perfect knowledge of an infinitude of things, not only of those which relate to God Himself and other intellectual matters, but also of those which pertain to corporeal nature in so far as it is the object of pure mathematics [which have no concern with whether it exists or not].

MEDITATION VI.

Of the Existence of Material Things, and of the real distinction between the Soul and Body of Man.

Nothing further now remains but to inquire whether material things exist. And certainly I at least know that these may exist in so far as they are considered as the objects of pure mathematics, since in this aspect I perceive them clearly and distinctly. For there is no doubt that God possesses the power to produce everything that I am capable of perceiving with distinctness, and I have never deemed that anything was impossible for Him, unless I found a contradiction in attempting to conceive it clearly. Further, the faculty of imagination which I possess, and of which, experience tells me, I make use when I apply myself to the consideration of material things, is capable of persuading me of their existence; for when I attentively consider what imagination is, I find that it is nothing but a certain application of the faculty of knowledge to the body which is immediately present to it, and which therefore exists.

And to render this quite clear, I remark in the first place the difference that exists between the imagination and pure intellection [or conception[1]]. For example, when I imagine a triangle, I do not conceive it only as a figure comprehended by three lines, but I also apprehend[2] these three lines as present by the power and inward vision of my mind[3], and this is what I call imagining. But if I desire to think of a chiliagon, I certainly conceive truly that it is a figure composed of a thousand sides, just as easily as I conceive

---

[1] 'Conception,' French version.   'intellectionem,' Latin version.
[2] intueor.   [3] acie mentis.

of a triangle that it is a figure of three sides only; but I cannot in any way imagine the thousand sides of a chiliagon [as I do the three sides of a triangle], nor do I, so to speak, regard them as present [with the eyes of my mind]. And although in accordance with the habit I have formed of always employing the aid of my imagination when I think of corporeal things, it may happen that in imagining a chiliagon I confusedly represent to myself some figure, yet it is very evident that this figure is not a chiliagon, since it in no way differs from that which I represent to myself when I think of a myriagon or any other many-sided figure; nor does it serve my purpose in discovering the properties which go to form the distinction between a chiliagon and other polygons. But if the question turns upon a pentagon, it is quite true that I can conceive its figure as well as that of a chiliagon without the help of my imagination; but I can also imagine it by applying the attention of my mind to each of its five sides, and at the same time to the space which they enclose. And thus I clearly recognise that I have need of a particular effort of mind in order to effect the act of imagination, such as I do not require in order to understand, and this particular effort of mind clearly manifests the difference which exists between imagination and pure intellection[1].

I remark besides that this power of imagination which is in one, inasmuch as it differs from the power of understanding, is in no wise a necessary element in my nature, or in [my essence, that is to say, in] the essence of my mind; for although I did not possess it I should doubtless ever remain the same as I now am, from which it appears that we might conclude that it depends on something which differs from me. And I easily conceive that if some body exists with which my mind is conjoined and united in such a way that it can apply itself to consider it when it pleases, it may be that by this means it can imagine corporeal objects; so that this mode of thinking differs from pure intellection only inasmuch as mind in its intellectual activity in some manner turns on itself, and considers some of the ideas which it possesses in itself; while in imagining it turns towards the body, and there beholds in it something conformable to the idea which it has either conceived of itself or perceived by the senses. I easily understand, I say, that the imagination could be thus constituted if it is true that body exists; and because I can discover no other

---

[1] intellectionem.

convenient mode of explaining it, I conjecture with probability that body does exist; but this is only with probability, and although I examine all things with care, I nevertheless do not find that from this distinct idea of corporeal nature, which I have in my imagination, I can derive any argument from which there will necessarily be deduced the existence of body.

But I am in the habit of imagining many other things besides this corporeal nature which is the object of pure mathematics, to wit, the colours, sounds, scents, pain, and other such things, although less distinctly. And inasmuch as I perceive these things much better through the senses, by the medium of which, and by the memory, they seem to have reached my imagination, I believe that, in order to examine them more conveniently, it is right that I should at the same time investigate the nature of sense perception, and that I should see if from the ideas which I apprehend by this mode of thought, which I call feeling, I cannot derive some certain proof of the existence of corporeal objects.

And first of all I shall recall to my memory those matters which I hitherto held to be true, as having perceived them through the senses, and the foundations on which my belief has rested; in the next place I shall examine the reasons which have since obliged me to place them in doubt; in the last place I shall consider which of them I must now believe.

First of all, then, I perceived that I had a head, hands, feet, and all other members of which this body—which I considered as a part, or possibly even as the whole, of myself—is composed. Further I was sensible that this body was placed amidst many others, from which it was capable of being affected in many different ways, beneficial and hurtful, and I remarked that a certain feeling of pleasure accompanied those that were beneficial, and pain those which were harmful. And in addition to this pleasure and pain, I also experienced hunger, thirst, and other similar appetites, as also certain corporeal inclinations towards joy, sadness, anger, and other similar passions. And outside myself, in addition to extension, figure, and motions of bodies, I remarked in them hardness, heat, and all other tactile qualities, and, further, light and colour, and scents and sounds, the variety of which gave me the means of distinguishing the sky, the earth, the sea, and generally all the other bodies, one from the other. And certainly, considering the ideas of all these qualities which presented themselves to my mind, and which alone I perceived properly or immediately, it was not without reason that I believed myself to perceive objects quite different from my thought, to wit, bodies from which those ideas proceeded; for I found by experience that these ideas presented themselves to me without my consent being requisite, so that I could not perceive any object, however desirous I might be, unless it were present to the organs of sense; and it was not in my power not to perceive it, when it was present. And because the ideas which I received through the senses were much more lively, more clear, and even, in their own way, more distinct than any of those which I could of myself frame in meditation, or than those I found impressed on my memory, it appeared as though they could not have proceeded from my mind, so that they must necessarily have been produced in me by some other things. And having no knowledge of those objects excepting the knowledge which the ideas themselves gave me, nothing was more likely to occur to my mind than that the objects were similar to the ideas which were caused. And because I likewise remembered that I had formerly made use of my senses rather than my reason, and recognised that the ideas which I formed of myself were not so distinct as those which I perceived through the senses, and that they were most frequently even composed of portions of these last, I persuaded myself easily that I had no idea in my mind which had not formerly come to me through the senses. Nor was it without some reason that I believed that this body (which by a certain special right I call my own) belonged to me more properly and more strictly than any other; for in fact I could never be separated from it as from other bodies; I experienced in it and on account of it all my appetites and affections, and finally I was touched by the feeling of pain and the titillation of pleasure in its parts, and not in the parts of other bodies which were separated from it. But when I inquired, why, from some, I know not what, painful sensation, there follows sadness of mind, and from the pleasurable sensation there arises joy, or why this mysterious pinching of the stomach which I call hunger causes me to desire to eat, and dryness of throat causes a desire to drink, and so on, I could give no reason excepting that nature taught me so; for there is certainly no affinity (that I at least can understand) between the craving of the stomach and the desire to eat, any more than between the perception of whatever causes pain and the thought of sadness which arises from this perception. And in the same way it appeared to me that I had learned from nature all the other judgments which I formed regarding the objects of my

senses, since I remarked that these judgments were formed in me
before I had the leisure to weigh and consider any reasons which
might oblige me to make them.

But afterwards many experiences little by little destroyed all
the faith which I had rested in my senses; for I from time to time
observed that those towers which from afar appeared to me to be
round, more closely observed seemed square, and that colossal
statues raised on the summit of these towers, appeared as quite
tiny statues when viewed from the bottom; and so in an infinitude
of other cases I found error in judgments founded on the external
senses. And not only in those founded on the external senses, but
even in those founded on the internal as well; for is there anything
more intimate or more internal than pain? And yet I have learned
from some persons whose arms or legs have been cut off, that they
sometimes seemed to feel pain in the part which had been amputated,
which made me think that I could not be quite certain that it was
a certain member which pained me, even although I felt pain in it.
And to those grounds of doubt I have lately added two others,
which are very general; the first is that I never have believed
myself to feel anything in waking moments which I cannot also
sometimes believe myself to feel when I sleep, and as I do not
think that these things which I seem to feel in sleep, proceed from
objects outside of me, I do not see any reason why I should have
this belief regarding objects which I seem to perceive while awake.
The other was that being still ignorant, or rather supposing myself
to be ignorant, of the author of my being, I saw nothing to prevent
me from having been so constituted by nature that I might be
deceived even in matters which seemed to me to be most certain.
And as to the grounds on which I was formerly persuaded of the
truth of sensible objects, I had not much trouble in replying to them.
For since nature seemed to cause me to lean towards many things
from which reason repelled me, I did not believe that I should trust
much to the teachings of nature. And although the ideas which
I receive by the senses do not depend on my will, I did not think
that one should for that reason conclude that they proceeded from
things different from myself, since possibly some faculty might be
discovered in me—though hitherto unknown to me—which produced
them.

But now that I begin to know myself better, and to discover
more clearly the author of my being, I do not in truth think that
I should rashly admit all the matters which the senses seem to

teach us, but, on the other hand, I do not think that I should doubt them all universally.

And first of all, because I know that all things which I apprehend clearly and distinctly can be created by God as I apprehend them, it suffices that I am able to apprehend one thing apart from another clearly and distinctly in order to be certain that the one is different from the other, since they may be made to exist in separation at least by the omnipotence of God ; and it does not signify by what power this separation is made in order to compel me to judge them to be different : and, therefore, just because I know certainly that I exist, and that meanwhile I do not remark that any other thing necessarily pertains to my nature or essence, excepting that I am a thinking thing, I rightly conclude that my essence consists solely in the fact that I am a thinking thing [or a substance whose whole essence or nature is to think]. And although possibly (or rather certainly, as I shall say in a moment) I possess a body with which I am very intimately conjoined, yet because, on the one side, I have a clear and distinct idea of myself inasmuch as I am only a thinking and unextended thing, and as, on the other, I possess a distinct idea of body, inasmuch as it is only an extended and unthinking thing, it is certain that this I [that is to say, my soul by which I am what I am], is entirely and absolutely distinct from my body, and can exist without it.

I further find in myself faculties employing modes of thinking peculiar to themselves, to wit, the faculties of imagination and feeling, without which I can easily conceive myself clearly and distinctly as a complete being ; while, on the other hand, they cannot be so conceived apart from me, that is without an intelligent substance in which they reside, for [in the notion we have of these faculties, or, to use the language of the Schools] in their formal concept, some kind of intellection is comprised, from which I infer that they are distinct from me as its modes are from a thing. I observe also in me some other faculties such as that of change of position, the assumption of different figures and such like, which cannot be conceived, any more than can the preceding, apart from some substance to which they are attached, and consequently cannot exist without it ; but it is very clear that these faculties, if it be true that they exist, must be attached to some corporeal or extended substance, and not to an intelligent substance, since in the clear and distinct conception of these there is some sort of extension found to be present, but no intellection at all.

There is certainly further in me a certain passive faculty of perception, that is, of receiving and recognising the ideas of sensible things, but this would be useless to me [and I could in no way avail myself of it], if there were not either in me or in some other thing another active faculty capable of forming and producing these ideas. But this active faculty cannot exist in me [inasmuch as I am a thing that thinks] seeing that it does not presuppose thought, and also that those ideas are often produced in me without my contributing in any way to the same, and often even against my will; it is thus necessarily the case that the faculty resides in some substance different from me in which all the reality which is objectively in the ideas that are produced by this faculty is formally or eminently contained, as I remarked before. And this substance is either a body, that is, a corporeal nature in which there is contained formally [and really] all that which is objectively [and by representation] in those ideas, or it is God Himself, or some other creature more noble than body in which that same is contained eminently. But, since God is no deceiver, it is very manifest that He does not communicate to me these ideas immediately and by Himself, nor yet by the intervention of some creature in which their reality is not formally, but only eminently, contained. For since He has given me no faculty to recognise that this is the case, but, on the other hand, a very great inclination to believe [that they are sent to me or] that they are conveyed to me by corporeal objects, I do not see how He could be defended from the accusation of deceit if these ideas were produced by causes other than corporeal objects. Hence we must allow that corporeal things exist. However, they are perhaps not exactly what we perceive by the senses, since this comprehension by the senses is in many instances very obscure and confused; but we must at least admit that all things which I conceive in them clearly and distinctly, that is to say, all things which, speaking generally, are comprehended in the object of pure mathematics, are truly to be recognised as external objects.

As to other things, however, which are either particular only, as, for example, that the sun is of such and such a figure, etc., or which are less clearly and distinctly conceived, such as light, sound, pain and the like, it is certain that although they are very dubious and uncertain, yet on the sole ground that God is not a deceiver, and that consequently He has not permitted any falsity to exist in my opinion which He has not likewise given me the faculty of correcting, I may assuredly hope to conclude that I have within

me the means of arriving at the truth even here. And first of all
there is no doubt that in all things which nature teaches me there
is some truth contained; for by nature, considered in general,
I now understand no other thing than either God Himself or else
the order and disposition which God has established in created
things; and by my nature in particular I understand no other thing
than the complexus of all the things which God has given me.

But there is nothing which this nature teaches me more expressly
[nor more sensibly] than that I have a body which is adversely
affected when I feel pain, which has need of food or drink when
I experience the feelings of hunger and thirst, and so on; nor can
I doubt there being some truth in all this.

Nature also teaches me by these sensations of pain, hunger,
thirst, etc., that I am not only lodged in my body as a pilot in a
vessel, but that I am very closely united to it, and so to speak so
intermingled with it that I seem to compose with it one whole.
For if that were not the case, when my body is hurt, I, who am
merely a thinking thing, should not feel pain, for I should perceive
this wound by the understanding only, just as the sailor perceives
by sight when something is damaged in his vessel; and when my
body has need of drink or food, I should clearly understand the
fact without being warned of it by confused feelings of hunger and
thirst. For all these sensations of hunger, thirst, pain, etc. are in
truth none other than certain confused modes of thought which
are produced by the union and apparent intermingling of mind
and body.

Moreover, nature teaches me that many other bodies exist
around mine, of which some are to be avoided, and others sought
after. And certainly from the fact that I am sensible of different
sorts of colours, sounds, scents, tastes, heat, hardness, etc., I very
easily conclude that there are in the bodies from which all
these diverse sense-perceptions proceed certain variations which
answer to them, although possibly these are not really at all similar
to them. And also from the fact that amongst these different sense-
perceptions some are very agreeable to me and others disagreeable,
it is quite certain that my body (or rather myself in my entirety,
inasmuch as I am formed of body and soul) may receive different
impressions agreeable and disagreeable from the other bodies which
surround it.

But there are many other things which nature seems to have
taught me, but which at the same time I have never really received

from her, but which have been brought about in my mind by a certain habit which I have of forming inconsiderate judgments on things; and thus it may easily happen that these judgments contain some error. Take, for example, the opinion which I hold that all space in which there is nothing that affects [or makes an impression on] my senses is void; that in a body which is warm there is something entirely similar to the idea of heat which is in me; that in a white or green body there is the same whiteness or greenness that I perceive; that in a bitter or sweet body there is the same taste, and so on in other instances; that the stars, the towers, and all other distant bodies are of the same figure and size as they appear from far off to our eyes, etc. But in order that in this there should be nothing which I do not conceive distinctly, I should define exactly what I really understand when I say that I am taught somewhat by nature. For here I take nature in a more limited signification than when I term it the sum of all the things given me by God, since in this sum many things are comprehended which only pertain to mind (and to these I do not refer in speaking of nature) such as the notion which I have of the fact that what has once been done cannot ever be undone and an infinitude of such things which I know by the light of nature [without the help of the body]; and seeing that it comprehends many other matters besides which only pertain to body, and are no longer here contained under the name of nature, such as the quality of weight which it possesses and the like, with which I also do not deal; for in talking of nature I only treat of those things given by God to me as a being composed of mind and body. But the nature here described truly teaches me to flee from things which cause the sensation of pain, and seek after the things which communicate to me the sentiment of pleasure and so forth; but I do not see that beyond this it teaches me that from those diverse sense-perceptions we should ever form any conclusion regarding things outside of us, without having [carefully and maturely] mentally examined them beforehand. For it seems to me that it is mind alone, and not mind and body in conjunction, that is requisite to a knowledge of the truth in regard to such things. Thus, although a star makes no larger an impression on my eye than the flame of a little candle there is yet in me no real or positive propensity impelling me to believe that it is not greater than that flame; but I have judged it to be so from my earliest years, without any rational foundation. And although in approaching fire I feel heat, and in approaching it a little too near I even feel pain, there is at the same time no reason in this which could persuade me that there is in the fire something resembling this heat any more than there is in it something resembling the pain; all that I have any reason to believe from this is, that there is something in it, whatever it may be, which excites in me these sensations of heat or of pain. So also, although there are spaces in which I find nothing which excites my senses, I must not from that conclude that these spaces contain no body; for I see in this, as in other similar things, that I have been in the habit of perverting the order of nature, because these perceptions of sense having been placed within me by nature merely for the purpose of signifying to my mind what things are beneficial or hurtful to the composite whole of which it forms a part, and being up to that point sufficiently clear and distinct, I yet avail myself of them as though they were absolute rules by which I might immediately determine the essence of the bodies which are outside me, as to which, in fact, they can teach me nothing but what is most obscure and confused.

But I have already sufficiently considered how, notwithstanding the supreme goodness of God, falsity enters into the judgments I make. Only here a new difficulty is presented—one respecting those things the pursuit or avoidance of which is taught me by nature, and also respecting the internal sensations which I possess, and in which I seem to have sometimes detected error [and thus to be directly deceived by my own nature]. To take an example, the agreeable taste of some food in which poison has been intermingled may induce me to partake of the poison, and thus deceive me. It is true, at the same time, that in this case nature may be excused, for it only induces me to desire food in which I find a pleasant taste, and not to desire the poison which is unknown to it; and thus I can infer nothing from this fact, except that my nature is not omniscient, at which there is certainly no reason to be astonished, since man, being finite in nature, can only have knowledge the perfectness of which is limited.

But we not unfrequently deceive ourselves even in those things to which we are directly impelled by nature, as happens with those who when they are sick desire to drink or eat things hurtful to them. It will perhaps be said here that the cause of their deceptiveness is that their nature is corrupt, but that does not remove the difficulty, because a sick man is none the less truly God's creature than he who is in health; and it is therefore as repugnant to God's goodness for the one to have a deceitful nature as it is for the other. And as a clock composed of wheels and counter-weights no less exactly observes the laws of nature when it is badly made, and does not show the time properly, than when it entirely satisfies the wishes of its maker, and as, if I consider the body of a man as being a sort of machine so built up and composed of nerves, muscles, veins, blood and skin, that though there were no mind in it at all, it would not cease to have the same motions as at present, exception being made of those movements which are due to the direction of the will, and in consequence depend upon the mind [as opposed to those which operate by the disposition of its organs], I easily recognise that it would be as natural to this body, supposing it to be, for example, dropsical, to suffer the parchedness of the throat which usually signifies to the mind the feeling of thirst, and to be disposed by this parched feeling to move the nerves and other parts in the way requisite for drinking, and thus to augment its malady and do harm to itself, as it is natural to it, when it has no indisposition, to be impelled to drink for its good by a similar cause. And although, considering the use to which the clock has been destined by its maker, I may say that it deflects from the order of its nature when it does not indicate the hours correctly; and as, in the same way, considering the machine of the human body as having been formed by God in order to have in itself all the movements usually manifested there, I have reason for thinking that it does not follow the order of nature when, if the throat is dry, drinking does harm to the conservation of health, nevertheless I recognise at the same time that this last mode of explaining nature is very different from the other. For this is but a purely verbal characterisation depending entirely on my thought, which compares a sick man and a badly constructed clock with the idea which I have of a healthy man and a well made clock, and it is hence extrinsic to the things to which it is applied ; but according to the other interpretation of the term nature I understand something which is truly found in things and which is therefore not without some truth.

But certainly although in regard to the dropsical body it is only so to speak to apply an extrinsic term when we say that its nature is corrupted, inasmuch as apart from the need to drink, the throat is parched ; yet in regard to the composite whole, that is to say, to the mind or soul united to this body, it is not a purely verbal predicate, but a real error of nature, for it to have thirst when drinking would be hurtful to it. And thus it still remains to inquire how the goodness of God does not prevent the nature of man so regarded from being fallacious.

In order to begin this examination, then, I here say, in the first place, that there is a great difference between mind and body, inasmuch as body is by nature always divisible, and the mind is entirely indivisible. For, as a matter of fact, when I consider the mind, that is to say, myself inasmuch as I am only a thinking thing, I cannot distinguish in myself any parts, but apprehend myself to be clearly one and entire ; and although the whole mind seems to be united to the whole body, yet if a foot, or an arm, or some other part, is separated from my body, I am aware that nothing has been taken away from my mind. And the faculties of willing, feeling, conceiving, etc. cannot be properly speaking said to be its parts, for it is one and the same mind which employs itself in willing and in feeling and understanding. But it is quite otherwise with corporeal or extended objects, for there is not one of these imaginable by me which my mind cannot easily divide into parts, and which conse-quently I do not recognise as being divisible ; this would be sufficient to teach me that the mind or soul of man is entirely different from the body, if I had not already learned it from other sources.

I further notice that the mind does not receive the impressions from all parts of the body immediately, but only from the brain, or perhaps even from one of its smallest parts, to wit, from that in which the common sense[1] is said to reside, which, whenever it is disposed in the same particular way, conveys the same thing to the mind, although meanwhile the other portions of the body may be differently disposed, as is testified by innumerable experiments which it is unnecessary here to recount.

I notice, also, that the nature of body is such that none of its parts can be moved by another part a little way off which cannot also be moved in the same way by each one of the parts which are between the two, although this more remote part does not act at all. As, for example, in the cord $ABCD$ [which is in tension] if we pull the last part D, the first part A will not be moved in any way differently from what would be the case if one of the intervening parts B or C were pulled, and the last part D were to remain unmoved. And in the same way, when I feel pain in my foot, my knowledge of physics teaches me that this sensation is communi-cated by means of nerves dispersed through the foot, which, being

---

[1] sensus communis.

extended like cords from there to the brain, when they are contracted in the foot, at the same time contract the inmost portions of the brain which is their extremity and place of origin, and then excite a certain movement which nature has established in order to cause the mind to be affected by a sensation of pain represented as existing in the foot. But because these nerves must pass through the tibia, the thigh, the loins, the back and the neck, in order to reach from the leg to the brain, it may happen that although their extremities which are in the foot are not affected, but only certain ones of their intervening parts [which pass by the loins or the neck], this action will excite the same movement in the brain that might have been excited there by a hurt received in the foot, in consequence of which the mind will necessarily feel in the foot the same pain as if it had received a hurt. And the same holds good of all the other perceptions of our senses.

I notice finally that since each of the movements which are in the portion of the brain by which the mind is immediately affected brings about one particular sensation only, we cannot under the circumstances imagine anything more likely than that this movement, amongst all the sensations which it is capable of impressing on it, causes mind to be affected by that one which is best fitted and most generally useful for the conservation of the human body when it is in health. But experience makes us aware that all the feelings with which nature inspires us are such as I have just spoken of; and there is therefore nothing in them which does not give testimony to the power and goodness of the God [who has produced them[1]]. Thus, for example, when the nerves which are in the feet are violently or more than usually moved, their movement, passing through the medulla of the spine[2] to the inmost parts of the brain, gives a sign to the mind which makes it feel somewhat, to wit, pain, as though in the foot, by which the mind is excited to do its utmost to remove the cause of the evil as dangerous and hurtful to the foot. It is true that God could have constituted the nature of man in such a way that this same movement in the brain would have conveyed something quite different to the mind; for example, it might have produced consciousness of itself either in so far as it is in the brain, or as it is in the foot, or as it is in some other place between the foot and the brain, or it might finally have produced consciousness of anything else whatsoever; but none of all this would have contributed so well to the conservation of the body. Similarly,

---

[1] Latin version only.   [2] spini dorsae medullam.

when we desire to drink, a certain dryness of the throat is produced which moves its nerves, and by their means the internal portions of the brain; and this movement causes in the mind the sensation of thirst, because in this case there is nothing more useful to us than to become aware that we have need to drink for the conservation of our health; and the same holds good in other instances.

From this it is quite clear that, notwithstanding the supreme goodness of God, the nature of man, inasmuch as it is composed of mind and body, cannot be otherwise than sometimes a source of deception. For if there is any cause which excites, not in the foot but in some part of the nerves which are extended between the foot and the brain, or even in the brain itself, the same movement which usually is produced when the foot is detrimentally affected, pain will be experienced as though it were in the foot, and the sense will thus naturally be deceived; for since the same movement in the brain is capable of causing but one sensation in the mind, and this sensation is much more frequently excited by a cause which hurts the foot than by another existing in some other quarter, it is reasonable that it should convey to the mind pain in the foot rather than in any other part of the body. And although the parchedness of the throat does not always proceed, as it usually does, from the fact that drinking is necessary for the health of the body, but sometimes comes from quite a different cause, as is the case with dropsical patients, it is yet much better that it should mislead on this occasion than if, on the other hand, it were always to deceive us when the body is in good health; and so on in similar cases.

And certainly this consideration is of great service to me, not only in enabling me to recognise all the errors to which my nature is subject, but also in enabling me to avoid them or to correct them more easily. For knowing that all my senses more frequently indicate to me truth than falsehood respecting the things which concern that which is beneficial to the body, and being able almost always to avail myself of many of them in order to examine one particular thing, and, besides that, being able to make use of my memory in order to connect the present with the past, and of my understanding which already has discovered all the causes of my errors, I ought no longer to fear that falsity may be found in matters every day presented to me by my senses. And I ought to set aside all the doubts of these past days as hyperbolical and ridiculous, particularly that very common uncertainty respecting sleep, which I could not distinguish from the waking state; for at present I find a very notable difference between the two, inasmuch as our memory can never connect our dreams one with the other, or with the whole course of our lives, as it unites events which happen to us while we are awake. And, as a matter of fact, if someone, while I was awake, quite suddenly appeared to me and disappeared as fast as do the images which I see in sleep, so that I could not know from whence the form came nor whither it went, it would not be without reason that I should deem it a spectre or a phantom formed by my brain [and similar to those which I form in sleep], rather than a real man. But when I perceive things as to which I know distinctly both the place from which they proceed, and that in which they are, and the time at which they appeared to me; and when, without any interruption, I can connect the perceptions which I have of them with the whole course of my life, I am perfectly assured that these perceptions occur while I am waking and not during sleep. And I ought in no wise to doubt the truth of such matters, if, after having called up all my senses, my memory, and my understanding, to examine them, nothing is brought to evidence by any one of them which is repugnant to what is set forth by the others. For because God is in no wise a deceiver, it follows that I am not deceived in this. But because the exigencies of action often oblige us to make up our minds before having leisure to examine matters carefully, we must confess that the life of man is very frequently subject to error in respect to individual objects, and we must in the end acknowledge the infirmity of our nature.

THE PRINCIPLES OF PHILOSOPHY

PREFATORY NOTE TO THE PRINCIPLES.

The *Principles of Philosophy* was published on six occasions by the Elzevirs in Holland. The first edition was brought out in 1644 in Latin, and it was the only one that appeared during Descartes' lifetime. His publisher indeed complained of the smallness of its sale. A visit to France was made just before the publication of the book, which he hoped would have taken place before he started, so that he might have taken with him copies for presenting to his friends. After paying visits of a business sort to his family, he found, on arriving at Paris, his friends Mersenne and Picot busy with the distribution of his book, which had appeared in excellent form as might have been expected from the reputation of the publishers. During a return journey to Holland, Descartes occupied himself with reading Picot's translation of his Principles into French —a translation which Baillet says he found much to his taste. It cannot, however, have been completed for some years later since Descartes wrote a preface on its completion in 1647. This translation is made from the Latin version collated with the French. The French version frequently differs considerably from the Latin, and when it seems desirable to indicate the difference this is done by means of square brackets. Only a part of the work is here translated, but the titles of the untranslated paragraphs have been given, and from these the nature of their contents can be gathered.

E. S. H.

SELECTIONS FROM THE PRINCIPLES OF PHILOSOPHY OF RENÉ DESCARTES.

Author's Letter to the Translator[1] of the book, which may here serve as Preface.

SIR,

The version of my Principles which you have taken the trouble to make is so polished and well-finished that it causes me to hope that the work may be read by more persons in French than in Latin, and that it will be better understood. My only apprehension is that the title may repel certain people who have not been nourished upon letters, or else who hold philosophy in evil esteem, because that which has been taught them has not satisfied them ; and this makes me think that it would be a good thing to add a preface which would expound the subject-matter of the book, the design I had in writing it, and the use to be derived from it. But although it should be my business to write this preface because I ought to know these things better than any one else, I can on my own account promise nothing but a summary of the principal points which seem to me as though they ought to be treated of in it ; and I leave it to your discretion to communicate to the public whatever you deem desirable.

I should have first of all desired to explain in it what philosophy is, beginning with the most ordinary matters, such as that this word philosophy signifies the study of wisdom, and that by wisdom we not only understand prudence in affairs, but also a perfect knowledge of all things that man can know, both for the conduct of his life and for the conservation of his health and the invention

---

[1] i.e. the translator into French, the Abbé Claude Picot.

of all the arts; and that in order that this knowledge should subserve these ends, it is essential that it should be derived from first causes, so that in order to study to acquire it (which is properly termed philosophising), we must begin with the investigation of these first causes, i.e. of the Principles. It is also necessary that these Principles should have two conditions attached to them; first of all they should be so clear and evident that the mind of man cannot doubt their truth when it attentively applies itself to consider them: in the second place it is on them that the knowledge of other things depends, so that the Principles can be known without these last, but the other things cannot reciprocally be known without the Principles. We must accordingly try to so deduce from these Principles the knowledge of the things that depend on them, that there shall be nothing in the whole series of the deductions made from them which shall not be perfectly manifest. It is really only God alone who has Perfect Wisdom, that is to say, who has a complete knowledge of the truth of all things; but it may be said that men have more wisdom or less according as they have more or less knowledge of the most important truths. And I think that in this there is nothing regarding which all the learned do not concur.

I should in the next place have caused the utility of this philosophy to be considered, and shown that since it extends over the whole range of human knowledge, we are entitled to hold that it alone is what distinguishes us from savages and barbarians, and that the civilisation and refinement of each nation is proportionate to the superiority of its philosophy. In this way a state can have no greater good than the possession of true philosophy. And, in addition, it would have been pointed out that as regards the individual, it is not only useful to live with those who apply themselves to this study, but it is incomparably better to set about it oneself; just as it is doubtless much better to avail oneself of one's own eyes for the direction of one's steps, and by the same means to enjoy the beauty of colour and light, than to close these eyes and trust to the guidance of another. But this last is better than to hold them closed, and not have any but oneself to act as guide. Speaking accurately, living without philosophy is just having the eyes closed without trying to open them; and the pleasure of seeing everything that is revealed to our sight, is not comparable to the satisfaction which is given by the knowledge of those things which are opened up to us by philosophy. And finally, this study is more necessary for the regulation of our manners and for our conduct in life, than is the use of our eyes in the guidance of our steps. The brute beasts who have only their bodies to preserve, devote their constant attention to the search for the sources of their nourishment; but men, in whom the principal part is the mind, ought to make their principal care the search after wisdom, which is its true source of nutriment. And I am likewise able to assure myself that there are many who would not fail to make the search if they had any hope of success in so doing, and knew to what an extent they were capable of it. There does not exist the soul so ignoble, so firmly attached to objects of sense, that it does not sometimes turn away from these to aspire after some other greater good, even although it is frequently ignorant as to wherein that good consists. Those most favoured by fortune, those who have abundance of health, honour and riches, are not exempt from this desire any more than others; on the contrary, I am persuaded that it is those very people who yearn most ardently after another good more perfect and supreme than all those that they possess already. And this sovereign good, considered by the natural reason without the light of faith, is none other than the knowledge of the truth through its first causes, i.e. the wisdom whose study is philosophy. And because all these things are absolutely true, it would not be difficult to persuade men of them, were they well argued and expressed.

But since we are prevented from believing these doctrines by experience, which shows us that those who profess to be philosophers are frequently less wise and reasonable than others who have never applied themselves to the study, I should here have succinctly explained in what all the knowledge we now possess consists, and to what degrees of wisdom we have attained. The first of these contains only notions which are of themselves so clear that they may be acquired without any meditation. The second comprehends all that which the experience of the senses shows us. The third, what the conversation of other men teaches us. And for the fourth we may add to this the reading, not of all books, but especially of those which have been written by persons who are capable of conveying good instruction to us, for this is a species of conversation held with their authors. And it seems to me that all the wisdom that we usually possess is acquired by these four means only; for I do not place divine revelation in the same rank, because it does not lead us by degrees, but raises us at a stroke to an infallible belief. There have indeed from all time been great men who have tried to find a fifth road by which to arrive at wisdom, incomparably more elevated and assured than these other four. That road is to seek out the first causes and the true principles from which reasons may be deduced for all that which we are capable of knowing; and it is those who have made this their special work who have been called philosophers. At the same time I do not know that up to the present day there have been any in whose case this plan has succeeded. The first and principal whose writings we possess, are Plato and Aristotle, between whom the only difference that exists is that the former, following the steps of his master Socrates, ingenuously confessed that he had never yet been able to discover anything for certain, and was content to set down the things that seemed to him to be probable, for this end adopting certain principles whereby he tried to account for other things. Aristotle, on the other hand, had less candour, and although he had been Plato's disciple for twenty years, and possessed no other principles than his master's, he entirely changed the method of stating them, and proposed them as true and certain although there was no appearance of his having ever held them to be such. But these two men had great minds and much wisdom acquired by the four methods mentioned before, and this gave them great authority, so that those who succeeded them were more bent on following their opinions than in forming better ones of their own. The main dispute between their disciples was as to whether every thing should be doubted, or whether there were some things which were certain. And this carried them, both on the one side and on the other, into extravagant errors; for certain of those who argued for doubt, extended it even to the actions of life, so that they omitted to exercise ordinary prudence in its conduct; and those who supported the doctrine of certainty, supposing it to depend on the senses, trusted to them entirely. To such a point was this carried that it is said that Epicurus ventured to affirm, contrary to all the reasonings of the astronomers, that the sun is no larger than it appears. A fault which may be observed in most disputes is that since the truth is a mean between the two opinions which are maintained, each disputant removes himself so much the farther from it the greater his desire to contradict. But the error of those who tended too much to the side of doubt, was not followed for long, and that of the others has been in some degree corrected by the recognition of the fact that in many instances the senses deceive us. At the same time I do not know that it has been entirely removed by showing that certainty is not in the senses, but only in the understanding, when it has evident perceptions ; and that while we only possess the knowledge which is acquired by the first four degrees of wisdom, we should not doubt those things that appear to be true in what concerns the conduct of life, while yet we should not hold them to be so certain that we may not change our minds regarding them when obliged to do so by the evidence of reason. From lack of having known this truth, or else, if there be those who have known it, from neglecting it, the greater part of those in later times who aspired to be philosophers, have blindly followed Aristotle, so that frequently they have corrupted the sense of his writings, attributing diverse opinions to him which he would not recognise as his, were he to return to this world ; and those who have not followed him (amongst whom many of the best minds are to be found) have yet been imbued with his teaching in their youth, for it forms the sole teaching in the Schools ; and these minds were so much occupied with this, that they were incapable of attaining to a knowledge of true Principles. And although I respect them all and would never wish to incur the odium of denouncing them, I can give a proof of my assertion which I do not think any one of them will gainsay, and this is that all have taken for granted some particular principle which they have not perfectly understood. For example I have known none of them who did not presuppose weight in terrestrial bodies, but although experiment proves to us very clearly that the bodies we call weighty descend towards the centre of the earth, we do not for all that know the nature of what is called gravity, that is, the reason or principle which causes bodies to descend thus, and we must derive it from elsewhere. The same may be said of the vacuum and of atoms, of heat and cold, of dryness and damp, and of salt, sulphur, mercury, and all other similar things which have been adopted as their principles by some. And none of the conclusions deduced from a principle which is not evident can be evident even though they are deduced from them in a manner which is evident and valid, and from this it follows that none of the reasonings which they rested on principles such as these could give them any certain knowledge of anything, nor in consequence cause them to advance one step in the search after wisdom. And if they have discovered any truth this has only come to pass by means of certain of the four methods above mentioned. All the same I do not desire one whit to detract from the honour to which each of them may aspire, I am only obliged to say for the consolation of those who have never studied, that just as in travelling while we turn our backs on the place to which we desire to go, the longer and quicker we walk the further we recede from the place we are making for, so that though we are afterwards put back into the right way, we cannot arrive at our destination as soon as if we had not walked in the wrong direction before ; so when our principles are bad, the more we cultivate them and the more carefully we apply ourselves to derive from them various consequences, thinking that we are philosophising very well, the further we are moving from the knowledge of the truth and from wisdom. From this we must conclude that those who have learnt least about all that which has hitherto been named philosophy, are the most capable of apprehending the truth.

After having made these matters very clear, I should have desired to set forth the reasons which serve to prove that the true principles by which we may arrive at that highest point of wisdom in which the sovereign good of the life of man consists, are those which I have put forward in this book. And only two are requisite for that, the first that the principles must be very clear, and the second that from them we may deduce all other things ; for there are but these two conditions that are essential in true principles. And I can easily prove that they are very clear, first of all by the manner in which I have found them, i.e. by rejecting all those propositions in respect to which I could find the slightest occasion for doubt ; for it is certain that those which could not be rejected in this way when application was made to their consideration, are the most evident and clear of all that the human mind can know. Thus in considering that he who would doubt all things cannot yet doubt that he exists while he doubts, and that what reasons so in being unable to doubt of itself and yet doubting all else, is not what we call our body but what we call our soul or thought, I have taken the being or existence of this thought as the first principle from which I have very clearly deduced the following : viz. that there is a God who is the author of all that is in the world, or who, being the source of all truth, has not created in us an understanding liable to be deceived in the judgments that it forms on matters of which it has a very clear and distinct perception. These comprise the whole of the principles of which I make use respecting immaterial or metaphysical things, from which I very clearly deduce those of corporeal or physical things, to wit, that there are bodies extended in length, breadth and depth, which have diverse figures and move in diverse ways. These, in sum, are all the principles from which I deduce the truth of other things. The other reason which proves the clearness of the principles is that they have been known from all time, and even received as true and indubitable by all men, with the sole exception of the existence of God, which has been placed in doubt by certain people because they have ascribed too much to the perceptions of the senses, and because God can neither be seen nor touched. But although all the truths which I place in my Principles have been known from all time and by all men, nevertheless there has never yet been any one, as far as I know, who has recognised them as the principles of philosophy, that is to say, as principles from which may be derived a knowledge of all things that are in the world : that is why it here remains to me to prove that they are such. And it appears to me that I cannot do better than cause this to be established by experience, that is to say, by inviting my readers to peruse this book. For although I have not treated of every thing, and although this is impossible, I consider that I have so explained all those matters with which I have had occasion to deal, that those who read them with attention will have reason to persuade themselves that there is no need to seek other principles than those I have brought forward, in order to arrive at all the most exalted knowledge of which the human mind is capable. And this will more especially be the case if, after having read my works, they take the trouble to consider how many diverse questions are therein explained, and if, perusing also the works of others, they observe how few are the probable reasons that can be given to explain the same questions by principles differing from mine. And in order that they may undertake this with greater ease, I should have been able to say to them that those who are imbued with my doctrines have much less trouble in understanding the works of others and in recognising their true value than those who are not so imbued ; and this is diametrically opposite to what I have just said of those who commenced with the ancient philosophy, i.e. that the more they have studied it the less are they fitted rightly to apprehend the truth.

I should also have here added a word of advice as regards the method of reading this book, which is that I should desire that it may first of all be run through in its entirety like a novel, without forcing the attention unduly upon it, or stopping at difficulties which may be met with, so that a general knowledge may be arrived at of the matters of which I have treated; and after that, if it is found that they deserve to be examined more carefully, and if the reader has the curiosity to inquire about their causes, it may be read a second time in order to notice the sequence of my reasoning. But though the reader cannot follow the argument adequately throughout, or understand the whole of its bearing, he must not therefore immediately cast it aside. It is only necessary to mark with a pen the places where difficulty is found, and continue to read without interruption to the end. Then if the book is taken up for a third time, I venture to say that he will discover the solution of the greater part of the difficulties which have formerly been marked, and that if certain still remain, their solution will be discovered on a further perusal.

I have noticed on examining the nature of many different minds, that there are almost none of them so dull or slow of understanding that they are incapable of high feelings, and even of attaining to all the profoundest sciences, were they trained in the right way. And that may also be proved by reason. For since the principles are clear and nothing must be deduced from them but by very evident reasoning, we have all sufficient intelligence to comprehend the conclusions that depend on them. But in addition to the drawbacks of prejudice from which no one is entirely exempt, although it is those who have studied the false sciences most deeply whom they harm the most, it almost always happens that those of moderate intelligence neglect to study because they do not consider themselves capable of doing so, and that the others who are more eager, hasten on too quickly. And from this it comes that they often accept principles which are not really evident, and from them derive consequences which are uncertain. That is why I desire to assure those who too greatly disparage their powers, that there is nothing in my writings which they are not capable of completely understanding if they take the trouble to examine them; while I also warn the others that even the most superior understanding will require much time and attention to comprehend all the matters which I have designed to embrace in them.

Following on this, and in order to make very clear the end I have had in view in publishing them, I would like to explain here what seems to me to be the order which should be followed in our self-instruction. To begin with, a man who as yet has merely the common and imperfect knowledge which may be acquired by the four methods before mentioned, should above all try to form for himself a code of morals sufficient to regulate the actions of his life, because this does not brook any delay, and we ought above all other things to endeavour to live well.   After that he should likewise study logic—not that of the Schools, because it properly speaking is only a dialectic which teaches how to make the things that we know understood by others, or even to repeat, without forming any judgment on them, many words respecting those that we do not know, thus corrupting rather than increasing good sense—but the logic that teaches us how best to direct our reason in order to discover those truths of which we are ignorant. And since this is very dependent on custom, it is good for him to practise the rules for a long time on easy and simple questions such as those of mathematics.   Then when he has acquired a certain skill in discovering the truth in these questions he should begin seriously to apply himself to the true philosophy, the first part of which is metaphysics, which contains the principles of knowledge, amongst which is the explanation of the principal attributes of God, of the immateriality of our souls, and of all the clear and simple notions which are in us.   The second is physics in which, after having found the true principles of material things, we examine generally how the whole universe is composed, and then in particular what is the nature of this earth and of all the bodies which are most commonly found in connection with it, like air, water and fire, the loadstone and other minerals.   It is thereafter necessary to inquire individually into the nature of plants, animals, and above all of man, so that we may afterwards be able to discover the other sciences which are useful to man.   Thus philosophy as a whole is like a tree whose roots are metaphysics, whose trunk is physics, and whose branches, which issue from this trunk, are all the other sciences.   These reduce themselves to three principal ones, viz. medicine, mechanics and morals—I mean the highest and most perfect moral science which, presupposing a complete knowledge of the other sciences, is the last degree of wisdom.

But just as it is not from the roots or the trunk of the trees that one culls the fruit, but only from the extremities of their branches, so the main use of philosophy is dependent on those of its parts that we cannot learn till the end.   Although, however, I am ignorant of almost all of these, the zeal which I have always shown in trying to render service to the public is the reason of my causing to be printed ten or twelve years ago certain essays on things which I appeared to have learned.   The first part of these essays was a *Discourse on the Method of rightly conducting one's Reason and seeking Truth in the Sciences*, where I summarised the principal rules of logic and of an imperfect system of morals which may be followed provisionally while we still know none better. The other parts were three Treatises : the first *Of the Dioptric* ; the second *Of Meteors*, and the last *Of Geometry*. In the *Dioptric* I intended it to be shown that we could make sufficient progress in philosophy to attain by its means a knowledge of those arts which are useful to life, because the invention of the telescope, which I there described, is one of the most difficult ever attempted. In the treatise on *Meteors* I endeavoured to make clear the difference which exists between the philosophy which I cultivate and that taught in the Schools, where the same subject is usually treated. Finally in the *Geometry* I professed to show that I had found certain matters of which men were previously ignorant, and thus to afford occasion for believing that many more may yet be discovered, in order by this means to incite all men to the search after truth. From this time onwards, foreseeing the difficulty which would be felt by many in understanding the foundations of metaphysics, I tried to explain the principal points in a book of *Meditations* which is not very large, but whose volume has been increased, and whose matter has been much illuminated, by the Objections which many very learned persons have sent me in their regard, and by the replies which I have made to them. Then, finally, when it appeared to me that these preceding treatises had sufficiently prepared the mind of readers to accept the *Principles of Philosophy*, I likewise published them, and I divided the book containing them into four parts, the first of which contains the principles of knowledge, which is what may be called the First Philosophy or Metaphysics. That is why it is better to read beforehand the Meditations which I have written on the same subject, in order that it may be properly understood. The other three parts contain all that is most general in Physics, i.e. an explanation of the first laws or principles of nature, the manner in which the heavens and fixed stars, the planets, the comets, and generally all the universe is composed. Then the nature of this earth, and of the air, water, fire, and the loadstone, is dealt with more particularly, for these are the bodies which may most commonly be found everywhere about it, as also all the qualities observed in these bodies, such as light, heat, weight, and such like. By this means I believe myself to have commenced to expound the whole of philosophy in its order without having omitted anything which ought to precede the last of which I have written. But in order to carry this plan to a conclusion, I should afterwards in the same way explain in further detail the nature of each of the other bodies which are on the earth, i.e. minerals, plants, animals, and above all man; then finally treat exactly of medicine, morals and mechanics. All this I should have to do in order to give to mankind a body of philosophy which is complete; and I do not feel myself to be so old, I do not so much despair of my strength, I do not find myself so far removed from a knowledge of what remains, that I should not venture to endeavour to achieve this design, were I possessed of the means of making all the experiments necessary to me in order to support and justify my reasoning. But seeing that for this end great expense is requisite to which the resources of an individual like myself could not attain were he not given assistance by the public, and not seeing that I can expect that aid, I conceive it to be henceforward my duty to content myself with studying for my own private instruction, trusting that posterity will pardon me if I fail henceforward to work for its good.

In order, however, to show in how far I believe myself to have already been of service to my fellowmen, I shall here state what are the fruits which I believe may be culled from my Principles. The first is the satisfaction which we must derive from discovering in them certain truths of which we have hitherto been ignorant; for although frequently the truth does not so much affect our imagination as does falsity and pretence, because it seems less wonderful and more simple, yet the satisfaction which it brings is always more lasting and solid. The second fruit is that in studying these Principles, we shall little by little accustom ourselves to judge better of all things with which we come in contact, and thus to become wiser. In this regard they will have an effect contrary to that of the ordinary philosophy, for it may easily be observed in those who are known as pedants, that it renders them less capable of reasoning than they would have been had they never learned it at all. The third fruit is that the truths which they contain, being perfectly clear and certain, will remove all subjects of dispute, and thus dispose men's minds to gentleness and concord. On the other hand the controversies of the Schools, by insensibly making those who practise themselves in them more captious and self-sufficient, are possibly the chief causes of the heresies and dissensions which now exercise the world. The last and principal fruit of these

Principles is that by cultivating them we may discover many truths which I have not expounded, and thus, passing little by little from one to the other, acquire in time a perfect knowledge of the whole of philosophy and attain to the highest degree of wisdom. For in all the arts we perceive how although at the first they are rude and imperfect, yet because they contain something that is true and whose effect is revealed by experience, they come little by little to perfection through practice. So, when we have true principles in philosophy we cannot fail, by following them, occasionally to meet with other truths; and there is no way in which we can better prove the falsity of those of Aristotle, than by pointing out that no progress has been attained by their means in all the centuries in which they have been followed.

I know very well that those who make such haste use so little circumspection in what they do, that even with quite solid foundations they cannot build anything that is firm and secure; and because it is commonly such men who are most ready to write books, they may in a short time spoil all that I have done, and if their writings are accepted as mine, or as representing my opinions, introduce uncertainty and doubt into my mode of philosophising, from which I have carefully tried to banish them. I have lately had experience as to this regarding one of them who might have been expected to have followed me most closely, and of whom I had even written 'that I was so assured of his intelligence that I did not believe him to have any opinion which I should not gladly have avowed as my own[1]'; for he published a year ago a book entitled *Fundamenta Physicae*[2] in which, although he had apparently said nothing regarding physics and medicine which he had not derived from my writings—from those published as well as from another still imperfect regarding the nature of animals which fell into his hands —yet because he had transcribed badly, changed the order, and denied certain truths of metaphysics upon which the whole of physics ought to rest, I am obliged entirely to disavow his work, and here to beg readers never to attribute to me any opinion unless they find it expressly stated in my works, and never to accept anything as true in my writings or elsewhere, unless they see it to be very clearly deduced from true Principles.

[1] *Epistola Renati* Des-Cartes *ad celeberrimum Virum D. Gisbertum* Voetium 1643: "...acutissimo et perspicacissimo ingenio Regii tantum tribuo, ut vix quicquam ab illo scriptum putem quod pro meo non libenter agnoscam." (Page 232, edit. *princeps*.)

[2] Henri Regii Ultrajectini, Fundamenta Physices. (*Amstelodami, apud Ludovicum Elzivirium.* A° 1646, in 8.)

I well know likewise that many centuries may pass until all the truths which may be deduced from these principles are so deduced, because the greater part of those which remain to be discovered depend on certain particular experiments which chance circumstances will never bring about, but which should be investigated with care and expense by the most intelligent of men, and because it will be unlikely that the same people who have the capacity of availing themselves of them will have the means of contriving them, and also because the majority of the best minds have formed such a bad conception of philosophy as a whole, owing to the defects which they have observed in that which has hitherto been in vogue, that they will not be able to discover a better. But finally, if the difference which is observable between these principles and those of all other men, and the great array of truths which may be deduced from them, causes them to perceive how important it is to continue in the search after these truths, and to observe to what a degree of wisdom, to what perfection of life, to what happiness they may lead us, I am convinced that no one will be found who will not attempt to occupy himself with so profitable a study, or at least will not favour and endeavour to assist with all his might those who employ themselves in this way with success. I trust that posterity may behold its happy issue.

Madam,

The great result which has accrued to me from the works which I have already published, has been that through them I have had the honour of coming under the notice of your Highness, and of being able occasionally to have converse with one whose qualities are so estimable that I conceive it to be a public service to set them before posterity for its example. It would ill become me to flatter, or even to write things as to which I have no certain knowledge, above all in this place in which I shall try to set down the Principles of truth. And the generous modesty which is seen in all the actions of your Highness suffices to assure me that the simple and unaffected judgment of one who writes but what he believes, will be more agreeable to you than the ornate praises of those who have studied the art of compliment. That is why I shall put nothing in this letter of which experience and reason has not rendered me certain, and here in the exordium, I shall write philosophically, just as in the rest of the book.

Great is the distinction between the apparent virtues and the true; there is also a distinction between those true virtues which proceed from an exact knowledge of the truth and others that are accompanied by ignorance. The virtues which I call apparent, are properly speaking but vices, which not being so frequent as other vices which are contrary to them, and being further removed from them than the virtues which occupy an intermediate position, are usually held in greater esteem than they. Thus since there are many more people who fear danger too much than those who fear it too little, temerity is often opposed to timidity as a virtue to a vice, and is more esteemed than true fortitude. Thus likewise the prodigal is much more frequently praised than the liberal, and nothing is more easy than for the superstitious and hypocritical to acquire a reputation for great piety.

Many of the true virtues do not proceed from true knowledge, but there are some which likewise proceed from a sort of error: thus it is frequently the case that simplicity is the cause of kindness, fear of devotion, and despair of courage. And the virtues which are thus accompanied by some imperfection differ from one another and have likewise been given different names. But those pure and perfect virtues which proceed from the knowledge of good alone, are all of the same nature, and may be comprised under the name of wisdom. For whoever forms a firm and constant resolve always to make use of reason to the best of his power, and in all his actions to do what he believes to be best, is truly wise, so far as his nature allows him to be so; and by this alone he is just, courageous, moderate, and possesses all the other virtues; but these are so united together that none take the predominance over others; and this is why, although they are much more perfect than the virtues that the admixture of some defect causes to shine forth, yet because the ordinary man remarks them less, they are not accorded the same praise.

Further, of two things requisite to the wisdom thus described, i.e. the perception of the understanding and the disposition of the will, it is only that which consists in the will that all men may alike possess, inasmuch as the understanding of some is not as good as that of others. But although those who are inferior in mind may be as wise as their nature permits, and may render themselves acceptable to God by their virtue, if they only form a firm and constant resolution to do what they judge to be right, and spare no effort in learning that of which they are ignorant, yet those who while possessing a constant desire to do well, and taking very special care in reference to their self-instruction, are endowed with a highly perspicacious intellect, will doubtless attain to a higher point of wisdom than the others.

And these three things are found perfectly in your Royal Highness, since in your case no diversions of the Court nor that mode of education which ordinarily condemns princesses to ignorance, have been capable of preventing your study of all that is best in the arts and sciences. And the incomparable excellence of your intellect is evident in the fact that in a very short time you have mastered the secrets of the sciences, and obtained a perfect knowledge of them all. But I have yet another proof very special to myself, inasmuch as I have never met any one who understood so generally and thoroughly all that is contained in my writings. For there are many who find them most obscure, even amongst the most learned and intelligent; and I notice in almost all that those who grasp things which pertain to metaphysics with ease have a dislike to geometry, while those who cultivate geometry have no propensity for the study of First Philosophy: and so true is this that I know of no mind but yours to which both studies are equally congenial, and which therefore merits to be termed incomparable. But what enhances my admiration most, is that so varied and perfect a knowledge of all the sciences does not reside in some ancient doctor who has for many years been given over to contemplation, but in a young Princess whose countenance and years would more fitly represent one of the Graces than a Muse or the sage Minerva.

Finally I not only remark in your Highness all that is requisite for a mind to attain to the highest and supremest wisdom, but also all that is requisite on the part of the will or the life. Benignity and gentleness are there so conjoined with majesty, that though fortune has perpetually attempted to injure you unjustly, it has failed to embitter you or cast you down. And this constrains me to accord such veneration that I consider this work not only due to you, since it treats of Philosophy (which is just the study of wisdom), but I also have no greater pride in my reputation as a philosopher, than I have in subscribing myself as

The devoted servant

Of your most Serene Highness,

Des-Cartes.

THE PRINCIPLES OF PHILOSOPHY.

FIRST PART.

OF THE PRINCIPLES OF HUMAN KNOWLEDGE.

PRINCIPLE I.

That in order to examine into the truth, it is necessary once in one's life to doubt of all things, so far as this is possible.

As we have once on a time been children and have judged of the things presented to our senses in various ways, while as yet we had not the entire use of our reason, many judgments thus precipitately formed prevent us from arriving at the knowledge of the truth, and apparently there seems no way in which we can deliver ourselves from these, unless we undertake once in our lives to doubt all things in which the slightest trace of incertitude can be found.

PRINCIPLE II.

That we ought to consider as false all these things of which we may doubt.

It will even be useful to reject as false all these things as to which we can imagine the least doubt to exist, so that we may discover with greater clearness which are absolutely true, and most easy to know.

PRINCIPLE III.

That we ought not to make use of this doubt for the conduct of our life meantime.

But in the meantime it is to be observed that we are to make use of this doubt only when we are engaged in contemplating the truth. For, as regards the conduct of our life, we are frequently obliged to follow opinions which are merely probable, because the opportunities for action would in most cases pass away before we could deliver ourselves from our doubts. And when, as frequently happens with two courses of action, we do not perceive the probability of the one more than the other, we must yet select one of them.

PRINCIPLE IV.

Why we may doubt of sensible things.

But because we desire to apply ourselves only to the search after truth, we shall in the first place doubt if, of all sensible things, or things which we have imagined, there are any that really exist : in the first place because we know that our senses have before deceived us, and that prudence directs us not to trust too much in what has even once deceived us : in the second place because in sleep we continually seem to feel or imagine innumerable things which have no existence. To those who thus resolve to doubt all, there is apparently no mark by which they can with certainty distinguish sleep from the waking state[1]

PRINCIPLE V.

Why we may likewise doubt of the demonstration of mathematics.

We shall also doubt of all the other things which have formerly seemed to us quite certain, even of the demonstrations of mathematics and of its principles which we formerly thought quite self-evident. One reason is that those who have fallen into error in reasoning on such matters, have held as perfectly certain and self-evident what we see to be false, but a yet more important reason is that we have been told that God who created us can do all that He desires. For we are still ignorant of whether He may not have desired to create us in such a way that we shall always be deceived, even in the things that we believe ourselves to know best ; since this does not seem less possible than our being occasionally deceived, which experience tells us is the case. And if we think that an omnipotent God is not the author of our being, and that we subsist of ourselves, or through some other, yet the less perfect we suppose the author to be, the more reason have we to believe that we are not so perfect that we cannot be continually deceived.

[1] 'Whether the thoughts that come to us in sleep are as false as are the others.' French version.

Principle VI.

That we possess a Free-Will which causes us to abstain from giving assent to dubious things, and thus prevents our falling into error.

But meanwhile whoever turns out to have created us, and even should he prove to be all-powerful and deceitful, we still experience a freedom through which we may abstain from accepting as true and indisputable those things of which we have not certain knowledge, and thus obviate our ever being deceived.

Principle VII.

That we cannot doubt our existence without existing while we doubt; and this is the first knowledge that we obtain when we philosophise in an orderly way.

While we thus reject all that of which we can possibly doubt, and feign that it is false, it is easy to suppose that there is no God, nor heaven, nor bodies, and that we possess neither hands, nor feet, nor indeed any body; but we cannot in the same way conceive that we who doubt these things are not; for there is a contradiction in conceiving that what thinks does not at the same time as it thinks, exist. And hence this conclusion *I think, therefore I am*, is the first and most certain of all that occurs to one who philosophises in an orderly way.

Principle VIII.

This furnishes us with the distinction which exists between the soul and the body, or between that which thinks and that which is corporeal.

This, then, is the best way to discover the nature of mind and the distinction between it and the body. For, in considering what we are who suppose that all things apart from ourselves [our thought] are false, we observe very clearly that there is no extension, figure, local motion, or any such thing which may be attributed to body, which pertains to our nature, but only thought alone; and consequently this notion of thought precedes that of all corporeal things and is the most certain; since we still doubt whether there are any other things in the world, while we already perceive that we think.

PRINCIPLE IX.

What thought[1] is.

By the word thought I understand all that of which we are conscious as operating in us. And that is why not alone understanding, willing, imagining, but also feeling, are here the same thing as thought. For if I say I see, or I walk, I therefore am, and if by seeing and walking I mean the action of my eyes or my legs, which is the work of my body, my conclusion is not absolutely certain; because it may be that, as often happens in sleep, I think I see or I walk, although I never open my eyes or move from my place, and the same thing perhaps might occur if I had not a body at all. But if I mean only to talk of my sensation[2], or my consciously seeming to see or to walk, it becomes quite true because my assertion now refers only to my mind, which alone is concerned with my feeling or thinking that I see and I walk.

PRINCIPLE X.

That conceptions which are perfectly simple and clear of themselves are obscured by the definitions of the Schools, and that they are not to be numbered as amongst those capable of being acquired by study [*but are inborn in us*].

I do not here explain various other terms of which I have availed myself or will afterwards avail myself, because they seem to me perfectly clear of themselves. And I have often noticed that philosophers err in trying to explain by definitions logically constructed, things which were perfectly simple in themselves; they thereby render them but more obscure. And when I stated that this proposition *I think, therefore I am* is the first and most certain which presents itself to those who philosophise in orderly fashion, I did not for all that deny that we must first of all know *what is knowledge, what is existence, and what is certainty,* and that *in order to think we must be,* and such like; but because these are notions of the simplest possible kind, which of themselves give us no knowledge of anything that exists, I did not think them worthy of being put on record.

---

[1] cogitatio.   [2] sensu.

PRINCIPLE XI.

How we may know our mind better than our body.

But in order to understand how the knowledge which we possess of our mind not only precedes that which we have of our body, but is also more evident, it must be observed that it is very manifest by the natural light which is in our souls, that no qualities or properties pertain to nothing; and that where some are perceived there must necessarily be some thing or substance on which they depend. And the same light shows us that we know a thing or substance so much the better the more properties we observe in it. And we certainly observe many more qualities in our mind than in any other thing, inasmuch as there is nothing that excites us to knowledge of whatever kind, which does not even much more certainly compel us to a consciousness of our thought. To take an example, if I persuade myself that there is an earth because I touch or see it, by that very same fact, and by a yet stronger reason, I should be persuaded that my thought exists; because it may be that I think I touch the earth even though there is possibly no earth existing at all, but it is not possible that I who form this judgment and my mind which judges thus, should be non-existent; and so in other cases.

PRINCIPLE XII.

The reason why everyone does not comprehend this in the same way.

Those who have not studied philosophy in an orderly way have held other opinions on this subject because they never distinguished their mind from their body with enough care. For although they had no difficulty in believing that they themselves existed, and that they had a greater assurance of this than of any other thing, yet because they did not observe that by themselves[1] they ought merely to understand their minds [when metaphysical certainty was in question], and since on the contrary they rather meant that it was their bodies which they saw with their eyes, touched with their hands, and to which they wrongly attributed the power of perception, they did not distinctly comprehend the nature of the mind.

[1] Per se ipsos.

Principle XIII.

In what sense the knowledge of all other things depends on the knowledge of God.

But when the mind which thus knows itself but still doubts all other things, looks around in order to try to extend its knowledge further, it first of all finds in itself the ideas of a multitude of things, and while it contemplates these simply and neither affirms nor denies that there is anything outside itself which corresponds to these ideas, it is beyond any danger of falling into error. The mind likewise discovers certain common ideas out of which it frames various demonstrations which absolutely convince us of their truth if we give attention to them. For example the mind has within itself the ideas of number and figure; it has also, amongst its ordinary conceptions this, that '*if equals are added to equals, the result is equal,*' and so on. From this it is easy to demonstrate that the three angles of a triangle are equal to two right angles, etc. Now mind perceives these and other facts to be true so long as the premises from which they are derived[1] are attended to. But since it cannot always devote this attention to them [when it remembers the conclusion and yet cannot recollect the order of its deduction], and conceives that it may have been created of such a nature that it has been deceived even in what is most evident, it sees clearly that it has great cause to doubt the truth of such conclusions, and to realise that it can have no certain knowledge until it is acquainted with its creator.

Principle XIV.

That the existence of God may be rightly demonstrated from the fact that the necessity of His existence is comprehended in the conception which we have of Him.

When mind afterwards considers the diverse conceptions which it has and when it there discovers the idea of a Being who is omniscient, omnipotent and absolutely perfect, which is far the most important of all; in it it recognises not merely a possible and contingent existence, as in all the other ideas it has of things which it clearly perceives, but one which is absolutely necessary and eternal. And just as it perceives that it is necessarily involved

---

[1] Praemissas ex quibus.

in the idea of the triangle that it should have three angles which are equal to two right angles, it is absolutely persuaded that the triangle has three angles equal to two right angles. In the same way from the fact that it perceives that necessary and eternal existence is comprised in the idea which it has of an absolutely perfect Being, it has clearly to conclude that this absolutely perfect Being exists.

PRINCIPLE XV.

That necessary existence is not similarly included in the notion we have of other things, but merely contingent existence.

The mind will be the better assured of the truth of this conclusion if it observes that it does not possess the idea of any other thing wherein existence is necessarily contained. And from this it realises that the idea of an absolutely perfect Being is not framed in it by means of itself, nor does it represent a chimera, but that it is a true and immutable nature, which cannot be non-existent, since in it existence is necessarily contained.

PRINCIPLE XVI.

That prejudice prevents many from knowing clearly the necessity for the existence of God.

Our mind would have no trouble in persuading itself of this truth if it were wholly free from prejudice to begin with; but inasmuch as we are accustomed to distinguish essence from existence in all other things, and as we can at will imagine many ideas of things which neither are nor have been, it may easily occur that when we do not steadily contemplate this absolutely perfect Being, we shall doubt whether the idea which we form of Him is not one of those which we frame at pleasure, or one to the essence of which existence does not pertain.

PRINCIPLE XVII.

That the more objective perfection there is in our ideas, the more should its cause also be more perfect.

Further, when we reflect on the various ideas that are in us, it is easy to perceive that there is not much difference between them when they are considered only as modes of thinking, but they are widely different in another way, since the one represents one thing, and the other another; and their cause must be more perfect as what they represent of their objects is more perfect. For this is just the same as in the case of someone said to have the idea of a machine in the construction of which there is much skill displayed, we have reason to ask how he obtained the idea, e.g. whether he saw somewhere a similar machine made by another, or whether he had a thorough knowledge of the science of mechanics, or whether he were endowed with such force of mind that he was able of himself to invent the machine without having seen anything similar anywhere else. For the whole of the ingenuity involved in the idea which is possessed by this man objectively, as in a picture, must exist in its first and principal cause whatever that may be, not only objectively or representatively, but also formally or eminently.

Principle XVIII.

That we may thus demonstrate that there is a God.

So, because we find within ourselves the idea of a God, or a supremely perfect Being, we are able to investigate the cause which produces this idea in us; but after, on considering the immensity of the perfection it possesses, we are constrained to admit that we can consider it only as emanating from an all-perfect Being, that is, from a God who truly exists. For it is not only made manifest by the natural light that nothing can be the cause of nothing whatever, and that the more perfect cannot proceed from the less perfect so as to be thus produced as by its efficient and total cause, but also that it is impossible for us to have any idea of anything whatever, if there is not within us or outside of us, an original, which as a matter of fact comprehends all the perfections. But as we do not in any way possess all those absolute perfections of which we have the idea, we must conclude that they reside in some other nature different from ours, and that is, in God; or at least that they were once in Him; and it follows from this most manifestly that they are there still.

Principle XIX.

That although we do not comprehend the whole Nature of God, there is yet nothing which we know so clearly as His perfections.

This is quite certain and manifest to those who have accustomed themselves to the contemplation of God and to turn their attention to His infinite perfections. For, though we do not comprehend them because the Nature of the Infinite is such that we, being finite, cannot comprehend them, we yet conceive them more clearly and distinctly than any material thing, because, being more simple and not being limited by anything that may obscure them, they occupy our mind more fully[1].

PRINCIPLE XX.

That we are not the cause of ourselves, but that God is, and that consequently there is a God.

But since everyone does not observe this, and because, when we have a notion of some machine in which there is much skill displayed, we sufficiently well know the manner in which we have acquired this knowledge, and because we cannot even recollect when the idea which we have of a God has been communicated to us by God, since it has always been present in us, we must yet inquire who then is the author of our Being, possessing as we do the idea of the infinite perfections which are in God. Because the light of nature makes it very clear that whoever knows something more perfect than himself cannot be the author of his being, because then he would have given himself all the perfections of which he had cognisance; and consequently he could not subsist by any other than by Him who possesses all these perfections in Himself, that is, by God.

PRINCIPLE XXI.

That the mere duration of our life suffices to prove the existence of God.

We cannot doubt the truth of this demonstration so long as we observe the nature of time or of the duration of things; for this is of such a kind that its parts do not depend one upon the other, and never co-exist; and from the fact that we now are, it does not follow that we shall be a moment afterwards, if some cause—the same that first produced us—does not continue so to produce us; that is to say, to conserve us. And we can easily recognise that

---

[1] Quia cogitationem nostram magis implent, L. The French version is different, viz. 'being more simple and not being limited, what we do conceive of them is much less confused.' A sentence is added 'There is also no specula-tion which can better aid in perfecting our understanding, and which is more important, than this, inasmuch as the consideration of an object unlimited in its perfections fills us with satisfaction and assurance.'

there is no strength in us whereby we may conserve ourselves, but that He who has so much power that He can conserve us out of Himself must by so much the greater reason conserve Himself, or rather not require to be conserved by any other, for, in fine, He is God.

PRINCIPLE XXII.

That in recognising the existence of God in the manner here explained, we also recognise all His attributes, in so far as they may be known by the light of nature alone.

We possess the great advantage in proving the existence of God in this way by His idea[1], that we recognise at the same time what He is in so far as the weakness of our nature permits. For when we reflect on the idea of Him which is implanted in us, we perceive that He is eternal, omniscient, omnipotent, the source of all goodness and truth, creator of all things, and that in fine he has in Himself all that in which we can clearly recognise any infinite perfection or good that is not limited by some imperfection.

PRINCIPLE XXIII.

That God is not corporeal, and does not perceive by means of the senses as we do, nor is He the originator of sin.

For there are many things in the world which are in some respects imperfect, although we remark in them certain perfections ; it is accordingly not possible that any of these exist in God. Thus in corporeal nature since divisibility is included in local extension, and divisibility indicates imperfection, it is certain that God is not body. And although it is of some advantage for us to have senses, yet because in all sensations there is passivity[2] and that indicates dependence, we conclude that God is possessed of no senses, but that He understands and wills—not indeed as we do, by operations which are in some way distinct one from another, but ever by one identical and very simple action, and that He understands and wills and effects everything : that is, everything that really exists ; for he does not will the evil of sin because that evil is nothing real.

---

[1] Per ejus scilicet ideam.
[2] Latin 'quia tamen in omni sensu passio est.' Fr. 'yet because the sensations that are in us are there through impressions which proceed from elsewhere.'

Principle XXIV.

That in passing from the knowledge that God exists, to the knowledge of his creatures, we must recollect that our understanding is finite, and the power of God infinite.

Being thus aware that God alone is the true cause of all that is or can be, we shall doubtless follow the best method of philosophising, if, from the knowledge which we possess of His nature, we pass to an explanation of the things which He has created, and if we try from the notions which exist naturally in our minds to deduce it, for in this way we shall obtain a perfect science, that is, a knowledge of the effects through their causes. But in order that we may undertake this task with most security from error, we must recollect that God, the creator of all things, is infinite and that we are altogether finite.

Principle XXV.

And that we must believe all that God has revealed, even though it is above the range of our capacities.

Thus if God reveals to us or to others certain things concerning Himself which surpass the range of our natural power of intelligence, such as the mysteries of the incarnation and the Trinity, we shall have no difficulty in believing them, although we may not clearly understand them. For we should not think it strange that in the immensity of His nature, as also in the objects of His creation, there are many things beyond the range of our comprehension.

Principle XXVI.

That we must not try to dispute about the infinite, but just consider that all that in which we find no limits is indefinite, such as the extension of the world, the divisibility of its parts, the number of the stars, etc.

We will thus never hamper ourselves with disputes about the infinite, since it would be absurd that we who are finite should undertake to decide anything regarding it, and by this means in trying to comprehend it, so to speak regard it as finite. That is why we do not care to reply to those who demand whether the half of an infinite line is infinite, and whether an infinite number is even or odd and so on, because it is only those who imagine their mind to be infinite who appear to find it necessary to investigate such questions. And for our part, while we regard things in which, in a certain sense, we observe no limits, we shall not for all that state that they are infinite, but merely hold them to be indefinite. Thus because we cannot imagine an extension so great that we cannot at the same time conceive that there may be one yet greater, we shall say that the magnitude of possible things is indefinite. And because we cannot divide a body into parts which are so small that each part cannot be divided into others yet smaller, we shall consider that the quantity may be divided into parts whose number is indefinite. And because we cannot imagine so many stars that it is impossible for God to create more, we shall suppose the number to be indefinite, and so in other cases.

Principle XXVII.

What is the difference between the indefinite and the infinite?

And we shall name these things indefinite rather than infinite in order to reserve to God alone the name of infinite, first of all because in Him alone we observe no limitation whatever, and because we are quite certain that He can have none, and in the second place in regard to other things, because we do not in the same way positively understand them to be in every part unlimited, but merely negatively admit that their limits, if they exist, cannot be discovered by us[1].

Principle XXVIII.

That we must not inquire into the final, but only into the efficient causes of created things.

Finally we shall not seek for the reason of natural things from the end which God or nature has set before him in their creation[2]; for we should not take so much upon ourselves as to believe that God could take us into His counsels. But regarding Him as the efficient cause of all things, we shall merely try to discover by the

---

[1] 'As regards other things we know that they are not thus absolutely perfect because although we observe in them certain properties which appear to have no limit, we yet know that this proceeds from our lack of understanding and not from their natures.' (This, the French, translation is to obviate the use of the terms positive and negative.)

[2] 'We shall not stop to consider the ends which God has set before Himself in the creation of the world and we shall entirely set aside from our philosophy the search for final causes.' French version.

light of nature that He has placed in us, applied to those attributes of which He has been willing we should have some knowledge, what must be concluded regarding the effects that we perceive by the senses ; but we must keep in mind what has been said, that we must trust to this natural light only so long as nothing contrary to it is revealed by God Himself[1].

PRINCIPLE XXIX.

That God is not the cause of our errors.

The first of God's attributes which falls to be considered here is that He is absolutely true and the source of all light, so that it is evidently a contradiction that He should deceive us, that is to say that He should be properly and positively[2] the cause of the errors to which we are conscious of being subject. For although the capacity for deceit would seem to be a mark of subtlety of mind amongst men, yet the will to deceive proceeds only from malice, or fear, or weakness, and it cannot consequently be attributed to God.

PRINCIPLE XXX.

And consequently all that we perceive clearly is true, and this delivers us from the doubts put forward above.

Whence it follows that the light of nature, or the faculty of knowledge which God has given us, can never disclose to us[3] any object which is not true, inasmuch as it comprehends it, that is, inasmuch as it apprehends it clearly and distinctly. Because we should have had reason to think God a deceiver if He had given us this faculty perverted, or such that we should take the false for the true [when using the faculty aright]. And this should deliver us from the supreme doubt which encompassed us when we did not know whether our nature had been such that we had been deceived in things that seemed most clear. It should also protect us against all the other reasons already mentioned which we had for doubting. The truths of mathematics should now be above suspicion, for they are of the clearest. And if we perceive anything by our senses, either waking or sleeping, if it is clear and distinct, and if we separate it from what is obscure and confused, we shall easily assure ourselves

---

[1] This clause is not in the French version, which is incomplete.
[2] Lat. Proprie ac positive.
[3] attingere Lat.; n'apperçoit, Fr. 'compass,' Veitch's Trans.

of what is the truth. I do not require to say more on this particular subject here, since I have treated of it fully in the Meditations on Metaphysics, and what I intend to say later will serve to explain it more accurately.

PRINCIPLE XXXI.

That our errors in respect of God are but negations, while in respect of ourselves they are privations or defects.

But as it happens that although God is not a deceiver we frequently fall into error, if we desire to investigate the origin and cause of our errors in order to guard against them, we must take care to observe that they do not depend so much on our intellect as on our will, and that they are not such as to require the actual assistance of God in order that they may be produced. In this way so far as He is concerned they are but negations, while in respect to us they are defects or privations.

PRINCIPLE XXXII.

That in us there are but two modes of thought, the perception of the understanding and the action of the will.

For all the modes of thinking that we observed in ourselves may be related to two general modes, the one of which consists in perception, or in the operation of the understanding, and the other in volition, or the operation of the will. Thus sense-perception[1], imagining, and conceiving things that are purely intelligible, are just different methods of perceiving[2]; but desiring, holding in aversion, affirming, denying, doubting, all these are the different modes of willing.

PRINCIPLE XXXIII.

That we deceive ourselves only when we form judgments about anything insufficiently known to us.

When we perceive anything, we are in no danger of misapprehending it, if we do not judge of it one way or the other; and even when we judge of it we should not fall into error, provided that we do not give our assent to what we do not know clearly and distinctly; but what usually misleads us is that we very frequently form a judgment although we have no very exact knowledge regarding that of which we judge.

---

[1] sentire.   [2] percipiendi.

Principle XXXIV.

That the will is requisite for judgment as well as the understanding.

I admit that we can judge of nothing unless our understanding is made use of, because there is no reason to suppose we can judge of what we in no wise apprehend ; but the will is absolutely essential for our giving our assent to what we have in some manner perceived. Nor, in order to form any judgment whatever, is it necessary that we should have a perfect and entire knowledge of a thing ; for we often give our assent to things of which we have never had any but a very obscure and confused knowledge.

Principle XXXV.

That the will is more extended than the understanding, and that our errors proceed from this cause.

Further, the perception of the understanding only extends to the few objects which present themselves to it, and is always very limited. The will, on the other hand, may in some measure be said to be the infinite, because we perceive nothing which may be the object of some other will, even of the immensity of the will that is in God, to which our will cannot also extend, so that we easily extend it beyond that which we apprehend clearly. And when we do this there is no wonder if it happens that we are deceived.

Principle XXXVI.

Our errors cannot be imputed to God.

And although God has not given us an understanding which is omnipotent, we must not for that reason consider that He is the originator of our errors. For all created understanding is finite, and it is of the nature of finite understanding not to embrace all things.

Principle XXXVII.

That the principal perfection of man is to have the power of acting freely or by will, and that this is what renders him deserving of either praise or blame.

That will should extend widely is in accordance with its nature, and it is the greatest perfection in man to be able to act by its means, that is freely, and by so doing we are in a peculiar way masters of our actions and thereby merit praise or blame. For we do not praise automatic machines although they respond exactly to the movements which they were destined to produce, since their actions are performed necessarily. We praise the workman who has made the machines because he has formed them with accuracy and has done so freely and not of necessity. And for the same reason when we choose what is true, much more credit is due to us when the choice is made freely, than when it is made of necessity.

Principle XXXVIII.

That our errors are the defects of our mode of action, but not of our nature; and that the faults of subordinates may often be attributed to other masters, but never to God.

It is very true that whenever we err there is some fault in our method of action, or in the manner in which we use our freedom; but for all that there is no defect in our nature, because it is ever the same whether our judgment be true or false. And even though God could have given us so incisive an intellect that we should never have fallen into error, we have no right for all that to demand this of Him. For although amongst us men, he who could prevent an impending evil and yet who does not so do, is judged to be its cause, the case is not the same with regard to God, who is not to be regarded as responsible for our errors though endowed with the power to prevent them. For the power which some men possess over others has been instituted for the purpose of their hindering evil from being done by others, while the power held over the universe by God is altogether absolute and free. This is why we should be grateful for the good things He has granted us and not complain that He does not bestow irom His bounty all that we knew He might have dispensed.

Principle XXXIX.

That freedom of the will is self-evident.

Finally it is so evident that we are possessed of a free will that can give or withhold its assent, that this may be counted as one of the first and most ordinary notions that are found innately in us. We had before a very clear proof of this, for at the same time as we tried to doubt all things and even supposed that He who created us employed His unlimited powers in deceiving us in every way, we perceived in ourselves a liberty such that we were able to abstain from believing what was not perfectly certain and indubitable. But that of which we could not doubt at such a time is as self-evident and clear as anything we can ever know.

PRINCIPLE XL.

That we likewise know certainly that everything is pre-ordained of God.

But because that which we have already learnt about God proves to us that His power is so immense that it would be a crime for us to think ourselves ever capable of doing anything which He had not already pre-ordained, we should soon be involved in great difficulties if we undertook to make His pre-ordinances harmonise with the freedom of our will, and if we tried to comprehend them both at one time.

PRINCIPLE XLI.

How the freedom of the will may be reconciled with Divine pre-ordination.

Instead of this, we shall have no trouble at all if we recollect that our thought is finite, and that the omnipotence of God, whereby He has not only known from all eternity that which is or can be, but also willed and pre-ordained it, is infinite. In this way we may have intelligence enough to come clearly and distinctly to know that this power is in God, but not enough to comprehend how He leaves the free action of man indeterminate ; and, on the other hand, we are so conscious of the liberty and indifference which exists in us, that there is nothing that we comprehend more clearly and perfectly. For it would be absurd to doubt that of which we inwardly experience and perceive as existing within ourselves, just because we do not comprehend a matter which from its nature we know to be incomprehensible.

PRINCIPLE XLII.

How, although we do not will to err, we yet err by our will.

But inasmuch as we know that all our errors depend on our will, and as no one desires to deceive himself we may wonder that we err at all. We must, however, observe that there is a great deal of difference between willing to be deceived and willing to give one's assent to opinions in which error is sometimes found. For although there is no one who expressly desires to err, there is hardly one who is not willing to give his assent to things in which unsuspected error is to be found. And it even frequently happens that it is the very desire for knowing the truth which causes those who are not fully aware of the order in which it should be sought for, to give judgment on things of which they have no real knowledge and thereby to fall into error.

Principle XLIII.

That we cannot err if we give our assent only to things that we know clearly and distinctly.

But it is certain that we shall never take the false as the true if we only give our assent to things that we perceive clearly and distinctly. Because since God is no deceiver, the faculty of knowledge that He has given us cannot be fallacious, nor can the faculty of will, so long at least as we do not extend it beyond those things that we clearly perceive. And even if this truth could not be rationally demonstrated, we are by nature so disposed to give our assent to things that we clearly perceive, that we cannot possibly doubt of their truth.

Principle XLIV.

That we shall always judge ill when we assent to what we do not clearly perceive, although our judgment may be true; and that it frequently is our memory that deceives us by leading us to believe that certain things had been satisfactorily established by us.

It is also quite certain that whenever we give our assent to some reason which we do not exactly understand, we either deceive ourselves, or, if we arrive at the truth, it is only by chance, and thus we cannot be certain that we are not in error. It is true that it happens but rarely that we judge of a matter at the same time as we observe that we do not apprehend it, because the light of nature teaches us that we must not judge of anything that we do not understand. But we frequently err when we presume we have known certain things as being stored up in our memory, to which on recollection we give our assent, and of which we have never possessed any knowledge at all.

Principle XLV.

What a clear and distinct perception is.

There are even a number of people who throughout all their lives perceive nothing so correctly as to be capable of judging of it properly. For the knowledge upon which a certain and incontrovertible judgment can be formed, should not alone be clear but also distinct. I term that clear which is present and apparent to an attentive mind, in the same way as we assert that we see objects clearly when, being present to the regarding eye, they operate upon it with sufficient strength. But the distinct is that which is so precise and different from all other objects that it contains within itself nothing but what is clear.

Principle XLVI.

It is shown from the example of pain that a perception may be clear without being distinct, but it cannot be distinct unless it is clear.

When, for instance, a severe pain is felt, the perception of this pain may be very clear, and yet for all that not distinct, because it is usually confused by the sufferers with the obscure[1] judgment that they form upon its nature, assuming as they do that something exists in the part affected, similar to the sensation of pain of which they are alone clearly conscious. In this way perception may be clear without being distinct, and cannot be distinct without being also clear.

Principle XLVII.

That in order to remove the prejudices of our youth, it must be considered what there is that is clear in each of our simple[2] notions.

Indeed in our early years, our mind was so immersed in the body, that it knew nothing distinctly, although it perceived much sufficiently clearly; and because it even then formed many judgments, numerous prejudices were contracted from which the majority of us can hardly ever hope to become free. But in order that we may now free ourselves from them I shall here enumerate all these simple notions which constitute our reflections, and distinguish whatever is clear in each of them from what is obscure, or likely to cause us to err.

---

[1] 'false,' French version.　　　[2] 'first,' French.

Principle XLVIII.

That all the objects of our perceptions are to be considered either as things or the affections of things, or else as eternal truths; and the enumeration of things.

I distinguish all the objects of our knowledge either into things or the affections of things[1], or as eternal truths having no existence outside our thought. Of the things we consider as real, the most general are *substance, duration, order, number,* and possibly such other similar matters as range through all the classes of real things. I do not however observe more than two ultimate classes of real things—the one is intellectual things, or those of the intelligence, that is, pertaining to the mind or to thinking substance, the other is material things, or that pertaining to extended substance, i.e. to body. Perception, volition, and every mode of knowing and willing, pertain to thinking substance; while to extended substance pertain magnitude or extension in length, breadth and depth, figure, movement, situation, divisibility into parts themselves divisible, and such like. Besides these, there are, however, certain things which we experience in ourselves and which should be attributed neither to mind nor body alone, but to the close and intimate union that exists between the body and mind as I shall later on explain in the proper place[2]. Such are the appetites of hunger, thirst, etc., and also the emotions or passions of the mind which do not subsist in mind or thought alone, as the emotions of anger, joy, sadness, love, etc.; and, finally all the sensations such as pain, pleasure, light and colour, sounds, odours, tastes, heat, hardness, and all other tactile qualities.

Principle XLIX.

That eternal truths cannot be enumerated thus, and that this is not requisite.

What I have hitherto enumerated are regarded either as the qualities of things or their modes.

[We must now talk of what we know as eternal truths.]

When we apprehend that it is impossible that anything can

---

[1] 'le premier contient toutes les choses qui ont quelque existence ; et l'autre, toutes les veritez qui ne sont rien hors de notre pensée,' French version. 'I distinguish all the objects of our knowledge into two species; the first contains all things which have an existence; the second all the truths which have no existence outside our thought.'

[2] Part IV. art. 189, 190 and 191.

be formed of nothing, the proposition *ex nihilo nihil fit* is not to be considered as an existing thing, or the mode of a thing, but as a certain eternal truth which has its seat in our mind, and is a common notion or axiom. Of the same nature are the following : 'It is impossible that the same thing can be and not be at the same time,' and that 'what has been done cannot be undone,' 'that he who thinks must exist while he thinks,' and very many other propositions the whole of which it would not be easy to enumerate. But [this is not necessary since] we cannot fail to recognise them when the occasion presents itself for us to do so, and if we have no prejudices to blind us.

Principle L.

That these eternal truths are clearly perceived, but not by all, by reason of prejudice.

As regards the common notions, indeed, there is no doubt that they may be clearly and distinctly perceived, for otherwise they would not deserve to bear this name ; but it is also true that there are some that do not in regard to all men deserve the name equally with others, because they are not equally perceived by all. Not, however, that I believe the faculty of knowledge to extend further with some men than with others ; it is rather that these common opinions are opposed to the prejudices of some who are thereby prevented from easily perceiving them, although they are perfectly manifest to those who are free from these prejudices.

Principle LI.

What substance is, and that it is a name which we cannot attribute in the same sense to God and to His creatures.

As regards these matters which we consider as being things or modes of things, it is necessary that we should examine them here one by one. By substance, we can understand nothing else than a thing which so exists that it needs no other thing in order to exist. And in fact only one single substance can be understood which clearly needs nothing else, namely, God. We perceive that all other things can exist only by the help of the concourse of God. That is why the word substance does not pertain *univoce* to God and to other things, as they say in the Schools, that is, no common signification for this appellation which will apply equally to God and to them can be distinctly understood.

PRINCIPLE LII.

That it may be attributed univocally to the soul and to body, and how we know substance.

Created substances, however, whether corporeal or thinking, may be conceived under this common concept; for they are things which need only the concurrence of God in order to exist. But yet substance cannot be first discovered merely from the fact that it is a thing that exists, for that fact alone is not observed by us. We may, however, easily discover it by means of any one of its attributes because it is a common notion that nothing is possessed of no attributes, properties, or qualities. For this reason, when we perceive any attribute, we therefore conclude that some existing thing or substance to which it may be attributed, is necessarily present

PRINCIPLE LIII.

That each substance has a principal attribute, and that the attribute of the mind is thought, while that of body is extension.

But although any one attribute is sufficient to give us a knowledge of substance, there is always one principal property of substance which constitutes its nature and essence, and on which all the others depend. Thus extension in length, breadth and depth, constitutes the nature of corporeal substance; and thought constitutes the nature of thinking substance. For all else that may be attributed to body presupposes extension, and is but a mode of this extended thing; as everything that we find in mind is but so many diverse forms of thinking. Thus, for example, we cannot conceive figure but as an extended thing, nor movement but as in an extended space; so imagination, feeling, and will, only exist in a thinking thing. But, on the other hand, we can conceive extension without figure or action, and thinking without imagination or sensation, and so on with the rest; as is quite clear to anyone who attends to the matter.

PRINCIPLE LIV.

How we may have clear and distinct notions of thinking substance, of corporeal substance, and of God.

We may thus easily have two clear and distinct notions or ideas, the one of created substance which thinks, the other of corporeal substance, provided we carefully separate all the attributes of thought from those of extension. We can also have a clear and distinct idea of an uncreated and independent thinking substance, that is to say, of God, provided that we do not suppose that this idea represents to us all that is exhibited in God, and that we do not mingle anything fictitious with it, but simply attend to what is evidently contained in the notion, and which we are aware pertains to the nature of an absolutely perfect Being. For no one can deny that such an idea of God exists in us, unless he groundlessly asserts that the mind of man cannot attain to a knowledge of God.

PRINCIPLE LV.

How we can also have a distinct understanding of duration, order, and number

We shall likewise have a very distinct understanding of *duration, order* and *number*, if, in place of mingling with the idea that we have of them what properly speaking pertains to the conception of substance, we merely consider that the duration of each thing is a mode under which we shall consider this thing in so far as it continues to exist; and if in the same way we think that order and number are not really different from the things that are ordered and numbered, but that they are only the modes under which we consider these things.

PRINCIPLE LVI.

What are modes, qualities, and attributes.

And, indeed, when we here speak of modes we mean nothing more than what elsewhere is termed *attribute* or *quality*. But when we consider substance as modified or diversified by them, I avail myself of the word *mode*; and when from the disposition or variation it can be named as of such and such a kind, we shall use the word *qualities* [to designate the different modes which cause it to be so termed]; and finally when we more generally consider that these modes or qualities are in substance we term them *attributes*. And because in God any variableness is incomprehensible, we cannot ascribe to Him modes or qualities; but simply attributes. And even in created things that which never exists in them in any diverse way, like existence and duration in the existing and enduring thing, should be called not qualities or modes, but attributes.

Principle LVII.

That there are attributes which pertain to things and others to thought; and what duration and time are.

Some of the attributes are in things themselves and others are only in our thought. Thus time, for example, which we distinguish from duration taken in its general sense and which we describe as the measure of movement, is only a mode of thinking[1]; for we do not indeed apprehend that the duration of things which are moved is different from that of the things which are not moved, as is evident from the fact that if two bodies are moved for the space of an hour, the one quickly, the other slowly, we do not count the time longer in one case than in the other, although there is much more movement in one of the two bodies than in the other. But in order to comprehend the duration of all things under the same measure, we usually compare their duration with the duration of the greatest and most regular motions, which are those that create years and days, and these we term time. Hence this adds nothing to the notion of duration, generally taken, but a mode of thinking.

Principle LVIII.

That number and all universals are simply modes of thought.

Similarly number when we consider it abstractly or generally and not in created things, is but a mode of thinking; and the same is true of all that which [in the schools] is named *universals*.

Principle LIX.

How Universals are formed and what are the five common ones:—genus, species, difference, property and accident.

Universals arise solely from the fact that we avail ourselves of one and the same idea in order to think of all individual things

---

[1] 'is only a mode of thinking that duration,' French version.

which have a certain similitude; and when we comprehend under the same name all the objects represented by this idea, that name is universal. For example, when we see two stones, and without thinking further of their nature than to remark that there are two, we form in ourselves an idea of a certain number which we term the number of two; and when afterwards we see two birds or two trees, and we observe without further thinking about their nature, that there are two of them, we again take up the same idea which we had before, which idea is universal; and we give to this number the universal name 'two.' And in the same way when we consider a three-sided figure we form a certain idea which we call the idea of a triangle; and we afterwards make use of it as a universal in representing to ourselves all the figures having three sides. But when we notice more particularly that of three-sided figures some have a right angle and others have not, we form the universal idea of a rectangular triangle, which being related to the preceding as to a more general, may be termed *species*; and the right angle is the universal *difference* by which right-angled triangles are distinguished from all others. If we further observe that the square of the side which subtends the right angle is equal to the squares of the two other sides, and that this property belongs only to this species of triangle, we may term it a [universal] property of the species. Finally if we suppose that certain of the triangles are moved, and others are not moved we should take that to be a universal *accident* of the same; and it is thus that we commonly enumerate the five universals, viz. genus, species, difference, property, accident.

Principle LX

Of distinctions, and firstly of real distinction.

But as to the number in things themselves, this proceeds from the distinction which exists between them; and *distinction* is of three sorts, viz. *real, modal,* and *of reason.* The *real* is properly speaking found between two or more substances; and we can conclude that two substances are really distinct one from the other from the sole fact that we can conceive the one clearly and distinctly without the other. For in accordance with the knowledge which we have of God, we are certain that He can carry into effect all that of which we have a distinct idea. That is why from the fact that we now have, e.g. the idea of an extended or corporeal substance, although we do not yet know certainly whether such really exists at all, we may yet conclude that it may exist ; and if it does exist, any one portion of it which we can demarcate in our thought must be distinct from every other part of the same substance. Similarly because each one of us is conscious that he thinks, and that in thinking he can shut off from himself all other substance, either thinking or extended, we may conclude that each of us, similarly regarded, is really distinct from every other thinking substance and from every corporeal substance. And even if we suppose that God had united a body to a soul so closely that it was impossible to bring them together more closely, and made a single thing out of the two, they would yet remain really distinct one from the other notwithstanding the union ; because however closely God connected them He could not set aside the power which He possessed of separating them, or conserving them one apart from the other, and those things which God can separate, or conceive in separation, are really distinct.

Principle LXI.

Of the modal distinction.

There are two sorts of *modal distinctions*, i.e. the one between the mode properly speaking, and the substance of which it is the mode, and the other between two modes of the same substance. The former we recognise by the fact that we can clearly conceive substance without the mode which we say differs from it, while we cannot reciprocally have a perception of this mode without perceiving the substance. There is, for example, a modal distinction between figure or movement and the corporeal substance in which both exist: there is also a distinction between affirming or recollecting and the mind. As to the other kind of distinction, its characteristic is that we are able to recognise the one mode without the other and *vice versâ*, but we can conceive neither the one nor the other without recognising that both subsist in one common substance. If, for example, a stone is moved and along with that is square, we are able to conceive the square figure without knowing that it is moved, and reciprocally, we may be aware that it is moved without knowing that it is square; but we cannot have a conception of this movement and figure unless we have a conception of the substance of the stone. As for the distinction whereby the mode of one substance is different from another substance, or from the mode of another substance, as the movement of one body is different from another body or from mind, or else as movement is different from duration[1]; it appears to me that we should call it real rather than modal; because we cannot clearly conceive these modes apart from the substances of which they are the modes and which are really distinct.

Principle LXII.

Of the distinction created by thought.

Finally the *distinction of reason* is between substance and some one of its attributes without which it is not possible that we should have a distinct knowledge of it, or between two such attributes of the same substance. This distinction is made manifest from the fact that we cannot have a clear and distinct idea of such a substance if we exclude from it such an attribute; or we cannot have a clear idea of the one of the two attributes if we separate from it the other. For example, because there is no substance which does not cease to exist when it ceases to endure, duration is only distinct from substance by thought[2]; and all the modes of thinking which we consider as though they existed in the objects, differ only in thought[3] both from the objects of which they are the thought and from each other in a common object[4]. I recollect having elsewhere conjoined this sort of distinction with modal distinction (near the end of the Reply made to the First Objection to the Meditations on the First Philosophy), but then it was not necessary to treat accurately of these distinctions, and it was sufficient for my purpose at the time simply to distinguish them both from the real.

Principle LXIII.

How we may have distinct conceptions of thought and extension, inasmuch as the one constitutes the nature of mind, and the other that of body.

We may likewise consider thought and extension as constituting the natures of intelligence and corporeal substance; and then they

---

[1] 'doute' in French version. In the Latin edition *dubitatione* is corrected to *duratio*.

[2] ratione.   [3] ratione.

[4] 'and generally all the attributes which cause us to have diverse thoughts of the same thing, such as the extension of body and its property of divisibility, do not differ from the body which is to us the object of them, or the one from the other, excepting so far as we sometimes think confusedly of the one without the other.' French version.

must not be considered otherwise than as the very substances that think and are extended, i.e. as mind and body; for we know them in this way very clearly and distinctly. It is moreover more easy to know a substance that thinks, or an extended substance, than substance alone, without regarding whether it thinks or is extended. For we experience some difficulty in abstracting the notions that we have of substance from those of thought or extension, for they in truth do not differ but in thought[1], and our conception is not more distinct because it comprehends fewer properties, but because we distinguish accurately that which it does comprehend from all other notions.

Principle LXIV.

How we may also conceive them as modes of substance.

We may likewise consider thought and extension as the modes which are found in substance; that is, in as far as we consider that one and the same mind may have many different thoughts, and that one body, retaining the same size, may be extended in many different ways, sometimes being greater in length and less in breadth or depth, and sometimes on the contrary greater in breadth and less in length. We then distinguish them modally from substance, and they may be conceived not less clearly and distinctly, provided that we do not think of them as substance or things separate from others, but simply as modes of things. Because when we regard them as in the substances of which they are the modes, we distinguish them from these substances, and take them for what they actually are; while, on the contrary, if we wish to consider them apart from the substances in which they are, that will have the effect of our taking them as self-subsisting things and thus confounding the ideas of mode and substance.

Principle LXV.

How we may likewise know their diverse modes.

We shall similarly best apprehend the diverse modes of thought such as understanding, imagining, recollecting, willing, etc., and the diverse modes of extension, or which pertain to extension, such as all figures, the situation of parts, and their movements, provided that we consider them simply as modes of the things in which they are; and as for motion we shall best understand it, if we inquire

[1] ratione.

only about locomotion, without taking into account the force that produces it, which I shall nevertheless endeavour to set forth in its own place.

Principle LXVI.

That we also have a clear knowledge of our sensations, affections, and appetites, although we frequently err in the judgments we form of them.

There remain our sensations, affections and appetites, as to which we may likewise have a clear knowledge, if we take care to include in the judgments we form of them that only which we know to be precisely contained in our perception of them, and of which we are intimately conscious. It is, however, most difficult to observe this condition, in regard to our senses at least, because we, everyone of us, have judged from our youth up that all things of which we have been accustomed to have sensation have had an existence outside our thoughts, and that they have been entirely similar to the sensation, that is the idea which we have formed of them. Thus, when, for example, we perceived a certain colour, we thought that we saw something which existed outside of us and which clearly resembled the idea of colour which we then experienced in ourselves, and from the habit of judging in this way we seemed to see this so clearly and distinctly as to be convinced that it is certain and indubitable.

Principle LXVII

That we frequently deceive ourselves in judging of pain itself.

The same is true in regard to all our other sensations, even those which have to do with agreeable sensation and pain. For although we do not believe that these feelings exist outside of us, we are not wont to regard them as existing merely in our mind or our perception, but as being in our hands, feet, or some other part of our body. But there is no reason that we should be obliged to believe that the pain, for example, which we feel in our foot, is anything beyond our mind which exists in our foot, nor that the light which we imagine ourselves to see in the sun really is in the sun [as it is in us]; for both these are prejudices of our youth, as will clearly appear in what follows.

Principle LXVIII.

How we may distinguish in such matters that which we know clearly from that in which we may err.

But in order that we may here distinguish that which is clear from that which is obscure we ought to observe that we have a clear or distinct knowledge of pain, colour, and other things of the sort when we consider them simply as sensations or thoughts. But when we desire to judge of such matters as existing outside of our mind, we can in no wise conceive what sort of things they are. And when anyone says that he sees colour in a body or feels pain in one of his limbs, it is the same as if he told us that he there saw or felt something but was absolutely ignorant of its nature, or else that he did not know what he saw or felt. For although when he examines his thoughts with less attention he perhaps easily persuades himself that he has some knowledge of it, because he supposes that there is something resembling the sensation of colour or pain which he experiences, yet if he investigates what is represented to him by this sensation of colour or pain appearing as they do to exist in a coloured body or suffering part, he will find that he is really ignorant of it.

Principle LXIX.

That we know magnitude, figure, etc. quite differently from colour and pain, etc.

This will be more especially evident if we consider that size in the body which is seen, or figure or movement (local movement at least, for philosophers by imagining other sorts of motion than this, have rendered its nature less intelligible to themselves), or situation, or duration, or number, and the like, which we clearly perceive in all bodies, as has been already described, are known by us in a quite different way from that in which colour is known in the same body, or pain, odour, taste, or any of the properties which, as hitherto mentioned, should be attributed to the senses. For although in observing a body we are not less assured of its existence from the colour which we perceive in its regard than from the figure which bounds it, we yet know this property in it which causes us to call it figured, with much greater clearness than what causes us to say that it is coloured.

Principle LXX.

That we may judge in two ways of sensible things, by one of which we shall avoid error, while by the other we shall fall into error.

It is thus evident when we say that we perceive colours in objects, that it is the same as though we said that we perceive something in the objects of whose nature we were ignorant, but which yet caused a very clear and vivid sensation in us, and which is termed the sensation of colours. But there is a great deal of difference in our manner of judging, for, so long as we believe that there is something in objects of which we have no knowledge (that is in things, such as they are, from which sensation comes to us), so far are we from falling into error that, on the contrary, we rather provide against it, for we are less likely to judge rashly of a thing which we have been forewarned we do not know. But when we think we perceive a certain colour in objects although we have no real knowledge of what the name colour signifies, and we can find no intelligible resemblance between the colour which we suppose to exist in objects and what we are conscious of in our senses, yet, because we do not observe this, or remark in these objects certain other qualities like magnitude, figure, number, etc., which we clearly know are or may be in objects, as our senses or understanding show us, it is easy to allow ourselves to fall into the error of holding that what we call colour in objects is something entirely resembling the colour we perceive, and then supposing that we have a clear perception of what we do not perceive at all.

Principle LXXI.

That the principal cause of error is found in the prejudices of childhood.

It is here that the first and principal of our errors is to be found. For in the first years of life the mind was so closely allied to body that it applied itself to nothing but those thoughts alone by which it was aware of the things which affected the body; nor were these as yet referred to anything existing outside itself, but the fact was merely that pain was felt when the body was hurt, or pleasure experienced when the body received some good, or else if the body was so [slightly] affected that no great good nor evil was experienced, such sensations were encountered as we call tastes, smells, sound, heat, cold, light, colours, etc., which in truth represent nothing to us outside of our mind, but which vary in accordance with the diversities of the parts and modes in which the body is affected[1]. The mind at the same time also perceived magnitudes, figures, movements and the like, which were exhibited to it not as sensations but as things or the modes of things existing, or at least capable of existing, outside thought, although it did not yet observe this distinction between the two. And afterwards when the machine of the body which has been so constituted by nature that it can of its own inherent power turn here and there, by turning fortuitously this way and the other, followed after what was useful and avoided what was harmful, the mind which was closely allied to it, reflecting on the things which it followed after or avoided, remarked first of all that they existed outside itself, and attributed to them not alone magnitudes, figures, movements, and other such properties which it apprehended as things or modes of things, but also tastes, smells, and the like, the sensations of which it perceived that these things caused in it. And as all other things were only considered in as far as they served for the use of the body in which it was immersed, mind judged that there was more or less reality in each body, according as the impressions made on body were more or less strong. Hence came the belief that there was much more substance or corporeal reality in rocks or metals than in air or water, because the sensations of hardness and weight were much more strongly felt. And thus it was that air was only regarded as anything when it was agitated by some wind, and we experienced it to be either hot or cold. And because the stars did not give more light than tiny lighted candles, it did not hold them to be larger than such flames. Moreover because it did not as yet remark that the earth turned on its own axis, and that the superficies was curved like a sphere, it was more ready to apprehend that it was immovable and that the surface was flat. And we have in this way been imbued with a thousand other such prejudices from infancy, which in later youth we quite forgot we had accepted without sufficient examination, admitting them as though they were of perfect truth and certainty, and as if they had been known by means of our senses or implanted in us by nature.

---

[1] 'which vary according to the movements which pass from all parts of our body to the part of the brain to which it is closely united.' French version.

Principle LXXII.

That the second cause of our errors is that we cannot forget these prejudices.

Though in coming to years of maturity, when the mind, being no longer wholly subject to the body, does not refer everything to it, but also inquires into the truth of things as they are in themselves, we find that much of the judgment that we before had formed is false, yet it is not easy to eradicate the false from our memory, and so long as it remains there it may be the cause of many errors. Thus, for example, since from our earliest years we imagined stars to be minute bodies, we have great difficulty in imagining anything different from this first conception, although astronomical reason tells us that they are amongst the largest—so greatly does prejudiced opinion affect our beliefs.

Principle LXXIII.

The third cause is that our mind fatigues itself when it applies its attention to the objects which are not present to the senses; and that we are therefore in the habit of judging of these not from present perceptions, but from preconceived opinions.

Further, since our mind cannot pause to consider any one thing with attention without difficulty and fatigue, and since of all objects it applies itself with the greatest difficulty to those which are present neither to the senses nor to the imagination, whether because it derives this nature from its union with the body, or because in the first years of our life we are so much occupied with feeling and imagining that we have acquired a greater facility for thinking in this way than in any other, besides acquiring the habit of so-doing, it comes about that many men are unable to believe that there is any substance unless it is imaginable and corporeal and even sensible. For they are ignorant that the only things that are imaginable are those that exist in extension, motion and figure, while there are many others that are intelligible; and they persuade themselves that there is nothing that can subsist but body, and finally, that there is no body which is not sensible. And since in truth we do not perceive any object as it is in itself by sense alone, as will be clearly shown later on, it comes to pass that most men in life perceive nothing but in a confused way.

Principle LXXIV.

The fourth cause is that we attach our concepts to words which do not accurately answer to the reality.

And finally, because we attach all our conceptions to words for the expression of them by speech, and as we commit to memory our thought in connection with these words; and as we more easily recall to memory words than things, we can scarcely conceive of anything so distinctly as to be able to separate completely that which we conceive from the words chosen to express the same. In this way most men apply their attention to words rather than things, and this is the cause of their frequently giving their assent to terms which they do not understand, either because they believe that they formerly understood them, or because they think that those who informed them correctly understood their signification. And although this is not the place in which to treat particularly of this matter, inasmuch as I have not yet dealt with the nature of the human body, nor even shown that any body exists at all, it yet appears to me that what I have already said may serve to enable us to distinguish those of our conceptions that are clear and distinct from those in which there is obscurity and confusion.

Principle LXXV.

A summary of all that has to be observed in order to philosophise correctly.

That is why, if we desire to philosophise seriously, and apply ourselves to the research of all the truths we are capable of knowing, we must, in the first place, rid ourselves of our prejudices, and must take great care sedulously to set aside all the opinions which we formerly accepted, until, on applying to them further examination, we discover them to be true. We should afterwards hold an orderly review of the conceptions which we have within us, and accept as true those and only those which present themselves to our apprehension as clear and distinct. In this way we shall know, first of all that we exist, inasmuch as our nature is to think, and at the same time that there is a God on whom we depend; and after having considered His attributes we shall be in a position to inquire into the truth of all other things, since God is their cause. In addition to the notions we have of God and our thoughts, we shall likewise find within us a knowledge of many propositions which are eternally true, as, for example, that nothing cannot be the cause of anything, etc. We shall also find there the idea of a corporeal or extended nature which may be moved, divided, etc., and also of the sensations which affect us, such as those of pain, colour, taste, etc., although we do not as yet know the cause of our being so affected. And comparing this [what we now know by examining those things in their order] with our former confused knowledge, we shall acquire the custom of forming clear and distinct conceptions of all that we can know. And in these few precepts it appears to me that the principles of human knowledge are contained.

Principle LXXVI.

That we ought to prefer the Divine authority to our perceptions[1], but, excluding this, we should not assent to anything which we do not clearly perceive.

Above all we should impress on our memory as an infallible rule that what God has revealed to us is incomparably more certain than anything else; and that we ought to submit to the Divine authority rather than to our own judgment even though the light of reason may seem to us to suggest, with the utmost clearness and evidence, something opposite. But in things in regard to which Divine authority reveals nothing to us, it would be unworthy of a philosopher to accept anything as true which he has not ascertained to be such, and to trust more to the senses, that is to judgments formed without consideration in childhood, than to the reasoning of maturity.

[1] 'reasonings.' French version.

SECOND PART.

OF THE PRINCIPLES OF MATERIAL THINGS.

PRINCIPLE I.

What are the reasons for our having a certain knowledge of material things?

Although we are all persuaded that material things exist, yet because we have doubted this before and have placed it in the rank of the prejudices of our childhood, it is now requisite that we should inquire into the reasons through which we may accept this truth with certainty. To begin with we feel that without doubt all our perceptions proceed from some thing which is different from our mind. For it is not in our power to have one perception rather than another, since each one is clearly dependent on the object which affects our senses. It is true that we may inquire whether that object is God, or some other different from God. But inasmuch as we perceive, or rather are stimulated by sense to apprehend clearly and distinctly a matter which is extended in length, breadth, and depth, the various parts of which have various figures and motions, and give rise to the sensations we have of colours, smells, pains, etc., if God immediately and of Himself presented to our mind the idea of this extended matter, or merely permitted it to be caused in us by some other object which possessed no extension, figure, or motion, there would be nothing to prevent Him from being regarded as a deceiver. For we clearly apprehend this matter as different from God, or ourselves, or our mind, and appear to discern very plainly that the idea of it is due to objects outside of ourselves to which it is absolutely similar. But God cannot deceive us, because deception is repugnant to His nature, as has been explained. And hence we must conclude that there is an object extended in length, breadth, and depth, and possessing all those properties which we clearly perceive to pertain to extended objects. And this extended object is called by us either body or matter.

PRINCIPLE II.

How we likewise know that the body of man is closely united to the mind.

It may be concluded also that a certain body is more closely united to our mind than any other, from the fact that pain and other of our sensations occur without our foreseeing them; and that mind is conscious that these do not arise from itself alone, nor pertain to it in so far as it is a thinking thing, but only in so far as it is united to another thing, extended and mobile, which is called the human body. But this is not the place to explain the matter further.

PRINCIPLE III.

That the perceptions of the senses do not teach us what is really in things, but merely that whereby they are useful or hurtful to man's composite nature.

It will be sufficient for us to observe that the perceptions of the senses are related simply to the intimate union which exists between body and mind, and that while by their means we are made aware of what in external bodies can profit or hurt this union, they do not present them to us as they are in themselves unless occasionally and accidentally. For [after this observation] we shall without difficulty set aside all the prejudices of the senses and in this regard rely upon our understanding alone, by reflecting carefully on the ideas implanted therein by nature.

PRINCIPLE IV.

That the nature of body consists not in weight, nor in hardness, nor colour and so on, but in extension alone.

In this way we shall ascertain that the nature of matter or of body in its universal aspect, does not consist in its being hard, or heavy, or coloured, or one that affects our senses in some other way, but solely in the fact that it is a substance extended in length, breadth and depth. For as regards hardness we do not know anything of it by sense, excepting that the portions of the hard bodies resist the motion of our hands when they come in contact with them ; but if, whenever we moved our hands in some direction, all the bodies in that part retreated with the same velocity as our hands approached them, we should never feel hardness; and yet we have no reason to believe that the bodies which recede in this way would on this account lose what makes them bodies. It follows from this that the nature of body does not consist in hardness. The same reason shows us that weight, colour, and all the other qualities of the kind that is perceived in corporeal matter, may be taken from it, it remaining meanwhile entire : it thus follows that the nature of body depends on none of these.

PRINCIPLE V.

That this truth regarding the nature of body is obscured by prejudices regarding rarefaction and the vacuum.

There still remain two reasons which may cause us to doubt whether the true nature of body consists solely in extension. The first is that prevalent opinion that most bodies are capable of being rarefied and condensed, so that when rarefied they have greater extension than when condensed ; and some have even subtilized to such an extent that they desire to distinguish the substance of a body from its quantity, and its quantity from its extension. The second reason is that when we conceive that there is extension in length, breadth and depth only, we are not in the habit of saying that there is a body, but only space and further empty space, which most people persuade themselves is a mere negation.

PRINCIPLE VI.

In what way rarefaction takes place.

But as regards rarefaction and condensation, whoever will examine his own thoughts and refuse to admit anything which he does not clearly perceive, will not allow that there is anything in these processes but a change of figure [in the body rarefied or condensed]: that is to say, rare bodies are those between whose parts there are many interstices filled with other bodies ; and those are called dense bodies, on the other hand, whose parts, by approaching one another, either render these distances less than they were, or remove them altogether, in which case the body is rendered so dense that it cannot be denser. And yet it does not possess less extension than when the parts occupied a greater space, owing to their being further removed from one another. For we ought not to attribute to a body the extension of the pores or the interstices which its parts do not occupy [when it is rarefied], but to the other bodies which occupy these interstices. Just as when we see a sponge filled with water or some other liquid, we do not suppose that for this reason each part of the sponge is more extended than when it is compressed and dry, but only that its pores are wider, and that it is therefore distributed over a larger space.

Principle VII.

That rarefaction cannot be intelligibly explained in any other way.

I am indeed unable to say why this rarefaction of bodies has been explained by some as the result of augmentation of quantity rather than by the example of the sponge. For although when air or water are rarefied we do not see any of the pores which are rendered large, nor any new body that is added to occupy them, it is yet less consonant with reason to suppose something that is unintelligible in order to give a merely verbal explanation of how bodies are rarefied, than to conclude in consequence of that rarefaction, that there are pores or interstices which become greater, and which are filled with some new body, although we do not perceive this new body with the senses. For there is no reason which obliges us to believe that we should perceive by our senses all the bodies which exist around us. And we perceive that it is very easy to explain rarefaction in this manner though not in any other. And finally it would be undoubtedly contradictory to suppose that any body should be increased by a fresh quantity or fresh extension, without the addition to it of a new extended substance, i.e. a new body. Because it is impossible to conceive any addition of extension or quantity, without the addition of a substance having quantity or extension, as will be more clearly shown below.

PRINCIPLE VIII.

That quantity and number differ only in thought[1] from what has quantity and is numbered.

For quantity differs from extended substance, or number from what is numbered, not in reality but only in our conception. Thus, to take an example, we may consider the whole nature of corporeal substance which is comprised within a space of ten feet, although we do not attend to this measure of ten feet; because it is clear that the thing conceived is the same in any one part of that space as in the whole. And *vice versâ*, we can comprehend the number ten, as also a continuous quantity of ten feet, without attending to any particular determinate substance, because the conception of the number of ten is plainly the same, whether considered in reference to the measure of ten feet, or to any other ten; and we cannot conceive a continuous quantity of ten feet without thinking of some extended substance of which it is the quantity, but yet we can conceive it without thinking of that determinate substance. In reality it is however impossible that even the least part of such quantity or extension can be taken away without taking away likewise an equal amount of substance; on the other hand, not the least part of the substance can be removed without our diminishing its quantity and extension by the same amount.

PRINCIPLE IX.

That corporeal substance, when distinguished from its quantity, is confusedly conceived as something incorporeal.

Although however, some express themselves otherwise on this subject, I cannot think that they regard it otherwise than as I have just said; for when they distinguish substance from extension or quantity, they either mean nothing by the word substance, or they merely form in their minds a confused idea of incorporeal substance which they falsely attribute to corporeal, and leave to extension, which they nevertheless call an accident, that true idea of this corporeal substance, and thus it is easy to see that their words are not in harmony with their thoughts.

[1] ratione.

Principle X.

What space or internal place is.

Space or internal place and the corporeal substance which is contained in it, are not different otherwise than in the mode in which they are conceived of by us. For, in truth, the same extension in length, breadth, and depth, which constitutes space, constitutes body; and the difference between them consists only in the fact that in body we consider extension as particular and conceive it to change just as body changes; in space, on the contrary, we attribute to extension a generic unity, so that after having removed from a certain space the body which occupied it, we do not suppose that we have also removed the extension of that space, because it appears to us that the same extension remains so long as it is of the same magnitude and figure, and preserves the same position in relation to certain other bodies, whereby we determine this space.

Principle XI.

In what sense it may be said that space is not different from corporeal substance.

And it will be easy for us to recognise that the same extension which constitutes the nature of body likewise constitutes the nature of space, nor do the two mutually differ, excepting as the nature of the genus or species differs from the nature of the individual, provided that, in order to discern the idea that we have of any body, such as stone, we reject from it all that is not essential to the nature of body. In the first place, then, we may reject hardness, because if the stone were liquefied or reduced to powder, it would no longer possess hardness, and yet would not cease to be a body; let us in the next place reject colour, because we have often seen stones so transparent that they had no colour; again we reject weight, because we see that fire although very light is yet body; and finally we may reject cold, heat, and all the other qualities of the kind either because they are not considered as in the stone, or else because with the change of their qualities the stone is not for that reason considered to have lost its nature as body. After examination we shall find that there is nothing remaining in the idea of body excepting that it is extended in length, breadth, and depth; and this is comprised in our idea of space, not only of that which is full of body, but also of that which is called a vacuum.

PRINCIPLE XII.

How space is different from body in our mode of conceiving it.

There is, however, some difference in our mode of conceiving them; for if we remove a stone from the space or place where it was, we conceive that the extension of this stone has also been removed from it, because we consider this to be singular, and inseparable from the stone itself. But meantime we suppose that the same extension of place occupied by the stone remains, though the place which it formerly occupied has been taken up with wood, water, air, and any other bodies, or even has been supposed to be empty, because we now consider extension in general, and it appears to us that the same is common to stones, wood, water, air, and all other bodies, and even to a vacuum, if there be such a thing, provided that it is of the same magnitude and figure as before, and preserves the same situation in regard to the external bodies which determine this space.

PRINCIPLE XIII.

What external place is.

The reason of this is that the words place and space signify nothing different from the body which is said to be in a place, and merely designate its magnitude, figure, and situation as regards other bodies. For it is necessary in order to determine this situation to observe certain others which we consider to be immovable; and according as we regard different bodies we may find that the same thing at the same time changes its place, and does not change it. For example, if we consider a man seated at the stern of a vessel when it is carried out to sea, he may be said to be in one place if we regard the parts of the vessel with which he preserves the same situation : and yet he will be found continually to change his position, if regard be paid to the neighbouring shores in relation to which he is constantly receding from one, and approaching another. And further, if we suppose that the earth moves, and that it makes precisely the same way from west to east as the vessel does from east to west, it will again appear to us that he who is seated at the stern does not change his position, because that place is determined by certain immovable points which we imagine to be in the heavens. But if at length we are persuaded that there are no points in the universe that are really immovable, as will presently be shown to be probable, we shall conclude that there is nothing that has a permanent place except in so far as it is fixed by our thought.

Principle XIV.

Wherein place and space differ.

The terms place and space are however different, because place indicates situation more expressly than magnitude or figure; while, on the contrary, we more often think of the latter when we speak of space. For we frequently say that a thing has succeeded to the place of another, although it does not possess exactly either its magnitude or its figure; but we do not for all that mean that it occupies the same space as the other; and when the situation is changed, we say that the place also is changed, although the same magnitude and figure exist as before. And hence if we say that a thing is in a particular place, we simply mean that it is situated in a certain manner in reference to certain other things; and when we add that it occupies a certain space or place, we likewise mean that it is of a definite magnitude or figure [so as exactly to fill the space].

Principle XV.

How external place is rightly taken to be the superficies of the surrounding body.

And thus we never distinguish space from extension in length, breadth and depth; but we sometimes consider place as in the thing placed, and sometimes as outside of it. Internal place is indeed in no way distinguished from space; but we sometimes regard external place as the superficies which immediately surrounds the thing placed in it. And it is to be observed that by superficies we do not here mean any portion of the surrounding body, but merely the extremity which is between the surrounding body and that surrounded, which is but a mode; or that we mean the common surface which is a surface that is not a part of one body rather than of the other, and that it is always considered the same, so long as it retains the same magnitude and figure. For although all the surrounding body with its superficies is changed, we should not imagine that the body which was surrounded by it had for all that changed its place, if it meanwhile preserved the same situation in regard to other bodies that are regarded as immovable. Thus if we suppose that a ship is carried along in one direction by the current of a stream, and is impelled by a contrary wind in another direction in an equal degree, so that its situation is not changed with regard to the banks, we are ready to admit that it remains in the same place although we see that the whole surrounding superficies is in a state of change.

PRINCIPLE XVI.

That it is contrary to reason to say that there is a vacuum or space in which there is absolutely nothing.

As regards a vacuum in the philosophic sense of the word, i.e. a space in which there is no substance, it is evident that such cannot exist, because the extension of space or internal place, is not different from that of body. For, from the mere fact that a body is extended in length, breadth, or depth, we have reason to conclude that it is a substance, because it is absolutely inconceivable that nothing should possess extension, we ought to conclude also that the same is true of the space which is supposed to be void, i.e. that since there is in it extension, there is necessarily also substance.

PRINCIPLE XVII.

That a vacuum, in the ordinary sense, does not exclude all body.

And when we take this word vacuum in its ordinary sense, we do not mean a place or space in which there is absolutely nothing, but only a place in which there are none of those things which we expected to find there. Thus because a pitcher is made to hold water, we say that it is empty when it contains nothing but air; or if there are no fish in a fish-pond, we say that there is nothing in it, even though it be full of water; similarly we say a vessel is empty, when, in place of the merchandise which it was designed to carry, it is loaded only with sand, so that it may resist the impetuous violence of the wind; and finally we say in the same way that a space is empty when it contains nothing sensible, even though it contain created matter and self-existent substance; for we are not wont to consider things excepting those with which our senses succeed in presenting us[1]. And if, in place of keeping in mind what we should comprehend by these words—vacuum and nothing— we afterwards suppose that in the space which is termed vacuum

[1] 'consider bodies near to us excepting in so far as they cause in our organs of sense impressions strong enough to enable us to perceive them.' French version.

there is not only nothing sensible, but nothing at all, we shall fall into the same error as if, because a pitcher is usually termed empty since it contains nothing but air, we were therefore to judge that the air contained in it is not a substantive thing.

Principle XVIII.

How the prejudice concerning the absolute vacuum is to be corrected.

We have almost all lapsed into this error from the beginning of our lives, for, seeing that there is no necessary connection between the vessel and the body it contains, we thought that God at least could remove all the body contained in the vessel without its being necessary that any other body should take its place. But in order that we may be able to correct this error, it is necessary to remark that while there is no connection between the vessel and that particular body which it contains, there is an absolutely necessary one between the concave figure of the vessel and the extension considered generally which must be comprised in this cavity; so that there is not more contradiction in conceiving a mountain without a valley, than such a cavity without the extension which it contains, or this extension without the substance which is extended, because nothing, as has already been frequently remarked, cannot have extension. And therefore, if it is asked what would happen if God removed all the body contained in a vessel without permitting its place being occupied by another body, we shall answer that the sides of the vessel will thereby come into immediate contiguity with one another. For two bodies must touch when there is nothing between them, because it is manifestly contradictory for these two bodies to be apart from one another, or that there should be a distance between them, and yet that this distance should be nothing; for distance is a mode of extension, and without extended substance it cannot therefore exist.

Principle XIX.

That this confirms what was said of rarefaction.

After we have thus remarked that the nature of material substance consists only in its being an extended thing, or that its extension is not different from what has been attributed to space however empty, it is easy to discover that it is impossible that any one of these parts should in any way occupy more space at one time than another, and thus that it may be rarefied otherwise than in the manner explained above; or again it is easy to perceive that there cannot be more matter or corporeal substance in a vessel when it is filled with gold or lead, or any other body that is heavy and hard, than when it only contains air and appears to be empty; for the quantity of the parts of matter does not depend on their weight or hardness, but only on the extension which is always equal in the same vessel.

PRINCIPLE XX.

That from this may be demonstrated the non-existence of atoms.

We also know that there cannot be any atoms or parts of matter which are indivisible of their own nature [as certain philosophers have imagined]. For however small the parts are supposed to be, yet because they are necessarily extended we are always able in thought to divide any one of them into two or more parts; and thus we know that they are divisible. For there is nothing which we can divide in thought, which we do not thereby recognise to be divisible; and therefore if we judged it to be indivisible, our judgment would be contrary to the knowledge we have of the matter. And even should we suppose that God had reduced some portion of matter to a smallness so extreme that it could not be divided into smaller, it would not for all that be properly termed indivisible. For though God had rendered the particle so small that it was beyond the power of any creature to divide it, He could not deprive Himself of His power of division, because it is absolutely impossible that He should lessen His own omnipotence as was said before. And therefore, absolutely speaking, its divisibility remains [to the smallest extended particle] because from its nature it is such.

PRINCIPLE XXI.

That extension of the world is likewise indefinite.

We likewise recognise that this world, or the totality of corporeal substance, is extended without limit, because wherever we imagine a limit we are not only still able to imagine beyond that limit spaces indefinitely extended, but we perceive these to be in reality such as we imagine them, that is to say that they contain in them corporeal substance indefinitely extended. For, as has been already shown very fully, the idea of extension that we perceive in any space whatever is quite evidently the same as the idea of corporeal substance.

PRINCIPLE XXII.

Thus the matter of the heavens and of the earth is one and the same, and there cannot be a plurality of worlds.

It is thus not difficult to infer from all this, that the earth and heavens are formed of the same matter, and that even were there an infinitude of worlds, they would all be formed of this matter; from which it follows that there cannot be a plurality of worlds, because we clearly perceive that the matter whose nature consists in its being an extended substance only, now occupies all the imaginable spaces where these other worlds could alone be, and we cannot find in ourselves the idea of any other matter.

PRINCIPLE XXIII.

That all the variety in matter, or all the diversity of its forms, depends on motion.

There is therefore but one matter in the whole universe, and we know this by the simple fact of its being extended. All the properties which we clearly perceive in it may be reduced to the one, viz. that it can be divided, or moved according to its parts, and consequently is capable of all these affections which we perceive can arise from the motion of its parts. For its partition by thought alone makes no difference to it; but all the variation in matter, or diversity in its forms, depends on motion. This the philosophers have doubtless observed, inasmuch as they have said that nature was the principle of motion and rest, and by nature they understood that by which all corporeal things become such as they are experienced to be.

PRINCIPLE XXIV.

What motion is in common parlance.

But motion (i.e. local motion, for I can conceive no other kind, and do not consider that we ought to conceive any other in nature), in the vulgar sense, is nothing more than the *action by which any body passes from one place to another*. And just as we have remarked above that the same thing may be said to change and not to change its place at the same time, we can say that it moves and does not move at the same time. For he who is seated in a ship setting sail, thinks he is moving when he looks at the shore he has left, and considers it as fixed, but not if he regards the vessel he is on, because he does not change his position in reference to its parts. Likewise, because we are accustomed to think that there is no motion without action and that in rest there is cessation of action, the person thus seated may more properly be said to be in repose than in motion, since he is not conscious of any action in himself.

Principle XXV.

What movement properly speaking is.

But if, looking not to popular usage, but to the truth of the matter, let us consider what ought to be understood by motion according to the truth of the thing; we may say, in order to attribute a determinate nature to it, that it is the *transference of one part of matter or one body from the vicinity of those bodies that are in immediate contact with it, and which we regard as in repose, into the vicinity of others.* By *one body* or by a *part of matter* I understand all that which is transported together, although it may be composed of many parts which in themselves have other motions. And I say that it is the *transportation* and not either the force or the action which transports, in order to show that the motion is always in the mobile thing, not in that which moves; for these two do not seem to me to be accurately enough distinguished. Further, I understand that it is a mode of the mobile thing and not a substance, just as figure is a mode of the figured thing, and repose of that which is at rest.

[The following are the titles of the subsequent propositions which have not been translated.]

Principle XXVI. *That more action is not required for movement than for rest.*

XXVII. *That movement and rest are merely two diverse modes of a body in motion.*

XXVIII. *That movement properly understood may be said only to relate to the bodies contiguous to that in motion.*

XLIV. *Movement is not contrary to movement, but to repose; and determination of a movement in one direction, to its determination on the other.*

XLV. *How it may be determined how much the movement of any bodies is altered by the impact of other bodies, and that by the following rules.*

XLVI. *The first.*

XLVII. „ *second.*

XLVIII. „ *third.*

XLIX. „ *fourth.*

L. „ *fifth.*

LI. „ *sixth.*

LII. „ *seventh.*

LIII. *That the application of these rules is difficult, because each body is affected by many others at the same time.*

LIV. *What are hard bodies, and what fluid bodies.*

LV. *That there is nothing that joins the parts of hard bodies excepting that they are in repose.*

LVI. *That the particles of fluid bodies are moved with equal force in all directions. And the slightest force suffices to move the hard bodies that exist in the fluid.*

LVII. *The proof of the above.*

LVIII. *That if any particles of a fluid move more slowly than a hard body existing in it, the fluid does not behave as a fluid in that part.*

LIX. *That a hard body, pushed by another hard one, does not receive all its motion from it, but a part also from the surrounding fluid.*

LX. *That yet it cannot receive a greater velocity from that fluid than it has from the hard body by which it is struck.*

LXI. *When a fluid body moves as a whole in any direction it necessarily bears with it a hard body which it contains in itself.*

LXII. *That we cannot say that a hard body moves, when it is carried along by a fluid.*

LXIII. *Why there are bodies so hard that although they are so small they are not easily divided by our hands.*

LXIV. *That I do not accept or desire any other principle in Physics than in Geometry or abstract Mathematics, because all the phenomena of nature may be explained by their means, and sure demonstration can be given of them.*

THIRD PART.

OF THE VISIBLE WORLD.

PRINCIPLE I.

That we cannot think too highly of the works of God.

Having now ascertained certain principles of material things which were derived, not from the prejudices of the senses, but from the light of reason, so that we cannot doubt of their truth, it is for us to examine whether from these alone we can explain all the phenomena of nature. And we shall commence with those which are the most general, and on which the others depend, such as the general structure of the visible world. But in order that we may philosophise correctly in this matter, two things are to be observed. The first is that we must ever keep before our minds the infinitude of the power and goodness of God, and not fear to fall into error by imagining His works to be too great, too beautiful, and too perfect, but that, on the contrary, we must take care lest, if we suppose any limits to exist in them of which we have no certain knowledge, we may seem to be insufficiently sensible of the greatness and power of the Creator.

PRINCIPLE II.

That we ought to beware lest we presume too much in supposing ourselves to understand the ends which God set before Himself in creating the world.

The second is that we ought to beware lest we think too highly of ourselves. This we should appear to do if we supposed the universe to have certain limits not presented to our knowledge without at the same time being assured of the fact by divine revelation, which would be making our knowledge extend beyond that which God has made; but this would be even more so if we persuaded ourselves that it was only for us that all things were created by God, or even were we to suppose that by the powers of our mind we could comprehend the ends which He set before Himself in creating the universe.

Principle III.

In what sense it can be said that all things were created for man.

For although it may be a pious thought, as far as Morals are concerned, to believe that God has created all things for us in as far as that incites us to a greater gratitude and affection toward Him, and although it is in some respect true, because there is nothing created from which we cannot derive some use, if it be but the exercise of our minds in considering it and the being incited to worship God by its means, it is yet not at all probable that all things have been created for us in such a manner that God has had no other end in creating them. And it seems to me that such a supposition would be certainly ridiculous and inept in reference to questions of Physics, for we cannot doubt that an infinitude of things exist, or did exist, though now they have ceased to exist, which have never been beheld or comprehended by man and which have never been of any use to him.

[The following are the titles of the subsequent propositions which have not been translated.]

Principle IV. *Of phenomena or experiments and what is their use in philosophy.*

V. *What is the ratio between the distances and magnitudes of sun, earth, and moon?*

VI. *What is the distance between the other planets and the sun?*

VII. *That we may suppose the fixed stars to be as remote as we like.*

VIII. *That the earth viewed from the heavens would not appear otherwise than as a planet less than Jupiter or Saturn.*

IX. *That the sun and fixed stars shine by their own light.*

X. *That the moon and the other planets derive light from the sun.*

XI.   *That the reason of the light of the earth and that of the planets is the same.*

XII.   *That the moon, when it is new, is illuminated by the earth.*

XIII.   *That the sun may be placed in the number of fixed stars, and the earth in the number of the planets.*

XIV.   *That the fixed stars remain always in the same position relatively to one another, but not so the planets.*

XV.   *That these same phenomena of the planets may be explained by various hypotheses.*

XVI.   *That the hypothesis of Ptolemy does not satisfactorily explain the phenomena.*

XVII.   *That the hypotheses of Copernicus and Tycho do not differ if they are regarded simply as hypotheses.*

XVIII.   *That in words Tycho ascribes less, but in reality more, motion to the earth than does Copernicus.*

XIX.   *That I deny the movement of the earth more carefully than Copernicus, and more truthfully than Tycho.*

XX.   *That we must suppose the fixed stars to be extremely far from Saturn.*

XXI.   *That the sun, like flame, consists of a material which is very mobile, but for all that it does not pass from one place to another.*

XXII.   *That the sun differs from the flame inasmuch as it has no need of aliment.*

XXIII.   *That all the fixed stars do not turn in the same sphere, but each one has a vast space around it void of other fixed stars.*

XXIV.   *That the heavens are fluid.*

XXV.   *That the heavens carry with them all the bodies that they contain.*

XXVI.   *That the earth rests in its own heaven, but that it is still carried along by it.*

XXVII.   *That the same may be considered true of all the planets.*

XXVIII.   *The earth, properly speaking, does not move, nor do any planets, although they are carried along.*

XXIX. *That movement must not be attributed to the earth, even in speaking improperly and according to vulgar usage; but we may correctly say that other planets are moved.*

XXX. *All the planets are carried round the sun by the heaven containing them.*

XXXI. *How the planets are carried along.*

XXXII. *How also are the spots on the sun.*

XXXIII. *How the earth also revolves round its own centre, and the moon round the earth.*

XXXIV. *The movement of the heavens is not perfectly circular.*

XXXV. *Of the aberrations of the planets latitudinally.*

XXXVI. *Of the longitudinal motion.*

XXXVII. *That all phenomena can be explained very easily by this hypothesis.*

XXXVIII. *According to the hypothesis of Tycho it ought to be said that the earth is moved round its own centre.*

XXXIX. *And it also is moved annually round the sun.*

XL. *That no change of position in the earth affects a change of aspect in regard to the fixed stars, on account of the greatness of their distance.*

XLI. *That this distance of the fixed stars is requisite for the motion of the comets which, it is now agreed, are celestial bodies.*

XLII. *All things that are seen in the earth may be counted as phenomena, but it is not necessary to consider them as a whole to begin with.*

XLIII. *That it can hardly be otherwise than that the causes from which all phenomena are clearly deduced are true.*

XLIV. *That I yet merely desire to assert that those which I set forth are to be regarded as hypotheses.*

XLV. *That I shall also here assume some propositions which are agreed to be false.*

XLVI. *The propositions which I here assume as explaining all phenomena.*

LXVI. *That the movement of these vortices must be somewhat deflected, in such a way that they work in harmony.*

LXVII. *That the poles of two vortices cannot touch one another.*

LXVIII. *That these vortices are of unequal magnitudes.*

LXIX. *That the matter of the first element flows from the poles of each vortex towards the centre, and from the centre toward the other parts.*

LXX. *That the same thing cannot be understood regarding the matter of the second element.*

LXXI. *What is the reason of this difference?*

LXXII. *How the matter which composes the sun is moved.*

LXXIII. *That there are various inequalities in the position of the body of the sun.*

LXXIV. *That there are various inequalities in the motion of its matter.*

LXXV. *That these inequalities do not prevent its figure being round.*

LXXVI. *Of the movements of the first element while it moves between the globules of the second.*

LXXVII. *How the light of the sun diffuses itself not only towards the ecliptic, but also towards the poles.*

LXXVIII. *How it diffuses itself towards the ecliptic.*

LXXIX. *How easily, on the motion of one small body, others as far remote as possible from it are moved.*

LXXX. *How the light of the sun tends towards the poles.*

LXXXI. *Whether its force is equal at the poles and at the ecliptic.*

LXXXII. *That the globules of the second element near the sun are smaller and are moved more quickly than those more remote up to a certain distance, beyond which all are of equal magnitude and for that reason are moved more quickly as they are farther from the sun.*

LXXXIII. *Why those farthest away are moved more quickly than those somewhat less far off.*

LXXXIV. *Why also those nearest to the sun are borne along more quickly than those slightly further off.*

LXXXV. *Why the same nearest to the sun are smaller than those more remote.*

LXXXVI. *Whence it is that the globules of the second element are moved in different ways at once, from which it follows that they are made clearly spherical.*

LXXXVII. *That there are various degrees of speed amongst the various particles of the first element.*

LXXXVIII. *That these minute particles of it that have the smallest velocity easily transfer what they have to others, and adhere one to another.*

LXXXIX. *That such minute particles adhering to one another are chiefly found in that matter of the first element which is borne from the poles to the centres of the vortices.*

XC. *What is the form of those minute particles which will henceforward be called striated particles?*

XCI. *That these particles coming from opposite poles are twisted contrariwise.*

XCII. *That there are only three stripes[1] in them.*

XCIII. *Among these striated particles and among the smallest of all there are various ones of different magnitudes in the case of the first element.*

XCIV. *How from these particles spots are generated on the surface of the sun or the stars.*

XCV. *From this the special properties of the spots may be learned.*

XCVI. *Why these spots are dissolved and new ones generated.*

XCVII. *How in the extremities of certain ones the colours of the rainbow appear.*

XCVIII. *How the spots are turned into faculae[2] or contrariwise.*

XCIX. *Into what kind of particles spots are dissolved.*

---

[1] 'strias' Latin.   [2] 'faculas' Latin; 'flames' French version.

C. *How from these the ether round the sun and stars is generated. And that this ether and these spots are referred to the third element.*

CI. *That the production and dissolution of spots depend on very uncertain causes.*

CII. *How the same spot can cover some one whole star.*

CIII. *Why the sun sometimes appears more obscure, and why the apparent magnitudes of certain stars change.*

CIV. *Why some fixed stars disappear or suddenly appear without warning.*

CV. *That there are many passages in the spots through which the striated particles easily pass.*

CVI. *What is the disposition of these passages, or why the striated particles cannot come back through them.*

CVII. *Why also those which come from one pole do not pass through the same passages as those which come from another.*

CVIII. *How the matter of the first element flows through those passages.*

CIX. *That other passages also intersect these crosswise.*

CX. *That the light of a star can hardly pass through a spot.*

CXI. *Description of a star unexpectedly appearing.*

CXII. *Description of a star slowly disappearing.*

CXIII. *That in all spots many of these passages are excavated by striated particles.*

CXIV. *That the same star can alternately appear and disappear.*

CXV. *That sometimes the whole vortex, in whose centre a star is, can be destroyed.*

CXVI. *How it can be destroyed before many spots have gathered around its star.*

CXVII. *How there can be very many spots around a star before its vortex is destroyed.*

CXVIII. *How these many spots are generated.*

[1] trabes, Latin; chevrons de feu, French.

PART IV.

OF THE EARTH.

[The titles only are given of the first CLXXXVII propositions.]

PRINCIPLE I. *That a false hypothesis which we have already used should be retained to explain the true nature of things.*

II. *What is the generation of the earth according to that hypothesis.*

III. *The division of the earth into three regions and the description of the first.*

IV. *Description of the second.*

V. *Description of the third.*

VI. *That the particles of the third element which are in this third region ought to be somewhat large.*

VII. *That these can be changed by the first and second element.*

VIII. *That they are greater than the globules of the second element, but less solid and less agitated than they.*

IX. *That from the beginning they have lain upon one another round the earth.*

X. *That various interstices of matter of the first and second element have been left around them.*

XI. *That the globules of the second element were originally the smaller, the nearer they were to the centre of the earth.*

XII. *That they have had narrower passages between them.*

XIII. *That the thicker were not always below the thinner.*

XIV.   *Of the first formation of various bodies in the third region of the earth.*

XV.   *Of the actions by whose agency these bodies were produced, and first of the general motion of the celestial globules.*

XVI.   *Of the first effect of this first action, that it makes bodies transparent.*

XVII.   *How the solid and hard body can have enough passages to transmit rays of light.*

XVIII.   *Of the second effect of this first action, viz. that it separates some bodies from others and purifies liquids.*

XIX.   *Of the third effect, that it makes drops of liquids round.*

XX.   *Explanation of the second action which is called gravity.*

XXI.   *That all parts of the earth, if they are considered singly, are not heavy, but light.*

XXII.   *In what the lightness of heavenly matter consists.*

XXIII.   *How all parts of the earth are drawn downwards by that heavenly matter, and thus become heavy.*

XXIV.   *How much gravity there is in each body.*

XXV.   *That this quantity does not answer to the quantity of matter in each body.*

XXVI.   *Why it is not in their natural places that bodies gravitate.*

XXVII.   *That gravity depresses bodies towards the centre of the earth.*

XXVIII.   *Of the third action, which is light; how it moves the particles of the air.*

XXIX.   *Of the fourth, which is heat; what it is, and how it continues when light is taken away.*

XXX.   *Why it penetrates further than light.*

XXXI.   *Why it rarefies almost all bodies.*

XXXII.   *Why the highest region of the earth was first divided into two different bodies.*

^{1} Diagram is shown here.

---

[1] Made from vitriol.

CII. *Why the flame from spirits of wine does not burn the wick.*

CIII. *Why spirits of wine burns most easily.*

CIV. *Why water with the greatest difficulty.*

CV. *Why the force of great fires is increased by water or salt thrown on them.*

CVI. *What sort of bodies are those which are easily burned.*

CVII. *Why certain bodies may take fire, others not.*

CVIII. *Why fire remains for some time in red hot coals.*

CIX. *Of gunpowder made from sulphur, nitre, and charcoal, and first of sulphur.*

CX. *Of nitre.*

CXI. *Of the combination of sulphur and nitre.*

CXII. *Of the motion of the particles of nitre.*

CXIII. *Why the flame of this powder is greatly dilated, and especially acts towards objects above.*

CXIV. *Of charcoal.*

CXV. *Of the grains of this powder in which its special force consists.*

CXVI. *Of lanterns burning for a very long time.*

CXVII. *Of the other effects of fire.*

CXVIII. *What bodies brought near it melt and boil.*

CXIX. *What bodies dry up and become hard.*

CXX. *Of waters burning, insipid, and acid.*

CXXI. *Of sublimates and oils.*

CXXII. *That when the degree of fire is altered, its effect is altered.*

CXXIII. *Of lime.*

CXXIV. *Of glass, how it is made.*

CXXV. *How its particles are joined together.*

CXXVI. *Why it is liquid when it is white-hot and easily assumes all shapes.*

CXXVII. *Why when it is cold it is very hard.*

CXXVIII.   *Why very brittle.*

CXXIX.   *Why its brittleness diminishes if it is cooled slowly.*

CXXX.   *Why it is transparent.*

CXXXI.   *How it becomes coloured.*

CXXXII.   *Why it is rigid like a bow, and in general why rigid bodies, when they are bent, of their own accord return to their former shape.*

CXXXIII.   *Of the magnet. Repetition of those things said before which are required for its explanation.*

CXXXIV.   *That there are no passages in air or in water fit for receiving striated particles.*

CXXXV.   *That there are also none in any bodies of the exterior of the earth, except in iron.*

CXXXVI.   *Why there are these passages in iron.*

CXXXVII.   *Why they are also in single filings[1] of it.*

CXXXVIII.   *How these passages are made fit to admit striated particles coming from either direction.*

CXXXIX.   *What is the nature of a magnet.*

CXL.   *How steel[2] and any sort of iron is made by melting.*

CXLI.   *Why steel is very hard, rigid, and brittle.*

CXLII.   *What is the difference between steel and other iron.*

CXLIII.   *How steel is tempered.*

CXLIV.   *What is the difference between the passages of a magnet, steel, and iron.*

CXLV.   *Enumeration of the properties of magnetic virtue.*

CXLVI.   *How striated particles flow through the passages of the earth.*

CXLVII.   *That they flow with greater difficulty through air, water and the exterior of the earth than through the interior.*

CXLVIII.   *That they go more easily through a magnet than through other bodies of the exterior of the earth.*

CXLIX.   *What the poles of a magnet are.*

[1] ramentis.   [2] chalybs.

CL.   *Why these poles turn towards the earth's poles.*

CLI.   *Why also they slope at a certain angle towards its centre.*

CLII.   *Why one magnet turns and inclines itself towards another magnet in the same way as towards the earth.*

CLIII.   *Why two magnets approach one another, and what is the sphere of activity of each.*

CLIV.   *Why they sometimes retreat from one another.*

CLV.   *Why parts of the segments of a magnet, which before being cut were joined, also retreat from one another.*

CLVI.   *Why two points which formerly were contiguous in the same magnet are poles of a different virtue.*

CLVII.   *Why there is the same force in each part of a magnet and in the whole.*

CLVIII.   *Why a magnet communicates its force to iron brought near it.*

CLIX.   *Why iron according to the various ways in which it is brought near to the magnet receives the force in different ways.*

CLX.   *Why an oblong piece of iron does not receive it except along its length.*

CLXI.   *Why a magnet loses nothing of its force, although it communicates its power to iron.*

CLXII.   *Why this force is communicated very quickly to iron, but is fixed in it by length of time.*

CLXIII.   *Why steel is fitter to receive it than baser iron.*

CLXIV.   *Why more is communicated to it by a more perfect magnet than by a less perfect.*

CLXV.   *Why even the earth itself gives magnetic force to iron.*

CLXVI.   *Why the magnetic force is weaker in the earth than in small magnets.*

CLXVII.   *Why needles touched by a magnet always have the poles of their virtue in their extremities.*

CLXVIII.   *Why poles of magnetic virtue do not always point accurately to the poles of the earth, but decline from them variously.*

CLXIX.   *Why even sometimes this declination alters with time.*

CLXX.   *Why in a magnet set up upon one of its poles, it can be smaller than when its poles are equidistant from the earth.*

CLXXI.   *Why a magnet attracts iron.*

CLXXII.   *Why an armed magnet sustains much more iron than a naked one.*

CLXXIII.   *Why its poles, although contrary, help each other to sustain iron.*

CLXXIV.   *Why the spinning of a wheel of iron is not hindered by the force of a magnet from which it is hung.*

CLXXV.   *How and why the force of one magnet increases or diminishes the force of another.*

CLXXVI.   *Why a magnet, however strong, cannot attract iron not near to it from a weaker magnet.*

CLXXVII.   *Why a weak magnet or iron can drag away iron near to it from a stronger magnet.*

CLXXVIII.   *Why in these northern regions the south pole of the magnet is stronger than the north.*

CLXXIX.   *Of the things which can be observed in iron filings scattered round a magnet.*

CLXXX.   *Why an iron plate joined to the pole of the magnet hinders its force of attracting or turning iron.*

CLXXXI.   *Why the interposition of no other body hinders this.*

CLXXXII.   *Why the unsuitable position of a magnet gradually diminishes its strength.*

CLXXXIII.   *Why rust, dampness and mouldiness also diminish it, and a strong fire entirely removes them.*

CLXXXIV.   *Of the force of attraction in amber, wax, resin and similar things.*

CLXXXV.   *What is the cause of this attraction in glass.*

CLXXXVI.   *The same cause of this is seen in the other bodies also.*

CLXXXVII.   *From what has been said we see what may be the causes of all other remarkable results which are usually referred to occult qualities.*

Principle CLXXXVIII.

Of what is to be borrowed from disquisitions on animals and man in order to advance the knowledge of material things.

I should add no more to this Fourth Part of the Principles of Philosophy, did I (as I had formerly in my mind) purpose writing other sections, viz. a Fifth and a Sixth Part, the fifth treating of living things, that is of animals and plants, and the sixth of man. But because I am not yet quite clear about all of the matters of which I should like to treat in these two last parts, and do not know whether I am likely to have sufficient leisure [or be able to make the experiments necessary] to complete them, I shall here add a little about the objects of the senses in order not to delay the earlier part too long to prevent [their lacking completeness or] anything being amissing which I should have reserved for the latter. For up to this point I have described the earth, and all the visible world, as if it were simply a machine in which there was nothing to consider but [the] figure and movements [of its parts], and yet our senses cause other things to be presented to us, such as colours, smells, sounds, and other such things, of which, if I did not speak, it might be thought that I had omitted the main part of the explanation of the objects of nature.

Principle CLXXXIX.

What sensation[1] is, and how it operates.

We must know, therefore, that although the mind of man informs[2] the whole body, it yet has its principal seat in the brain, and it is there that it not only understands and imagines, but also perceives ; and this by means of the nerves which are extended like filaments from the brain to all the other members, with which they are so connected that we can hardly touch any part of the human body without causing the extremities of some of the nerves spread over it to be moved; and this motion passes to the other extremities of those nerves which are collected in the brain round the seat of the soul, as I have just explained quite fully enough in the fourth chapter of the Dioptrics. But the movements which are thus excited in the brain by the nerves, affect in diverse ways the soul or mind, which is intimately connected with the brain, according to the diversity of the motions themselves. And the diverse

---

[1] sensus. [2] ' is united with,' French version.

affections of our mind, or thoughts that immediately arise from these motions, are called perceptions of the senses[1], or, in common language, sensations[2].

Principle CXC.

The different kinds of sensation; and firstly of the internal, that is, of the passions or affections[3] of the mind and of the natural appetites.

The diversities of these sensations depend firstly on the diversity in the nerves themselves, and then on the diversities of the motions which occur in the individual nerves. We have not, however, so many individual senses as individual nerves; it is enough merely to distinguish seven chief different kinds, two of which belong to internal senses, and five to the external. The nerves which extend to the stomach, œsophagus, the fauces, and the other interior parts that serve for the satisfaction of our natural wants, constitute one of our internal senses, which is called the natural appetite[4]. The minute nerves, which extend to the heart and the neighbourhood of the heart, operate in the other internal sense which embraces all the emotions[5] of the mind or passions, and affections such as joy, sadness, love, hate and the like. For, to take an example, when the blood is pure and well-tempered, so that it dilates in the heart more readily and strongly than usual, this so enlarges and moves the little nerves scattered around the orifices, that there is thence a corresponding movement in the brain which affects the mind with a certain natural sense of cheerfulness ; and as often as these same nerves are moved in the same way, even although it be from other causes, they excite in us this same feeling[6]. Thus the imagination of the fruition of some good does not contain in itself the sensation of joy, but it causes the animal spirits to pass from the brain to the muscles in which these nerves are inserted ; and thus dilating the orifices of the heart, it causes these small nerves to move in the manner which necessarily produces the sensation of joy. Thus, when we are given news the mind first judges of it, and if it is good it rejoices with that intellectual joy which is independent of any emotion[7] of the body, and which the Stoics did not deny to their wise man [although they wished to regard him as free from all passion]. But as soon as this spiritual joy proceeds [from the

---

[1] sensuum perceptiones.   [2] sensus.   [3] affectibus.
[4] appetitus naturalis.   [5] commotiones.   [6] sensus, sentiment de joye.
[7] commotio.

understanding] to the imagination, the spirits flow from the brain to the muscles about the heart and these excite a movement in the small nerves by which another motion is excited in the brain which gives the soul the sensation of animal joy[1]. In the same way when the blood is so thick that it flows badly into the ventricles of the heart, and is not there sufficiently dilated, it excites in the same nerves a movement quite different from the preceding, which, communicated to the brain, gives a sensation of sadness to the mind, although it is itself perhaps ignorant of the cause of the sadness. And the other causes [which move these little nerves in the same way] may likewise give the same sensation to the soul. But the other movements of the same small nerves produce other affections, such as those of love, hate, fear, anger, &c. in as far as they are merely affections or passions of the mind, that is, in as far as they are confused thoughts which the mind does not have from itself alone, but because it is intimately united to the body, receiving its impressions therefrom. For there is the greatest difference between these passions and the distinct thoughts which we have of what ought to be loved, chosen, or shunned [although they are often found together]. The natural appetites such as hunger, thirst, &c., are likewise sensations excited in the mind by means of the nerves of the stomach, fauces, &c. and are entirely different from the will which we have to eat, drink, &c. [and to do all that we think proper for the conservation of the body]; but because this will or appetition nearly always accompanies them, they are called appetites.

Principle CXCI.

Of the external senses and first of all of the sense of touch.

As regards the external senses, everyone acknowledges five, because there are five different kinds of objects that stimulate the nerves which are their organs, and because there is the same number of kinds of confused thoughts excited in the soul by these motions in the nerves. In the first place there are nerves terminating in the skin all over the body. The skin serves as a medium by which the nerves can come in contact with any material body whatever, and be moved by these wholes, in one way by their hardness, in another by their gravity, in another by their heat, in another by their humidity &c.; and these nerves excite as many different

---

[1] laetitia animalis.

sensations in the mind as there are different modes by which they are moved, or their ordinary motion is prevented, and from this a corresponding number of tactile qualities derive their names. Besides this, when these nerves are moved a little more vehemently than usual, and yet in such a way that our body is in nowise injured, this causes a sense of gratification which is naturally agreeable to the mind, inasmuch as it gives evidence of the powers of the body to which it is closely joined. But if this action [be strong enough to] cause our body to be in some way hurt, that gives us the sensation of pain. And in this way we see why corporeal pleasure and pain, though absolutely contrary sensations, are almost similar in the objects causing them.

PRINCIPLE CXCII.

Of Taste.

In the next place the other nerves spread over the tongue and the neighbouring parts, are diversely moved by the particles of the bodies which are separated from one another and float in the saliva in the mouth, and thus cause the diverse tastes to be felt according to the diversity of their own figures.

PRINCIPLE CXCIII.

Of Smell.

In the third place two nerves or appendages to the brain, for they do not go beyond the skull, are moved by the corporeal particles separated and flying in the air—not indeed by any particles whatsoever, but only by those which, when drawn into the nostrils, are subtle and lively enough to enter the pores of the bones we call the spongy, and thus to reach the nerves. And from the diverse motions of these particles, the diverse sensations of smell arise.

PRINCIPLE CXCIV.

Of Hearing.

Fourthly, two other nerves hidden in the inward cavities of the ears receive the tremors and vibrations of the whole circumjacent air, for the air agitating the small membranes of the tympanum at the same time disturbs a chain of little bones which are attached, and to which these nerves adhere, and from the diversity of these movements the sensations of different sounds arise.

Principle CXCV.

Of Sight.

Finally the extremities of the optic nerves, composing the covering of the eyes called the retina, are not moved by the air, nor by any other material object, but only by the globules of the second element, from which we derive the sense of light and colours, as I have already sufficiently explained in the Dioptrics and Meteors.

Principle CXCVI.

That the soul does not perceive excepting in as far as it is in the brain.

It is however easily proved that the soul feels those things that affect the body not in so far as it is in each member of the body, but only in so far as it is in the brain, where the nerves by their movements convey to it the diverse actions of the external objects which touch the parts of the body [in which they are inserted]. For, in the first place, there are many maladies which, though they affect the brain alone, yet either disorder or altogether take away from us the use of our senses; just like sleep itself which affects the brain alone, and yet every day takes from us during a great part of our time the faculty of perception, which is afterwards restored to us on awakening. Secondly, from the fact that though the brain be healthy [as well as the members in which the organs of the external senses are to be found], if the paths by which the nerves pass from the external parts to the brain are obstructed, that sensation is lost in these external parts of the body. And finally we sometimes feel pain as though it were in certain of our members, and yet its cause is not in these members where it is felt, but in others through which the nerves pass that extend to the brain from the parts where the pain is felt. And this I could prove by innumerable experiments; here, however, one will suffice. When a girl suffering from a serious affection of the hand was visited by the surgeon, her eyes were usually bandaged lest seeing the dressing should have a bad effect upon her. After some days, as gangrene set in, her arm had to be cut off from the elbow and several linen cloths tied together were substituted in place of the amputated limb, in such a way that she was quite ignorant of what had been done; meanwhile, however, she had various pains, sometimes in one of the fingers of the hand which was cut off, and sometimes in another. This could clearly only happen because the nerves which previously had been carried all the way from the brain to the hand, and afterwards terminated in the arm near the elbow, were there affected in the same way as it was their function to be stimulated for the purpose of impressing on the mind residing in the brain the sensation of pain in this and that finger. [And this shows clearly that pain in the hand is not felt by the mind inasmuch as it is in the hand, but as it is in the brain.]

Principle CXCVII.

That mind is of such a nature that from the motion of the body alone the various sensations can be excited in it.

It may, in the next place, be [easily] proved that our mind is of such a nature that the motions which are in the body are alone sufficient to cause it to have all sorts of thoughts, which do not give us any image of any of the motions which give rise to them; and specially that there may be excited in it those confused thoughts called feelings or sensations[1]. For [first of all] we observe that words, whether uttered by the voice or merely written, excite in our minds all sorts of thoughts and emotions. On the same paper, with the same pen and ink, by moving the point of the pen ever so little over the paper in a certain way, we can trace letters which bring to the minds of our readers thoughts of battles, tempests or furies, and the emotions of indignation and sadness; while if the pen be moved in another way, hardly different, thoughts may be given of quite a different kind, viz. those of quietude, peace, pleasantness, and the quite opposite passions of love and joy. Someone will perhaps reply that writing and speech do not immediately excite any passions in the mind, or imaginations of things different from the letters and sounds, but simply so to speak various acts of the understanding; and from these the mind, making them the occasion[2], then forms for itself the imaginations of a variety of things. But what shall we say of the sensations of what is painful and pleasurable? If a sword moved towards our body cuts it, from this alone pain results which is certainly not less different from the local movement of the sword or of the part of the body

---

[1] sensus, sive sensationes.
[2] 'understanding the meaning of these words.' French version.

which is cut, than are colour or sound or smell or taste. And therefore, as we see clearly that the sensation of pain is easily excited in us from the fact alone that certain parts of our body are locally disturbed by the contact with certain other bodies, we may conclude that our mind is of such a nature that certain local motions can excite in it all the affections belonging to all the other senses.

Principle CXCVIII.

That there is nothing known of external objects by the senses but their figure, magnitude or motion.

Besides this, we observe in the nerves no difference which may cause us to judge that some convey to the brain from the organs of the external sense any one thing rather than another, nor again that anything is conveyed there excepting the local motion of the nerves themselves. And we see that this local motion excites in us not alone the sensations of pleasure or pain, but also the sensations of sound and light. For if we receive a blow in the eye hard enough to cause the vibration to reach the retina, we see myriads of sparks which are yet not outside our eye ; and when we place our finger on our ear to stop it, we hear a murmuring sound whose cause cannot be attributed to anything but the agitation of the air which is shut up within it. Finally we can likewise frequently observe that heat and the other sensible qualities, inasmuch as they are in objects, and also the forms of these bodies which are purely material, such as e.g. the forms of fire, are produced in them by the motions of certain other bodies, and that these again also produce other motions in other bodies. And we can very well conceive how the movement of one body can be caused by that of another, and diversified by the size, figure, and situation of its parts, but we can in nowise understand how these same things (viz. size, figure and motion) can produce something entirely different in nature from themselves, such as are those substantial forms and real qualities which many suppose to exist in bodies ; nor likewise can we understand how these forms or qualities possess the force adequate to cause motion in other bodies. But since we know that our mind is of such a nature that the diverse motions of body suffice to produce in it all the diverse sensations that it has, and as we see by experience that some of the sensations are really caused by such motions, though we do not find anything but these movements to pass through the organs of the external senses to the brain, we may conclude that we in no way likewise apprehend that in external objects like light, colour, smell, taste, sound, heat, cold, and the other tactile qualities, or what we call their substantial forms, there is anything but the various dispositions of these objects which have the power of moving our nerves in various ways.

Principle CXCIX.

That there is no phenomenon in nature which has not been dealt with in this treatise.

And thus by a simple enumeration it may be deduced that there is no phenomenon in nature whose treatment has been omitted in this treatise.   For there is nothing that can be counted as a phenomenon of nature, excepting what we are able to perceive by the senses.   And with the exception of motion, magnitude and figure [or the situation of the parts of each body], which things I have explained as they exist in every body, we perceive nothing outside us by means of our senses, but light, colours, smells, tastes, sounds and the tactile qualities; and of all these I have just proved that they are nothing more, as far as is known to us, than certain dispositions of objects consisting of magnitude, figure, and motion [so well have I demonstrated that there is nothing in all the visible world, in as far as it is merely visible or sensible, but the things I have there explained].

Principle CC.

That there are no principles in this treatise which are not accepted by all men; and that this philosophy is not new, but is the most ancient and most common of all.

But I likewise desire that it should be observed that although I have here tried to give an explanation of the whole nature of material things, I have nevertheless made use of no principle which has not been approved by Aristotle and by all the other philosophers of every time; so that this philosophy, instead of being new, is the most ancient and common of all.   For I have only considered the figure, motion and magnitude of each body, and examined what must follow from their mutual concourse according to the laws of mechanics, confirmed as they are by certain and daily experience. But no one ever doubted that bodies were mixed and have diverse magnitudes and figures, according to the diversity of which their motions also vary, and that from mutual collision those that are larger are divided into many smaller, and thus change their figure. We have experience of this not alone by one single sense, but by several, e.g. by touch, sight and hearing; we also distinctly imagine and understand this. This cannot be said of other things that come under our senses, such as colours, sounds, and the like, which are perceived not by means of several senses, but by single ones; for their images are always confused in our minds, nor do we know what they are.

Principle CCI.

That certain sensible bodies are composed of insensible particles.

I consider that there are many particles in each body which cannot be perceived by our senses, and this will perhaps not be approved by those who take their senses as a measure of the things they can know. [But it seems to me to be doing great wrong to human reason if we do not consider that knowledge goes beyond the seen]; for no one can doubt that there are bodies so small that they cannot be perceived by any of our senses, if only we consider what is being added each moment to those bodies which increase little by little, and what is removed from those which diminish in the same fashion. We day by day see a tree grow, and it is impossible to comprehend how it becomes larger than it was before, unless by conceiving that some body is added to it. But who has ever observed by means of the senses what are the small bodies which are each day added to the plant that grows? Those at least who hold quantity to be finitely divisible should acknowledge that the particles may become so small as to be absolutely imperceptible. And indeed it should not be wondered at that we are unable to perceive very minute bodies, for the nerves, which must be moved by objects in order to cause us to perceive, are not very minute, but are like small cords which consist of a quantity of yet smaller fibres, and thus they cannot be moved by the minutest of bodies. Nor do I think that anyone who uses his reason will deny that we do much better to judge of what takes place in small bodies which their minuteness alone prevents us from perceiving, by what we see occurring in those that we do perceive [and thus explain all that is in nature, as I have tried to do in this treatise], than, in order to explain certain given things, to invent all sorts of novelties, that have no relation to those that we perceive [such as are first matter, substantial forms, and all the great array of qualities which many are in the habit of assuming, any of which it is more difficult to understand than all the things which we profess to explain by their means].

PRINCIPLE CCII.

That the philosophy of Democritus is not less different from ours than from the vulgar[1].

But Democritus also imagined that there were certain corpuscles that had various figures, sizes and motions, from the heaping together and mutual concourse of which all sensible bodies took their origin; and nevertheless his philosophy is by common consent universally rejected. To this I reply that it never was rejected by anyone because in it he considered bodies smaller than those that can be perceived by the senses, and attributed to them various sizes, figures and motions, for no one can doubt that there are in reality many such, as has been already shown. But this philosophy was rejected in the first place, because it presupposed certain indivisible corpuscles, which hypothesis I also completely reject; in the second place it was rejected because Democritus imagined a void about them, which I demonstrate to be an impossibility; in the third place because he attributed to them gravity, the existence of which I deny in any body in so far as it is considered by itself, because this is a quality depending on the relationship in respect of situation and motion which bodies bear to one another; and finally because he had not explained in detail how all things arose from the concourse of the corpuscles alone, or, if he explained it in regard to certain cases, his reasoning was not in all cases by any means coherent [or such as was capable of proving to us that all nature can be explained in the same way]. If we are to judge of his opinions from what has been preserved regarding his opinions, this at least is the verdict we must give on his philosophy. I leave it to others to judge as to whether what I have written in philosophy possesses sufficient coherence in itself [and whether it is fertile enough in yielding us conclusions. And inasmuch as because the consideration of figure, magnitude and motion has been admitted by Aristotle and all others, as well as by Democritus, and as I reject all that the

---

[1] 'from that of Aristotle and others.' French version.

latter has supposed with this one exception, while I reject practically
all that has been supposed by the others, it is clear that this method
of philosophising has no more affinity with that of Democritus than
with any of the other particular sects.]

Principle CCIII.

How we may arrive at a knowledge of the figures [*magnitudes*]
and motions of the insensible particles of bodies.

But since I assign determinate figures, magnitudes and motions
to the insensible particles of bodies, as if I had seen them, whereas
I admit that they do not fall under the senses, someone will perhaps
demand how I have come to my knowledge of them. To[1] this I
reply that I first considered generally the most simple and best
understood principles implanted in our understanding by nature,
and examined the principal differences that could be found between
the magnitudes, figures and situations of bodies insensible on
account of their smallness alone, and what sensible effects could be
produced by the various ways in which they impinge on one another.
And finally, when I found like effects in the bodies perceived by our
senses, I considered that they might have been produced from a
similar concourse of such bodies, especially as no other mode of
explaining them could be suggested. And for this end the example
of certain bodies made by art was of service to me, for I can
see no difference between these and natural bodies, excepting that
the effects of machines depend for the most part on the operation
of certain instruments, which, since men necessarily make them, must
always be large enough to be capable of being easily perceived
by the senses. The effects of natural causes, on the other hand,
almost always depend on certain organs minute enough to escape
every sense. And it is certain that there are no rules in mechanics
which do not hold good in physics, of which mechanics forms a part
or species [so that all that is artificial is also natural] ; for it is not
less natural for a clock, made of the requisite number of wheels, to

---

[1] The first clause of this sentence is amplified in the French version as
follows : ' To this I reply that I first considered generally all the most clear and
distinct notions of material things to be found in our understanding, and that
finding none but those we possess of figures, magnitudes and motions, and the
rules whereby these three things can be diversified by one another, which rules
are the principles of Geometry and Mechanics, I judged that all the knowledge
man can have of nature must be derived from this source alone, because all the
notions that we have of sensible things, being confused and obscure, cannot
serve to give us any acquaintanceship with anything outside ourselves, but may
on the other hand serve to impede it.'

indicate the hours, than for a tree which has sprung from this or that seed, to produce a particular fruit. Accordingly, just as those who apply themselves to the consideration of automata, when they know the use of a certain machine and see some of its parts, easily infer from these the manner in which others which they have not seen are made, so from considering the sensible effects and parts of natural bodies, I have endeavoured to discover the nature of the imperceptible causes and insensible parts contained in them.

Principle CCIV.

That touching the things which our senses do not perceive, it is sufficient to explain what the possibilities are about the nature of their existence, though perhaps they are not what we describe them to be [*and this is all that Aristotle has tried to do*].

But here it may be said that although I have shown how all natural things can be formed, we have no right to conclude on this account that they were produced by these causes. For just as there may be two clocks made by the same workman, which though they indicate the time equally well and are externally in all respects similar, yet in nowise resemble one another in the composition of their wheels, so doubtless there is an infinity of different ways in which all things that we see could be formed by the great Artificer [without it being possible for the mind of man to be aware of which of these means he has chosen to employ]. This I most freely admit; and I believe that I have done all that is required of me if the causes I have assigned are such that they correspond to all the phenomena manifested by nature [without inquiring whether it is by their means or by others that they are produced]. And it will be sufficient for the usages of life to know such causes, for medicine and mechanics and in general all these arts to which the knowledge of physics subserves, have for their end only those effects which are sensible, and which are accordingly to be reckoned among the phenomena of nature[1]. And lest it be supposed that Aristotle did, or desired to do, more than this, it must be recollected that he expressly says in the first book of the *Meteorologics*, in the beginning

---

[1] 'have for their end merely the application of certain sensible bodies to one another, so that by the operation of natural causes certain sensible effects are produced; and one will be able to accomplish this quite as well by considering the succession of certain causes thus imagined, although false, as if they were true, since this succession is supposed to be similar so far as sensible effects are concerned.' French version.

of the seventh chapter, that with regard to things not manifest to the senses, he considers that he supplies sufficient explanations and demonstrations of them, if he merely shows that they may be such as he explains them to be.

Principle CCV.

That nevertheless there is a moral certainty that everything is such as it has been shown to be.

But nevertheless, that I may not injure the truth, we must consider [two kinds of uncertainty and] first of all what has moral certainty; that is, a certainty which suffices for the conduct of life, though if we regard the absolute power of God, what is morally certain may be uncertain. [So those who have never visited Rome do not doubt its being a city in Italy, although it may very well be that all those from whom they have heard about it have deceived them. Again,] if, for instance, anyone wishing to read a letter written in Latin characters that are not placed in their proper order, takes it into his head to read B wherever he finds A and C where he finds B, thus substituting for each letter the one following it in the alphabet, and if he in this way finds that there are certain Latin words composed of these, he will not doubt that the true meaning of the writing is contained in these words, though he may discover this by conjecture, and although it is possible that the writer did not arrange the letters in this order of succession, but on some other, and thus concealed another meaning in it: for this is so unlikely to occur [especially when the cipher contains many words] that it seems incredible. But they who observe how many things regarding the magnet, fire, and the fabric of the whole world, are here deduced from a very small number of principles, although they considered that I had taken up these principles at random and without good grounds, they will yet acknowledge that it could hardly happen that so much would be coherent if they were false.

Principle CCVI.

That we possess even more than a moral certainty.

And further there are some, even among natural things, which we judge to be absolutely, and more than morally, certain[1]. This

---

[1] 'of which we judge that it is impossible that the thing should be other than as we think it.' French version.

certainty is founded on the metaphysical ground that as God is supremely good and cannot err, the faculty which He has given us of distinguishing truth from falsehood, cannot be fallacious so long as we use it aright, and distinctly perceive anything by it. Of this nature are mathematical demonstrations[1], the knowledge that material things exist, and the evidence of all clear reasoning that is carried on about them. Amongst these truths it seems to me that there should be counted those conclusions which have been arrived at in this treatise, if it be considered that they are derived in a continual series from the first and most simple principles of human knowledge. And this is specially so, if it be sufficiently understood that we can perceive no external objects unless some local motion be excited by them in our nerves; and that such motion cannot be excited by the fixed stars, owing to their immense distance from us, unless a motion be also produced in them, and in the whole intervening heavens[2]; for these facts being admitted, all the others, at least the more general doctrines which I have advanced about the world and earth, appear to be the only possible explanations of the phenomena they present.

PRINCIPLE CCVII.

Nevertheless all my opinions are submitted to the authority of the church.

At the same time, recalling my insignificance, I affirm nothing, but submit all these opinions to the authority of the Catholic Church, and to the judgment of the more sage; and I wish no one to believe anything I have written, unless he is personally persuaded by the force and evidence of reason.

---

[1] 'for we see clearly that it is impossible that two or three should together form less than five or that a square should not have four sides &c.' French version.

[2] The French version states that the fluidity of the heavens follows from this as explained in Part III, § xlvi.

THE END.

THE SEARCH AFTER TRUTH

PREFATORY NOTE TO 'THE SEARCH AFTER TRUTH.'

This unfinished Dialogue, Descartes' biographer Baillet tells us, was intended to form two volumes written in French. A Latin translation appeared in an edition of 1701 published at Amsterdam. Leibniz was known to have 'a Dialogue in French' amongst the unpublished papers of Descartes, and this French text was sought for in vain by MM. Adam and Tannery at the Royal Library of Hanover where it was likely to be found. A young student named Jules Sire was, however, fortunate enough to discover, not Leibniz's original copy but another. Leibniz was in Paris with Tschirnhaus, and he took Tschirnhaus to see Clerselier, who had what remained of Descartes' papers. Tschirnhaus copied 'The Search after Truth' and sent it to Leibniz, and this was the copy discovered by Sire. We do not know whether Clerselier's copy was incomplete, or Tschirnhaus' transcription of it, but it does not give more than half of the Latin version of 1701. Leibniz himself added at the end, 'I have the rest elsewhere.' MM. Adam and Tannery thus published Tschirnhaus's copy of the original in French, completing it from the Latin, and this is the edition here used. The date of the work is unknown.

E. S. H.

THE SEARCH AFTER TRUTH BY THE
LIGHT OF NATURE.

*The Search after Truth by means of the Light of Nature which
alone, and without the assistance of Religion or Philosophy, determines
what are the opinions which a good man should hold on all matters
which may occupy his thoughts, and which penetrate into the secrets
of the most curious of the sciences.*

A good man has no need to have read every book, nor to have
carefully learned all that which is taught in the Schools; it would
even be a defect in his education were he to have devoted too much
of his time to the study of letters. There are many other things to
do in life, and he has to direct that life in such a manner that the
greater part of it shall remain to him for the performance of good
actions which his own reason ought to teach him, even supposing
that he were to receive his lessons from it alone. But he comes
into the world in ignorance, and as the knowledge of his earliest
years rests only on the weakness of the senses and the authority of
masters, he can scarcely avoid his imagination being filled with an
infinite number of false ideas, before his reason has the power of
taking his conduct into its own hands; in consequence he requires
to have good natural endowments or else instruction from a wise
man, both in order to rid himself of the false doctrines with which
his mind is filled, and for building the first foundations of a solid
knowledge, and discovering all the means by which he may carry
his knowledge to the highest point to which it can possibly attain.

In this work I propose to show what these means are, and to
bring to light the true riches of our souls, by opening to each one
the road by which he can find in himself, and without borrowing
from any, the whole knowledge which is essential to him in the
direction of his life, and then by his study succeed in acquiring
the most curious forms of knowledge that the human reason is
capable of possessing.

But in order that the greatness of my scheme may not to begin with seize your minds with an astonishment so great that confidence in my words can no longer find therein a place, I warn you that what I undertake is not as difficult as might be imagined. Those branches of knowledge which do not extend beyond the capacities of the human mind are, as a matter of fact, united by a bond so marvellous, they are capable of being deduced from one another by sequences so necessary, that it is not essential to possess much art or address in order to discover them, provided that by commencing with those that are most simple we learn gradually to raise ourselves to the most sublime. That is what I shall try to show you here by a system of reasoning so clear and yet so simple, that every one will be able to judge for himself that if he has not observed the same things, it is solely because he has not cast his eyes in the right direction, nor fixed his thoughts on the same considerations as I, and that no more glory is due to me for having discovered them, than is due to a casual passer-by for having accidentally discovered under his feet a rich treasure which had for long successfully eluded the searches of many.

And certainly I am surprised that amongst so many distinguished minds which in a matter of this description should have succeeded much better than I, none have had the patience to find their way out of their difficulties ; and that nearly all have followed in the footsteps of these travellers who, abandoning the main route in favour of a cross-road, find themselves lost amongst briars and precipices.

But I do not desire to examine into what others have known or have been ignorant of. It will suffice for me to note that even if all the knowledge which we can desire is to be found in books, that which they contain of good is mingled with so many futilities, and confusedly dispersed in such a mass of great volumes, that, in order to read them, more time would be requisite than human life can supply us with, and more talent in discovering the useful than would be required in ascertaining it for ourselves.

That is what makes me hope that the reader will not be vexed by here finding an easier path, and that the facts which I shall advance will not be the less well received, even although I do not borrow them from Plato or Aristotle, but show that they have current value in the world, just as has money which is in nowise of less value when it proceeds from the purse of a peasant than when it comes from the treasury. I have even made it my business to make them equally useful to all men; and I have not been able to discover a style better adapted to this end than that of genuine conversation, wherein each one familiarly explains to his friends the best of his thoughts. And under the names Eudoxus, Polyander, and Epistemon, I assume that a man endowed with ordinary mental gifts, but whose judgment is not spoiled by any false ideas, and who is in possession of his whole reason in all the purity of its nature, receives as his guests in the country house which he inhabits, two men the most distinguished and interesting of their time, one of whom has studied not at all, while the other is well acquainted with all that can be learnt in the Schools And there (in the midst of other discourse which each one can imagine for himself, as well as the local conditions and particular surroundings from which I shall frequently cause them to take examples in order to make their conceptions more clear), they thus introduce the subject of which they will afterwards treat to the end of these two books.

Polyander, Epistemon, Eudoxus.

Polyander. I consider you are so fortunate in having discovered all these wonderful things in the Greek and Latin books, that it seems to me that if I had studied as much as you, I should be as different from what I now am, as angels are from you. And I cannot excuse the folly of my parents who, being persuaded that the study of letters would enfeeble the mind, sent me to the court and camps at so early an age, that I should all my life have had to bewail my ignorance, had I not learned something from my association with you.

Epistemon. The best thing that you could be taught on this subject is that the desire for knowledge, which is common to all men, is an evil which cannot be cured, for curiosity increases with knowledge; and as the deficiencies that are present in our soul only trouble us in so far as we recognise them, you have a certain advantage over us, in that you do not see as we do, that many things are lacking to you.

Eudoxus. Can it be, Epistemon, that you who are so well instructed, can believe that there is in nature any evil so universal that there is no remedy to be applied to it? As for me, I consider that just as there are in each country sufficient fruits and rivers to appease the hunger and thirst of all men, so there are truths that can be known in every matter sufficient to satisfy fully the curiosity of healthy minds ; and I think that the body of a dropsical patient is not further removed from its normal condition than the mind of those who are perpetually worked upon by an insatiable curiosity.

Epistemon. I have, it is true, heard in former times that our desires could not extend naturally to things that seemed to us impossible, and that it ought not to do so to those that are vicious or useless ; but so many things can be known which appear possible to us, and which are not only good and agreeable, but also very necessary in the conduct of life, that I cannot believe that anyone ever knew enough of them not to have legitimate reasons always to desire to know more.

Eudoxus. What, then, would you say of me, if I tell you that I no longer feel any desire to learn anything at all, and that I am as happy with my small knowledge as Diogenes used to be with his tub, and all this without my having any need of his philosophy ? For the knowledge of my neighbours is not the limit of my own, as are their fields which here surround the small piece of ground that I possess ; and my mind at its own will disposing of all the truths which it comes across, does not dream that there are others to discover. For it enjoys the same repose that the king of an isolated country would have were he so separated from all others as to imagine that beyond his frontiers there was nothing but unfertile deserts and uninhabitable mountains.

Epistemon. If any other but you spoke to me thus, I should regard him as one whose mind was either very vain or else too little given to curiosity; but the retreat which you have chosen in this solitude, and the small amount of pains that you take to become known, removes from you the charge of vanity ; and the time you have hitherto consecrated to journeyings, visiting learned men, and examining everything that is most difficult in each science, suffices to assure us that you are not lacking in curiosity. I can hence say nothing but that I consider you very happy and that I am convinced that you must be in the possession of a knowledge much more perfect than that of others.

Eudoxus. I thank you for the good opinion in which you hold me, but I do not desire to abuse your courtesy to the point of desiring that you should believe what I have just said, solely on the faith of my words. We must not advance opinions so far removed from vulgar beliefs, without at the same time being able to demonstrate certain effects from so doing ; that is why I beg you both to be good enough to spend this delightful season here, so that I may have the opportunity of openly showing you some part of the things that I know. For I venture to flatter myself that not alone will you recognise that I have some reason for being happy in this knowledge, but, in addition, that you yourselves will have much happiness from the things that you will have learned.

Epistemon. I would not wish to refuse a favour that already I so ardently desired of you.

Polyander. And I shall have great pleasure in being present at this discussion, not that I believe myself capable of deriving any good from it.

Eudoxus. On the contrary, Polyander, believe me it will be you who will derive advantage from it, because you are quite unprejudiced, and it will be easier for me to guide aright any one with an open mind than Epistemon, whom we shall often find in opposition to us. But in order to make you more easily understand the nature of the knowledge of which I am going to treat, I beg you to observe a difference which exists between the sciences and those simple forms of knowledge which can be acquired without the aid of reasoning, such as languages, history, geography, &c., or to speak generally, everything that depends on experience alone. I am ready to grant that the life of a man would not suffice to acquire a knowledge of all that the world contains; but I am also persuaded that it would be folly to desire that it should be so, and that it is no more the duty of an ordinary well-disposed man to know Greek and Latin than it is to know the languages of Switzerland or Brittany; or that the history of the Empire should be known any more than that of the smallest state in Europe. And I consider that such a one should consecrate his leisure to good and useful things alone, and occupy his memory only with those that are most necessary. As to those sciences which are nothing but the judgments which we base on some knowledge previously acquired, some are deduced from common objects of which every one is cognisant, and others from rare and well thought out experiments. And I confess likewise that it would be impossible for us to treat in detail each one of these last; for we should first of all have to examine all the herbs and stones brought to us from the Indies; we should have to have beheld the phœnix, and in a word to be ignorant of none of the marvellous secrets of nature. But I shall believe myself to have sufficiently fulfilled my promise if, in explaining to you the truths which may be deduced from common things known to each one of us, I make you capable of discovering all the others when it pleases you to take the trouble to seek them.

Polyander. For my part I believe that this is likewise all that it is possible to desire, and I would have been satisfied if you had merely taught me a certain number of propositions which are so celebrated that no one can be ignorant of them, such as those that concern the Deity, the rational soul, the virtues, their reward, &c., propositions which I compare with those ancient families which every one recognises as the most illustrious, although the titles of their nobility are concealed under the ruins of antiquity. For I do not really doubt that those who first of all induced the human race to believe in all these things had excellent reasons for proving them ; but their arguments have been so rarely repeated since, that no one knows them any longer : and yet they are truths so important, that the dictates of prudence tell us that we should believe them blindly at the risk of being deceived, rather than that we should await a future life in order to be further instructed in them.

Epistemon. As far as I am concerned I am a little more curious, and I should like you to explain to me certain particular difficulties which suggest themselves to me in each branch of knowledge, and principally in what concerns the secrets of the human arts, apparitions, illusions, and in a word all the wonderful effects attributed to magic. For I believe it to be useful to know all that, not in order to make use of the knowledge, but in order that one should not allow one's judgment to be beguiled by wonder at an unknown thing.

Eudoxus. I shall try to satisfy you in regard to both ; and, in order to adopt an order which we may make use of to the end, I wish first of all, Polyander, to talk with you of all things that the world contains, considering them in themselves, on the understanding that Epistemon shall interrupt our talk as little as possible, because his observations would often force us to leave our subject. We shall finally consider all these things anew, though under another aspect, in so far as they are in relation with us, and as they may be termed true or false, good or evil ; and it is here that Epistemon will find occasion to set forth all the difficulties which will remain to him from the preceding discourses.

Polyander. Tell us, then, the order that you will follow in your explanations.

Eudoxus. We must commence with the human soul because all our knowledge depends on it ; and after having considered its

nature and effects, we shall reach its author ; and when we come to
know who He is and how He has created all things in the world,
we shall observe what is most certain regarding other creatures ;
and we shall inquire how our senses perceive things, and how our
reflections become false or true. Then I shall place before your
eyes the works of man upon corporeal objects, and after having
struck wonder into you by the sight of machines the most powerful,
and automata the most rare, visions the most specious, and tricks
the most subtle that artifice can invent, I shall reveal to you secrets
which are so simple that you will henceforward wonder at nothing
in the works of our hands. After that I shall reach the works of
nature, and, after having shown you the cause of all its changes,
the diversity of its qualities, and the reason why the soul of plants
and animals differs from ours, I shall place under your consideration
the whole building up of sensible things. The phenomena of the
heavens, and those certain conclusions which we may derive from
them being observed, I shall pass on to most sane conjectures
regarding what man cannot determine positively, in order to try
to give an account of the relation sensible things bear to intellectual, and both to the Creator, of the immortality of the creatures,
and of their state after the end of Time. Then we shall come
to the second part of this discourse in which we shall treat in
detail of all the sciences, selecting in each that which is most solid,
and we shall support a method whereby they may be carried on
much further, and find of ourselves, with a mind of ordinary ability,
what those most subtle can discover. After having thus prepared
our minds for judging perfectly of the truth, we must also apply
ourselves to the direction of our wills in respect of distinguishing
good from evil, and observing the true difference between virtue
and vice. That being done, I trust that your desire for knowledge
will not be so violent, and that all that I shall have said to you will
seem so well established that you will come to believe that a man
with a healthy mind, had he been brought up in a desert and never
received more than the light of nature to illumine him, could not if
he carefully weighed all the same reasons, adopt an opinion different
from ours. In order to begin this discourse we must inquire as to
what is the first knowledge man arrives at, in what part of the soul
it is to be found, and why it is so imperfect to begin with.

Epistemon. All that seems to me to explain itself very clearly
if we compare the imagination of children to a *tabula rasa* on
which our ideas, which resemble portraits of each object taken from

nature, should depict themselves. The senses, the inclinations, our masters and our intelligence, are the various painters who have the power of executing this work; and amongst them, those who are least adapted to succeed in it, i.e. the imperfect senses, blind instinct, and foolish nurses, are the first to mingle themselves with it. There finally comes the best of all, intelligence, and yet it is still requisite for it to have an apprenticeship of several years, and to follow the example of its masters for long, before daring to rectify a single one of their errors. In my opinion this is one of the principal causes of the difficulty we experience in attaining to true knowledge. For our senses really perceive that alone which is most coarse and common; our natural instinct is entirely corrupted; and as to our masters, although there may no doubt be very perfect ones found amongst them, they yet cannot force our minds to accept their reasoning before our understanding has examined it, for the accomplishment of this end pertains to it alone. But it is like a clever painter who might have been called upon to put the last touches on a bad picture sketched out by prentice hands, and who would find it vain to employ all the rules of his art in correcting little by little first a trait here, then a trait there, and finally be required to add to it from his own hand all that was lacking, and who yet could not prevent great faults from remaining in it, because from the beginning the picture would have been badly conceived, the figures badly placed, and the proportions badly observed.

Eudoxus. Your comparison places perfectly under our eyes the first obstacle which stands in our way; but you do not show the means of which we must avail ourselves if we wish to avoid it. And according to me it is this, that just as your artist would have done much better, after having effaced by drawing over it a sponge all the features of the picture, to begin it entirely over again rather than lose his time in correcting it, so each one who has reached a certain term of years known as the age of knowledge, should set himself once for all to remove from his imagination all the inexact ideas which have hitherto succeeded in engraving themselves upon it, and seriously begin to form new ones, applying thereto all the strength of his intelligence with such zeal that if he does not bring them to perfection, the fault will not at least be laid on the weakness of the senses, or on the errors of nature.

Epistemon. That would be an excellent remedy if we could easily employ it; but you are not ignorant that the opinions first received by our imagination remain so deeply imprinted there, that our will alone, if it did not employ the aid of certain strong reasons, could not arrive at effacing them.

Eudoxus. It is certain of these reasons that I hope to teach you; and if you wish to derive some fruit from this our intercourse, you must give me your whole attention, and allow me to converse a little with Polyander in order that I may begin by upsetting all the knowledge he has hitherto acquired. And as it is not sufficient to satisfy him, and it cannot but be bad, I may compare it to a badly constructed edifice whose foundations are not solid. I know no better remedy than absolutely to rase it to the ground, in order to raise a new one in its stead. For I do not wish to be placed amongst the number of these insignificant artisans, who apply themselves only to the restoration of old works, because they feel themselves incapable of achieving new. We can, however, Polyander, while we are busy destroying this edifice, at the same time form the foundations which may serve our purpose, and prepare the best and most solid materials that are necessary in order to succeed in our task; provided you are in any degree willing to examine with me which of all the truths men can know, are those that are most certain and easy of knowledge.

Polyander. Is there anyone who can doubt that sensible things (I mean thereby those that can be seen and touched) are much more certain than the others? As for me I should be very much astonished if you would show me as clearly some of those things that are said of God and our soul.

Eudoxus. That, however, is what I hope to do, and it seems to me surprising that men are credulous enough to base their knowledge on the certitude of the senses, when there is no one who is unaware that they frequently deceive us, and that we have good reason for always mistrusting those that have once betrayed us.

Polyander. I am well aware that the senses sometimes deceive us when they are ill affected, just as a sick person thinks that all food is bitter; when they are too far from the object this is also so, just as when we look at the stars they never appear to us as large as they really are; and in general when they do not act freely according to the constitution of their nature. But all their errors are easily known, and do not prevent my being now perfectly persuaded that I see you, that we walk in a garden, that the sun gives light, and, in a word, that all that my senses usually offer to me is true.

Eudoxus. Since it is not sufficient for me to tell you that the senses deceive us in certain cases where you perceive it, in order to make you fear being deceived by them on other occasions when you are not aware of it, I shall go further and ask if you have ever seen a melancholic man of the nature of those who believe themselves to be vases, or who think some part of their body is of enormous size; they would swear that they see and touch that which they imagine they do. And it is true that any ordinary man would be indignant if anyone were to say to him that he could not have any more reason than they to be certain of his opinion, since it rests equally with theirs on what the senses and his imagination represent to him. But you cannot be annoyed if I ask you whether you are not like other men subject to sleep, and if you cannot think when you sleep that you see me, that you walk in this garden, that the sun gives light, in a word all these other things that you imagine yourself now to be certain of. Have you never heard in comedies this expression for astonishment, "*Am I awake or asleep?*" How can you be certain that your life is not a perpetual dream and that all that you imagine you learn by means of your senses is not as false now as it is when you sleep? More particularly as you have learned that you have been created by a superior Being to whom as omnipotent it would not have been more difficult to make us such as I have described, than such as you believe yourself to be?

Polyander. Certainly these are reasons sufficient to upset all the knowledge of Epistemon if he is contemplative enough to give his attention to it; as for me, I should fear becoming in some degree crazy, if, never having applied my mind to study, or accustomed myself to turn my mind away from the things of the senses, I was going to apply myself to meditations which, as far as I am concerned, a little exceed my capacities.

Epistemon. I think it very dangerous to proceed too far in this mode of reasoning. General doubts of this kind lead us straight to the ignorance of Socrates, or the uncertainty of the Pyrrhonists, which resembles water so deep that one cannot find any footing in it.

Eudoxus. I confess that it is not without great danger that one ventures without a guide when one does not know the ford, and many have lost their way in doing so; but you have no reason to fear if you follow after me. It is such fears, indeed, that have prevented many learned men from attaining to the knowledge of a doctrine which is solid and certain enough to deserve the name of science; when, imagining that there was nothing on which they could rest their faith more firm and solid than the things that we perceive by the senses, they built on this foundation of sand rather than by digging down further finding a firm substratum of rock or clay. It is not here that we must stop. There is more; even if you did not wish further to examine the reasons which I have just stated, they would yet already in their principal effect have attained to the goal I wished to reach, so long as they had so affected your imagination as to place you on your guard against them. That is an indication to show you that your knowledge is not so infallible that you may not fear to see its foundations shattered since they make you doubt all; and consequently you are made to doubt your very knowledge itself, and this proves that I have accomplished my end, which was to upset your knowledge by showing you its uncertainty. From fear, however, that you may lack more courage and refuse to follow me further, I declare to you that those doubts which alarmed you to begin with, are like those phantoms and vain images which appear in the night by the uncertain glimmer of a feeble light. Fear pursues you if you flee, but if you approach and touch them, you will find nought but wind and shadow, and you will ever after be better able to meet whatever may arrive.

Polyander. Convinced by your reasoning I desire then to set before myself all these difficulties in the strongest manner possible, and to apply myself to doubt whether I have not been dreaming all my life, and whether even all these ideas that I thought could only enter into my mind by the door of the senses, might not have been formed of themselves, just as similar ideas are formed when I sleep, or when I am certain that my eyes are shut, my ears closed, and, in a word, that none of my senses are in operation. In this way I shall be uncertain not only as to whether you are in the world, if a world exists, if there be a sun, but also whether I have eyes, ears, a body, even whether I talk with you, whether you address me, in short I shall doubt all things[1].

Eudoxus. There you are, well prepared, and this is the very point I wished to bring you to; but this is the very moment for your giving your attention to the consequences which I wish to derive from your argument. You see very well that you can reasonably doubt all things, the knowledge of which comes to you by the senses alone; but can you doubt of your doubt and remain uncertain whether you doubt or not?

---

[1] This completes the original French manuscript. The rest is taken from the Latin translation of the original.

Polyander. I confess that this astonishes me, and the little sagacity which a sufficiently small amount of common sense gives me brings it to pass that I do not without stupefaction find myself forced to confess that I know nothing with certainty, but that I doubt all things and am certain of nothing. But what conclusions do you wish to derive from this? I do not see to what use this universal astonishment can serve, nor by what reason a doubt of this kind can be a principle which is able to carry us very far. Quite on the contrary, you have made the end of this our converse relief from all our doubts, and the discovery of truths of which Epistemon, wise as he is, may very well have been ignorant.

Eudoxus. Just give me your attention; I am going to conduct you further than you think. For it is really from this universal doubt which is like a fixed and unchangeable point, that I have resolved to derive the knowledge of God, of yourself, and of all that the world contains.

Polyander. You certainly make great promises and provided you carry them out it would certainly be worth our while to grant what you ask for. Keep, then, your promises and we will keep those we made to you.

Eudoxus. Since, then, you cannot deny that you doubt, and that it is on the other hand certain that you doubt, and so certain that you cannot even doubt of that, it is likewise true that you are, you who doubt; and that is so true that you can no longer doubt of it any more.

Polyander. I agree with you, for if I did not exist I could not doubt.

Eudoxus. You are, then, and you know that you are, and you know it because you doubt.

Polyander. All that is very true.

Eudoxus. But in order that you may not be turned aside from your plan, go on little by little, and as I have said to you, you will feel yourself drawn on further than you think. You are, and you know that you are, and you know that because you know that you doubt. But you, who doubt all and who cannot doubt of yourself, what are you?

Polyander. The reply is not difficult and I see very well that you have chosen me in place of Epistemon so that I may respond to your questions. You had no mind to put any question to which it is not quite easy to reply. I shall then tell you that I am a man.

Eudoxus. You pay no attention to my question, and the reply that you make to me, simple as it may appear to you, will bring us into a labyrinth of difficulties, if I try ever so little to press you. Were I for example to ask Epistemon himself what a man is, and were he to reply, as is done in the Schools, that a man is a rational animal; and if, in addition, in order to explain these two terms which are not less obscure than the first, he were to conduct us by all the steps which are termed metaphysical, we should be dragged into a maze from which it would be impossible for us to emerge. As a matter of fact, from this question two others arise, the first is what is an animal? The second, what is reasonable And further, if, to explain what an animal is he were to reply that it is a living thing possessed of sensations, that a living thing is an animate body, that a body is a corporeal substance, you see that the question, like the branches of a genealogical tree, would go on increasing and multiplying; and finally all these wonderful questions would finish in pure tautology, which would clear up nothing, and would leave us in our original ignorance.

Epistemon. I am sorry to see that you despise this tree of Porphyry which has always excited the admiration of the learned, and I am vexed that you wish to show Polyander what he is by another method than the one which for so long has been admitted by the Schools. In fact until now no better means has been found, nor a means more calculated to teach us what we are, than that of placing in sequence under our eyes all the successive items which constitute the totality of our nature, so that by this means, by ascending and descending all the steps, we may be made aware of what we have in common with other beings, and of that in which we differ. That is the highest point to which our knowledge can attain.

Eudoxus. I neither have nor should I ever have any intention of condemning the method employed in the Schools; it is to it that I am indebted for the little that I know, and it is of its assistance that I have availed myself, in order to become aware of the uncertainty of all that I have learned there. Therefore although my teachers taught me nothing that was certain, I yet owe to them my thanks for having been taught by them to acknowledge this; and I now owe them all the greater thanks in that the things they taught me were doubtful, than had they been more in conformity with reason; for in that latter case I might possibly have contented myself with the small amount of reason that I should have discovered there, and that would have rendered me less zealous in the search after truth. The admonition that I gave to Polyander serves less to dissipate the obscurity into which his reply cast you than to make him more attentive to my question. I return then to my subject, and in order that we may not digress further I ask him a second time what he is, he who can doubt all things and cannot doubt of himself.

Polyander. I thought I had satisfied you by saying to you that I was a man, but I now see that I did not calculate well. I see very well that this answer does not satisfy you, and, truth to say, I confess that it does not now satisfy myself, more especially since you have shown me the embarrassment and uncertainty into which it can throw us if we wish to get light upon it and understand it. As a matter of fact, whatever Epistemon may say, I observe great obscurity in all these metaphysical steps. If, for instance, we say that a body is a corporeal substance without saying what a corporeal substance is, these two words will not teach us more than the word body. In the same way if we say that what lives is an animate body without having first explained what body is, and what animate is, and if we likewise enquire into all the other metaphysical degrees, it may be to put forward words in a certain order, but it is to express nothing; for it indicates nothing that can be conceived or that can form a clear and distinct idea in our mind. Even when, in order to reply to your question, I said that I was a man, I did not think of all the scholastic entities of which I was ignorant, and of which I had never even heard, and which, as far as I am concerned, exist only in the imagination of those who have invented them. But I spoke of the things that we see, that we touch, that we feel, that we experience in ourselves, in a word, of the things that the simplest of men know as well as the greatest philosopher in the world, that is to say that I am a certain whole composed of two arms, two legs, a head, and all the parts which constitute what we call the human body, and which in addition is nourished, walks, feels, and thinks.

Eudoxus. I saw at once by your reply that you had not quite understood my question, and that you replied to more things than I asked of you. But as you have just numbered in the things of which you doubt, the arms, legs, head, and all the other parts composing the human body, I did not wish to interrogate you on any of these things of whose existence you are not sure. Tell me, then, what you really are inasmuch as you doubt. It is on this point alone, the only one which you can know with certainty, that I desired to question you.

Polyander. I now see that I have been mistaken in my reply and that I have gone further than I should, inasmuch as I did not properly understand your idea. That will render me more circumspect in future and at the same time it causes me to marvel at the exactitude of your method, whereby you conduct us little by little by simple and easy paths to the knowledge of the things that you wish to teach us. I have however reason to call the error that I have committed happy, since, thanks to it, I know very well that what I am inasmuch as I doubt, is in no wise what I call my body. And more than that, I do not even know that I have a body, since you have shown me that I might doubt of it. In addition to this I may add that I cannot even absolutely deny that I have a body. Yet, while entirely setting aside all these suppositions, this will not prevent my being certain that I exist. On the contrary, they confirm me yet more in the certainty that I exist and that I am not a body; otherwise, doubting of my body I should at the same time doubt of myself, and this I cannot do; for I am absolutely convinced that I exist, and I am so much convinced of it, that I can in no wise doubt of it.

Eudoxus. That is beautifully expressed and you bring out the matter so well that I should not do better myself. I see very well that all that now remains is to leave you entirely to yourself, merely taking care to set you on the right road. Nay, further: I think that in order to find the most difficult truths, provided we are well guided, the only necessity is to have common sense, to put it vulgarly; and, as I find you very well provided with that, as I had hoped, all I have to do is to show you the road you should henceforward follow. Continue then to deduce by yourself the consequences which flow from this first principle.

Polyander. This principle seems to me so fertile, and it offers me so many things at once, that it seems as though I should want a great deal of work to reduce them to order. This one admonition that you have given me to consider who I who doubt am, and not to confound myself with what I formerly believed to be me, has thrown such a flood of light upon my mind, and so dissipated the mists, that by the light of this torch I see more accurately in myself what is not visible to the eyes, and that I am more persuaded that I possess what cannot be touched, than I ever have been of possessing a body.

Eudoxus. This warmth pleases me infinitely well although it may displease Epistemon who, because you have not shewn him his error, or placed under his eyes a part of the things that you say are contained in this principle, will always believe, or will at least fear, that the torch offered to you is similar to those wandering fires that are extinguished and vanish away when they are approached, and that so you may fall into your original darkness, i.e. into your former ignorance. And it certainly would be marvellous if you who have never studied nor opened books of philosophy, should all at once gain wisdom at such a small cost. So we should not be astonished that Epistemon judges in this way.

Epistemon. Yes, I confess I took that to be the result of mere enthusiasm, and I thought that Polyander who has never meditated on the great truths which philosophy teaches, was so transported by the discovery of the least of them that he could not prevent himself from letting you know of it by his shouts of joy. But those who like you[1] have travelled this road for long, have expended much oil and trouble in reading and re-reading the writings of the ancients, and in unravelling and expounding all that is most complicated in the philosophers, are no longer astonished by this enthusiasm, and make no more of it than they do of the vain hopes which frequently lay hold of one in commencing mathematics, when the threshold of the temple alone has so far been saluted. These novices have scarcely been given the line and the circle, and shown what is a straight line and a curved, when they believe that they are going to square the circle and duplicate the cube. But we have so frequently refuted the opinion of the Pyrrhonists, and they themselves have derived so little fruit from this method of philosophizing, that they have been in error all their lives, and have not been able to get free of the doubts which they have introduced into philosophy. They thus seem never to have worked for anything but learning to doubt: that is why, with Polyander's permission, I shall doubt whether he himself can derive anything better from it.

Eudoxus. I see very clearly that you speak to Polyander in order to spare me; your pleasantries are all the same evidently directed against me; but let Polyander speak and after that we shall see which of us will laugh last.

Polyander. I will do so willingly; nay, I fear that this dispute will become hot between you two and that if you plunge into the matter too deeply, I shall end by understanding nothing at all.

[1] The French editors conjecture 'like me.'

Thus shall I lose the fruit which I promise myself in returning to to my original studies. I pray then that Epistemon may permit me to nourish this hope for so long as it pleases Eudoxus to lead me by the hand in the path in which he has placed me.

Eudoxus. You have already clearly recognized in considering yourself simply as doubting, that you are not body, and that as such you would not find within you any of the parts which constitute the human machine : that is to say, that you have neither arms, nor legs, nor head, nor eyes, nor ears, nor any organ which may serve for a sense of any kind. But notice whether in the same way you cannot reject all the things that you formerly understood by the description which you gave of the idea which in former times you had of man. For, as you judiciously remarked, that was a fortunate error that you committed in passing beyond the limits of my question. Thanks really to it, you can arrive at a knowledge of what you are by removing from you and rejecting all that you perceive clearly does not belong to you, and by simply admitting what so necessarily pertains to you that you are as certain of it as of your existence and doubt.

Polyander. I thank you for thus setting me on my way ; I did not know any longer where I was. I said first of all that I was a whole formed of arms, legs, a head, and all the parts which form the human body, besides which I walk, am nourished, feel and think. It has been necessary for me, in order to consider myself simply as I know myself to be, to set aside all these parts or all these members which constitute the human machine; that is to say, I must consider myself as without arms, legs, head, and, in a word, without body. But it is true that what in me doubts is not what we call our body ; so then it is also true that I, inasmuch as I doubt, do not eat or walk, for neither of these two things can be done without body. Further, I cannot even state that I, inasmuch as I doubt, can feel. As feet really serve for walking, so do eyes for seeing, and ears for hearing. But as I have none of these organs because I have not body, I cannot say that I feel. In addition to that, I have often in dreaming thought I felt many things that I did not really feel at all, and as I resolved to admit nothing here but what was so true that I could not doubt of it, I cannot say that I am a perceiving thing, that is, one that sees with eyes and hears with ears. It might indeed be that I thought I perceived although none of these things happened.

Eudoxus. I cannot prevent myself from stopping you here, not to turn you aside, but to encourage you, and make you consider what common sense can do if it is well directed. As a matter of fact, is there anything in all this which is not exact, which is not legitimately argued, and well deduced from what precedes? And all that is said and done without logic, or rule, or a formula for the argument, but with the simple light of reason and with a just sense which, acting alone and of itself, is less exposed to error than when it anxiously tries to follow a thousand diverse routes which art and human idleness have discovered, less to bring it to perfection than to corrupt it. Epistemon even seems to be in this matter of our opinion; for while saying nothing of the matter, he gives us to understand that he approves what we have said. Go on, then, Polyander, and show him how far good sense can carry us, and at the same time what consequences can be derived from our principle.

Polyander. Of all the attributes which I bestowed upon myself, only one remains for me to examine and that is thought; and I see that it is the only one that I cannot separate from myself. For if it is true that I doubt just because I cannot doubt that I do so, it is also equally true that I think; for what is doubting but thinking in a certain way? And in fact if I did not think, I could not know whether I doubt or exist. Yet I am, and I know that I am, and I know it because I doubt, that is to say because I think. And better, it might be that if I ceased for an instant to think I should cease at the same time to be. Likewise the sole thing that I cannot separate from me, that I know certainly to be me and that I can now affirm without fear of deception—that one thing, I repeat, is that I am a thinking thing.

Eudoxus. What, Epistemon, do you think of what Polyander has just said? Do you find his argument to be halting or inconsequent? Should you have thought that an unlettered man, and one who had not studied, would have reasoned so well and followed out his ideas so rigorously? Here, if I do not mistake, you must begin to see that he who knows how properly to avail himself of doubt can deduce from it absolutely certain knowledge, better, more certain, and more useful than that derived from this great principle which we usually establish as the basis or centre to which all other principles are referred and from which they start forth, viz. *it is impossible that one and the same thing should both be and not be.* I shall perhaps have occasion to demonstrate the utility of it to you. But let us not interrupt Polyander's discourse, or remove ourselves from our subject; as to you, see if you have anything to say or any objection to make.

Epistemon. Since you lay the blame on me and even exasperate me, I shall show you what logic can do when it is roused, and at the same time I shall raise difficulties and obstacles of such a nature that not only Polyander but you yourself will have much difficulty in getting free of them. Let us then go no further, but stop here and severely examine your principles and deductions. As a matter of fact with the aid of true logic, and after your own principles, I shall show that nothing of what Polyander has said rests on a legitimate foundation or brings about any conclusion. You say that you are and that you know that you are, that you know it because you doubt and because you think. But do you know what doubting or what thinking is? And as you do not desire to admit anything of which you are not certain and do not know perfectly, how can you be certain that you are by means of attributes so obscure and consequently so uncertain? It would have been better first of all to have taught Polyander what doubt is, what thought is, what existence is, so that his reasoning might have the strength of a demonstration, and that he might first of all understand himself before applying himself to make others comprehend.

Polyander. That is beyond me, so I give it up leaving you to unravel this knot with Epistemon.

Eudoxus. For this occasion I undertake it with pleasure, but on the condition that you will be judge of our differences; for I dare not hope that Epistemon will give way to my reasoning. He who is like him, full of opinions and prepossessed with a hundred prejudices, finds it difficult to hand himself over to the light of nature alone; for long he has been accustomed to yield to authority rather than to lend his ear to the dictates of his own reason. He likes better to interrogate others, to weigh what the ancients have written, than to consult himself on the judgment which he should form; and as from his childhood he has taken as reason what rested only on the authority of preceptors, now he gives his authority as a reason and desires that others should pay to him the tribute which he formerly paid them. But I shall have reason to be content and I shall believe myself to have sufficiently answered the objections which have been proposed to you by Epistemon, if you give your assent to what I shall say, and if your reason convinces you of it.

Epistemon. I am not so rebellious nor so difficult to persuade, nor is it so difficult to satisfy me as you think. And further, although I had reasons for mistrusting Polyander, I would willingly submit our case to his arbitration; and as soon as he favours you I promise you to confess myself vanquished. But he must guard himself from being deceived and falling into the error for which he reproaches others, that is to say, from taking as a motive for persuasion the esteem which he has formed for you.

Eudoxus. If he allowed himself to rest on so feeble a support he would look badly after his own interests and I presume that he will attend to them. But let us return to our subject matter. I am quite of your opinion, Epistemon, that we must know what doubt is, what thought is, before being fully convinced of the truth of this reasoning *I doubt therefore I am*; or, what comes to the same, *I think therefore I am*. But do not go and imagine that in order to know this we must do violence to our mind and put it to torture in order to ascertain the *proximate species* and the *essential difference*, and form from it a definition by rule. All that must be left to him who is going to be a professor or to dispute in the Schools. But whoever desires to examine things by himself and judge of them as he conceives them, cannot be so devoid of mental power not to see clearly whenever he is willing to give attention to it, what doubt is, or thought or existence, and to be required to learn their distinctions. Further I declare that there are certain things which we render more obscure by trying to define them, because, since they are very simple and clear, we cannot know and perceive them better than by themselves. Nay, we must place in the number of those chief errors that can be committed in the sciences, the mistakes committed by those who would try to define what ought only to be conceived, and who cannot distinguish the clear from the obscure, nor discriminate between what, in order to be known, requires and deserves to be defined, from what can be best known by itself. And in the number of the things which are clear in the way above explained and which can be known by themselves, we must place doubt, thought, and existence.

I do not think that anyone has ever existed who is stupid enough to have required to learn what existence is before being able to conclude and affirm that he is; the same holds true of thought and doubt. Indeed I add that one learns those things in no other way than by one's self and that nothing else persuades us of them except our own experience and this knowledge and internal testimony that each one finds within himself when he examines things. In vain shall we define what white is in order to make it comprehensible to him who sees absolutely nothing, while in order to know it, it is only requisite to open one's eyes and see the white; in the same way in order to know what doubt is, or thought, it is only requisite to doubt and think. That teaches us all that we can know of it, and explains more respecting it than even the most exact definitions. It is thus true that Polyander ought to have known these things, before being able to draw the conclusions which he has advanced; but since we have chosen him as judge, ask him if he has ever been ignorant of what is.

Polyander. I certainly confess that it is with the greatest pleasure that I have heard you disputing regarding a thing which you have not been able to know but from me, and it is not without some joy that I see, at least on this occasion, that it is necessary for me to be recognised as your master and for you to recognise yourselves as my pupils. Therefore in order to put both of you out of pain and quickly to resolve your difficulty (as a matter of fact we say that a thing is promptly done when it is done beyond all hope and expectation), I can state for certain that I never doubted what doubt is, although I never began to know it, or rather to think of it until the time when Epistemon desired to place it in doubt. You no sooner showed me the small amount of certainty which we have as to the existence of things which are only known to us by the evidence of the senses, than I commenced to doubt of them, and that sufficed to make me know doubt and at the same time my certainty of it, in such a way that I can affirm that as soon as I commenced to doubt I commenced to know with certainty. But my doubt and my certainty did not relate to the same object; my doubt regarded things only which existed outside me, my certainty concerned me and my doubt. Eudoxus then spoke truly when he asserted that there are things that we cannot know without seeing them; therefore to learn what doubt is, what thought is, it is necessary only that we ourselves should think and doubt. The same holds good of existence; it is only necessary to know what we understand by this word; we know at the very same moment what the thing is, at least in so far as we can know it, and there is no necessity here for a definition, which will more confuse than clear up the matter.

Epistemon. Since Polyander is satisfied I likewise give my assent, and I shall not push the dispute further. However I do not see that during the two hours that we have been here and that we have been arguing, he has advanced much. All that Polyander has learnt by the help of this wonderful method of which you so boast, consists solely of the fact that he doubts that he thinks and that he is a thinking thing. A wonderful knowledge in truth! Many words for small results! as much could be said in four words and we should have all given our assent. As for me if I had to employ as many words and as much time in learning something of so small an importance, I confess I should not resign myself to it without regret. Those who are our instructors tell us much more about the matter; they are much more confident; nothing stops them; they take everything upon them and decide about all. Nothing turns them aside from their plan, nothing astonishes them, whatever happens; when they feel themselves pressed too hard, an equivocation or the *distinguo* saves them from all embarrassment. And more, be certain that their method will always be preferred to that of one like you who doubts all and who fears so much to trip that he keeps treading the same spot and thus makes no advance.

Eudoxus. I never intended to prescribe to anyone the method he ought to follow in the search after truth, but merely to expound that of which I have availed myself, so that if it were found bad it would be set aside; if it were found good and useful others would avail themselves of it in turn; and I always left full liberty to all to set it aside or to admit it. If it is now said that it has advanced me little, it is for experience to decide as to that; and I am certain, provided that you continue to lend me your attention, you will yourself confess that we cannot take too many precautions in the establishment of our bases, and that once they are well established we shall push the consequences further and with much more facility than we had dared to promise ourselves; so that I believe that all the errors which are found in the sciences come from the fact that we have in the beginning formed our judgments too precipitately by admitting as principles obscure things of which we had no clear and distinct notion. The truth of this is shown by the modicum of progress that we have made in the sciences whose principles are certain and known by all; for, on the other hand, in the others, whose principles are obscure or uncertain, those who desire sincerely to express their thought will be forced to confess that after having employed much time, and having read many great volumes, they have to recognise that they know nothing and have learnt nothing.

It must not then appear astonishing to you, my dear Epistemon, if, desiring to lead Polyander in the way that is surer than that in which I was trained to walk, I am so careful and exact that I hold that only to be true of which I have a certainty equal to that with which I am aware that I am, I think, I am a thinking thing.

Epistemon. You seem to me to resemble these tumblers who always fall back on their feet, so ceaselessly do you return to your principle. Yet if you proceed by this path you will go neither far nor quickly. How, as a matter of fact, shall you always find truths of which you are as certain as of your existence?

Eudoxus. That is not as difficult as you think ; for all the truths succeed one another and are united by a common bond ; the whole secret consists simply in beginning with the first and most simple, and in rising little by little, and so to speak by gradations, to those more remote and complicated. Who now will doubt that what I have set forth as first principle is the first of the things which we might come to know with the help of a method? It is certain that we cannot doubt it, even were we to doubt of all things in the world. As then we are certain of having begun well, we must take pains not to deceive ourselves in what follows, we must apply our whole care not to admit that to be true which is liable to the smallest doubt. Pursuing this plan we must in my opinion allow Polyander to speak ; for as he follows no guidance but that of his common sense, and as his reason is corrupted by no prejudices, it is difficult for him to be deceived, or at any rate he would easily perceive that this was so, and he would without any trouble return to the right road. Let him then speak, and set forth what he himself alleges he has seen in your principle.

Polyander. So many things are contained in the idea of a thinking thing that whole days would be required to develope them. We shall only treat of the principal ones and those that can make the notion clearer and hinder our confounding it with what bears no relationship to it. I mean by a thinking being[1]....

---

[1] The Amsterdam Latin Version here inserts 'The rest is wanting.'

THE PASSIONS OF THE SOUL

PREFATORY NOTE TO 'THE PASSIONS OF THE SOUL.'

THE work entitled 'The Passions of the Soul' was written in French during the winter of 1645-6, four years before its author's death. It was the last work published by Descartes, who, indeed, expressed himself as very unwilling to appear again in print; the publication of the work was probably due to the urgent entreaties of Clerselier, Chanut, and other friends. Baillet, his biographer, says Descartes never published without regretting it, and certainly his publishers did not encourage him to do so, for complaints were constant as to the small sale of his books. The 'Passions' was sent to Queen Christina of Sweden, with whom Descartes had carried on a correspondence on the subjects allied to those discussed in this book. The first sketch had been sent to his other royal friend, Princess Elizabeth of Palatine in April, 1646, and she suggested some slight alterations upon it. The manuscript was placed in Clerselier's hands[1] in August, 1649 and was printed in Amsterdam in the end of November by Louis Elzevir, while Henry le Gras issued it at the same time in Paris. The author was at this period in Sweden, where he died, but he had probably revised the proofs before leaving Holland. He received copies of the book before his death, which was accelerated by the early morning lessons given in the depth of winter to Queen Christina at Stockholm.

E. S. H.

[1] Baillet says Clerselier, but M. Adam thinks it is more likely to have been the Abbé Picot.

THE PASSIONS¹ OF THE SOUL.

PART FIRST.

OF THE PASSIONS IN GENERAL, AND INCIDENTALLY OF THE WHOLE NATURE OF MAN.

ARTICLE I.

That what in respect of a subject is passion, is in some other regard always action.

There is nothing in which the defective nature of the sciences which we have received from the ancients appears more clearly than in what they have written on the passions; for, although this is a matter which has at all times been the object of much investigation, and though it would not appear to be one of the most difficult, inasmuch as since every one has experience of the passions within himself, there is no necessity to borrow one's observations from elsewhere in order to discover their nature; yet that which the ancients have taught regarding them is both so slight, and for the most part so far from credible, that I am unable to entertain any hope of approximating to the truth excepting by shunning the paths which they have followed. This is why I shall be here obliged to write just as though I were treating of a matter which no one had ever touched on before me; and, to begin with, I consider that all that which occurs or that happens anew, is by the philosophers, generally speaking, termed a passion, in as far as the subject to which it occurs is concerned, and an action in respect of him who causes it to occur. Thus although the agent and the recipient [patient] are frequently very different, the action and the

¹ The expression 'Passions' is in this Treatise of course used in its etymological significance.

passion are always one and the same thing, although having different names, because of the two diverse subjects to which it may be related.

ARTICLE II.

That in order to understand the passions of the soul its functions must be distinguished from those of body.

Next I note also that we do not observe the existence of any subject which more immediately acts upon our soul than the body to which it is joined, and that we must consequently consider that what in the soul is a passion is in the body commonly speaking an action; so that there is no better means of arriving at a knowledge of our passions than to examine the difference which exists between soul and body in order to know to which of the two we must attribute each one of the functions which are within us.

ARTICLE III.

What rule we must follow to bring about this result.

As to this we shall not find much difficulty if we realise that all that we experience as being in us, and that to observation may exist in wholly inanimate bodies, must be attributed to our body alone; and, on the other hand, that all that which is in us and which we cannot in any way conceive as possibly pertaining to a body, must be attributed to our soul.

ARTICLE IV.

That the heat and movement of the members proceed from the body, the thoughts from the soul.

Thus because we have no conception of the body as thinking in any way, we have reason to believe that every kind of thought which exists in us belongs to the soul; and because we do not doubt there being inanimate bodies which can move in as many as or in more diverse modes than can ours, and which have as much heat or more (experience demonstrates this to us in flame, which of itself has much more heat and movement than any of our members), we must believe that all the heat and all the movements which are in us pertain only to body, inasmuch as they do not depend on thought at all.

ARTICLE V.

That it is an error to believe that the soul supplies the movement and heat to body.

By this means we shall avoid a very considerable error into which many have fallen ; so much so that I am of opinion that this is the primary cause which has prevented our being able hitherto satisfactorily to explain the passions and the other properties of the soul. It arises from the fact that from observing that all dead bodies are devoid of heat and consequently of movement, it has been thought that it was the absence of soul which caused these movements and this heat to cease ; and thus, without any reason, it was thought that our natural heat and all the movements of our body depend on the soul : while in fact we ought on the contrary to believe that the soul quits us on death only because this heat ceases, and the organs which serve to move the body disintegrate.

ARTICLE VI.

The difference that exists between a living body and a dead body.

In order, then, that we may avoid this error, let us consider that death never comes to pass by reason of the soul, but only because some one of the principal parts of the body decays ; and we may judge that the body of a living man differs from that of a dead man just as does a watch or other automaton (i.e. a machine that moves of itself), when it is wound up and contains in itself the corporeal principle of those movements for which it is designed along with all that is requisite for its action, from the same watch or other machine when it is broken and when the principle of its movement ceases to act.

ARTICLE VII.

A brief explanation of the parts of the body and some of its functions.

In order to render this more intelligible, I shall here explain in a few words the whole method in which the bodily machine is composed. There is no one who does not already know that there are in us a heart, a brain, a stomach, muscles, nerves, arteries, veins, and such things. We also know that the food that we eat descends into the stomach and bowels where its juice, passing into the liver and into all the veins, mingles with, and thereby increases the quantity of the blood which they contain. Those who have acquired even the minimum of medical knowledge further know how the heart is composed, and how all the blood in the veins can easily flow from the vena cava into its right side and from thence pass into the lung by the vessel which we term the arterial vein, and then return from the lung into the left side of the heart, by the vessel called the venous artery, and finally pass from there into the great artery, whose branches spread throughout all the body. Likewise all those whom the authority of the ancients has not entirely blinded, and who have chosen to open their eyes for the purpose of investigating the opinion of Harvey regarding the circulation of the blood, do not doubt that all the veins and arteries of the body are like streams by which the blood ceaselessly flows with great swiftness, taking its course from the right cavity of the heart by the arterial vein whose branches are spread over the whole of the lung, and joined to that of the venous artery by which it passes from the lung into the left side of the heart; from these, again, it goes into the great artery whose branches, spread throughout all the rest of the body, are united to the branches of the vein, which branches once more carry the same blood into the right cavity of the heart. Thus these two cavities are like sluices through each of which all the blood passes in the course of each circuit which it makes in the body. We further know that all the movements of the members depend on the muscles, and that these muscles are so mutually related one to another that when the one is contracted it draws toward itself the part of the body to which it is attached, which causes the opposite muscle at the same time to become elongated; then if at another time it happens that this last contracts, it causes the former to become elongated and it draws back to itself the part to which they are attached. We know finally that all these movements of the muscles, as also all the senses, depend on the nerves, which resemble small filaments, or little tubes, which all proceed from the brain, and thus contain like it a certain very subtle air or wind which is called the animal spirits.

ARTICLE VIII.

What is the principle of all these functions?

But it is not usually known in what way these animal spirits and these nerves contribute to the movements and to the senses, nor what is the corporeal principle which causes them to act. That is why, although I have already made some mention of them in my other writings, I shall not here omit to say shortly that so long as we live there is a continual heat in our heart, which is a species of fire which the blood of the veins there maintains, and that this fire is the corporeal principle of all the movements of our members.

ARTICLE IX.

How the movement of the heart is carried on.

Its first effect is to dilate the blood with which the cavities of the heart are filled; that causes this blood, which requires a greater space for its occupation, to pass impetuously from the right cavity into the arterial vein, and from the left into the great artery; then when this dilation ceases, new blood immediately enters from the vena cava into the right cavity of the heart, and from the venous artery into the left; for there are little membranes at the entrances of these four vessels, disposed in such a manner that they do not allow the blood to enter the heart but by the two last, nor to issue from it but by the two others. The new blood which has entered into the heart is then immediately afterwards rarefied, in the same manner as that which preceded it; and it is just this which causes the pulse, or beating of the heart and arteries; so that this beating repeats itself as often as the new blood enters the heart. It is also just this which gives its motion to the blood, and causes it to flow ceaselessly and very quickly in all the arteries and veins, whereby it carries the heat which it acquires in the heart to every part of the body, and supplies them with nourishment.

ARTICLE X.

How the animal spirits are produced in the brain.

But what is here most worthy of remark is that all the most animated and subtle portions of the blood which the heat has rarefied in the heart, enter ceaselessly in large quantities into the cavities of the brain. And the reason which causes them to go there rather than elsewhere, is that all the blood which issues from the heart by the great artery takes its course in a straight line towards that place, and not being able to enter it in its entirety, because there are only very narrow passages there, those of its parts which are the most agitated and the most subtle alone pass through, while the rest spreads abroad in all the other portions of the body. But these very subtle parts of the blood form the animal spirits;

and for this end they have no need to experience any other change in the brain, unless it be that they are separated from the other less subtle portions of the blood; for what I here name spirits are nothing but material bodies and their one peculiarity is that they are bodies of extreme minuteness and that they move very quickly like the particles of the flame which issues from a torch. Thus it is that they never remain at rest in any spot, and just as some of them enter into the cavities of the brain, others issue forth by the pores which are in its substance, which pores conduct them into the nerves, and from there into the muscles, by means of which they move the body in all the different ways in which it can be moved.

ARTICLE XI.

How the movements of the muscles take place.

For the sole cause of all the movements of the members is that certain muscles contract, and that those opposite to them elongate, as has already been said; and the sole cause of one muscle contracting rather than that set against it, is that there comes from the brain some additional amount of animal spirits, however little it may be, to it rather than to the other. Not that the spirits which proceed immediately from the brain suffice in themselves to move the muscles, but they determine the other spirits which are already in these two muscles, all to issue very quickly from the one of them and to pass into the other. By this means that from which they issue becomes longer and more flaccid, and that into which they enter, being rapidly distended by them, contracts, and pulls the member to which it is attached. This is easy to understand provided that we know that there are but very few animal spirits which continually proceed from the brain to each muscle, but that there are always a quantity of others enclosed in the same muscle, which move there very quickly, sometimes by only turning about in the place where they are,—that is, when they do not find any passage open from which to issue forth from it—and sometimes by flowing into the opposite muscle; and inasmuch as there are little openings in each of these muscles by which the spirits can flow from one to the other, and which are so arranged that when the spirits that come from the brain to one of them have ever so little more strength than those that proceed to the other, they open all the entrances by which the spirits of the other muscle can pass into this one, and at the same time close all those by which the spirits of this last can pass into the other. By this means all the spirits formerly contained in these two muscles very quickly collect in one of them and then distend and shorten it, while the other becomes elongated and flaccid.

ARTICLE XII.

How outside objects act upon the organs of the senses.

We have still to understand the reasons why the spirits do not flow always from the brain into the muscles in the same fashion, and why occasionally more flow towards some than towards others. For in addition to the action of the soul which is truly in our case one of these causes, as I shall subsequently explain, there are two others which depend only on the body, and of these we must speak. The first consists in the diversity of movements which are excited in the organs of sense by their objects, and this I have already explained fully enough in the Dioptric; but in order that those who see this work may not be necessitated to read others, I shall here repeat that there are three things to consider in respect of the nerves, i.e. first of all their marrow or interior substance, which extends in the form of little filaments from the brain, from which it originates, to the extremities of the other members to which these filaments are attached; secondly the membranes which surround them, and which, being conterminous with those which envelope the brain, form the little tubes in which these little filaments are enclosed; and finally the animal spirits which, being carried by these same tubes from the brain to the muscles, are the reason of these filaments remaining there perfectly free and extended, so that the least thing that moves the part of the body to which the extremity of any one of them is attached, causes by that same means the part of the brain from which it proceeds to move, just as when one draws one end of a cord the other end is made to move.

ARTICLE XIII.

That this action of outside objects may lead the spirits into the muscles in diverse ways.

And I have explained in the Dioptric how all the objects of sight communicate themselves to us only through the fact that they move locally by the intermission of transparent bodies which are between them and us, the little filaments of the optic nerves which are at the back of our eyes, and then the parts of the brain from which these nerves proceed; I explained, I repeat, how they move them in as many diverse ways as the diversities which they cause us to see in things, and that it is not immediately the movements which occur in the eye, but those that occur in the brain which represent these objects to the soul. To follow this example, it is easy to conceive how sounds, scents, tastes, heat, pain, hunger, thirst and generally speaking all objects of our other external senses as well as of our internal appetites, also excite some movement in our nerves which by their means pass to the brain; and in addition to the fact that these diverse movements of the brain cause diverse perceptions to become evident to our soul, they can also without it cause the spirits to take their course towards certain muscles rather than towards others, and thus to move our limbs, which I shall prove here by one example only. If someone quickly thrusts his hand against our eyes as if to strike us, even though we know him to be our friend, that he only does it in fun, and that he will take great care not to hurt us, we have all the same trouble in preventing ourselves from closing them; and this shows that it is not by the intervention of our soul that they close, seeing that it is against our will, which is its only, or at least its principal activity; but it is because the machine of our body is so formed that the movement of this hand towards our eyes excites another movement in our brain, which conducts the animal spirits into the muscles which cause the eyelids to close.

ARTICLE XIV.

That the diversity which exists between the animal spirits may also cause a diversity in the course they take.

The other cause which serves to conduct the animal spirits differently into the muscles, is the unequal agitation of these spirits and the diversity of their parts. For when some of their parts are more coarse and more agitated than others, they pass further forward in a straight line into the cavities and pores of the brain, and by this means are conducted into other muscles than those they would enter if they had less force.

ARTICLE XV.

The causes of their diversity.

And this inequality may proceed from the diverse matters of which they are composed, as we see in the case of those who have drunk much wine—that the vapours of this wine entering quickly into the blood, rise from the heart to the brain, where they become converted into animal spirits, which, being stronger and more abundant than those ordinarily there, are capable of moving the body in many strange fashions. This inequality of spirits may also proceed from diverse dispositions of the heart, liver, stomach, spleen, and all other parts which contribute to their production; for we must here notice principally certain little nerves inserted in the base of the heart, which serve to enlarge and diminish the entrances of its cavities, whereby the blood dilating there more or less forcibly, produces spirits disposed in diverse ways. We must also notice that although the blood which enters the heart comes there from all other parts of the body, it nevertheless often happens that it is more forcibly driven from some parts than from others, because the nerves and muscles which lead to these particular parts press or agitate it to a greater extent; and that, according to the diversity of the parts from which it comes the most, it dilates variously in the heart and then produces spirits which have different qualities. Thus, for example, that which comes from the lower part of the liver where is the gall, dilates in another fashion in the heart than that which comes from the spleen, and this one again differently from what comes from the veins of the arms or legs, and this finally quite otherwise than the juice of the food when, having newly issued from the stomach and bowels, it at once passes by the liver to the heart.

Article XVI.

How all the members may be moved by the objects of the senses and by the animal spirits without the aid of the soul.

We must finally remark that the machine of our body is so formed that all the changes undergone by the movement of the spirits may cause them to open certain pores in the brain more than others, and reciprocally that when some one of the pores is opened more or less than usual (to however small a degree it may be) by the action of the nerves which are employed by the senses, that changes something in the movement of the spirits and causes them to be conducted into the muscles which serve to move the body in the way in which it is usually moved when such an action takes place. In this way all the movements which we make without our will contributing thereto (as frequently happens when we breathe, walk, eat, and in fact perform all those actions which are common to us and to the brutes), only depend on the conformation of our members, and on the course which the spirits, excited by the heat of the heart, follow naturally in the brain, nerves, and muscles, just as the movements of a watch are produced simply by the strength of the springs and the form of the wheels.

Article XVII.

What the functions of the soul are.

After having thus considered all the functions which pertain to the body alone, it is easy to recognise that there is nothing in us which we ought to attribute to our soul excepting our thoughts, which are mainly of two sorts, the one being the actions of the soul, and the other its passions. Those which I call its actions are all our desires, because we find by experience that they proceed directly from our soul, and appear to depend on it alone : while, on the other hand, we may usually term one's passions all those kinds of perception or forms of knowledge which are found in us, because it is often not our soul which makes them what they are, and because it always receives them from the things which are represented by them.

Article XVIII.

Of the Will.

Our desires, again, are of two sorts, of which the one consists of the actions of the soul which terminate in the soul itself, as when we desire to love God, or generally speaking, apply our thoughts to some object which is not material ; and the other of the actions which terminate in our body, as when from the simple fact that we have the desire to take a walk, it follows that our legs move and that we walk.

Article XIX.

Of the Perceptions.

Our perceptions are also of two sorts, and the one have the soul as a cause and the other the body. Those which have the soul as a cause are the perceptions of our desires, and of all the imaginations or other thoughts which depend on them. For it is certain that we cannot desire anything without perceiving by the same means that we desire it ; and, although in regard to our soul it is an action to desire something, we may say that it is also one of its passions to perceive that it desires. Yet because this perception and this will are really one and the same thing, the more noble always supplies the denomination, and thus we are not in the habit of calling it a passion, but only an action.

ARTICLE XX.

Of the imaginations and other thoughts which are formed by the soul.

When our soul applies itself to imagine something which does not exist, as when it represents to itself an enchanted palace or a chimera, and also when it applies itself to consider something which is only intelligible and not imaginable, e.g. to consider its own nature, the perceptions which it has of these things depend principally on the act of will which causes it to perceive them. That is why we usually consider them as actions rather than passions.

ARTICLE XXI.

Of the imaginations which have the body only as a cause.

Amongst the perceptions which are caused by the body, the most part depend on the nerves; but there are also some which do not depend on them, and which we name imaginations, such as those of which I have just spoken, from which they yet differ inasmuch as our will has no part in forming them; and this brings it to pass that they cannot be placed in the number of the actions of the soul. And they only proceed from the fact that the spirits being agitated in diverse ways and meeting with traces of diverse preceding impressions which have been effected in the brain, take their course there fortuitously by certain pores rather than by others. Such are the illusions of our dreams, and also the day-dreams which we often have when awake, and when our thought wanders aimlessly without applying itself to anything of its own accord. But, although some of these imaginations are the passions of the soul, taking this word in its most correct and perfect significance, and since they may all be thus termed if we take it in a more general significance, yet, because they have not a cause of so notable and determinate a description as the perceptions which the soul receives by the intermission of the nerves, and because they appear to be only a shadow and a picture, we must, before we can distinguish them very well, consider the difference prevailing among these others.

Article XXII.

Of the difference which exists among the other perceptions.

All the perceptions which I have not yet explained come to the soul by the intermission of the nerves, and there is between them this difference, that we relate them in the one case to objects outside which strike our senses, in the other to our soul.

Article XXIII.

Of the perceptions which we relate to objects which are without us.

Those which we relate to the things which are without us, to wit to the objects of our senses, are caused, at least when our opinion is not false, by these objects which, exciting certain movements in the organs of the external senses, excite them also in the brain by the intermission of the nerves, which cause the soul to perceive them. Thus when we see the light of a torch, and hear the sound of a bell, this sound and this light are two different actions which, simply by the fact that they excite two different movements in certain of our nerves, and by these means in the brain, give two different sensations to the soul, which sensations we relate to the subjects which we suppose to be their causes in such a way that we think we see the torch itself and hear the bell, and do not perceive just the movements which proceed from them.

Article XXIV.

Of the perceptions which we relate to our body.

The perceptions which we relate to our body, or to some of its parts, are those which we have of hunger, thirst, and other natural appetites, to which we may unite pain, heat, and the other affections which we perceive as though they were in our members, and not as in objects which are outside us ; we may thus perceive at the same time and by the intermission of the same nerves, the cold of our hand and the heat of the flame to which it approaches ; or, on the other hand, the heat of the hand and the cold of the air to which it is exposed, without there being any difference between the actions which cause us to feel the heat or the cold which is in our hand, and those which make us perceive that which is without us, excepting that from the one of these actions following upon the other, we judge that the first is already in us, and what supervenes is not so yet, but is in the object which causes it.

Article XXV.

Of the perceptions which we relate to our soul.

The perceptions which we relate solely to the soul are those whose effects we feel as though they were in the soul itself, and as to which we do not usually know any proximate cause to which we may relate them : such are the feelings of joy, anger, and other such sensations, which are sometimes excited in us by the objects which move our nerves and sometimes also by other causes. But, although all our perceptions, both those which we relate to objects which are outside us, and those which we relate to the diverse affections of our body, are truly passions in respect of our soul, when we use this word in its most general significance, yet we are in the habit of restricting it to the signification of those alone which are related to soul itself; and it is only these last which I have here undertaken to explain under the name of the passions of the soul.

Article XXVI.

That the imaginations which only depend on the fortuitous movements of the spirits, may be passions just as truly as the perceptions which depend on the nerves.

It remains for us to notice here that all the same things which the soul perceives by the intermission of the nerves, may also be represented by the fortuitous course of the animal spirits, without there being any other difference excepting that the impressions which come into the brain by the nerves are usually more lively or definite than those excited there by the spirits, which caused me to say in Article XXI that the former resemble the shadow or picture of the latter. We must also notice that it sometimes happens that this picture is so similar to the thing which it represents that we may be mistaken therein regarding the perceptions which relate to objects which are outside us, or at least those which relate to certain parts of our body, but that we cannot be so deceived regarding the passions, inasmuch as they are so close to, and so entirely within our soul, that it is impossible for it to feel them without their being actually such as it feels them to be. Thus often when we sleep, and sometimes even when we are awake, we imagine certain things so forcibly, that we think we see them before us, or feel them in our body, although they do not exist at all ; but although we may be asleep, or dream, we cannot feel sad or moved by any other passion without its being very true that the soul actually has this passion within it.

Article XXVII.

The definition of the passions of the soul.

After having considered in what the passions of the soul differ from all its other thoughts, it seems to me that we may define them generally as the perceptions, feelings, or emotions of the soul which we relate specially to it, and which are caused, maintained, and fortified by some movement of the spirits.

Article XXVIII.

Explanation of the first part of this definition.

We may call them perceptions when we make use of this word generally to signify all the thoughts which are not actions of the soul, or desires, but not when the term is used only to signify clear cognition; for experience shows us that those who are the most agitated by their passions, are not those who know them best; and that they are of the number of perceptions which the close alliance which exists between the soul and the body, renders confused and obscure. We may also call them feelings because they are received into the soul in the same way as are the objects of our outside senses, and are not otherwise known by it; but we can yet more accurately call them emotions of the soul, not only because the name may be attributed to all the changes which occur in it— that is, in all the diverse thoughts which come to it, but more especially because of all the kinds of thought which it may have, there are no others which so powerfully agitate and disturb it as do these passions.

Article XXIX.

Explanation of the second part.

I add that they particularly relate to the soul, in order to distinguish them from the other feelings which are related, the one to outside objects such as scents, sounds, and colours; the others to our body such as hunger, thirst, and pain. I also add that they are caused, maintained, and fortified by some movement of the spirits, in order to distinguish them from our desires, which we may call emotions of the soul which relate to it, but which are caused by itself; and also in order to explain their ultimate and most proximate cause, which plainly distinguishes them from the other feelings.

ARTICLE XXX.

That the soul is united to all the portions of the body conjointly.

But in order to understand all these things more perfectly, we must know that the soul is really joined to the whole body, and that we cannot, properly speaking, say that it exists in any one of its parts to the exclusion of the others, because it is one and in some manner indivisible, owing to the disposition of its organs, which are so related to one another that when any one of them is removed, that renders the whole body defective; and because it is of a nature which has no relation to extension, nor dimensions, nor other properties of the matter of which the body is composed, but only to the whole conglomerate of its organs, as appears from the fact that we could not in any way conceive of the half or the third of a soul, nor of the space it occupies, and because it does not become smaller owing to the cutting off of some portion of the body, but separates itself from it entirely when the union of its assembled organs is dissolved.

ARTICLE XXXI.

That there is a small gland in the brain in which the soul exercises its functions more particularly than in the other parts.

It is likewise necessary to know that although the soul is joined to the whole body, there is yet in that a certain part in which it exercises its functions more particularly than in all the others; and it is usually believed that this part is the brain, or possibly the heart: the brain, because it is with it that the organs of sense are connected, and the heart because it is apparently in it that we experience the passions. But, in examining the matter with care, it seems as though I had clearly ascertained that the part of the body in which the soul exercises its functions immediately is in nowise the heart, nor the whole of the brain, but merely the most inward of all its parts, to wit, a certain very small gland which is situated in the middle of its substance and so suspended above the duct whereby the animal spirits in its anterior cavities have communication with those in the posterior, that the slightest movements which take place in it may alter very greatly the course of these spirits; and reciprocally that the smallest changes which occur in the course of the spirits may do much to change the movements of this gland.

Article XXXII.

How we know that this gland is the main seat of the soul.

The reason which persuades me that the soul cannot have any other seat in all the body than this gland wherein to exercise its functions immediately, is that I reflect that the other parts of our brain are all of them double, just as we have two eyes, two hands, two ears, and finally all the organs of our outside senses are double; and inasmuch as we have but one solitary and simple thought of one particular thing at one and the same moment, it must necessarily be the case that there must somewhere be a place where the two images which come to us by the two eyes, where the two other impressions which proceed from a single object by means of the double organs of the other senses, can unite before arriving at the soul, in order that they may not represent to it two objects instead of one. And it is easy to apprehend how these images or other impressions might unite in this gland by the intermission of the spirits which fill the cavities of the brain : but there is no other place in the body where they can be thus united unless they are so in this gland.

Article XXXIII.

That the seat of the passions is not in the heart.

As to the opinion of those who think that the soul receives its passions in the heart, it is not of much consideration, for it is only founded on the fact that the passions cause us to feel some change taking place there; and it is easy to see that this change is not felt in the heart excepting through the medium of a small nerve which descends from the brain towards it, just as pain is felt as in the foot by means of the nerves of the foot, and the stars are perceived as in the heavens by means of their light and of the optic nerves; so that it is not more necessary that our soul should exercise its functions immediately in the heart, in order to feel its passions there, than it is necessary for the soul to be in the heavens in order to see the stars there.

ARTICLE XXXIV.

How the soul and the body act on one another.

Let us then conceive here that the soul has its principal seat in the little gland which exists in the middle of the brain, from whence it radiates forth through all the remainder of the body by means of the animal spirits, nerves, and even the blood, which, participating in the impressions of the spirits, can carry them by the arteries into all the members. And recollecting what has been said above about the machine of our body, i.e. that the little filaments of our nerves are so distributed in all its parts, that on the occasion of the diverse movements which are there excited by sensible objects, they open in diverse ways the pores of the brain, which causes the animal spirits contained in these cavities to enter in diverse ways into the muscles, by which means they can move the members in all the different ways in which they are capable of being moved; and also that all the other causes which are capable of moving the spirits in diverse ways suffice to conduct them into diverse muscles; let us here add that the small gland which is the main seat of the soul is so suspended between the cavities which contain the spirits that it can be moved by them in as many different ways as there are sensible diversities in the object, but that it may also be moved in diverse ways by the soul, whose nature is such that it receives in itself as many diverse impressions, that is to say, that it possesses as many diverse perceptions as there are diverse movements in this gland. Reciprocally, likewise, the machine of the body is so formed that from the simple fact that this gland is diversely moved by the soul, or by such other cause, whatever it is, it thrusts the spirits which surround it towards the pores of the brain, which conduct them by the nerves into the muscles, by which means it causes them to move the limbs.

ARTICLE XXXV.

Example of the mode in which the impressions of the objects unite in the gland which is in the middle of the brain.

Thus, for example, if we see some animal approach us, the light reflected from its body depicts two images of it, one in each of our eyes, and these two images form two others, by means of the optic nerves, in the interior surface of the brain which faces its cavities; then from there, by means of the animal spirits with which its cavities are filled, these images so radiate towards the little gland which is surrounded by these spirits, that the movement which forms each point of one of the images tends towards the same point of the gland towards which tends the movement which forms the point of the other image, which represents the same part of this animal. By this means the two images which are in the brain form but one upon the gland, which, acting immediately upon the soul, causes it to see the form of this animal.

ARTICLE XXXVI

Example of the way in which the passions are excited in the soul.

And, besides that, if this figure is very strange and frightful— that is, if it has a close relationship with the things which have been formerly hurtful to the body, that excites the passion of apprehension in the soul and then that of courage, or else that of fear and consternation according to the particular temperament of the body or the strength of the soul, and according as we have to begin with been secured by defence or by flight against the hurtful things to which the present impression is related. For in certain persons that disposes the brain in such a way that the spirits reflected from the image thus formed on the gland, proceed thence to take their places partly in the nerves which serve to turn the back and dispose the legs for flight, and partly in those which so increase or diminish the orifices of the heart, or at least which so agitate the other parts from whence the blood is sent to it, that this blood being there rarefied in a different manner from usual, sends to the brain the spirits which are adapted for the maintenance and strengthening of the passion of fear, i.e. which are adapted to the holding open, or at least reopening, of the pores of the brain which conduct them into the same nerves. For from the fact alone that these spirits enter into these pores, they excite a particular movement in this gland which is instituted by nature in order to cause the soul to be sensible of this passion ; and because these pores are principally in relation with the little nerves which serve to contract or enlarge the orifices of the heart, that causes the soul to be sensible of it for the most part as in the heart.

ARTICLE XXXVII.

How it seems as though they are all caused by some movement of the spirits.

And because the same occurs in all the other passions, to wit, that they are principally caused by the spirits which are contained in the cavities of the brain, inasmuch as they take their course towards the nerves which serve to enlarge or contract the orifices of the heart, or to drive in various ways to it the blood which is in the other parts, or, in whatever other fashion it may be, to carry on the same passion, we may from this clearly understand why I have placed in my definition of them above, that they are caused by some particular movement of the animal spirits.

Article XXXVIII.

Example of the movements of the body which accompany the passions and do not depend on the soul.

For the rest, in the same way as the course which these spirits take towards the nerves of the heart suffices to give the movement to the gland by which fear is placed in the soul, so, too, by the simple fact that certain spirits at the same time proceed towards the nerves which serve to move the legs in order to take flight, they cause another movement in the same gland, by means of which the soul is sensible of and perceives this flight, which in this way may be excited in the body by the disposition of the organs alone, and without the soul's contributing thereto.

Article XXXIX.

How one and the same cause may excite different passions in different men.

The same impression which a terrifying object makes on the gland, and which causes fear in certain men, may excite in others courage and confidence ; the reason of this is that all brains are not constituted in the same way, and that the same movement of the gland which in some excites fear, in others causes the spirits to enter into the pores of the brain which conduct them partly into the nerves which serve to move the hands for purposes of self-defence, and partly into those which agitate and drive the blood towards the heart in the manner requisite to produce the spirits proper for the continuance of this defence, and to retain the desire of it.

Article XL.

The principal effect of the passions.

For it is requisite to notice that the principal effect of all the passions in men is that they incite and dispose their soul to desire those things for which they prepare their body, so that the feeling of fear incites it to desire to fly, that of courage to desire to fight, and so on.

Article XLI.

The power of the soul in regard to the body.

But the will is so free in its nature, that it can never be constrained; and of the two sorts of thoughts which I have distinguished in the soul (of which the first are its actions, i.e. its desires, the others its passions, taking this word in its most general significance, which comprises all kinds of perceptions), the former are absolutely in its power, and can only be indirectly changed by the body, while on the other hand the latter depend absolutely on the actions which govern and direct them, and they can only indirectly be altered by the soul, excepting when it is itself their cause. And the whole action of the soul consists in this, that solely because it desires something, it causes the little gland to which it is closely united to move in the way requisite to produce the effect which relates to this desire.

Article XLII.

How we find in the memory the things which we desire to remember.

Thus when the soul desires to recollect something, this desire causes the gland, by inclining successively to different sides, to thrust the spirits towards different parts of the brain until they come across that part where the traces left there by the object which we wish to recollect are found; for these traces are none other than the fact that the pores of the brain, by which the spirits have formerly followed their course because of the presence of this object, have by that means acquired a greater facility than the others in being once more opened by the animal spirits which come towards them in the same way. Thus these spirits in coming in contact with these pores, enter into them more easily than into the others, by which means they excite a special movement in the gland which represents the same object to the soul, and causes it to know that it is this which it desired to remember.

Article XLIII.

How the soul can imagine, be attentive, and move the body.

Thus when we desire to imagine something we have never seen, this desire has the power of causing the gland to move in the manner requisite to drive the spirits towards the pores of the brain by the opening of which pores this particular thing may be represented; thus when we wish to apply our attention for some time to the consideration of one particular object, this desire holds the gland for the time being inclined to the same side. Thus, finally, when we desire to walk or to move our body in some special way, this desire causes the gland to thrust the spirits towards the muscles which serve to bring about this result.

ARTICLE XLIV.

That each desire is naturally united to some movement of the gland; but that, by intentional effort or by custom, it may be united to others.

At the same time it is not always the desire to excite in us some movement, or bring about some result which is able so to excite it, for this changes according as nature or custom have diversely united each movement of the gland to each particular thought. Thus, for example, if we wish to adjust our eyes so that they may look at an object very far off, this desire causes their pupils to enlarge; and if we wish to set them to look at an object very near, this desire causes them to contract; but if we think only of enlarging the pupil of the eye we may have the desire indeed, but we cannot for all that enlarge it, because nature has not joined the movement of the gland which serves to thrust forth the spirits towards the optic nerve, in the manner requisite for enlarging or diminishing the pupil, with the desire to enlarge or diminish it, but with that of looking at objects which are far away or near. And when in speaking we think only of the sense of what we desire to say, that causes us to move the tongue and lips much more quickly and much better than if we thought of moving them in all the many ways requisite to utter the same words, inasmuch as the custom which we have acquired in learning to speak, caused us to join the action of the soul (which, by the intermission of the gland can move the tongue and lips), with the significance of words which follow these movements, rather than with the movements themselves.

ARTICLE XLV.

What is the power of the soul in reference to its passions.

Our passions cannot likewise be directly excited or removed by the action of our will, but they can be so indirectly by the representation of things which are usually united to the passions which we desire to have, and which are contrary to those which we desire to set aside. Thus, in order to excite courage in oneself and remove fear, it is not sufficient to have the will to do so, but we must also apply ourselves to consider the reasons, the objects or examples which persuade us that the peril is not great; that there is always more security in defence than in flight; that we should have the glory and joy of having vanquished, while we could expect nothing but regret and shame for having fled, and so on.

ARTICLE XLVI.

The reason which prevents the soul from being able wholly to control its passion.

And there is a special reason which prevents the soul from being able at once to change or arrest its passions, which has caused me to say in defining them that they are not only caused, but are also maintained and strengthened by some particular movement of the spirits. This reason is that they are nearly all accompanied by some commotion which takes place in the heart, and in consequence also in the whole of the blood and the animal spirits, so that until this commotion has subsided, they remain present to our thought in the same manner as sensible objects are present there while they act upon the organs of our senses. And as the soul, in rendering itself very attentive to some other thing, may prevent itself from hearing a slight noise or feeling a slight pain, but cannot prevent itself in the same way from hearing thunder or feeling the fire which burns the hand, it may similarly easily get the better of the lesser passions, but not the most violent and strongest, excepting after the commotion of the blood and spirits is appeased. The most that the will can do while this commotion is in its full strength is not to yield to its effects and to restrain many of the movements to which it disposes the body. For example, if anger causes us to lift our hand to strike, the will can usually hold it back; if fear incites our legs to flee, the will can arrest them, and so on in other similar cases.

ARTICLE XLVII.

In what the strife consists which we imagine to exist between the lower and higher part of the soul.

And it is only in the repugnance which exists between the movements which the body by its animal spirits, and the soul by its will, tend to excite in the gland at the same time, that all the strife which we are in the habit of conceiving to exist between the inferior part of the soul, which we call the sensuous, and the superior which is rational, or as we may say, between the natural appetites and the will, consists. For there is within us but one soul, and this soul has not in itself any diversity of parts ; the same part that is subject to sense impressions is rational, and all the soul's appetites are acts of will. The error which has been committed in making it play the part of various personages, usually in opposition one to another, only proceeds from the fact that we have not properly distinguished its functions from those of the body, to which alone we must attribute every thing which can be observed in us that is opposed to our reason ; so that there is here no strife, excepting that the small gland which exists in the middle of the brain, being capable of being thrust to one side by the soul, and to the other by the animal spirits, which are mere bodies, as I have said above, it often happens that these two impulses are contrary, and that the stronger prevents the other from taking effect. We may, however, distinguish two sorts of movement excited by the animal spirits in the gland—the one sort represents to the soul the objects which move the senses, or the impressions which are met with in the brain, and makes no attempt to affect its will ; the others do make an effort to do so—i.e. those which cause the passions or the movements of the body which accompany the passions. And as to the first, although they often hinder the actions of the soul, or else are hindered by them, yet, because they are not directly contrary to them, we do not notice any strife between them. We only notice the strife between the latter and the acts of will which conflict with them : e.g. between the effort with which the spirits impel the gland in order to cause a desire for something in the soul, and that with which the soul repels it again by the desire which it has to avoid the very same thing. And what causes this strife to come into evidence for the most part is that the will, not having the power to excite the passions directly, as has just been said, is constrained to use its best endeavours, and to apply itself to consider successively several things as to which, though it happens that one has the power to change for a moment the course taken by the spirits, it may come to pass that that which succeeds does not have it, and that they immediately afterwards revert to that same course because the disposition which has before held its place in the nerves, heart, and blood has not changed, and thus it comes about that the soul feels itself almost at the same time impelled to desire and not to desire the same thing. It is from this that occasion has been taken to imagine in the soul two powers which strive one with the other. At the same time we may still conceive a sort of strife to exist, inasmuch as often the same cause which excites some passion in the soul, also excites certain movements in the body to which the soul does not contribute, and which it stops, or tries to stop, directly it perceives them; as we see when what excites fear also causes the spirits to enter into the muscles which serve to move the legs with the object of flight, and when the wish which we have to be brave stops them from doing so

ARTICLE XLVIII.

How we recognise the strength or infirmity of souls, and what is lacking in those that are most feeble.

And it is by success in these combats that each individual can discover the strength or the weakness of his soul; for those in whom by nature the will can most easily conquer the passions and arrest the movements of the body which accompany them, without doubt possess the strongest souls. But there are those people who cannot bring their strength to the test, because they never cause their will to do battle with its proper arms, but only with those with which certain passions furnish it in order to resist certain others. That which I call its proper arms consists of the firm and determinate judgments respecting the knowledge of good and evil, in pursuance of which it has resolved to conduct the actions of its life; and the most feeble souls of all are those whose will does not thus determine itself to follow certain judgments, but allows itself continually to be carried away by present passions, which, being frequently contrary to one another, draw the will first to one side, then to the other, and, by employing it in striving against itself, place the soul in the most deplorable possible condition. Thus when fear represents death as an extreme evil, and one which can only be avoided by flight, ambition on the other hand sets forth the infamy of this flight as an evil worse than death. These two passions agitate the will in diverse ways; and in first obeying one and then the other, it is in continual opposition to itself, and thus renders the soul enslaved and unhappy.

Article XLIX.

That the strength of the soul does not suffice without the knowledge of the truth.

It is true that there are very few men so weak and irresolute that they desire nothing except what their passion dictates to them. The most part have determinate judgments, in pursuance of which they regulate a part of their actions; and although often their judgments are false or even founded on certain passions by which the will formerly allowed itself to be vanquished or led astray, yet, because it continues to follow them when the passion which has caused them is absent, they may be considered as its proper arms, and we may reflect that souls are stronger or weaker by reason of the fact that they are able to follow these judgments more or less closely, and resist the present passions which are contrary to them. Yet there is a great difference between the resolutions which proceed from a false opinion, and those which are founded only on the knowledge of the truth, inasmuch as if we follow the latter we are assured that we shall never regret nor repent it, whereas we do so always when we have followed the first-mentioned, and hence discovered our error in doing so.

Article L.

That there is no soul so feeble that it cannot, if well directed, acquire an absolute power over its passions.

And it is useful here to know that, as has already been said above, although each movement of the gland seems to have been joined by nature to each one of our thoughts from the beginning of our life, we may at the same time join them to others by means of custom, as experience shows us in the case of words which excite movements in the gland, which, so far as the institution of nature is concerned, do not represent to the soul more than their sound when they are uttered by the voice, or the form of their letters when they are written, and which, nevertheless, by the custom which has been acquired in thinking of what they signify when their sound has been heard or their letters have been seen, usually make this signification to be understood rather than the form of their letters or the sound of their syllables. It is also useful to know that although the movements both of the gland and of the spirits of the brain, which represent certain objects to the soul, are naturally joined to those which excite in it certain passions, they can at the same time be separated from these by custom, and joined to others which are very different; and also that this custom can be acquired by a solitary action, and does not require long usage. Thus when we unexpectedly meet with something very foul in food that we are eating with relish, the surprise that this event gives us may so change the disposition of our brain, that we can no longer see any such food without horror, while we formerly ate it with pleasure. And the same thing is to be noticed in brutes, for although they have no reason, nor perhaps any thought, all the movements of the spirits and of the gland which excite the passions in us, are none the less in them, and in them serve in maintaining and strengthening not, as in our case, the passions, but the movements of the nerves and muscles which usually accompany them. So when a dog sees a partridge he is naturally disposed to run towards it, and when he hears a gun fired, this sound naturally incites him to flight. But nevertheless setters are usually so trained that the sight of a partridge causes them to stop, and the sound which they afterwards hear when a shot is fired over them, causes them to run up to us. And these things are useful in inciting each one of us to study to regard our passions; for since we can with a little industry change the movement of the brain in animals deprived of reason, it is evident that we can do so yet more in the case of men, and that even those who have the feeblest souls can acquire a very absolute dominion over all their passions if sufficient industry is applied in training and guiding them.

PART SECOND.

OF THE NUMBER AND ORDER OF THE PASSIONS AND AN EXPOSITION OF THE SIX PRIMITIVE PASSIONS

ARTICLE LI.

What are the first causes of the passions.

We know from what has been said above that the ultimate and most proximate cause of the passions of the soul is none other than the agitation with which the spirits move the little gland which is in the middle of the brain. But that does not suffice to distinguish one from another; it is necessary to investigate their sources, and to examine their first causes: and, although they may sometimes be caused by the action of the soul which determines itself to conceive of this or that object, and also simply by the temperament of the body or by the impressions which are fortuitously met with in the brain, as happens when we feel sad or joyous without being able to give a reason, it yet appears by what has been said, that in all cases the same passions can also be excited by the objects which move the senses, and that these objects are their most ordinary and principal causes; from which it follows that in order to find them all, it is sufficient to consider all the effects of these objects.

ARTICLE LII.

What is their mode of operation and how they may be enumerated.

I notice besides, that the objects which move the senses do not excite diverse passions in us because of all the diversities which are in them, but only because of the diverse ways in which they may harm or help us, or in general be of some importance to us; and that the customary mode of action of all the passions is simply this, that they dispose the soul to desire those things which nature tells us are of use, and to persist in this desire, and also bring about that same agitation of spirits which customarily causes them to dispose the body to the movement which serves for the carrying into effect of these things ; that is why, in order to enumerate them, we must merely examine in their order in how many diverse ways which are significant for us, our senses can be moved by their objects ; and I shall here make an enumeration of all the principal passions according to the order in which they may thus be found.

THE ORDER AND ENUMERATION OF THE PASSIONS.

ARTICLE LIII.

Wonder.

When the first encounter with some object surprises us, and we judge it to be new or very different from what we formerly knew, or from what we supposed that it ought to be, that causes us to wonder and be surprised ; and because that may happen before we in any way know whether this object is agreeable to us or is not so, it appears to me that wonder is the first of all the passions ; and it has no opposite, because if the object which presents itself has nothing in it that surprises us, we are in nowise moved regarding it, and we consider it without passion

ARTICLE LIV.

Esteem and disdain, generosity or pride and humility or poor-spiritedness.

To wonder is united esteem or disdain according as it is at the greatness of an object or its smallness that we wonder. And we may thus esteem or despise ourselves, from which come the passions, and then the habitudes, of magnanimity or pride, and of humility or poor-spirit.

ARTICLE LV.

Veneration and disdain.

But when we esteem or think little of other objects which we consider as free causes capable of doing good or evil, from esteem proceeds veneration and from simple absence of esteem, disdain.

Article LVI.

Love and hatred.

And all the preceding passions may be excited in us without our in any way perceiving if the object which causes them is good or evil. But when a matter is presented as relatively to us good, i.e. as agreeable to us, that causes us to have love for it, and when it is represented as evil or hurtful to us, that excites hatred in us.

Article LVII.

Desire.

From the same consideration of good and evil all the other passions originate; but in order to place them in order I make distinctions as to time, and considering that they lead us to regard much more the future than the present or the past, I commence with desire. For not only when we desire to acquire a good which we do not yet have, or avoid an evil which we judge may occur; but also when we only anticipate the conservation of a good or absence of an evil, which is as far as this passion may extend, it is evident that it ever regards the future.

Article LVIII.

Hope, fear, jealousy, confidence and despair.

It suffices to reflect that the acquisition of a good or removal of an evil is possible in order to be incited to desire it. But when besides that we consider whether there is much or little prospect that we shall obtain what we desire, that which represents to us that there is much probability of this excites in us hope, and that which represents to us that there is little, excites fear, of which jealousy is a species. When hope is excessive it changes its nature and is called confidence or assurance. Just as on the other hand extreme fear becomes despair.

Article LIX.

Irresolution, courage, bravery, emulation, cowardice, and terror.

And we can thus hope and fear although the issue of what we expect in no way depends on us; but when it is represented to us as dependent there may be a difficulty in the selection of the means or in carrying them into execution. From the first proceeds the irresolution which disposes us to deliberate and take council. To the latter courage or bravery is opposed, of which emulation is a species. And cowardice is contrary to courage, as fear or terror is to bravery.

Article LX.

Remorse.

And if one is moved to act before irresolution has passed away, that causes remorse of conscience to arise, which does not concern the time to come like the preceding passions, but the present or the past.

Article LXI.

Joy and sadness.

And the consideration of the present good excites joy in us, and that of evil, sadness, when it is a good or an evil which is represented as belonging to us.

Article LXII.

Mockery, envy, pity.

But when it is represented to us as pertaining to other men, we may esteem them either as worthy or unworthy of it; and when we esteem them worthy, that does not excite in us any other passion but joy, inasmuch as it is some satisfaction to us to see that things happen as they should. There is only this difference, that the joy that comes from what is good is serious, while what comes from evil is accompanied by laughter and mockery. But if we esteem them unworthy of it, the good excites envy and the evil pity, which are species of sadness. And we must notice that the same passions which relate to present good or evil things may often likewise be related to those which are to come, since our belief that they will come represents them as if they were present.

Article LXIII.

Self-satisfaction and repentance.

We may also consider the cause of the good or evil, present as well as past. And the good which has been done by ourselves gives us an internal satisfaction which is the sweetest of all the passions; while the evil excites repentance, which is the most bitter.

ARTICLE LXIV.

Favour and gratitude.

But the good which has been done by others causes us to regard them with favour although it is not to us that it has been done, and if it is to us, we join to the favour gratitude.

ARTICLE LXV.

Indignation and anger.

In the same way the evil done by others and not having any relation to us, only causes us to be indignant with them ; and when it is so related it likewise arouses anger.

ARTICLE LXVI.

Pride[1] and shame.

Further, the good which is or has been in us, being referred to the opinion which others may have of it, excites a feeling of glory or pride in us, and the evil, shame.

ARTICLE LXVII.

Disgust, regret, and gaiety[2].

And sometimes the duration of the good brings about tedium or disgust, while that of evil diminishes sadness. And finally from past good, regret proceeds, and this is a species of sadness ; and from past evil comes gaiety[2], which is a species of joy.

ARTICLE LXVIII.

Why this enumeration of the passions is different from that which is commonly received.

Here we have the order which seems to me to be the best for the enumeration of the passions. In this I know well that I am parting company with all those who have written on this subject before, but it is not without great reason that I do so. For these derive their enumeration from the fact that they distinguish in the sensitive part of the soul two appetites which they name the *concupiscent* and *irascible* respectively. And because in the soul I recognise no distinction of parts, as I have said above, this seems to me to signify nothing but that it has two faculties, the one of desire,

---

[1] 'La gloire.'   [2] allégresse F.

and the other of anger, and because in the same way it has the faculties of wondering, loving, hoping, fearing, and thus of receiving in itself every other passion, or else bringing about actions to which these passions urge it, I do not see why they have desired to refer them all to concupiscence or anger.   And besides their enumeration does not comprehend all the principal passions, as I believe this one does. I speak only of the principal, because we may further distinguish many other more particular ones, and their number is indefinite.

Article LXIX.

That there are only six primitive passions.

But the number of those which are simple and primitive is not very large.   For, in making a review of all those which I have enumerated, we may easily notice that there are but six which are such, i.e. wonder, love, hatred, desire, joy and sadness; and that all the others are composed of some of these six, or are species of them. That is why, in order that their multitude may not embarrass my readers, I shall here treat the six primitive passions separately; and afterwards I shall show in what way all the others derive from them their origin.

Article LXX.

Of wonder; its definition and cause.

Wonder is a sudden surprise of the soul which causes it to apply itself to consider with attention the objects which seem to it rare and extraordinary.   It is thus primarily caused by the impression we have in the brain which represents the object as rare, and as consequently worthy of much consideration; then afterwards by the movement of the spirits, which are disposed by this impression to tend with great force towards the part of the brain where it is, in order to fortify and conserve it there ; as they are also disposed by it to pass thence into the muscles which serve to retain the organs of the senses in the same situation in which they are, so that it is still maintained by them, if it is by them that it has been formed.

Article LXXI.

That in this passion no change occurs in the heart or in the blood.

And this passion has this particular characteristic, that in it we do not notice that it is accompanied by any change which occurs in the heart and blood like the other passions. The reason of this is that not having good or evil as its object, but only the knowledge of the thing that we wonder at, it has no relation with the heart and blood on which all the good of the body depends, but only with the brain where are the organs of the senses which are the instruments of this knowledge.

Article LXXII.

In what the strength of wonder consists.

That does not prevent its having much strength because of the surprise, i.e. the sudden and unexpected arrival of this impression which changes the movement of the spirits, which surprise is proper and peculiar to this passion ; so that when surprise is met with in other passions as it is usually met with in almost all, thus increasing them, what happens is that wonder is united to them. And the strength depends on two things, i.e. on the novelty, and on the fact that the movement which it causes possesses its entire strength from its commencement. For it is certain that such a movement has more effect than those which, being feeble to begin with, and only increasing little by little, can easily be turned aside. It is likewise certain that the objects of sense which are new, affect the brain in certain parts in which it is not usually affected, and that the fact that these parts are more tender or less firm than those which a frequent agitation has solidified, increases the effect of the movements which they there excite. And we shall not find this incredible if we consider that it is a similar reason which brings it about that, the soles of our feet being accustomed to a contact which is rough enough owing to the weight of the body which they bear, we feel this contact but little when we walk, while another much slighter and more gentle touch, when they are tickled, is almost insupportable because it is unusual to us.

Article LXXIII.

What astonishment is.

And this surprise has so much power in causing the spirits which are in the cavities of the brain to take their way from thence to the place where is the impression of the object which we wonder at, that it sometimes thrusts them all there, and causes them to be so much occupied in preserving this impression that there are none which pass from thence into the muscles, nor even which in any way turn themselves away from the tracks which they originally pursued in the brain: and this causes the whole body to remain as immobile as a statue, and prevents our perceiving more of the object than the first face which is presented, or consequently of acquiring a more particular knowledge of it. That is what we commonly call being astonished, and astonishment is an excess of wonder which can never be otherwise than bad.

Article LXXIV.

The end which the passions serve, and to what they are detrimental.

And it is easy to understand from what has been said above, that the utility of all the passions consists alone in their fortifying and perpetuating in the soul thoughts which it is good it should preserve, and which without that might easily be effaced from it. And again, all the harm which they can cause consists in the fact that they fortify and conserve these thoughts more than necessary, or that they fortify and conserve others on which it is not good to dwell.

Article LXXV.

In what wonder particularly consists.

And we may say more particularly of wonder that it is useful, inasmuch as it causes us to learn and retain in our memory things of which we were formerly ignorant; for we shall only wonder at that which appears rare and extraordinary to us, and nothing can so appear excepting because we have been ignorant of it, or also because it is different from the things which we have known; for it is this difference which causes it to be called extraordinary. Now although a thing which was unknown to us, presents itself anew to our understanding or our senses, we do not for all that retain it in our memory, unless the idea which we have of it is strengthened in our brain by some passion or else by the application of our understanding which our will determines to a particular attention and reflection. And the other passions may serve to make us remark things which seem good or evil; but we have only wonder for those which appear but seldom. We also see that those who have no natural inclination towards this passion are usually very ignorant.

Article LXXVI.

In what it may do harm, and how we may make good its deficiency and correct its excess.

But it much more frequently occurs that we wonder too much, and that we are astonished in perceiving things which deserve little or no consideration, than that we wonder too little. And this may entirely prevent or pervert the use of the reason. That is why, although it is good to be born with some inclination towards this passion, because that disposes us for the acquisition of the sciences, we must at the same time afterwards try to free ourselves from it as much as possible. For it is easy to supplement its defects by special reflection and attention which our will can always oblige our understanding to give on these occasions when we judge that the matter which presents itself is worth the trouble. But there is no other remedy to prevent our wondering to excess than that of acquiring a knowledge of various matters and exercising ourselves in the consideration of all those which may appear the most rare and strange.

Article LXXVII.

That it is neither the most stupid nor the most clever who are most carried away by wonder.

For the rest, although it is only those who are dull and stupid who are in nowise impelled by their nature to wonder, that is not to say that those who are best supplied with wits are always those who are most disposed to it. As a matter of fact it is principally those who, although they have a fairly good supply of common sense, have at the same time no high opinion as to their sufficiency.

Article LXXVIII.

That its excess may pass into a matter of habit when we fail to correct it.

And although this passion seems to diminish with use, because the more we meet with rare things which we wonder at, the more we accustom ourselves to cease to wonder at them, and to think that all those which may afterwards present themselves are common, still, when it is excessive, and causes us to arrest our attention solely on the first image of the objects which are presented, without acquiring any other knowledge of them, it leaves behind it a custom which disposes the soul in the same way to pause over all the other objects which present themselves, provided that they appear to it to be ever so little new. And this is what causes the continuance of the malady of those who suffer from a blind curiosity—that is, who seek out things that are rare solely to wonder at them, and not for the purpose of really knowing them : for little by little they become so given over to wonder, that things of no importance are no less capable of arresting their attention than those whose investigation is more useful.

ARTICLE LXXIX.

The definition of love and hate.

Love is an emotion of the soul caused by the movement of the spirits which incites it to join itself willingly to objects which appear to it to be agreeable. And hatred is an emotion caused by the spirits which incite the soul to desire to be separated from the objects which present themselves to it as hurtful. I say that these emotions are caused by the spirits in order to distinguish love and hate, which are passions and depend on the body, both from the judgments which also induce the soul by its free will to unite itself with the things which it esteems to be good, and to separate itself from those it holds to be evil, and from the emotions which these judgments excite of themselves in the soul.

ARTICLE LXXX.

What it is to join or separate oneself by one's free will.

For the rest, by the word will I do not here intend to talk of desire, which is a passion apart, and one which relates to the future, but of the consent by which we consider ourselves from this time forward as united with what we love, so that we imagine a whole of which we conceive ourselves as only constituting one part, while the thing loved constitutes another part. In the case of hatred, on the other hand, we consider ourselves only and as a whole, entirely separated from the matter for which we possess an aversion.

ARTICLE LXXXI.

Of the distinction usually made between the love belonging to concupiscence and that of benevolence.

And two sorts of love are usually distinguished, the one of which is named the love of benevolence, that is to say the love which incites us to wish well to what we love; the other is named the love of concupiscence, that is to say the love that causes us to desire the thing that is loved. But it appears to me that this distinction concerns the effects of love alone, and not its essence ; for as soon as we are willingly joined to some object, of whatever nature it may be, we have for it a feeling of benevolence, i.e. we also join to it willingly the things which we believe to be agreeable to it : and this is one of the principal effects of love. And if we judge that it is a desirable thing to possess it, or to be associated with it in some other manner than through the will, we desire it : and this is likewise one of the most ordinary effects of love.

Article LXXXII.

How very different passions agree, inasmuch as they participate in love.

There is also no need to distinguish as many kinds of love as there are diverse objects which we may love; for, to take an example, although the passions which an ambitious man has for glory, a miser for money, a drunkard for wine, a brutal man for a woman whom he desires to violate, a man of honour for his friend or mistress, and a good father for his children, may be very different, still, inasmuch as they participate in love, they are similar. But the four first only have love for the possession of the objects to which their passion relates, and do not have any for the objects themselves, for which they only have desire mingled with other particular passions. But the love which a good father has for his children is so pure that he desires to have nothing from them, and does not wish to possess them otherwise than he does, nor to be united with them more closely than he already is. For, considering them as replicas of himself, he seeks their good as his own, or even with greater care, because, in setting before himself that he or they form a whole of which he is not the best part, he often prefers their interests to his, and does not fear losing himself in order to save them. The affection which honourable men have for their friends is of this nature even though it is rarely so perfect ; and that which they have for their mistress participates largely in it, but it also participates a little in the others.

Article LXXXIII.

Of the difference which exists between simple affection, friendship, and devotion.

We may, it seems to me, find differences in love according to the esteem which we bear to the object loved as compared with oneself: for when we esteem the object of love less than ourselves, we have only a simple affection for it; when we esteem it equally with ourselves, that is called friendship; and when we esteem it more, the passion which we have may be called devotion. Thus we may have affection for a flower, a bird, a horse; but unless we have a very ill-regulated mind, we can have friendship for men alone. And they are so truly the object of this passion, that there is no man so imperfect that we cannot have for him a very perfect friendship, when we are loved by him, and when we have a truly noble and generous soul, in accordance with what will be afterwards explained in Articles CLIV and CLVI. As to the meaning of devotion, its principal object is no doubt the supreme Divinity to whom we cannot fail to be devoted when we know Him as we should; but we may also have devotion for our prince, country, town, and even for a particular man, when we esteem him much more than ourselves. Now the difference which exists between these three sorts of love is shown principally by their effects; for inasmuch as in all of them we consider ourselves as joined and united to the thing loved, we are always ready to abandon the lesser portion of the whole into which we both enter, in order to preserve the other portion. This brings it to pass that in simple affection we always prefer ourselves to the object loved; and, on the other hand, in devotion the thing loved is so much preferred to the self, that we do not fear death in order to preserve it. We have frequently seen examples of this in the case of those who have exposed themselves to a certain death in the defence of their prince or their town, and in some cases even for the private persons to whom they were devoted.

Article LXXXIV.

That there are not as many kinds of hate as of love.

For the rest, although hatred is directly opposed to love, we do not always divide it into so many species because we do not to the same extent notice the difference which exists between the evils from which we are separated by our will, as we do that which exists between the good things to which we are joined.

Article LXXXV

Of delight and revulsion[1].

And I only find one distinct characteristic of any note which is alike in both. It consists in the fact that the objects both of love and hatred may be represented to the soul by the external senses, or else by the internal, and by its own reason : for we commonly denominate good or evil that which our interior senses or our reason make us judge to be agreeable or the contrary to our nature ; but we term beautiful or ugly that which is so represented to us by our outward senses, principally by that of sight, which alone is more considered than the others ; hence two sorts of love originate, i.e. that which we have for good things, and that which we have for beautiful things, to which we may give the name of attraction or delight in order not to confound it with the other, nor yet with desire, to which we often attribute the name of love. And from thence also, two kinds of hatred in the same way take their rise, the one of which relates to evil things, the other to ugly things ; and this last may be called horror or aversion in order to distinguish it. But what is most remarkable here is that these passions of delight and detestation or horror are usually more violent than the other sorts of love or hate, because what comes to the soul by the senses touches it more forcibly than what is represented to it by its reason, and that even though these first passions have usually less truth ; so that of all the passions it is these which deceive the most, and against which we should guard ourselves most carefully.

Article LXXXVI.

The definition of Desire.

The passion of desire is an agitation of the soul caused by the spirits which dispose it to wish for the future the things which it represents to itself as agreeable. Thus we do not only desire the presence of the absent good, but also the conservation of the present, and further, the absence of evil, both of that which we already have, and of that which we believe we might experience in time to come.

Article LXXXVII.

That it is a passion which has no opposite.

I know very well that usually in the Schools the passion which makes for the search after the good which alone is called desire is

[1] De l'agrément et de l'horreur.

opposed to that which makes for the avoidance of evil, which is called aversion. But inasmuch as there is no good whose privation is not an evil, nor any evil considered in a positive sense, whose privation is not a good, and that in investigating riches, for example, we necessarily shun poverty, in fleeing from sickness we make for health, and so on with other things, it seems to me that it is always an identical movement which makes for the search after good, and at the same time for the avoidance of the evil which is contrary to it. I merely remark this difference in it, that the desire which we have when we make for some good is accompanied by love, and then by hope and joy; while the same desire, when it tends to remove itself from evil contrary to this good, is accompanied by hate, fear and sadness; which is the cause of our judging it to be contrary to itself. But if we wish to consider it when at the same time it relates equally to some good with the view of seeking it, and to an opposed evil in order to avoid it, we may very clearly see that it is but one passion which brings about both the one and the other.

Article LXXXVIII.

Its different species.

There would be more reason in distinguishing desire into as many different species as there are different objects sought after; since, for example, curiosity, which is none other than a desire for knowledge, differs much from desire for glory, and this again from desire for vengeance, and so on in the case of other objects. But it is here sufficient to know that there are as many species of the passions as there are of love and hatred, and that the most important and strongest are those which take their rise from the emotions of delight and revulsion.

Article LXXXIX.

The desire which springs from revulsion.

Now, although it is only one and the same desire which makes for the search after a good and the escape from an evil which is contrary to it, as has been said, the desire which originates from delight cannot fail to be very different from that which springs from revulsion; for this delight and revulsion which are truly contrary to one another, are not the good and the evil which serve as objects for those desires, but only two emotions of the soul, which dispose it to seek after two very different things. That is, revulsion is instituted by nature to represent to the soul a sudden and unexpected death, so that although it is sometimes but the touch of a grub, or the sound of a trembling leaf, or one's own shadow, which causes us to be seized with horror, we at once feel as much emotion as though a very evident peril of death offered itself to the senses; and this is what suddenly produces the agitation which causes the soul to employ all its forces in order to avoid an evil so present; and it is this kind of desire which we commonly call avoidance and aversion.

ARTICLE XC.

That which springs from delight.

On the other hand, delight is specially instituted by nature to represent the enjoyment of that which gives pleasure as the greatest of all the good things which pertain to man, which causes us to desire this enjoyment very ardently. It is true that there are various sorts of delight and that the desires which take their origin in these diverse varieties are not all equally powerful. For, to take an example, the beauty of flowers incites us only to look at them, and that of fruits to eat them. But the principal one is that which proceeds from the perfections which we imagine in a person whom we think may become another self; for with the difference of sex which nature has placed in men, as in the animals without reason, it has also placed certain impressions in the brain which bring it to pass that at a certain age, and in a certain time, they consider themselves defective, and as though they were but the half of a whole, of which an individual of the other sex should be the other half. In this way the acquisition of this half is confusedly represented by nature as the greatest of all imaginable goods. And although we see many persons of this other sex, we do not for all that desire several at the same time, inasmuch as nature does not cause us to imagine that we have need of more than one half. But when we observe something in one which is more agreeable than what we at the same time observe in others, that determines the soul to feel only for the first all the inclination which nature gives it to seek for the good which that nature represents to it as the greatest that can be possessed; and this inclination or desire which thus springs from delight more usually receives the name of love than the passion of love which has above been described. It has likewise stranger effects and it is what provides the principal material for the writers of romances and for poets.

The definition of Joy.

Joy is an agreeable emotion of the soul in which consists the enjoyment that the soul possesses in the good which the impressions of the brain represent to it as it own. I say that it is in this emotion that the enjoyment of the good consists; for as a matter of fact the soul receives no other fruits from all the good things that it possesses; and while it has no joy in these, it may be said that it does not enjoy them more than if it did not possess them at all. I add also that it is of the good which the impressions of the brain represent to it as its own, in order not to confound this joy, which is a passion, with the joy that is purely intellectual, and which comes into the soul by the action of the soul alone, and which we may call an agreeable emotion excited in it, in which the enjoyment consists which it has in the good which its understanding represents to it as its own. It is true that while the soul is united to the body this intellectual joy can hardly fail to be accompanied by that which is a passion; for as soon as our understanding perceives that we possess some good thing, even although this good may be so different from all that pertains to body that it is not in the least capable of being imagined, imagination does not fail immediately to make some impression in the brain from which proceeds the movement of the spirits which excites the passion of joy.

ARTICLE XCII

The definition of Sadness.

Sadness is a disagreeable languor in which consists the discomfort and unrest which the soul receives from evil, or from the defect which the impressions of the brain set before it as pertaining to it. And there also is an intellectual sadness which is not passion, but which hardly ever fails to be accompanied by it.

ARTICLE XCIII.

The causes of these two passions.

But when intellectual joy or sadness thus excites that which is a passion their cause is evident enough; and we see from their definitions that joy proceeds from the belief that we have of possessing some good, and sadness from the belief that we have of possessing some evil or defect. It often, however, happens that we feel sad or joyful without being thus able distinctly to observe the good or evil which are the causes of it; e.g. when this good or this evil form their impressions in the brain without the intermission of the soul, sometimes because they only pertain to the body, and sometimes, too, although they pertain to the soul, because it does not consider them as good and evil, but under some other form the impression of which is joined to that of good and of evil in the brain.

Article XCIV.

How these passions are excited by things good and evil which only concern the body, and in what pleasurable stimulation and pain consists.

Thus when we are in full health and the weather is more serene than usual, we feel a gaiety within us which proceeds from no function of the understanding, but only from the impressions which the movement of the spirits causes in the brain; and we never feel sad in the same way except when the body is indisposed, even although we do not know that it is so. Thus the titillation of the senses is so nearly followed by joy, and pain by sadness, that the greater part of mankind does not distinguish the two. And yet they differ so much that pains may sometimes be suffered with joy, or pleasurable sensations received which cause displeasure. But the cause which brings it to pass that in a general way joy follows pleasurable sensation, is the fact that all that we call pleasurable sensation or agreeable sentiment is simply due to the fact that the objects of sense excite some movement in the nerves which would be capable of harming them had they not strength sufficient to resist the movement, or were the body not well disposed; and this produces in the brain an impression which, being instituted by nature to give evidence to this good disposition and this strength, represents that to the soul as a good pertaining to it, inasmuch as it is united to body and thus excites in it joy. It is almost the same reason which brings it about that we naturally take pleasure in being moved by all sorts of passions, even by sadness and hatred, when these passions are only caused by the strange adventures which we see represented in a theatre, or by other similar means which, not being able to harm us in any way, seem pleasurably to excite our soul in affecting it. And the cause which brings it to pass that pain usually produces sadness, is that the feeling which we call pain always proceeds from some action which is so violent that it hurts our nerves; in this way, being instituted by nature to signify to the soul the injury which the body receives by this action, and its weakness in not being able to resist it, it represents both to it as evils, which are always disagreeable to it, excepting when they bring about certain good results which it esteems more than these.

Article XCV.

How they may also be excited by the things good and evil which the soul does not notice even although they belong to it, such as the pleasure taken in encountering risk or in the recollection of a past evil.

Thus the pleasure which young people often take in undertaking difficult tasks and in exposing themselves to great perils, even although they hope for no profit or glory by doing so, proceeds in their case from the fact that the reflection which they make that what they undertake is difficult, makes an impression in their brain which, being united to that which they might form were they to think that it is a good thing to feel sufficiently courageous, happy, skilful, or strong to dare to risk themselves to such an extent, is the cause of their taking pleasure in so-doing. And the happiness which old people have when they recollect the evils which they have suffered, proceeds from the fact that they represent to themselves that it is a good thing to survive in spite of them all.

Article XCVI.

The movements of the blood and the spirits to which the five preceding passions are due.

The five passions which I have here commenced to explain are so united or opposed the one to the other, that it is easier to consider them all together than to treat each of them separately, as wonder has been treated; and their cause is not, as is that of the latter, in the brain alone, but also in the heart, the spleen, the liver, and in all the other portions of the body in as far as they serve for the production of the blood and consequently of the spirits. For, although all the veins conduct the blood which they contain towards the heart, yet it sometimes happens that the blood of certain of them is driven there with greater strength than that of others; it also happens that the openings by which it enters into the heart, or else those by which it issues out, are more enlarged or contracted on one occasion than on the other.

ARTICLE XCVII.

The chief experiences that furnish us with the knowledge of these movements in Love.

Now in considering the various alterations which experience causes us to observe in our body while our soul is agitated by various passions, I notice in love that when it occurs alone, that is, when it is unaccompanied by any strong joy, desire, or sadness, the beating of the pulse is equal and much fuller and stronger than is usually the case, that we feel a gentle heat in the breast, and that the digestion of food is accomplished very quickly in the stomach. In this way this passion is useful to health.

ARTICLE XCVIII.

In Hatred.

I notice, on the other hand, that in hatred the pulse is unequal, feebler, and often quicker; that we have fits of cold interspersed with a severe and biting heat in the breast difficult to describe; that the stomach ceases to fulfil its functions and is inclined to vomit and reject the food that has been eaten, or at least to corrupt them and convert them into evil humours.

ARTICLE XCIX.

In Joy.

In joy, that the pulse is equal and quicker than usual, but that it is not so strong or full as in love, and that we feel an agreeable heat which is not only in the breast, but also spreads throughout all the other exterior parts of the body with the blood which we see present there in abundance; and yet that we sometimes lose our appetite because the digestion is not so active as usual.

ARTICLE C.

In Sadness.

In sadness, that the pulse is feeble and slow, and that we feel as it were constrictions round the heart which press upon it, and icy chills which congeal it and communicate their cold to the rest of the body; and that nevertheless we continue in certain cases to have a good appetite and to feel that the stomach does not fail to do its duty, provided that there is no hatred mingled with the sadness.

Article CI.

In Desire.

I finally notice this peculiarity about desire, that it agitates the heart more violently than any of the other passions, and furnishes more spirits to the brain, which, passing from thence into the muscles, render all the senses more acute, and all the parts of the body more mobile.

Article CII.

The movement of the blood and spirits in Love.

These observations, and many others which would be too lengthy to transcribe, have caused me to judge that when the understanding represents to itself some object of love, the impression which this reflection makes in the brain leads the animal spirits, by the nerves of the sixth part, towards the muscles which are around the intestines and stomach in the manner requisite to cause the juice of the food, which converts itself into new blood, to pass quickly towards the heart without stopping in the liver; and that being driven thither with more strength than any that is in the other parts of the body, it enters in greater abundance and excites there a stronger heat because it is coarser than that which has already been several times rarefied in passing and repassing through the heart. And this causes the spirits also to be sent to the brain, whose parts are coarser and more agitated than usual. And these spirits, fortifying the impression which the first thought of the agreeable object there makes, oblige the soul to pause over this reflection; and it is in this that the passion of love consists.

Article CIII.

In Hatred.

In hatred, on the other hand, the first thought of the object which brings about aversion so conducts the animal spirits which are in the brain towards the muscles of the stomach and intestines, that they prevent the juice of the food from mingling with the blood by closing up all the openings by which it usually flows there;

and it also conducts them in such a way toward the little nerves of the spleen and of the lower portion of the liver, where is the receptacle of the bile, that the portions of the blood which are usually thrown back towards these parts issue from them and flow with that which is in the branches of the vena cava towards the heart; and this causes many inequalities in its heat, insomuch that the blood which comes from the spleen hardly heats and rarefies itself at all, while on the contrary that which comes from the lower part of the liver, where the gall always is, enflames and dilates very quickly. In consequence of this the animal spirits which go to the brain also have very unequal parts and very extraordinary movements, from whence it comes about that they strengthen the ideas of hatred which are found to be already imprinted there, and dispose the soul to reflections which are full of sharpness and bitterness.

ARTICLE CIV.

In Joy.

In joy it is not so much the nerves of the spleen, the liver, or the stomach, or the intestines, which are active, as those which are in the whole of the rest of the body, and particularly that which is round the orifices of the heart, which, opening and enlarging these orifices, supplies the means whereby the blood which the other nerves drive from the veins to the heart may enter there and issue forth in a larger quantity than usual. And because the blood which then enters the heart has already passed and repassed there several times, having come from the arteries to the veins, it dilates very easily and produces spirits whose parts, being very equal and subtle, are proper for the formation and fortification of the impressions of the brain which give to the soul thoughts which are gay and peaceful.

ARTICLE CV.

In Sadness.

In sadness, on the contrary, the openings of the heart are much contracted by the small nerve which surrounds them, and the blood of the veins is in nowise agitated, which brings it to pass that very little of it goes towards the heart and yet the passages by which the juice of the food flows from the stomach and the intestines towards the liver remain open, which causes the appetite not to diminish at all, excepting when hatred, which is often united to sadness, closes them.

ARTICLE CVI.

In Desire.

Finally, to the passion of desire the following fact is proper, namely, that the wish which we have to obtain some good, or to avoid some evil, promptly sends the animal spirits from the brain to all the portions of the body which may be of service in the actions requisite for this effect, and particularly to the heart and the parts which furnish it with most blood, so that in receiving greater abundance than usual, it sends a greater quantity of spirits towards the brain, both in order to maintain and fortify there the idea of this wish, and to pass from thence into all the organs of the senses and all the muscles which may be employed in obtaining that which we desire.

ARTICLE CVII.

What is the cause of its movements in Love.

And I deduce the reasons for all this from what has been said above, that there is a connection between our soul and our body such that when we have once joined some corporeal action with some thought, the one of the two never after presents itself to us without the other presenting itself at the same time. We see in the case of those who have in illness taken some concoction with great aversion, that they can neither drink nor eat afterwards any thing approaching it in taste without the same aversion coming back to them; and similarly they cannot think of the aversion in which the medicines are held, without the same taste coming back to them in thought. For it seems to me that the earliest passions that our soul had had when first it was joined to our body must be due to the fact that sometimes the blood or other juice which entered into the heart was a more suitable nutriment than usual for the maintenance there of heat, which is the principle of life, and that was the cause of the soul uniting itself to this nutriment of its own free will, that is to say liking it, and at the same time the animal spirits flowed from the brain to the muscles which might press or agitate the parts from which it had come to the heart, in order to cause them to send it yet more; and these parts were the stomach and the intestines, the agitation of which increases our appetite, or else the liver and lung likewise, which the muscles of the diaphragm may compress. That is why this same movement of animal spirits has always since accompanied the passion of love.

Article CVIII.

In Hatred.

Sometimes, on the other hand, there comes to the heart some juice of a foreign nature which was not qualified to maintain heat, or which even was capable of extinguishing it, and this was the reason that the spirits which rose from the heart to the brain excited in the soul the passion of hatred; and at the same time also these spirits went from the brain to the nerves which were able to drive the blood of the spleen and of the small veins of the liver towards the heart in order to prevent this hurtful juice from entering therein; and further they went towards these nerves which could drive back this juice to the intestines and stomach, or sometimes likewise oblige the stomach to vomit: and from this it results that these same movements usually accompany the passion of hatred. And our eye shows us that there are in the liver numbers of veins or ducts of sufficient width by which the juice of the food could pass from the portal vein into the vena cava and from thence to the heart without delaying at all in the liver. But there is also an infinitude of others that are smaller, where it might stop, and which always contains blood in reserve as does the spleen also; which blood being coarser than that which is in the other portions of the body is capable of serving better as nourishment to the fire which is in the heart, when the stomach and intestines fail to supply it with nutriment.

Article CIX.

In Joy.

It has also sometimes happened in the beginning of our life that the blood contained in the veins was a nourishment sufficiently well suited to maintain the heat of the heart, and that they contained it in such a quantity that there was no need to derive any nourishment from elsewhere. And this has excited in the soul the passion of joy, and has at the same time caused the orifices of the heart to be more open than usual; it has also brought it to pass that the animal spirits (flowing abundantly from the brain, not alone into the nerves which serve for opening these orifices, but also generally speaking into all the others which drive the blood of the veins to the heart) prevent any fresh blood from coming from the liver, spleen, intestines and stomach. That is why these same movements accompany joy.

ARTICLE CX

In Sadness.

Sometimes on the contrary it has happened that the body has lack of nourishment, and it is this that must give the soul its first experience of sadness—that sadness at least which is as yet free from intermixture with hatred. The same reason has also caused the orifices of the heart to be contracted, because they receive only a small quantity of blood; and a sufficiently notable proportion of the blood from the spleen is present because it is so to speak the ultimate reservoir which serves to furnish blood to the heart when enough does not come to it from elsewhere. That is why the movements of the spirits and of the nerves which serve to contract thus the cavities of the heart and to conduct there the blood of the spleen, invariably accompany sadness.

ARTICLE CXI.

Of Desire.

To conclude, all the first desires which the soul can have had when it was newly joined to the body have been desires of receiving the things that were suitable to it, and of repelling those which were hurtful; and it has been to bring about these same effects that the spirits have henceforth commenced to produce movements in all the muscles and all the organs of the senses, in every method in which they can move them. And this is the cause that now, when the soul desires something, the whole body becomes more agile and more disposed towards movement than it customarily is apart from desire. And when it further happens that the body is so disposed, that renders the desires of the soul stronger and more ardent.

ARTICLE CXII.

The external signs of these Passions.

That which I have set down here makes sufficiently clear the cause of the differences in the pulse and of all the other properties which I have above attributed to these passions, without there being any necessity for me to pause in order to explain them further. But because I have only remarked in each that which may be observed to accompany it when it is alone, and which serves for a knowledge of the movements of the blood and the spirits which produce them, it still remains for me to treat of the several exterior signs which usually accompany them, and which are much better observed when several are mingled with one another as they usually are, than when they are separated. The principal of these signs are the actions of the eyes and face, changes of colour, tremors, languor, swooning, laughter, tears, groans and sighs.

ARTICLE CXIII.

Of the actions of the Eyes and Face.

There is no passion that is not evidenced by some particular action of the eyes. And that is so manifest in certain emotions that even the stupidest servants can remark by the eye of their master if he is or is not angry with them. But although these actions of the eyes are easily perceived, and that which they signify is known, it is not, for all that, easy to describe them, since each is composed of many changes which take place in the movement and shape of the eye which are so unique and so slight that we cannot perceive each one separately, although the result of their conjunction is very easily observed. We may say almost the same of the actions of the face which also accompany the passions, for although they are of greater extent than those of the eyes, it is at the same time hard to distinguish them; and they are so little different that there are men who present almost the same mien when they weep as when they laugh. It is true that there are some which are remarkable enough, as are the seams in the forehead which come in anger, and certain movements of nose and lips in indignation and scorn; but they do not so much appear to be natural as voluntary. And generally speaking all actions, whether of face or eyes, may be changed by the soul when, desiring to hide a passion, it vigorously calls up the image of a contrary one: so that we may make use of these actions as well in dissimulating our passions as in evidencing them.

ARTICLE CXIV.

Of changes of Colour.

We cannot so easily prevent ourselves from flushing or becoming pale when some passion disposes us to do so, because these changes do not depend on the nerves and muscles, as do the preceding, and because they proceed more immediately from the heart, which may be called the source of the passions, inasmuch as it prepares the blood and the spirits for producing them. It is, however, certain that the colour of the face only proceeds from the blood which, continually flowing from the heart by the arteries into all the veins, and from all the veins into the heart, produces more or less colour in the face, according as it to a larger or less extent fills the small veins which are towards its surface.

Article CXV.

How Joy causes us to flush.

Joy thus makes the colour more vivid and more ruddy, because in opening the sluices of the heart it causes the blood to flow more quickly in all the veins, and because, becoming warmer and more subtle, it moderately distends all the parts of the face, and thus gives it a more cheerful and lively expression.

Article CXVI.

How Sadness causes paleness.

Sadness, on the contrary, in contracting the orifices of the heart, causes the blood to flow more slowly in the veins, and, becoming colder and thicker, the blood requires less space there, so that, retreating into those that are widest and which are nearest to the heart, it leaves the more remote; and since the most conspicuous of these are in the face, this causes it to become pale and sunk, more especially when the sadness is great, or when it supervenes quickly, as we see in sudden fright when the surprise increases the action which constricts the heart.

Article CXVII.

How we often flush though we are sad.

But it often happens that we do not become pale in sadness, but on the contrary become red, which must be attributed to other passions which unite themselves to sadness, to wit, possibly desire, and sometimes also hatred. These passions, heating or agitating the blood which proceeds from the liver, intestines and other interior parts, drive it towards the heart, and from thence by the great artery to the veins of the face, without the sadness which closes more or less the orifices of the heart being able to prevent it, excepting when it is an extreme sadness. But although it be only moderate, it easily prevents the blood thus come into the veins of the face from descending towards the heart, while love, desire, or hatred, force into it other portions of the blood coming from the internal parts. That is why this blood, being arrested around the face, renders it red and even redder than during joy, because the colour of the blood appears so much the more as it flows less quickly, and also because it can thus better collect in the veins of the face than when the orifices of the heart are more open. This is principally seen in shame, which is made up of self-love and a pressing desire to avoid present disgrace which causes the blood of the interior parts to come towards the heart and then from thence by the arteries to the face, and there is also present a moderate amount of sadness which prevents this blood from returning to the heart. The same thing usually appears when we weep, for, as I shall afterwards maintain, it is love joined to sadness which most frequently causes tears; and the same thing is evidenced in anger, where frequently a prompt desire for vengeance is mingled with love, hatred and sadness.

ARTICLE CXVIII.

Of Tremors.

Tremors have two different causes; the one is that sometimes too little of the spirits in the brain passes into the nerves, and the other is that sometimes there comes too much to permit of the exact closing of the small passages of the muscle, which, in pursuance of what has been said in Article XI, ought to be closed in order to determine the movements of the members. The first cause is evidenced in sadness and fear, as also when we tremble with cold; for these passions may, just as well as the coldness of the air, so thicken the blood that it does not furnish enough spirits to the brain to permit of the despatch of some of them into the nerves. The other cause often appears in those who ardently desire something, and in those who are strongly moved by prayer, as also in those who are drunken. For these two passions, as well as wine, sometimes cause so many animal spirits to proceed to the brain that they cannot be conducted in a properly regulated way from thence to the muscles.

ARTICLE CXIX.

Of Languor.

Languor is a tendency to relax and be motionless, and this is experienced in all the members; like tremors, it proceeds from the fact that sufficient animal spirits do not go into the nerves, but in a different way. For the cause of tremors is that there are not sufficient spirits in the brain in order to carry out the determinations of the gland when it drives them towards some muscle, while langour proceeds from the fact that the gland does not determine them to go towards any particular muscle more than to others.

Article CXX.

How it is caused by love and by desire.

And the passion which most usually causes this effect is love joined to the desire for a thing whose acquisition is not imagined to be at the time possible; for love so occupies the soul in considering the object loved that it employs all the spirits which are in the brain in representing to it its image, and it checks all the movements of the glands which do not contribute to this result. And we must notice regarding desire that the property which I have attributed to it of rendering the body the more mobile, only belongs to it when we imagine the object desired to be such that we can from this time forth do something which serves towards its acquisition. For if we imagine, on the other hand, that it is impossible at this time to do anything which is useful for that end, all the agitation of desire remains in the brain, without in any way passing into the nerves : and, being entirely employed in there strengthening the idea of the desired object, it leaves the rest of the body languid

Article CXXI.

That it may also be caused by other passions.

It is true that hatred, sadness, and even joy, may also cause some languor when they are very violent, because they occupy the soul entirely in considering their object, principally when the desire of a thing to whose acquisition we cannot contribute anything at the present time is united to it. But because we pause much longer over the consideration of the objects to which we ally ourselves by our own free-will than those which we dissociate therefrom, and than any others, and as languor does not rest on a sudden surprise but requires some time in its formation, it is to be met with much more in love than in all the other passions.

Article CXXII.

Of Swooning.

A swoon is not far removed from death, for death results when the fire which is in our heart is extinguished altogether, and we only fall into a faint when it is stifled in such a way that there still remain some traces of heat which may afterwards rekindle it. There are, however, several indispositions of the body which cause us thus to fall into a faint, but amongst the passions it is only extreme joy which we observe as having the power to do so. And the manner in which I believe it to bring about this effect is that, by opening the orifices of the heart to an unusual extent, the blood of the veins enters so suddenly, and in so large a quantity, that it cannot be rarefied there by the heat promptly enough to raise the little membranes which close the entrances of these veins, and thus it quenches the fire which it usually maintains when it only enters the heart in moderation.

Article CXXIII.

Why grief does not cause us to swoon.

It would seem that a great grief falling on us suddenly ought so to close the orifices of the heart as to be able also to extinguish its fire, but nevertheless we do not observe that to happen, or if it does happen it is very rarely the case. From this I argue that the reason is that there can scarcely be so little blood in the heart as to be insufficient to maintain heat when its orifices are almost closed.

Article CXXIV.

Of Laughter.

Laughter consists in the fact that the blood, which proceeds from the right orifice in the heart by the arterial vein, inflating the lungs suddenly and repeatedly, causes the air which they contain to be constrained to pass out from them with an impetus by the windpipe, where it forms an inarticulate and explosive utterance ; and the lungs in expanding equally with the air as it rushes out, set in motion all the muscles of the diaphragm from the chest to the neck, by which means they cause motion in the facial muscles, which have a certain connection with them. And it is just this action of the face with this inarticulate and explosive voice that we call laughter.

Article CXXV.

Why it does not accompany the greatest joys.

But although it seems as though laughter were one of the principal signs of joy, nevertheless joy cannot cause it except when it is moderate and has some wonder or hate mingled with it. For we find by experience that when we are extraordinarily joyous the subject of this joy never causes us to burst into laughter, and we cannot even be so easily induced to do so by some other cause as when we are sad. And the reason of this is that in great joys the lung is always so full of blood that it cannot be further inflated by repeated gushes.

Article CXXVI.

What are its principal causes.

And I can only observe two causes which make the lung thus inflate suddenly. The first is the surprise of admiration or wonder, which, being united to joy, may open the orifices of the heart so quickly that a great abundance of blood suddenly entering on its right side by the *vena cava*, rarefies there, and, passing from thence by the arterial vein, inflates the lung. The other is the admixture of some liquor which increases the rarefaction of the blood, and I can find nothing which could do that but the most liquid part of that which proceeds from the spleen, which part of the blood being driven to the heart by some slight emotion of hatred, assisted by the surprise of wonder, and mingling itself there with the blood which proceeds from the other parts of the body which joy causes to enter there in abundance, may cause this blood to dilate there much more than usual. We observe the same thing in many other liquids which, when on the fire, suddenly dilate when we throw a little vinegar into the vessel where they are ; for the most liquid portion of the blood which comes from the spleen is in nature similar to vinegar. Experience also causes us to see that in all the possible occurrences which can produce this explosive laughter which proceeds from the lung, there is always some little element of hatred, or at least of wonder. And those whose spleen is not in a very healthy condition are subject to being not alone more sad, but also at intervals more gay and more disposed to laughter than the others, inasmuch as the spleen sends two sorts of blood to the heart, the one thick and coarse, which causes sadness, the other very fluid and subtle, which causes joy. And often, after having laughed much, we feel ourselves naturally inclined to sadness because the more fluid portion of the blood of the spleen being exhausted, the other, more coarse, follows it towards the heart.

ARTICLE CXXVII.

Its cause in indignation.

As to the laughter which sometimes accompanies indignation, it is usually artificial and feigned ; but when it is natural, it appears to proceed from the joy that we have in observing the fact that we cannot be hurt by the evil at which we are indignant, and, along with that, from the fact that we find ourselves surprised by the novelty or by the unexpected encountering of this evil. In this way joy, hatred and wonder contribute to it. At the same time I would fain believe that it may also be produced without any joy, by the movement of aversion alone, which sends blood from the spleen to the heart, where it is rarefied and driven from thence to the lung ; and this it easily inflates when it finds it almost empty. And speaking generally, all that can suddenly inflate the lung in this way causes the outward action laughter, excepting when sadness changes it into that of groans, and the cries which accompany tears. In reference to which Vives[1] writes of himself regarding a time when he had been long without eating, that the first pieces of food which he placed in his mouth caused him to laugh ; and this might proceed from the fact that his lung, emptied of blood by lack of nourishment, was promptly inflated by the first juice which passed from his stomach to his heart, and which the mere imagination of eating could conduct there, even before the arrival of the food he was eating.

ARTICLE CXXVIII.

Of the origin of Tears.

As laughter is never caused by the greatest joys, so tears do not proceed from an extreme sadness but only from that which is moderate and accompanied or followed by some feeling of love or likewise of joy. And in order to understand their origin properly, we must remark that although a mass of vapours continually escapes from all the portions of our body, there are at the same time none from which so much issues as the eyes, because of the size of the

[1] In the margin of the first edition : "I. L. Vives, 3. de Animâ. cap. de Risu."

optic nerves and the multitude of little arteries by which the vapours reach them; and as the sweat is simply composed of vapours which, issuing from the other parts of the body, are converted into water on their surface, so tears are formed from the vapours which issue from the eyes.

Article CXXIX.

Of the manner in which vapours change into water.

Now, as I have said in the Meteors, in explaining the manner in which the vapours of the air are converted into rain, that this proceeds from the fact that they are less agitated or more abundant than usual, so I believe that when those that issue from the body are much less agitated than usual, although they are not so abundant, they do not any the less convert themselves into water, which causes the cold sweats which sometimes come from weakness when we are ill. And I believe that when they are much more abundant, provided that they are not also more agitated, they also convert themselves into water, which is the cause of the sweat which comes when we perform a certain amount of exercise. But then the eyes do not perspire, because during the exercise of the body, since the greater part of the animal spirits go into the muscles which serve to move it, less goes by the optic nerve to the eyes. And it is one and the same matter which forms blood when found in the veins or arteries, and spirits, when it is in the brain, nerves, or muscles, and vapours when it issues forth in the form of air, and finally sweat or tears when it condenses into water on the surface of the body or the eyes.

Article CXXX.

How that which causes pain in the eye excites it to tears.

And I can only observe two causes which make the vapours which issue from the eyes change into tears. The first is when the figure of the pores by which they pass is changed by some accident or other; for that, retarding the movement of these vapours and changing their order, may cause them to be converted into water. Thus the falling into the eyes of the tiniest mite suffices to draw some tears from them, because in exciting pain in them it changes the disposition of their pores in such a manner that when some become more contracted, the small portion of the vapours pass by less quickly; and instead of their issuing forth as before at equal distances the one from the other, and thus remaining separate, they come into contact with one another, because the order of these pores is put out, and by this means they join one another and thus become converted into tears.

Article CXXXI.

How we weep owing to sadness.

The other cause is sadness followed by love or joy, or generally speaking by some cause which makes the heart to drive forth much blood through the arteries. Sadness is requisite in weeping, because by chilling all the blood, it contracts the pores of the eyes; but since in proportion as it contracts them, it also diminishes the quantity of the vapours which they should allow to pass, that does not suffice to produce tears if the quantity of these vapours is not at the same time increased by some other cause. And there is nothing which increases it more than the blood which is sent to the heart in the passion of love; we see likewise that those who are sad do not continually shed tears, but only at intervals, when they make some new reflection on the objects of their affection.

Article CXXXII.

Of the groans which accompany tears.

And then the lungs are also sometimes inflated suddenly by the abundance of the blood which enters them, and which drives out from them the air which they contained, which, issuing by the windpipe, begets the groans and cries which usually accompany tears. And these cries are as a rule shriller than those which accompany laughter, although they are produced almost in the same way. The reason of this is that the nerves which serve to enlarge or contract the organs of the voice in order to make it louder or sharper, being united to those which open the orifices of the heart in joy, and contract them in sadness, cause these organs to enlarge or contract at the same time.

Article CXXXIII.

Why children and old people easily weep.

Children and old people are more disposed to weep than those of middle age, but for different reasons. Old people often weep from affection and joy; for these two passions united together send much blood to the heart and hence much vapour to the eyes; and the agitation of these vapours is so much retarded by the coldness of their bodily disposition[1], that they easily convert themselves into tears, even although no sadness has preceded. And if some old people also weep very easily from vexation, it is not so much the temperament of their body as that of their mind that disposes them to do so ; and it only happens to those who are so feeble that they allow themselves to be entirely overcome by small causes of sorrow, fear or pity. The same occurs with children who never cry with joy, but much more frequently owing to sadness, even when it is not accompanied with love ; for they have always enough blood to produce much vapour, the movement of which, being retarded by sadness, is converted into tears.

Article CXXXIV.

Why some children become pale instead of crying.

At the same time there are some who become pale instead of weeping, when they are angry, which may demonstrate in them an extraordinary judgment and courage, that is to say, when it proceeds from their considering the greatness of the evil and preparing themselves for a stout resistance, in the same way as do older people. But more usually it is a mark of an evil disposition, at least when it proceeds from a tendency towards hatred or fear, for these are passions which diminish the material of tears. And, on the contrary, we see that those who weep very easily are inclined to love and pity.

Article CXXXV.

Of Sighs.

The cause of sighing is very different from that of tears, even though like the latter it presupposes sadness. For, our tendency to weep when the lungs are full of blood is replaced by a tendency to sigh when they are almost empty, and when some imagination of hope or joy opens the orifices of the venous artery which sadness had contracted ; because then the small amount of blood which remains in the lungs, suddenly falling into the left side of the heart by this venous artery and being driven thence by the desire of arriving at this joy, which agitates all the muscles of the diaphragm and chest at the same time, the air is promptly driven through the mouth into the lungs, in order there to fill the place left by this blood , and that is what we call sighing.

[1] leur naturel Fr.

Article CXXXVI.

From whence proceed the effects of the passions which are peculiar to certain men.

For the rest, in order in a few words to supply all that can be added regarding the diverse effects or diverse causes of the passions, I shall content myself with repeating the principle on which all that I have written about them rests, *i.e.* that there is a connection between our soul and our body of such a nature that when we have once connected some corporeal action with some thought, the one of the two does not present itself to us afterwards without the other presenting itself also; and that it is not always the same actions which are connected with the same thoughts. For that suffices to provide a reason for the whole of that which each of us can observe as peculiar to himself or to others regarding this matter, and which has not been here explained. And, for example, it is easy to reflect that the strange aversions of certain people which prevent their being able to endure the scent of roses or the presence of a cat, or things of that sort, only proceed from the fact that at the beginning of their lives they have suffered much unpleasantness through some such objects, or else have shared in the feelings of their mother who has so suffered before they were born. For it is certain that there is a relation between all the movements of the mother and those of the child in her womb, inasmuch as what is harmful to the one is hurtful to the other. And the scent of roses may have caused a severe headache to a child while still in the cradle, or a cat may have terrified him without anyone having been aware of it, or of any memory remaining of it afterwards, although the idea of aversion which he then had for these roses or for this cat remain imprinted on his brain to the end of his life.

Article CXXXVII.

Of the function of the five passions here explained inasfar as they relate to the body.

After having given definitions of love, of hatred, of desire, of joy, and of sadness, and having treated of all the corporeal movements, which cause or accompany them, we only have here to consider their function. And regarding this it must be observed that, in accordance with the institutions of nature they all relate to body, and are only bestowed on the soul in so far as it is united to body. In this way their natural use is to incite the soul to consent and contribute to the actions which may serve to maintain the body, or to render it in some manner more perfect. And from this point of view sadness and joy are the two foremost that are employed. For those things that are hurtful to the body are immediately made known to the soul only by the feeling of pain which it experiences, and which first of all produces in it the passion of sadness, then the hatred of what causes this pain, and, in the third place, the desire to rid oneself of it. Similarly, likewise, the soul is only immediately notified of things useful to the body by some sort of pleasant stimulation which causes joy within it, then causes the love of that which is believed to be its cause to arise, and finally brings about the desire to acquire what is capable of causing a continuance of that joy, or else causes us to rejoice again in the future after a similar sensation. And this shows us that they are all five very useful relatively to the body, and even that sadness in some way ranks higher and is more essential than joy, and hatred than love, because it is of more importance to repel the things which injure and may destroy, than to acquire those which add some perfection without which we may subsist.

Article CXXXVIII.

Of their faults and the means of correcting them.

But, although this use of the passions is the most natural which they can have, and though all the animals devoid of reason direct their lives simply by bodily movements similar to those which in our case usually follow these passions, and to which they incite our soul to consent, it is nevertheless not always good, inasmuch as there are many things hurtful to the body which cause no sadness at the first, or which even produce joy, and others which are useful to it although at first they are distasteful. And, in addition to that, they almost always cause the good things, as well as the evil, to seem much greater and more important than they are ; so that they incite us to seek after the one and flee from the others with more ardour and care than is desirable, just as we also see that the brutes are often deceived by baits, and that, in order to evade small evils, they precipitate themselves into greater evils. That is why we should make use of experience and reason in order to distinguish good from evil, and to recognize their just value, so that we may not take the one for the other, or rush into anything too violently.

Article CXXXIX.

Of the function of the same passions inasfar as they pertain to the soul, and to begin with, of love.

This would be sufficient if we had in us body only, or did it form the better part of us, but inasmuch as it is only the lesser part, we should chiefly consider the passions in so far as they pertain to the soul, with respect to which love and hatred proceed from knowledge and precede joy and sadness, excepting when these last two hold the place of the knowledge of which they are species. And when this knowledge is true, that is to say when the things which it constrains us to love are truly good, and those which it constrains us to hate are truly evil, love is incomparably better than hatred; it can never be too great, and it never fails to produce joy. I assert that this love is extremely good, because, uniting to us what is truly good, it in so far adds perfection to us. I also assert that it cannot be too great, for all that which the most excessive love can do is to unite us so perfectly to these good things, that the love which we have in particular for ourselves, places no distinction therein; this I believe can never be bad. And it is necessarily followed by joy, because it represents to us what we love as a good which pertains to us.

Article CXL.

Of Hatred.

Hatred, on the contrary, cannot be so small that it does not hurt; and it is never devoid of sadness. I assert that it cannot be too small because we are not incited to any action by the hatred of evil to which we cannot be yet more stimulated by the love of good to which it is opposed, at least when this good and this evil are sufficiently known. For I confess that the hatred of evil which pain alone calls forth, is necessary in respect to body; but I speak here only of that which proceeds from a clearer knowledge, and I only relate it to the soul. I assert also that it is never without sadness, because evil, being merely a privation, cannot be conceived without some real subject in which it subsists; and there is nothing real which has not some goodness in it, and so the hatred which removes us from some evil, by the same means removes us from the good to which it is united, and the privation of this good being represented to our soul as a defect which pertains to it, excites sadness therein. For example, the hatred which removes from us the evil habits of someone, by the same means removes us from his company in which we might independently of that find some good of which we are vexed at being deprived. And similarly in all the other hatreds we may observe some element of sadness.

ARTICLE CXLI.

Of Desire, Joy, and Sadness.

As to desire, it is evident that, when it proceeds from a true knowledge, it cannot be bad, provided that it is not excessive, and that this knowledge rules it. It is also evident that joy cannot fail to be good, nor sadness to be bad when we view them in their relation to the soul, because it is in the latter that consists all the inconveniences and embarrassments which the soul obtains from evil, and in the former that consists all the enjoyment of good which pertains to it. And thus, if we had no body, I should venture to say that we could not too greatly abandon ourselves to love, joy, nor too much avoid hatred and sadness; but the corporeal movements which accompany them may all be hurtful to health when they are very violent, and, on the contrary, be useful to it when they are only moderate.

ARTICLE CXLII.

Of Joy and Love, compared with Sadness and Hatred.

For the rest, since hatred and sadness should be rejected by the soul, even when they proceed from a true knowledge, this should with greater reason be the case when they proceed from some false opinion. But people may doubt whether love and joy are good or not, when they are thus established on a bad foundation; and it appears to me that if they are only considered precisely as they are in themselves in reference to the soul, it may be said that, although joy is less solid, and love less advantageous, than when they have a better foundation, they do not cease to be preferable to sadness and hatred equally badly founded. In this way, in the vicissitudes of life where we cannot avoid the risk of being deceived, we always do much better to incline towards the passions which make for good, rather than towards those which relate to evil, even if it be only to avoid it; and even a false joy is often of more value than a sadness whose cause is true. But I dare not say the same of love in respect of hate; for when hatred is just, it only removes us from the subject which contains the evil from which it is good to be separated, while the love which is unjust unites us to things which may hurt, or at least which do not deserve to be so much considered by us as they are, which demeans and degrades us.

Article CXLIII.

Of the same passions inasmuch as they relate to Desire.

And we must be very careful to remark that what I have just said of these four passions takes place only when they are considered precisely in themselves, and do not incite us to any action. For in so far as they excite in us desire by means of which they regulate our habits, it is certain that all those whose cause is false may harm, and that on the contrary all those whose cause is just may be of use, and, even when they are equally badly founded, joy is usually more hurtful than sadness, since the latter, by providing restraint and fear, disposes in a certain degree to prudence, while the other makes those who abandon themselves to it rash and imprudent.

Article CXLIV.

Of Desires whose accomplishment depends only on us.

But because these passions can only bring us to any kind of action by the intervention of the desire which they excite, it is this desire particularly which we should be careful to regulate, and it is in this that the principal use of morality consists. And, as I have just said that desire is always good when it follows a true knowledge, so it cannot fail to be bad when it is founded on some error. And it seems to me that the error which we most ordinarily commit in respect to desires is that of not sufficiently distinguishing the things which entirely depend on us from those which do not so depend. For as to those which only depend on us, *i.e.* on our free will, it is sufficient to know that they are good, not to have it in our power to desire them with too much ardour, because it is following after virtue to perform good actions which depend on ourselves, and it is certain that we cannot have a too ardent desire for virtue. Besides which, since that which we in this way desire is incapable of failing to succeed with us, as it is on ourselves alone that it depends, we shall always receive from it all the satisfaction that we have expected from it. But the fault which is usually committed in this is never in desiring too much, but only in desiring too little; and the sovereign remedy against that is to free the mind as much as possible from all kinds of other less useful desires, and then to try to know very clearly and to consider with attention the goodness of that which is to be desired.

ARTICLE CXLV

Of those Desires which depend only on other things, and what is the meaning of chance.

As to the things which in nowise depend on us, good as they may be, we should never desire them with passion, not only because they may not happen and thus may vex us so much the more in proportion to the strength of our desire for them, but principally because, in occupying our thought, they turn us away from applying our affection to other things, the acquisition of which depends on us. And there are two general remedies for these vain desires : the first is generosity, of which I shall speak later : the second is that we ought frequently to cause ourselves to reflect on divine Providence and represent to ourselves that it is impossible that anything should happen in any other way than as it has been determined by this Providence from all eternity. In this way it is, so to speak, a fatality or an immutable necessity, which must be opposed to chance, in order to destroy it by treating it as a chimera which only proceeds from the error of our understanding. For we can desire nothing but that which we hold to be in some manner possible, and we can only hold to be possible those things that do not depend on us, in so far as we reflect that they depend on chance, *i.e.* that we judge that they may happen, and that similar things have formerly happened. And this opinion is founded only on the fact that we do not know all the facts that contribute to each effect ; for when a thing that we have judged to depend on chance does not come to pass, that shows that some one of the causes that were necessary in order to produce it has failed, and in consequence that it was absolutely impossible, and that no such thing has ever happened—that is, a thing in the production of which a similar cause was also lacking—so that if we had not been ignorant of that beforehand, we should not have ever judged it possible, nor consequently have desired it.

Article CXLVI.

Of those that depend on us and on others.

We must, then, entirely set aside the vulgar opinion that there is outside of us a Fortune which causes things to happen or not to happen in accordance with its pleasure, and we must recognize that all is conducted by divine Providence, whose eternal decree is so infallible and immutable, that, excepting the things that this same decree has willed to leave dependent on our free will, we ought to reflect that in relation to us nothing happens which is not necessary, and so to speak decreed by fate, and that thus we cannot without error desire that it should happen otherwise. But because the greater part of our desires extends to things which do not depend entirely on us, nor entirely on others, we ought to distinguish exactly in them what depends only on us, in order to extend our desire to that alone; and as to what remains, although we ought in this to hold success to be absolutely decreed by fate and immutable, in order that our desire may not occupy itself therewith, we should not omit to consider the reasons which make it more or less to be hoped for, in order that they may serve to regulate our actions. Thus, to take an example, if we have business in some particular place to which we may go by two different roads, the one of which is usually much safer than the other, although the decree of Providence is perhaps such that, if we go by the road which we judge to be safest, we shall not escape being robbed by so doing, while, on the other hand, we might pass by the other without danger, we should not for all that be indifferent as to which one we choose, nor rest on the immutable fatality of the said decree. But reason desires us to choose the road which is usually most safe, and our desire should be accomplished in respect to that when we have followed it, whatever evil may thus befall us, because this evil, having been relatively to us inevitable, we have had no reason to expect exemption from it, but merely claim to have done the best that our understanding has been able to point out, as I suppose to have been the case. And it is certain that when we exercise ourselves in thus distinguishing fatality from fortune, we easily accustom ourselves so to regulate our desires, that, in as far as their accomplishment depends only on us, they may always provide us with complete satisfaction.

Article CXLVII.

Of the interior emotions of the soul.

I shall only add here a consideration which, it seems to me, we shall find of much service in preventing us from suffering any inconvenience from the passions ; and that is that our good and our harm depend mainly on the interior emotions which are only excited in the soul by the soul itself, in which respect they differ from its passions, which always depend on some movement of the spirits. And, although these emotions of the soul are frequently united to the passions which are similar to them, they may likewise often be met with along with others, and even take their origin from those which are contrary to them. For example, when a husband laments his dead wife whom (as sometimes happens) he would be sorry to see brought to life again, it may be that his heart is oppressed by the sadness that the appurtenances of woe and the absence of one to whose conversation he was used excite in him ; and it may be that some remnants of love or pity which present themselves to his imagination draw sincere tears from his eyes, notwithstanding that he yet feels a secret joy in the inmost parts of his heart, the emotion of which possesses so much power that the sadness and the tears which accompany it can do nothing to diminish its force. And when we read of strange adventures in a book, or see them represented in a theatre, which sometimes excite sadness in us, sometimes joy, or love, or hatred, and generally speaking all the passions, according to the diversity of the objects which are offered to our imagination ; but along with that we have pleasure in feeling them excited in us, and this pleasure is an intellectual joy which may as easily take its origin from sadness as from any of the other passions.

Article CXLVIII.

That the exercise of virtue is a sovereign remedy against the passions.

And, inasmuch as these inward emotions touch us most nearly, and in consequence have much more power over us than the passions from which they differ, and which are met with in conjunction with them, it is certain that, provided our soul is always possessed of something to content itself with inwardly, none of the troubles that come from elsewhere have any power to harm it, but rather serve to increase its joy, inasmuch as, seeing that it cannot be harmed by them, it is made sensible of its perfection. And in order that our soul may thus have something with which to be content, it has no need but to follow exactly after virtue. For whoever has lived in such a way that his conscience cannot reproach him for ever having failed to perform those things which he has judged to be the best (which is what I here call following after virtue) receives from this a satisfaction which is so powerful in rendering him happy that the most violent efforts of the passions never have sufficient power to disturb the tranquillity of his soul.

PART THIRD.

OF PARTICULAR PASSIONS.

ARTICLE CXLIX.

Of Esteem and Disdain.

After having explained the six primitive passions which are so to speak the genera of which all the others are species, I shall here observe succinctly what in particular there is in each of these others, and I shall keep to the same order in which I have before enumerated them. The two first are esteem and disdain; for although their names usually signify only passionless opinions on our part as to the value of a particular thing, still, at the same time, because there often arises from these opinions passions to which we have not given particular names, it seems to me that such may be attributed to them. And esteem, in so far as it is a passion, is an inclination which the soul possesses to represent to itself the value of the thing esteemed, which inclination is caused by a particular movement of the animal spirits conducted into the brain in such a way that they there fortify the impression which serve for this end. The passion of disdain, on the contrary, is an inclination possessed by the soul to consider the baseness or smallness of that which it disdains, caused by the movement of the spirits which fortify the idea of this smallness.

ARTICLE CL.

That these two passions are only species of wonder or admiration.

These two passions are thus only species of wonder; for when we do not wonder at the greatness or smallness of an object, we do not make more or less of it than reason tells us that we ought to do in its regard, so that we then esteem or disdain it without passion.

And, although often the esteem is excited in us by love, and the disdain by hate, that is not universally so, and only proceeds from the fact that we are more or less inclined to consider the greatness or smallness of an object because of our having more or less affection for it.

Article CLI.

That we may esteem or disdain ourselves.

Now these two passions may generally speaking relate to all sorts of objects ; but they are chiefly remarkable when we relate them to ourselves, i.e. when it is our own merit that we esteem or despise. And the movement of the spirits which causes them is then so manifest, that it even changes the mien, the gestures, the gait, and generally speaking all the actions of those who have a better or a worse opinion of themselves than usual.

Article CLII.

For what reasons we may esteem ourselves.

And because one of the principal parts of wisdom is to know in what way and for what cause each person ought to esteem or despise himself, I shall here try to place on record my opinion on the matter. I only remark in us one thing which might give us good reason to esteem ourselves, to wit, the use of our free will, and the empire which we possess over our wishes. Because it is for those actions alone which depend on this free will that we may with reason be praised or blamed ; and this in a certain measure renders us like God in making us masters of ourselves, provided that we do not through remissness lose the rights which He gives us.

Article CLIII.

In what Generosity consists.

Thus I think that true generosity which causes a man to esteem himself as highly as he legitimately can, consists alone partly in the fact that he knows that there is nothing that truly pertains to him but this free disposition of his will, and that there is no reason why he should be praised or blamed unless it is because he uses it well or ill ; and partly in the fact that he is sensible in himself of a firm and constant resolution to use it well, that is to say, never to fail of his own will to undertake and execute all the things which he judges to be the best—which is to follow perfectly after virtue.

ARTICLE CLIV.

That Generosity prevents our despising others.

Those who have this knowledge and feeling about themselves easily persuade themselves that every other man can also have them in his own case, because there is nothing in this that depends on another. That is why they never despise anyone; and, although they often see that others commit faults which make their feebleness apparent, they are at the same time more inclined to excuse than to blame them, and to believe that it is rather by lack of knowledge than by lack of good-will that they commit them. And, as they do not think of themselves as being much inferior to those who have more goods or honours, or even who have more mental gifts, more knowledge, more beauty, or, generally speaking, who surpass them in some other perfections, they do not at the same time esteem themselves much above those whom they surpass, because all these things seem to them to be of very small account as compared with the good-will for which alone they esteem themselves, and which they also suppose to exist, or at least to be capable of, existing in all other men.

ARTICLE CLV.

In what consists a virtuous humility.

The most high-minded are thus usually the most humble; and virtuous humility simply consists in the fact that the reflection which we make on the infirmity of our nature and on the faults which we may formerly have committed, or are capable of committing, which are not less than those which may be committed by others, is the reason that we do not prefer ourselves to any one else, and that we think that others, having their free-will as well as we, can likewise use it as well as we.

ARTICLE CLVI.

What are the properties of generosity, and how it serves as a remedy against the disorders of the passions.

Those who are generous in this way are naturally impelled to do great things and at the same time to undertake nothing of which they do not feel themselves capable. And because they do not hold anything more important than to do good to other men and to disdain their individual interests, they are for this reason always perfectly courteous, affable and obliging towards everyone. And along with that, they are entirely masters of their passions, particularly of the desires, of jealousy and envy, because there is nothing the acquisition of which does not depend on them, which they think of sufficient worth to merit being much sought after; they are likewise free of hatred to other men because they hold all in esteem; and of fear, because the confidence which they have in their virtue assures them; and finally of anger, because, esteeming very little all those things that depend on others, they never give so much advantage to their enemies as to recognise that they are hurt by them.

Article CLVII.

Of Pride.

All those who form a good opinion of themselves for some other reason, whatever it may be, have not a true generosity, but merely a pride which .is always very vicious, although it is all the more so, the more the cause for which we esteem ourselves is unjust. And the most unjust cause of all is when we are proud without any reason, that is to say, without our thinking so far as this goes that there is in us any merit for which we ought to be esteemed, simply taking the view that merit is not taken into consideration at all, and that as glory is regarded as nothing but usurpation, those who ascribe most of it to themselves really possess the greatest amount of it. This vice is so unreasonable and absurd, that I should scarcely have believed that there were men who could allow themselves to give way to it, if no one were ever unjustly praised; but flattery is everywhere so common that there is no man so defective that he does not often see himself esteemed for things that do not merit any praise, or even that merit blame; and this gives occasion to the most ignorant and stupid to fall into this species of pride.

Article CLVIII.

That its effects are contrary to those of generosity.

But whatever may be the reason for which we esteem ourselves, if it is other than the will which we feel in ourselves always to make good use of our free-will, from which I have stated that generosity proceeds, it always produces a very reprehensible pride, which is so different from this true generosity that it has effects entirely contrary to it. For all those other gifts such as cleverness, beauty, riches, honours, &c. usually being esteemed so much the more highly as they are found in the smaller number of persons, and being even for the most part of such a nature that they cannot be communicated to many persons, that causes the proud to try to depreciate all other men, and, being slaves to their desires, they have a soul incessantly agitated by hatred, envy, jealousy or anger.

Article CLIX.

Of vicious humility.

As to abjectness or a vicious humility, it consists principally in the fact that men are feeble or have a lack of resolution, and that, as though they had not the entire use of their free-will, they cannot prevent themselves doing things of which they know that they will afterwards repent; it also consists in their considering that they cannot subsist by themselves nor do without many things the acquisition of which depends on others. It is thus directly opposed to noble-mindedness, and it often happens that those who have the most abject minds are the most arrogant and haughty, just as the most noble-minded are the most modest and humble. But while it is the case that those whose minds are strong and noble do not change in disposition in respect of the prosperity or adversity that comes to them, those whose minds are feeble and abject are led simply by Fortune, and prosperity does not puff them up less than adversity makes them humble. Frequently we even observe that they abase themselves with every mark of shame in the presence of those from whom they expect some profit or fear some ill, and, at the same time, that they insolently place themselves above those from whom they neither hope nor fear anything.

Article CLX.

What is the movement of the animal spirits in these passions.

For the rest, it is easy to recognise that pride and poor spirit are not only vices, but also passions, because the emotions attached to them readily appear outwardly in those who are suddenly puffed up or cast down by some new occasion that produces them; but we may doubt whether generosity and humility, which are virtues, may likewise be passions, because their movements appear to be less, and because it seems that virtue has not so much in common with passion as has vice[1]. At the same time I see no reason preventing the same movement of the spirits which serves to strengthen a thought when it has a foundation which is bad, from also fortifying it when it has one which is just. And, since pride and generosity consist only in the good opinion which we have of ourselves, and only differ inasmuch as this opinion is unjust in the one case and just in the other, it appears to me that we may relate them to one and the same passion, which is excited by a movement composed of the passions of wonder, of joy and of love, both of that which we have for ourselves, and of that which we have for the thing which causes us to hold ourselves in estimation. On the other hand, the movement which excites humility, whether virtuous or vicious, is composed of the passions of wonder, sadness, and of the love which we have for ourselves, mingled with the hatred which we have for the faults which cause us to disdain ourselves. And the whole difference which I observe in these movements is that the passion of wonder has two properties—the first being that surprise renders it strong from its commencement, and the other that it is equal in its continuance, i.e. that the spirits continue to move according to the same tenor in the brain. Of these properties the first is met with much more in pride and poor spiritedness than in generosity and virtuous humility; and, on the other hand, the second is better seen in the latter than in the other two. The reason of this is that vice usually proceeds from ignorance, and that it is those who know themselves the least who are the most subject to become proud and to humiliate themselves more than they ought to do; because all that happens to them anew surprises them, and brings it to pass that in attributing it to themselves they wonder at themselves, and esteem or despise themselves according as they judge that what happens to them is to their advantage or is not so. But because often after a thing which has made them proud, another follows which humiliates them, the movement of their passions is variable. There is, on the contrary, nothing in generosity which is not consistent with virtuous humility or anything else which might change them, and this causes their movements to be firm, constant, and always very similar to themselves. But they are not due so much to surprise because those who esteem themselves in this way are sufficiently aware what are the causes which make

[1] 'Ne symbolise par tant avec la Passion, que fait le vice' F. V. Latin: 'nec videtur ita virtuti cum Passionibus convenire ac vitio.'

them esteem themselves; at the same time we may say that these things are so wonderful (i.e. the power of making use of one's free-will, which causes us to value ourselves, and the infirmities of the subject in whom this power rests, which cause us not to place too high a regard on ourselves) that on every occasion on which we present them to ourselves anew, they always supply a new cause for wonder.

Article CLXI.

How Generosity may be acquired.

And it must be observed that what we commonly name virtues are habitudes in the soul, which dispose it to certain thoughts in such a way that they are different from these thoughts, but can produce them, and reciprocally can be produced by them. It must also be observed that these thoughts may be produced by the soul alone, but that it often happens that some movement of the spirits fortifies them, and that then they are actions of virtue, and at the same time passions of the soul. Thus, while there is no virtue to which it appears as though good native qualities contribute so much as to that which causes us only to esteem ourselves at a just value, and as it is easy to believe that all the souls that God places in human bodies are not equally noble and strong (which is the reason for my having called this virtue generosity, following the usage of our language, rather than magnanimity, following the usage of the Schools where it is not much known) it is yet certain that good instruction serves much in correcting the faults of birth, and that, if we frequently occupy ourselves in the consideration of what free-will is, and how great are the advantages which proceed from a firm resolution to make a good use of it, as also, on the other hand, how vain and useless are all the cares which exercise the ambitions, we may excite in ourselves the passion, and then acquire the virtue of generosity, which, being so to speak the key of all other virtues, and a general remedy for all the disorders of the passions, it appears to me that this consideration is well worthy of notice.

Article CLXII.

Of Veneration.

Veneration, or respect, is an inclination of the soul not only to esteem the object which it reveres, but also to submit itself thereto with some fear, in order to try to render it favourably inclined. In this way we possess veneration only for free causes which we judge

to be capable of doing good or evil to us, without our knowing
which of the two they may do. For we have love and devotion
rather than a simple veneration for those from whom we expect
nothing but good, and we have hatred for those from whom we expect
only evil. And, if we do not believe that the cause of this good
or evil is free, we do not submit ourselves to it in order to
render it favourable to us. Thus when the pagans had veneration for woods, fountains, or mountains, it was not properly
speaking these dead things which they revered, but the divinities
which they believed to preside over these. And the movement
of the animal spirits which excites veneration is composed of that
which excites wonder and that which excites fear, of which I shall
speak later.

Article CLXIII.

Of Disdain.

At the same time what I call disdain is the inclination which
the soul has to despise a free cause, in judging that, although in
its nature it is capable of doing good or evil, it is nevertheless so
much below us that to us it can do neither. And the movement
of the spirits which excites it is composed of those which excite
wonder and security or assurance.

Article CLXIV.

Of the functions of these two passions.

And it is the noble-mindedness and feebleness of soul or poor
spirit, which determine the good and the evil employment of these
two passions; for the more noble and generous our soul is, the
more inclination we have to render to each man what pertains to
him; and thus we have not only a very profound humility in
regard to God, but we also render without any repugnance all the
honour and respect which is due to each man according to the rank
and authority which he has in the world, and we disdain nothing
but vices. Those who have a low and feeble mind, on the contrary,
are subject to sin by excess, sometimes inasmuch as they revere
and fear things which are worthy of disdain alone, and sometimes inasmuch as they insolently despise those which most merit
reverence; and they often pass very quickly from extreme impiety to superstition, and then from superstition to impiety, so
that there is no vice nor disorder of the mind of which they are
not capable.

Article CLXV.

Of Hope and Fear.

Hope is a disposition of the soul to persuade itself that what it desires will come to pass : and this is caused by a particular movement of the spirits, i.e. by that of joy and that of desire mingled together ; and fear is another disposition of the soul which persuades it that the thing hoped for will not come to pass ; and it must be observed that, although these two passions are contrary, we can nevertheless have them both at the same time, that is to say, when we represent to ourselves different reasons at the same time, some of which cause us to judge that the accomplishment of desire is easy, while the others make it seem difficult.

Article CLXVI.

Of Confidence and Despair.

And no one of these passions ever accompanies desire without its giving place in some way to the other ; for when hope is so strong that it entirely drives away fear, it changes its nature and is called security or confidence ; and when we are assured that what we desire will come to pass, though we continue to desire that it shall come to pass, we nevertheless cease to be agitated by the passion of desire, which made its accomplishment be regarded with anxiety. In the same way, when fear is so extreme that it removes all place for hope, it converts itself into despair ; and this despair, representing the matter as impossible, entirely extinguishes desire, which only relates to things that are possible.

Article CLXVII.

Of Jealousy.

Jealousy is a species of fear which is related to the desire we have to preserve to ourselves the possession of some thing ; and it does not so much proceed from the strength of the reasons that suggest the possibility of our losing that good, as from the high estimation in which we hold it, and which is the cause of our examining even the minutest subjects of suspicion, and taking them to be very considerable reasons for anxiety.

Article CLXVIII.

In how far this passion is right.

And because we ought to have more care in preserving these good possessions that are very great than those which are less, this passion may be just and right in some circumstances. Thus, for example, a captain who is defending a position of great importance has the right to be jealous of it, that is to say, to be mistrustful of all the means by which it might be surprised; and a good woman is not blamed for being jealous of her honour, that is, when she is not only guarding herself against acting wrongly, but also avoiding even the slightest reason for scandal.

Article CLXIX.

In what it is blameworthy.

But we scorn a miser when he is jealous of his treasure, that is, when he gloats over it, and desires never to be away from it for fear he may be robbed of it; for money is not worthy of being guarded with so much care. And we despise a man who is jealous of his wife, because it shows that he does not love her in the right way, and that he has a bad opinion of himself or of her. I repeat that he does not love her in the right way, since if he had a true love for her, he would not have any inclination to distrust her; but it is not properly speaking she whom he loves, but just the good which he conceives as consisting in having sole possession of her, and he would not fear to lose this good did he not judge himself to be unworthy of it, or else conceive that his wife is unfaithful. For the rest this passion only relates to suspicions and distrust, since it is not properly speaking being jealous to try to avoid some evil when we have just cause for fearing it.

Article CLXX.

Of Irresolution.

Irresolution is likewise a species of fear, which, holding the soul so to speak in a state of suspension between the many actions which it may perform, is the cause for its executing none, and thus for its having time for choosing before deciding, and this function is truly of a certain value. But when it lasts longer than it ought to do, and causes the time requisite for action to be employed in deliberation, it is very bad. And I assert that it is a species of fear, notwithstanding that it may happen, when we have a choice of several things the excellence of which seems to be very equal, that we remain uncertain and irresolute without our having for all that any fear; for this kind of irresolution proceeds only from the object presented, and not from any movement of the animal spirits; chat is why this is not a passion unless it be that the fear we have of choosing wrongly augments our uncertainty. But this fear is so common and so strong in some people that often, although they have nothing to choose, and see only one thing which they may take or leave, it keeps them back and causes them to stop futilely and seek for something else; and then it is an excess of irresolution which proceeds from a too great desire to do right and from a feebleness of understanding, which, having no clear and distinct conceptions, simply has many confused ones. That is why the remedy against this excess is to accustom oneself to form certain and determinate judgments concerning all things that present themselves, and to believe that we always do our duty when we do what we judge to be best, although we may possibly judge very badly.

Article CLXXI

Of Courage and Bravery.

Courage, when it is a passion and not a custom or natural inclination, is a certain heat or agitation which disposes the soul forcibly to bend itself powerfully to the execution of the things which it desires to do, of whatever nature they may be; and bravery is a species of courage which disposes the soul to the execution of the things that are the most dangerous.

Article CLXXII.

Of Emulation.

And emulation is also a species of courage, but in another sense; for we may consider courage as a *genus* which divides into as many species as there are different objects, and into as many others as it has causes; in the first aspect bravery is a species, and in the second, emulation. And this last is none other than a heat which disposes the soul to undertake things which it hopes to be able on its own account to succeed in, because it sees them succeed with others; and thus it is a species of courage of which the external cause is example. I repeat the external cause, because it must ever have in addition to that an inward cause, which consists in the fact that the body is so constituted that desire and hope have more power in causing a quantity of blood to pass to the heart than has fear or despair to prevent it.

Article CLXXIII.

How Bravery depends on hope.

For it must be remarked that although the object of bravery is difficulty, from which there usually follows fear, or even despair, so that it is in matters the most dangerous and desperate that we employ most bravery or courage, it is yet essential that we should hope, or even that we should be assured, that the end which is proposed will succeed, in order to oppose with vigour the difficulties that we meet with. But this end is different from this object of bravery; for we could not be assured of and hopeless of the same thing at the same time. Thus when the Decii threw themselves against their enemies and rushed to certain death, the object of their bravery was the difficulty of preserving their life during this action, for which difficulty they had only despair, for they were certain of perishing; but their end was to animate their soldiers by their example, and to cause them to win the victory, for which they had hope; or again their end also was to obtain after their death a glory of which they were assured.

Article CLXXIV.

Of Cowardice and Fear.

Cowardice is directly opposed to courage, and it is a languor or coldness which prevents the soul from proceeding to the execution of things which it would do were it exempt from this passion; and fear or terror, which is contrary to bravery, is not only a coldness, but also a perturbation and astonishment of the soul, which takes from it the power of resisting the evils which it thinks lie at hand.

Article CLXXV.

Of the uses of Cowardice.

And, although I cannot persuade myself that nature has given to men any passion which is always vicious and has no good and praiseworthy use, I have yet much trouble in guessing what end these two can serve. It merely seems to me that cowardice has some use when it exempts us from taking the pains which we might be incited to take by probable reasons, if other more certain reasons, which have caused them to be judged useless, had not excited this passion; for besides the fact that it exempts the soul from these pains, it is secondly useful also for the body, inasmuch as, in restraining the movement of the spirits, it prevents us from dissipating our forces. But usually it is very hurtful, because it turns away the will from useful actions; and because it only proceeds from the fact that we have not enough hope or desire, we only need to augment within us these two passions in order to correct it.

ARTICLE CLXXVI.

Of the uses of Fear.

As to the significance of fear or terror, I do not see that it can ever be praiseworthy or useful; it likewise is not a special passion, but merely an excess of cowardice, astonishment and fear, which is always vicious, just as bravery is an excess of courage which is always good, provided that the end proposed is good; and because the principal cause of fear is surprise, there is nothing better for getting rid of it than to use premeditation and to prepare oneself for all eventualities, the fear of which may cause it.

ARTICLE CLXXVII.

Of Remorse.

Remorse of conscience is a species of sadness which comes from the doubt which we have that a thing which we are doing or have done is good; and it necessarily presupposes doubt. For if we were entirely assured that what we are doing was bad, we should abstain from doing it, inasmuch as the will only tends towards things which have some appearance of goodness; and if we were assured that what we have already done was bad, we should experience repentance for it, not simply remorse. And the use of this passion is to make us examine whether that of which we doubt is good or not, or to prevent our doing it another time so long as we are not certain that it is good. But because it presupposes evil, the better part would be never to have occasion to feel it; and we may prevent it by the same means as those whereby we may exempt ourselves from irresolution.

ARTICLE CLXXVIII.

Of Scorn.

Derision or scorn is a sort of joy mingled with hatred, which proceeds from our perceiving some small evil in a person whom we consider to be deserving of it ; we have hatred for this evil, we have joy in seeing it in him who is deserving of it ; and when that comes upon us unexpectedly, the surprise of wonder is the cause of our bursting into laughter, in accordance with what has been said above of the nature of laughter[1]. But this evil must be small, for if it is great we cannot believe that he who has it is deserving of it, unless when we are of a very evil nature or bear much hatred towards him.

ARTICLE CLXXIX.

Why the least perfect are usually most given to mockery.

And we notice that people with very obvious defects such as those who are lame, blind of an eye, hunched-backed, or who have received some public insult, are specially given to mockery ; for, desiring to see all others held in as low estimation as themselves, they are truly rejoiced at the evils which befall them, and they hold them deserving of these.

ARTICLE CLXXX.

Of the function of ridicule.

As regards the modest bantering which is useful in reproving vices by making them appear ridiculous, so long as we do not laugh at them ourselves or bear any hatred towards the individuals concerned, it is not a passion, but a quality pertaining to the well disposed man which gives evidence of the gaiety of his temper and the tranquillity of his soul, which are characteristic marks of virtue ; it often also shows the ingenuity of his mind in knowing how to present an agreeable appearance to the things which he ridicules.

ARTICLE CLXXXI.

Of the function of laughter in ridicule.

And it is not wrong to laugh when we hear the jests of another ; these jests may even be such that it would be difficult not to laugh at them ; but when we ourselves jest, it is more fitting to abstain from laughter, in order not to seem to be surprised by the things that are said, nor to wonder at the ingenuity we show in inventing them. And that makes those who hear them all the more surprised.

[1] p. 386.

Article CLXXXII.

Of Envy.

What we usually call envy is a vice which consists in a perversion of nature which causes certain people to be annoyed with the good which they see coming to others, but I here use the word to signify a passion which is not always vicious. Envy, then, in so far as it is a passion, is a kind of sadness mingled with hatred, which proceeds from our seeing good coming to those whom we consider unworthy of it; and we cannot think this with any reason excepting in relation to the good things of fortune. For as regards those of the soul, or even of the body, inasmuch as we possess them from birth, it is sufficient so far as worthiness is concerned that we have received them from God before being capable of committing any evil.

Article CLXXXIII.

How it may be either just or unjust.

But when fortune sends good things to some one who is truly unworthy of them, and envy is only excited in us because, naturally loving justice, we are vexed that it is not observed in the distribution of these good things, our sentiments may be excusable, more especially when the good which we envy in others is of such a kind that it may be converted into evil in their hands, as when it is some charge or office in whose exercise they may comport themselves ill. When we desire the same good for ourselves and are prevented from having it because others who are less worthy possess it, this passion is rendered more violent; and it does not cease to be excusable provided that the hatred which it contains relates solely to the bad distribution of the good which we envy, and not to the persons who possess it or distribute it. But there are few who are sufficiently generous and just not to bear hatred to those who get the better of them in the acquisition of a good which is not communicable to many, and which they had desired for themselves, although those who acquired it are as worthy or even more so. And what is usually most envied is glory; for although the glory of others does not prevent our being able to aspire to it, it yet renders access to it more difficult, and heightens the price we must pay for it.

Article CLXXXIV.

From whence it comes that the envious are subject to have a leaden complexion.

For the rest, there is no vice which so detracts from the happiness of men as that of envy; for, in addition to the fact that those who are tainted with it distress themselves, they also disturb to the utmost of their power the pleasure of others; and usually they have a leaden hue, that is to say, one of mingled yellow and black like battered blood, whence envy is in Latin called *livor*, which accords very well with what has been said above regarding the movements of the blood in sadness and hatred. For the former causes the yellow bile which proceeds from the lower portion of the liver, and the black which proceeds from the spleen, to expand from the heart by the arteries into all the veins, and the latter causes the blood in the veins to have less heat, and to flow more slowly than usual, which suffices to render the colour livid. But because the bile, yellow as well as black, may also be sent into the veins by many other causes, and because envy does not send them there in sufficiently great quantity to change the shade of the colour, except when it is great and of long duration, we must not think that all those in whom we observe this colour are inclined thereto.

Article CLXXXV.

Of Pity.

Pity is a species of sadness, mingled with love or good-will towards those whom we see suffering some evil of which we consider them undeserving. It is thus contrary to envy by reason of its object, and to scorn because it considers its objects in another way.

Article CLXXXVI.

Those who are the most given to pity.

Those who feel themselves very feeble and subject to the adversities of fortune appear to be more disposed to this passion than others, because they represent the evil of others as possibly occurring to themselves; and then they are moved to pity more by the love that they bear to themselves than by that which they bear to others.

ARTICLE CLXXXVII.

How the most noble-minded are touched by this passion.

Nevertheless those who are most generous and strongest in mind, inasmuch as they fear no ill for themselves and hold themselves to be beyond the powers of fortune, are not exempt from compassion when they see the infirmity of other men and hear their plaints; for it is a part of generosity to wish well to one and all. But the sadness of this pity is no longer bitter, and, like that caused by the tragic actions which we see represented in a theatre, it is more external and in the senses than in the interior of the soul, which has yet the satisfaction of thinking that it does its duty in compassionating the afflicted. And there is this difference here that while the ordinary man has compassion on those who lament their lot because he thinks that the evils from which they suffer are very vexatious, the principal object of the pity of the greatest men is the weakness of those whom they see bemoaning their fate, because they do not consider that any accident which might possibly happen would be so great an ill as is the cowardice of those who cannot endure it with constancy; and although they hate vices, they do not for all that hate those whom they see subject to them, but only pity them.

ARTICLE CLXXXVIII

Who are those who are not touched by it.

But it is only the evilly disposed and envious, who naturally hate all men, or those who are so brutal and blinded by good fortune, or rendered so desperate by evil fortune that they do not consider that any evil can happen to them, who are insensible to pity.

ARTICLE CLXXXIX.

Why this passion moves us to weep.

For the rest we weep very easily in this passion because love, sending much blood towards the heart, causes many vapours to issue from the eyes, and the coldness of sadness, retarding the agitation of these vapours, causes them to change into tears, in accordance with what has been said above.

ARTICLE CXC.

Of Self-Satisfaction.

The satisfaction which those who pursue virtue constantly have, is a habitude of their soul which is called tranquillity and repose of conscience; but that which is newly acquired, when we have just done some action which we think good, is a passion, i.e. a species of joy which I consider to be the sweetest of all joys, because its cause depends only on ourselves. At the same time when this cause is not just, i.e. when the actions from which we derive much satisfaction are not of great importance or are even vicious, it is absurd, and only serves to produce pride and an impertinent arrogance; and this we observe particularly in those who, believing themselves to be pious, are merely bigoted and given over to superstitions. That is to say they are those who, under the pretence that they go frequently to church, that they recite many prayers, that they wear their hair short, that they fast, that they give alms, think themselves to be absolutely perfect, and imagine themselves to be such close friends of God that they can do nothing to displease Him, and that all that their passion presents is well-directed zeal, although it sometimes guides them into the greatest crimes that can be committed by men, such as the betrayal of towns, the assassination of princes, the extermination of entire peoples, for the sole reason that they do not follow *their* opinions.

ARTICLE CXCI.

Of Repentance.

Repentance is directly opposed to self-satisfaction and is a species of sadness which comes from our believing ourselves to have committed some evil action; and it is very bitter because its cause proceeds from ourselves alone, though this does not prevent its being very useful when it is the case that the action of which we repent is evil, and when we have a certain knowledge of it, because it incites us to do better another time. But it often happens that feeble minds repent of the things they have done without knowing assuredly that they are evil; they only persuade themselves because they fear it is so, and if they had done the opposite, they would have repented in the same way; and this is an imperfection in them deserving of pity. The remedies for this fault are the same as those which serve to remove irresolution.

ARTICLE CXCII.

Of Favour.

Favour is, properly speaking, a desire to see good coming to some one for whom one has good will: but here I make use of this word to signify this will inasmuch as it is excited in us by some good action on the part of him for whom we have it. For we are naturally impelled to love those who do the things which we esteem to be good, even though no good comes to us by so doing. In this sense favour is a species of love, not of desire, although the desire to see good come to him whom one favours always accompanies it; and it is usually united to pity because the tribulations which we see falling upon the unfortunate are the cause of our reflecting all the more on their merits.

ARTICLE CXCIII.

Of Gratitude.

Gratitude is also a species of love excited in us by some action on the part of him for whom we have it, by which also we believe that he has done us some good or at least had that intention. It has thus the same content as favour, and so much the more in that it is founded on an action which affects us, and of which we have the desire to make a return. That is why it has much more strength, especially in the minds of those who are, to however small a degree, noble and generous.

ARTICLE CXCIV.

Of Ingratitude.

As to ingratitude it is not a passion, for nature has not placed in us any movement of the spirits which excites it; it is merely a vice directly opposed to gratitude, inasmuch as the former is always virtuous and one of the principal bonds that bind together human society. That is why this vice is found only in men who are brutal and very arrogant, and who think that all things are their due; or in stupid people, who never reflect on the benefits that they receive; or feeble and abject persons who, being sensible of their infirmity and need, basely seek the help of others, and after they have received it, hate their benefactors because, not having the will to render them the like, or despairing to be able to do so, and imagining that every one is as mercenary as they, and that no good thing is accomplished without the hope of recompense, they think they have deceived them.

ARTICLE CXCV.

Of Indignation.

Indignation is a species of hatred or aversion which we have by nature against those who do some evil of whatever sort it be; and it is often mingled with envy or pity, but yet it has a very different object. For we are indignant only with those who do good or evil to persons who are undeserving of it; but we are envious of those who receive this good, and we pity those who receive the evil. It is true that it is in some ways doing evil to possess a good of which we are not worthy [*digne*]; and this may be the reason why Aristotle and his successors, supposing envy to be always a vice, have termed by the name indignation that passion which is not vicious.

ARTICLE CXCVI.

Why it is sometimes united to pity, and sometimes to scorn.

It is likewise in some way receiving evil to do evil, from whence it comes that some unite pity to their indignation, and others scorn, according as they are disposed to good will or evil towards those whom they observe committing faults; and it is thus that the laughter of Democritus and the tears of Heraclitus have proceeded from the same cause.

ARTICLE CXCVII.

That it is often accompanied by wonder and is not incompatible with joy.

Indignation is often likewise accompanied by wonder; for we usually suppose that all things will be done in the manner we judge they ought to be done, that is, in the way we esteem to be good; that is why, when it happens otherwise, it surprises us, and we wonder at it. It is also not incompatible with joy, although it is more usually united to sadness; for when the evil as to which we are indignant cannot hurt us, and we consider that we would not desire to do the same, that gives us some pleasure; and it is possibly one of the causes of the laughter which sometimes accompanies this passion.

Article CXCVIII.

Of its Use.

For the rest, indignation is noticed much more in those who wish to appear virtuous than in those who really are so; for, although those who love virtue cannot without aversion see the vices of others, they do not become impassioned excepting against those that are greatest and most extraordinary. It is being ill-tempered[1] and fretful to have much indignation for things of slight importance; it is being unjust, to have it for things not blameworthy at all; and it is being impertinent and absurd not to restrict this passion to the actions of men and to extend them to the works of God or nature, as do those who, never being content with their condition or fortune, dare to find subject for criticism in the conduct of the world and in the secrets of Providence.

Article CXCIX.

Of Anger.

Anger is also a species of hatred or aversion which we have towards those who have done some evil to or have tried to injure not any chance person but more particularly ourselves. Thus it has the same content as indignation, and all the more so in that it is founded on an action which affects us, and for which we desire to avenge ourselves, for this desire almost always accompanies it; and it is directly opposed to gratitude, as indignation is to favour. But it is incomparably more violent than these three other passions, because the desire to repel harmful things and to revenge oneself, is the most persistent of all desires. It is desire, united to self-love, which furnishes to anger the agitation of the blood that courage and bravery can cause; and hatred brings it to pass that it is mainly the bilious blood coming from the spleen and the small veins of the liver that experiences this agitation and enters into the heart, where, because of its abundance and of the nature of the bile with which it is mingled, it excites a heat which is more severe and ardent than is that which may be excited by love or by joy.

[1] difficile Fr.

Article CC.

Why those whom it makes flush are less to be feared than those whom it makes blanch.

And the external signs of this passion are different according to the difference of personal temperaments and the diversity of the other passions which compose it or unite themselves with it. We thus see people who become pale or who tremble when they become angry, and we see others who become flushed or who even weep ; and we usually judge that the anger of those who grow pale is more to be feared than the anger of those who become red. And the reason of this is that when we do not desire to, or are unable to revenge ourselves otherwise than by our expression and words, we employ all our heat and all our strength from the commencement of our emotion, and this is the reason that we become red, besides which sometimes the regret and self-pity that we have, since we cannot avenge ourselves otherwise, is the reason why we weep. And, on the other hand, those who hold themselves in and make up their minds to a greater vengeance, become sad from thinking themselves obliged to behave so by the action which angers them ; and they are sometimes also afraid by reason of the evils which may follow on the resolution which they have taken, which renders them pale, cold and trembling to begin with. But when they afterwards come to execute their vengeance, they become warm again in proportion as they had been cold to begin with, just as we notice that fevers which commence with chill usually become the most severe.

Article CCI.

That there are two sorts of anger, and that those who have the most goodness are most subject to the former.

This shows us that we can distinguish two kinds of anger : the one which is very hasty and manifests itself very much on the surface, but which yet has little effect and can be easily appeased ; the other which does not show itself so much to begin with, but which all the more powerfully gnaws the heart and has more dangerous effects. Those who have much goodness and much love are most subject to the first, for it does not proceed from a profound hatred, but from an instant aversion, which surprises them, because, being impelled to imagine that all things should go in the way which they judge to be best, so soon as it happens otherwise, they wonder and frequently are displeased, even although the matter does not affect them personally, because, having much affection, they interest themselves for those whom they love in the same way as for themselves. Thus what would only be cause for indignation in the case of another, is for them a cause of anger; and because the inclination which they have to love causes them to have much heat and much blood in their heart, the aversion which surprises them cannot send there bile in so small a quantity that it does not cause at first a great commotion in this blood. But this commotion does not last, because the strength of the surprise does not continue, and because, as soon as they perceive that the subject which has vexed them ought not to affect them so much, they repent of it.

ARTICLE CCII.

That it is weak and base spirits which most permit themselves to give way to the latter.

The other kind of anger in which hatred and sadness predominate, is not so apparent at first if it be not perhaps that it causes the face to grow pale; but its strength is little by little increased by the agitation of an ardent desire to avenge oneself excited in the blood, which, being mingled with the bile which is sent towards the heart from the lower part of the liver and spleen, excites there a very keen and ardent heat. And as it is the most generous souls who have most gratitude, it is those who have most pride, and who are most base and infirm, who most allow themselves to be carried away by this kind of anger; for the injuries appear so much the greater as pride causes us to esteem ourselves more, and likewise the more we esteem the good things which they remove; which last we value so much the more, as our soul is the more feeble and base, because they depend on others.

ARTICLE CCIII.

That noble-mindedness serves as a remedy against its excesses.

For the rest, although this passion is useful in giving us strength in repelling injuries, there is yet no passion an excess of which we should more carefully avoid, because, in disturbing our judgment, they often cause us to commit faults of which we have afterwards to repent, and they even sometimes prevent our repelling these injuries as well as we might have done had we suffered less emotion. But as there is nothing which makes it excessive so much as pride, so I think that noble spirit is the best remedy which can be found against its excesses, because, causing us to esteem very little all the good things which may be taken away, and on the other hand to esteem highly the liberty and absolute dominion over self that we cease to have when we allow ourselves to be offended by some one, it brings it to pass that we have nothing but disdain, or at the most indignation, for those injuries which others are wont to resent angrily.

ARTICLE CCIV.

Of Glory.

What I here call by the name glory is a species of joy founded on self-love, which proceeds from the belief or hope we have of being praised by certain others. It is thus different from the internal satisfaction that comes from our belief that we have performed some good action; for we are sometimes praised for things which we do not believe to be good, and blamed for those we believe to be better. But both are species of self-esteem as well as species of joy; for seeing that we are esteemed by others is a reason for esteeming ourselves.

ARTICLE CCV.

Of Shame.

Shame, on the contrary, is a species of sadness, also founded on self-love, which proceeds from the apprehension or the fear which we possess of being blamed; besides that it is a species of modesty or humility and mistrust of self. For when we esteem ourselves so highly that we cannot imagine ourselves to be disdained by any, we cannot easily be ashamed.

ARTICLE CCVI.

Of the uses of these two passions.

Glory and shame have the same functions in so far as they incite us to virtue, the one by hope, and the other by fear. It is only necessary to inform one's judgment as to what is truly worthy of being blamed or praised in order that we may not be ashamed of doing well or make our vices a source of vanity, as happens in the case of many. But it is not good to rid oneself entirely of these passions as the Cynics used to do; for although common people judge very ill, yet because we cannot live without others and it is important to us to be esteemed by them, we ought frequently to follow their opinions rather than ours respecting the external aspect of our actions.

ARTICLE CCVII.

Of Impudence

Impudence or effrontery, which is a disdain of shame and frequently of glory also, is not a passion, because there is not in us any special movement of the spirits which excites it; but it is a vice opposed to shame and also to glory, inasmuch as both are good, just as ingratitude is opposed to gratitude and cruelty to pity. And the principal cause of effrontery proceeds from a man's having frequently received great affronts; for there is no one who does not in his youth imagine that praise is a good, and infamy an evil, much more important to life than it is found by experience to be, when, on receiving some signal affronts, he sees himself to be entirely deprived of honour and disdained by all men. That is why such men become shameless who, only estimating good or evil by their bodily well-being, see that after these affronts they flourish just as much as before or even sometimes much more, because they are free from many trammels imposed upon them by honour, and because they discover that if the loss of their goods is united to their disgrace, charitable people are always found who give to them.

ARTICLE CCVIII.

Of Disgust.

Disgust is a species of sadness which proceeds from the same cause as that from which joy earlier proceeded. For we are so constituted that the greater part of the things as to which we rejoice are only good in our regard for a time, and afterwards become tiresome. This is specially true in respect of eating and drinking which are useful only so long as we have an appetite, and are hurtful when we have it no longer; and because they then cease to be agreeable to the taste[1] this passion is termed disgust[1].

---

[1] goût and dégoût, Fr.

Article CCIX.

Of Regret.

Regret is also a kind of sadness which has a particular bitterness inasmuch as it is always united to a certain despair and to the memory of the pleasure which gave us joy, for we regret nothing but the good things regarding which we rejoiced and which are so lost that we have no hope of recovering them at the time and in the guise in which we regret them.

Article CCX

Of Cheerfulness.

Finally, what I call cheerfulness is a species of joy in which there is this peculiarity, that its sweetness is increased by the recollection of the evils which we have suffered, and of which we are relieved, in the same way as we feel freed of some heavy burden which we have for a long time borne on our shoulders. And I observe nothing very remarkable in these three passions, nor have I placed them here but in order to follow the enumeration which I made above; yet it seems to me that this enumeration has been useful in order to show that we have omitted none which were worthy of particular consideration.

Article CCXI.

A general remedy against the Passions.

And now that we are acquainted with them all, we have much less reason to fear them than we formerly had. For we see that they are all good in their nature and that we have nothing to avoid but their evil uses or their excesses, against which the remedies which I explained might suffice, if each one of us took sufficient heed to practise them. But because I have placed amongst these remedies the forethought and diligence whereby we can correct our natural faults in exercising ourselves in separating within us the movements of the blood and spirits from the thoughts to which they are usually united. I confess that there are few people who are sufficiently prepared in this way to meet all the accidents of life, and that these movements excited in the blood by the objects of the passions follow so promptly from these single impressions that are made in the brain and from the disposition of the organs, although the soul contributes in no wise to them, that there is no human wisdom capable of resisting them when sufficient preparation is not made for doing so. Thus many people cannot prevent themselves from laughing on being tickled, even though they have no pleasure in it; for the impression of joy and surprise which caused them formerly to laugh for the same reason, being once more awakened in their imagination, causes their lung to be suddenly inflated in spite of themselves by the blood which the heart sends to it. In this way those who are naturally much carried away by their disposition towards emotions of joy or pity, or fear or anger, cannot prevent themselves from fainting, weeping, or trembling, or from having their blood agitated just as though they had a fever, when their imagination is violently affected by the object of some one of these passions. But what we can always do on such occasions, and what I think I can here put forward as the most general remedy and that most easy to practise against all excesses of the passions, is that, when we feel our blood to be thus agitated, we should be warned of the fact, and recollect that all that presents itself before the imagination tends to delude the soul and causes the reasons which serve to urge it to accomplish the object of its passion to appear much stronger than they are, and those which serve to dissuade it to be much weaker. And when the passions urge us only towards things the execution of which necessitates some delay, we ought to abstain from pronouncing any judgment on the spot, and to divert ourselves by other thoughts until time and rest shall have entirely calmed the emotion which is in the blood. And finally, when it incites us to actions regarding which it is requisite that an immediate resolution should be taken, the will must make it its main business to consider and follow up the reasons which are contrary to those set up by the passions, although they appear to be less strong; just as when we are suddenly attacked by some enemy, the occasion does not permit of our taking time to deliberate. But it seems to me that what those who are accustomed to reflect on their actions can always do when they feel themselves to be seized with fear, is to try to turn their thoughts away from the consideration of danger by representing to themselves the reasons which prove that there is much more certainty and honour in resistance than in flight. And on the other hand, when they feel that the desire of vengeance and anger incites them to run thoughtlessly towards those who attack them, they will recollect that it is imprudence to lose their lives when they can without dishonour save themselves, and that, if the match is very unequal, it is better to beat an honourable retreat or ask quarter, than to expose oneself doggedly to certain death.

ARTICLE CCXII.

That it is on them alone that all the good and evil of this life depends.

For the rest, the soul may have pleasures of its own, but as to those which are common to it and the body, they depend entirely on the passions, so that the men whom they can most move are capable of partaking most of enjoyment in this life. It is true that such men may also find most bitterness when they do not know how to employ them well, or fortune is contrary to them. But the principal use of prudence or self-control is that it teaches us to be masters of our passions, and to so control and guide them that the evils which they cause are quite bearable, and that we even derive joy from them all.

NOTES DIRECTED AGAINST A CERTAIN PROGRAMME

PREFATORY NOTE TO THE NOTAE IN PROGRAMMA.

THE former friend and now opponent of Descartes, Regius or Le Roy, had issued from Utrecht in anonymous form a sort of poster or manifesto on the nature of the human mind. Descartes undertook a refutation written in Latin which is here translated. It was printed, apparently without his knowledge, in December 1647, and was accompanied by Verses and a Preface which had not his approbation. Neither the Verses nor the Preface are reproduced here. This is the last writing on Descartes' part which concerns the relationship between him and his former disciple at Utrecht. The latter, however, did not confess himself defeated but returned later to the charge.

E. S. H.

RENÉ DESCARTES: NOTES DIRECTED AGAINST A CERTAIN PROGRAMME PUBLISHED IN BELGIUM AT THE END OF THE YEAR 1647 UNDER THIS TITLE

An Explanation of the Human Mind or Rational Soul: What it is and what it may be.

A few days ago I received two pamphlets attacking me, one openly and directly, the other only covertly and by implication. Of the first I make no account; indeed I am indebted to the author, for by the very fact that with all his inordinate labour he has succeeded in collecting nothing but groundless revilings and calumnies that none could credit, he has borne me witness that he could find nothing in my writings to which he could reasonably take exception, and thus has corroborated their truth better than he would have done by praising them, and moreover has effected this at the expense of his own reputation. The other pamphlet troubles me more, though I am not mentioned openly in the discussion, and it is published without the name of author or printer; for it contains opinions which I deem pernicious and erroneous and is issued in the shape of a Programme which may be affixed to Church doors, and exposed to the view of any chance reader. It is said, however, that it was previously printed in another form, with the name appended (purporting to be the author's)[1], of one whose doctrine is believed by many to be identical with my own. I am constrained to expose his errors, lest, perchance, they be attributed to me myself by those who happen to come across these papers, and have not read my writings.

[1] Regius.

The following is the Programme in the form in which it finally saw the light:—

AN EXPLANATION of the Human Mind or Rational Soul: What it is, and what it may be.

I. *The Human Mind is that wherein the processes of thought[1] are first accomplished by man; and it consists of the faculty of thinking alone, and the inward principle.*

II. *So far as the laws of nature are concerned, they seem to allow that the mind may be either a substance, or a mode of a corporeal substance, or, if we follow some other philosophers who state that extension and thought are attributes inherent in certain substances, as in subjects, then, as these attributes are not mutually opposed but diverse, there is no reason why mind should not be an attribute co-existing in the same subject with extension, though the one attribute is not comprised in the concept of the other. Whatever we can conceive can exist. But mind can be conceived, so that it can be any one of the aforesaid, for none of them involves a contradiction. Therefore it may be any one of these things.*

III. *Hence they are in error who assert that we conceive the human mind clearly and distinctly, as though it were necessarily[2] and really distinct from the body.*

IV. *The fact that mind is in truth nothing other than a substance, or an entity really distinct from body, in actuality separable from it, and capable of existing apart and independently[3], is revealed to us in Holy Scripture, in many places. And thus what in the view of some, the study of nature leaves doubtful[4] is already placed beyond all doubt for us through divine revelation in Scripture.*

V. *Nor is it any objection that we may have doubts about the body, but in nowise about the mind. For this only proves that, so long as we doubt about body, we cannot say that mind is a mode of body.*

VI. *The human mind, though it is a substance really distinct from body, is nevertheless, so long as it is in the body, organic in all its activities. And therefore as there are diverse dispositions of the body, so there are correspondingly diverse processes[5] of the mind.*

---

[1] actiones cogitativae.
[2] Sive actu (note in the first edition). [3] per se.
[4] Si accuratam et non moralem rerum veritatem et cognitionem quæramus (note in first edition). [5] cogitationes.

VII. *As mind is of a nature diverse from body, and from the disposition of body, and cannot arise from this disposition, therefore it is incorruptible.*

VIII. *As it has no parts and no extension in its concept, it is idle to speculate whether it exists as a whole in the whole, and is present as a whole in each individual part.*

IX. *As mind can be affected in equal degree by things imaginary and by things real, hence[1] the study of Nature leaves us doubtful whether any material things are really perceived by us. But even this doubt is banished by divine revelation in Holy Writ, whereby it is beyond all doubt that God created heaven and earth, and all that in them is, and even now conserves them.*

X. *The bond which maintains body and soul in union is the law of the unchangeableness of Nature whereby every individual thing persists in the state in which it is, until it is thrown out of that state by some other thing.*

XI. *As mind is a substance and is first brought into existence at the moment of generation, the most accurate opinion seems to be that of those who hold that the rational soul is brought into existence by God, at generation, by an immediate act of creation.*

XII. *The mind has no need of innate ideas, or notions, or axioms, but of itself the faculty of thinking suffices for the accomplishment of its processes[2].*

XIII. *Therefore all common notions, engraven on the mind, owe their origin to the observation of things or to tradition.*

XIV. *In fact the very idea of God which is implanted in the mind, is the outcome of divine revelation, or of tradition, or of observation.*

XV. *Our concept of God, or the idea of God which exists in our mind, is not an argument strong enough to prove the existence of God, since all things do not exist of which concepts are observed within us; and this idea, as conceived by us, and that imperfectly, does not, more than the concept of any other thing, transcend our proper powers of thought.*

---

[1] Non moraliter, sed exquisitam et accuratam rerum veritatem quærenti (note in first edition).

[2] actiones.

XVI.   *The thought of the mind is twofold : intellect and will.*

XVII.   *Intellect is perception and judgment.*

XVIII.   *Perception is sense, memory, and imagination.*

XIX.   *All sensation is the perception of some corporeal movement, which requires no intentional images*[1] *and it is effected, not in the outward channels of sense, but in the brain alone.*

XX.   *The will is free, and inclines indifferently to opposites in nature, as our self-consciousness bears us witness.*

XXI.   *Will is self-determined, and is to be termed blind no more than vision is to be termed deaf.*

'No men more easily attain a great reputation for piety than the superstitious and the hypocrites[2].'

The following is an examination of the programme.

Notes to the Title.

I observe *in the title*[3] a promise is made, not of bare assertions regarding the rational soul, but of an explanation of it, so that we must needs believe that in this programme are contained all, or at least, the principal arguments[4], which the author had, not only for proving his propositions, but also for unfolding them, and that no other arguments are to be expected from him. In that he terms the *rational soul 'the human mind*[5],' he has my approbation, for thus he avoids the ambiguity of the word *soul*[6] and in this point follows me.

Notes to the Individual Articles.

In the first article[7] he seems to aim at a *definition* of the rational soul, with imperfect success, for he omits the genus (i.e. that it is a substance, or a mode, or something else) and he expounds only the *differentia*, which he has borrowed from me, for no one before me, so far as I know, asserted that mind consisted in *one thing alone*, namely the *faculty of thinking and the inward source* (sc. of thinking).

In the second article[8] he begins to speculate about its genus, and

---

[1] species intentionales.
[2] vide 'Principles,' Vol. I, p. 217.   This aphorism reproduced at the end of Regius' poster is a saying of Descartes.
[3] p. 432.   [4] rationes.   [5] p. 432.   [6] anima.
[7] p. 432.   [8] p. 432.

says that '*the laws of nature seem to allow that the human mind may be either a substance, or a mode of a corporeal substance.*'

This assertion involves a contradiction, no less than if he had said, 'The laws of nature allow that a mountain can exist with or without a valley.' For a distinction must be drawn between things which from their nature can change, like the facts that I am at present either writing or not writing, that one man is prudent, another imprudent; and things which never change, such as are all the things that pertain to the essence of anything, as is generally acknowledged by philosophers. Of course there is no doubt that it can be said of contingent things that the laws of nature permit these things to be either one way or another—for instance, the fact that I am at present either writing or not writing. But when the point at issue is the essence of something, it is manifestly foolish and contradictory to say that the laws of nature allow that it may be after any fashion save the fashion after which it really is. Nor does it more pertain to the nature of a mountain that it cannot exist without a valley, than to the nature of the human mind that it is what it is, namely, that it is a substance, if substance it be, or, indeed, that it is a mode of a corporeal substance, if in truth it be such a mode. Of this *our friend* endeavours at this point to convince us, and to prove it throws in these words, '*or if we are to follow some other philosophers* etc.[1],' while by '*other philosophers*' he obviously means myself, for I was the first to consider thought the predominant attribute of immaterial substance, and extension the predominant attribute of material substance. But I did not say that these attributes were inherent in the substances, as in subjects diverse from themselves. Here we must beware of understanding by the word 'attribute' nothing other than 'mode.' Whenever we see a quality assigned to anything by nature, whether it be a mode that can suffer change, or the very essence of that thing, manifestly unchangeable, we term that quality its attribute. Thus in God there are many attributes, but no modes. Thus too one of the attributes of any substance is this, that it exists *per se*. Thus the extension of any body can, within itself, admit diverse modes, for it is one mode of its extension, if that body be spherical, another if it be square; but extension itself, which is the subject of these modes, is not in itself a mode of material substance, but an attribute, because it constitutes the essence and nature of material substance.

[1] p. 432.

Thus, finally, the modes of thought are diverse, for affirmation is a different mode of thought from negation, and so on; but thought itself, being the inward source[1] from which these modes arise, and in which they are inherent, is not conceived as a mode, but as an attribute which constitutes the nature of a substance. Whether thought be material, or immaterial, is the question at present before us.

He adds that '*these attributes are not mutually opposed, but diverse*[2].' In these words again there is a contradiction, for when the question concerns attributes that constitute the essence of substances, there can be no greater opposition between them than the fact that they are different. Once it is admitted that 'this is different from that,' it is equivalent to saying that 'this is not that'; but to be and not to be are contraries. '*Since they are not mutually opposed,*' he says, '*but different, there is no reason why mind should not be an attribute co-existing in the same subject with extension, though the one attribute is not comprised in the concept of the other.*' In these words there is an obvious fallacy, for he comes to a conclusion with regard to every possible attribute, which can be valid only in the case of modes properly so called; and yet he nowhere proves that the mind, or inward principle of thought, is such a mode. On the contrary, from his own words in *Article* V I will soon demonstrate that it is not so. Of the other attributes which constitute the natures of things, it cannot be said that those which are different, and of which neither is contained in the concept of the other, are co-existent in one and the same subject, for that is equivalent to saying that one and the same subject has two different natures, and this involves a contradiction, at least so long as the subject in question is simple and not composite—as in the present case.

Three points are to be noted here, a sufficient grasp of which would have prevented this writer from falling into such obvious errors.

First: It belongs to the theory of modes that, though we can easily comprehend a substance apart from a mode, we cannot, conversely, clearly comprehend a mode unless at the same time we conceive the substance of which it is a mode (as I have explained in the *first part of the Principles, Article* LXI[3]), and on this point all philosophers are agreed. That *our friend* however paid no respect

---

[1] Principium.　　　　[2] p. 432.　　　　[3] Vol. i, pp. 239, 240.

to this rule, is manifest from his *5th Article*. In that passage he admits that '*we can doubt about the existence of the body, while, at the same time, we do not doubt about the existence of the mind*[1].' Hence it follows that the mind can be comprehended by us apart from the body, and, accordingly, is not a mode of the body.

The *second point* which I would note here is the difference between simple and composite entities[2]. A composite entity is one in which are found two or more attributes, any one of which can be comprehended distinctly apart from the other, for it is from the fact that one can be thus cognised without the other, that each of these constituent elements is seen to be, not a mode of the others, but a thing, or the attribute of a thing which can exist without that attribute. A simple entity is one in which such attributes are not found. Hence it is clear that that subject in which we understand extension only, with the various modes of extension, is a simple entity. So, too, is a subject in which we comprehend thought only, with the various modes of thought. But that in which we observe extension and thought co-existent is a composite entity, to wit, a Man, who consists of soul and body. *Our author* seems to assume that man is body alone and that mind is but a mode of body.

Finally, we must note here that in subjects compounded of several substances there is frequently one substance predominant. This we contemplate in such a way as to treat any of the remaining substances which we connect with it as nothing more than a mode. Thus a *man* clad may be contemplated as a compound of man and clothes, but the being clad, in comparison with the man, is only a mode, although garments are substances. In the same way *our author* might, in the case of man, who is a compound of soul and body, consider body the predominant element, in relation to which the being animate, or the possession of thought, is nothing other than a mode. But it is foolish to infer from that, that the mind itself, or that through which the body thinks, is not a substance different from the body.

This dictum he endeavours to corroborate by means of the following syllogism: '*Whatever we can conceive can exist. But the mind can be conceived as one of the aforesaid* (viz. a substance, or a mode of a corporeal substance); *for none of these things involves a contradiction. Therefore etc.*' Here it must be noted that though the rule, '*whatever we can conceive can exist,*'

---

[1] Vol. I, p. 432.   [2] *entia.*

is mine, and true, so long as the question concerns a clear and distinct concept, in which is contained the possibility of the thing to be realised[1] (because God can bring into being everything which we clearly perceive to be possible), nevertheless we must not make rash use of it. A man might quite easily imagine that he rightly understood something which in reality he did not understand, being utterly blinded by some sort of prejudice. This is the case of *our author* when he maintains that there is no contradiction involved in the statement that one and the same thing possesses either of two natures which are utterly incompatible, to wit, that it is a substance, *or* a mode. If he had only said that he perceived no reasons for believing the human mind to be an immaterial substance rather than a mode of a material substance, his ignorance might have been excused. If he had said that no reasons could be found by the brain of man to prove either alternative, his arrogance would certainly have been reprehensible, but his statement would have evinced no contradiction. But when he says that the '*laws of nature allow that the same thing may be a substance, or a mode,*' his words are altogether self-contradictory and betray the irrationality of his brain.

In the third article he makes known his judgment concerning me. For it was *I* who wrote that 'the human mind can be clearly and distinctly perceived as a substance different from corporeal substance.' *Our friend,* however, though he relies on no other arguments than those self-contradictory ones which he has unfolded in the preceding article, proclaims that I am in error. Of that I make no account. Nor do I examine the words '*of necessity*' or '*in actuality,*' which contain a certain ambiguity; for they are not of great moment.

Moreover, I scruple to examine the statements regarding Holy Writ in the *fourth article*[2], lest I should appear to assume the right of investigating another man's religion. Thus much I will say : Here one must distinguish between three types of questions. Certain things are believed through faith alone. Such are the mystery of the Incarnation, the Trinity, and the like. Others, however, though they have a certain bearing on faith, can nevertheless be investigated by the natural reason[3]. Among these are generally ranked by the orthodox theologians the existence of God, and the distinction of mind from body. Finally, there are others which

---

[1] rei.   [2] p. 432.   [3] ratio naturalis.

belong in no wise to the sphere of faith, but only to the sphere of human reason, e.g. the question of the squaring of the circle or of making gold by the art of alchemy. And even as these men abuse the words of Holy Scripture, who, from a distorted interpretation of it presume to elicit these last questions, so do those others diminish its authority who undertake to solve the first type of question by arguments sought from philosophy alone. Nevertheless all theologians contend that these questions should be shown to be in nowise incompatible with the light of nature[1], and to this end they direct their most zealous endeavours. As for questions of the second class, not only do they deem them in no way incompatible with the light of nature, but they even exhort philosophers to solve these questions, so far as in them lies, by theories evolved from the mind of man. But never have I seen any one who would affirm that the laws of nature allow that anything should be otherwise than Holy Scripture teaches, unless he wished to show indirectly that he had no faith in Scripture. For as we were born men before we became Christians, it is beyond belief that any man should seriously embrace opinions which he thinks contrary to that right reason that constitutes a man, in order that he may cling to the faith through which he is a Christian.

But perhaps *our author* does not imply this, for his words are, '*Through study of nature some may find doubtful that which is already placed beyond all doubt for us by the Divine Revelation in Holy Writ.*' In these words I find a two-fold contradiction. In the first place, in that he assumes the doctrine that the essence of one and the same thing, which must be assumed always to remain the same (because, if it be supposed to become different, it will be by this very fact a different thing, to be indicated by a different name), is nevertheless, so far as the study of Nature goes, doubtful, and accordingly changeable. The second contradiction is in the word '*some*,' because, as Nature is the same for all men[2] a thing that can be doubtful only to 'some' is not doubtful according to Nature's showing[3].

The fifth article is to be related to the second rather than to the *fourth*, for in it the *author* is concerned, not with Divine Revelation, but with the nature of mind—the question as to whether it is a substance or a mode. To prove the defensibility of the view that mind is nothing other than a mode, he attempts to refute an

---

[1] lumen naturale.   [2] omnium eadem.   [3] per naturam.

objection taken from my writings. I wrote that we could not doubt that our mind existed, because, from the very fact that we doubted, it followed that our mind existed, but that meantime we might doubt whether any material things existed; whence I deduced and demonstrated that mind was clearly perceived by us as an existence, or substance, even supposing we had no concept whatever of the body, and denied that any material things had existence; and, accordingly, that the concept of mind did not involve any concept of body. This argument he thinks to explode by saying that '*it only proves that, so long as we doubt about the body, we cannot term mind a mode of body*[1].' Here he shows that he is utterly ignorant of what it is that philosophers term a 'mode'; for the nature of a mode consists in this, that it can by no means be comprehended, except it involve in its own concept the concept of the thing of which it is a mode—as I have explained above[2]. *Our friend*, however, admits that mind can sometimes be cognized apart from body, to wit, when there are doubts about the body; whence it assuredly follows that mind cannot be termed a mode of body. And what is sometimes true about the essence or nature of a thing is always true. Nevertheless he affirms that *the laws of nature allow that mind may be only a mode of body*[3]. These two statements are manifestly irreconcilable.

In the sixth article[4] I fail to apprehend his meaning. Certainly I remember hearing in the Schools that the *mind is an activity*[5] *of the organic body*, but till this day I never heard the mind itself termed 'organic.' For this reason I crave *our author's* indulgence, to the end that, as I have nothing certain to base my remarks on at this point, I may expound my conjectures, not as though they were true to fact, but simply as conjectures. I seem to observe two irreconcilable statements. One of these is to the effect that the human mind is a substance really distinct from the body. This *the author* openly states, but, so far as he can, waives argument on the point, and contends that it can be proved only by the authority of Holy Scripture. The other statement is that that same human mind, in all its activities, is *organic* or instrumental, that is to say, such that it does not act[6] of itself, but is used by the body as though it were something that strengthened its members[7] and other corporeal modes, and so he affirms in effect, if not in so many words, that *the mind is nothing other than a mode of body*, as though he

---

[1] p. 432. [2] p. 436. [3] p. 432. [4] p. 432.
[5] actus. [6] nihil agat. [7] membrorum suorum confirmatione.

had drawn up his whole artillery of argument to prove this point and this alone. These two statements are so manifestly contraries that I do not think *the author* wished them both, at one and the same time, to find credence with readers, but deliberately coupled them together, so that he might in some sort give satisfaction to the more simple-minded, and to his friends the theologians, by his citation of Scriptural authority, and that, meantime, his more keen-witted readers might realize that, when he said '*mind is distinct from body*,' he was speaking in irony, and that he was heart and soul of the opinion that mind is nothing but a mode.

In the seventh article again, *and the eighth*[1], he seems to be speaking merely in irony. And he retains the same Socratic figure of speech in *the latter part of article IX*[2]. But *in the first part* he appends a reason to his assertion, and thus, it would seem, is to be taken seriously in this passage. He teaches that, *so far as nature shows, it is doubtful whether any material things are really perceived by us*, and submits as his reason the statement that '*the mind can be affected in the same degree by things imaginary as by things real*.' If this theory is to be received as true, it must be granted that we have use of no understanding[3] properly so called, but only of that faculty which is usually termed the '*common sense*[4]' whereby impressions are received of things imaginary as much as of things real, so that they affect the mind—a faculty which philosophers commonly allow even to the brute creation. But surely those who have understanding, and are not fashioned like the horse or mule, even although they are affected not only by images of real things but also by those which occur in the brain from other causes (as happens in sleep), can distinguish the one kind of image from the other with the utmost clearness, by the light of reason. The method in which this happens, surely and infallibly, I have explained *in my writings*, so accurately that I am convinced that no one who has read them throughout, and is capable of understanding them, can be a sceptic.

In *the tenth and eleventh articles*[5] it is still possible to suspect him of irony. If the soul be believed to be a substance, it is foolish and ridiculous to say '*the bond which maintains body and soul in union is the law of the unchangeableness of nature, whereby every individual thing persists in the state in which it is*[6].' For it is equally true of things disunited as of things united that they persist in the same state so long as nothing changes that state.

---

[1] p. 433. [2] p. 433. [3] intellectus. [4] sensus communis.
[5] p. 433. [6] p. 433.

This is not at present the point at issue. The question is, how it happens that the mind is united with the body, and not dissevered from it. But if soul be supposed to be a mode of body, it is rightly said that no bond of union need be sought other than the fact that it persists in the state in which it is, since modes have no other state than that present to the things of which they are modes.

In article twelve[1] he appears to dissent from me only in words, for when he says that *the mind has no need of innate ideas, or notions, or axioms*, and at the same time allows it the faculty of thinking (to be considered natural or innate), he makes an affirmation in effect identical with mine, but denies it in words. For I never wrote or concluded that the mind required innate ideas which were in some sort different from its faculty of thinking; but when I observed the existence in me of certain thoughts which proceeded, not from extraneous objects nor from the determination of my will, but solely from the faculty of thinking which is within me, then, that I might distinguish the ideas or notions (which are the forms of these thoughts) from other thoughts *adventitious* or *factitious*, I termed the former '*innate*.' In the same sense we say that in some families generosity is innate, in others certain diseases like gout or gravel, not that on this account the babes of these families suffer from these diseases in their mother's womb, but because they are born with a certain disposition or propensity for contracting them.

The conclusion which he deduces in *article* XIII[2] from the preceding article is indeed wonderful. '*For this reason*,' he says (i.e. because the mind has no need of innate ideas, but the faculty of thinking of itself is sufficient), '*all common notions, engraven on the mind, owe their origin to the observation of things or to tradition*'— as though the faculty of thinking could of itself execute nothing, nor perceive nor think anything save what it received from observation or tradition, that is, from the senses. So far is this from being true, that, on the contrary, any man who rightly observes the limitations of the senses, and what precisely it is that can penetrate through this medium to our faculty of thinking must needs admit that no ideas of things, in the shape in which we envisage them by thought, are presented to us by the senses. So much so that in our ideas there is nothing which was not innate in the mind, or

---

[1] p. 432.   [2] p. 432.

faculty of thinking, except only these circumstances which point to experience—the fact, for instance, that we judge that this or that idea, which we now have present to our thought, is to be referred to a certain extraneous thing, not that these extraneous things transmitted the ideas themselves to our minds through the organs of sense, but because they transmitted something which gave the mind occasion to form these ideas, by means of an innate faculty, at this time rather than at another. For nothing reaches our mind from external objects through the organs of sense beyond certain corporeal movements, as *our author* himself affirms, in *article* XIX[1], taking the doctrine from my *Principles*; but even these movements, and the figures which arise from them, are not conceived by us in the shape they assume in the organs of sense, as I have explained at great length in my *Dioptrics*. Hence it follows that the ideas of the movements and figures are themselves innate in us. So much the more must the ideas of pain, colour, sound and the like be innate, that our mind may, on occasion of certain corporeal movements, envisage these ideas, for they have no likeness to the corporeal movements. Could anything be imagined more preposterous than that all common notions which are inherent in our mind should arise from these movements, and should be incapable of existing without them ? I should like *our friend* to instruct me as to what corporeal movement it is which can form in our mind any common notion, e.g. the notion that '*things which are equal to the same thing are equal to one another,*' or any other he pleases ; for all these movements are particular, but notions are universal having no affinity with movements and no relation to them.

He goes on to affirm, *in article* XIV[2], that even the idea of God which is in us is the outcome, not of our faculty of thinking, as being native to it, but of *Divine Revelation or tradition, or observation.* The error of this assertion we shall the more readily realise if we reflect that anything can be said to be the outcome of another, either because this other is its proximate and primary cause, without which it could not exist, or only because it is a remote and accidental cause, which, certainly, gives the primary cause occasion to produce its effect at one time rather than at another. Thus all workmen are the primary and proximate causes of their works, but those who give them orders, or promise them reward, that they may perform these works, are accidental and remote causes, because, probably, they would not have performed the tasks unbidden. There is no doubt that tradition or observation is a remote cause, inviting us to bethink ourselves of the idea which we may have of God, and to present it vividly to our thought. But no one can maintain that this is the proximate and efficient[1] cause, except the man who thinks that we can apprehend nothing regarding God save this name '*God*,' and the corporeal figure which painters exhibit to us as a representation of God. For observation, if it takes place through the medium of sight, can of its own proper power present nothing to the mind beyond pictures, and pictures consisting only of a permutation of corporeal movements, as *our author* himself instructs us. If it takes place through the medium of hearing, it presents nothing beyond words and voices; if through the other senses, it has nothing in it which can have reference to God. And surely it is manifest to every man that sight, of itself and by its proper function, presents nothing beyond pictures, and hearing nothing beyond voices or sounds, so that all these things that we think of, beyond these voices or pictures, as being symbolised by them, are presented to us by means of ideas which come from no other source than our faculty of thinking, and are accordingly together with that faculty innate in us, that is, always existing in us potentially; for existence in any faculty is not actual but merely potential existence, since the very word 'faculty' designates nothing more or less than a potentiality. But that with regard to God we can comprehend nothing beyond a name or a bodily effigy, no one can affirm, save a man who openly professes himself an atheist, and moreover destitute of all intellect.

After expounding his opinion concerning God, *our author*[2], *in article* XV, thinks to refute all the arguments by which I have proved God's existence. At this point it occurs to one to marvel at the man's self-confidence, in that he imagines that he can so easily and in so few words overturn all that I have built up by dint of long and concentrated meditation, and to the explanation of which I have devoted a whole volume. But all the arguments which I have adduced in this matter can be subordinated to *two*. *In the first place* I have shown that we have a notion or idea of God such that, when we sufficiently attend to it and ponder the matter in the manner I have expounded[3], we realise from this contemplation alone, that it cannot be but that God exists, since

---

[1] effectrix.   [2] p. 433.   [3] 'Medit.' Vol. I, p. 179.

existence, not merely possible or contingent as in the ideas of all other things, but altogether necessary and actual, is contained in this concept. This argument, which is held as certainly and obviously proved, not only by myself but by several others, and these men pre-eminent in learning and genius who have sedulously investigated the matter—this argument, I say, *the author of the Programme* thinks to refute in this fashion : ' *Our concept of God, or the idea of God which exists in our mind, is not an argument sufficiently strong to prove the existence of God, since all things do not exist of which concepts are observed within us*[1].' By these words he shows that he has read my writings, but has in nowise had either the power or the will to understand them. For the point of my argument is, not the idea in general, but its peculiar property, a property which is evident in the highest degree in the idea we have of God, and which can be found in the concept of no other thing, namely, the necessity of existence, which is required as that crown of perfections without which we cannot comprehend God. *The other* argument by which I proved the existence of God, I deduced from my clear proof of the fact that we should not have had the faculty for conceiving all the perfections which we recognise in God, had it not been true that God existed, and that we were created by Him[2]. This argument *our friend* thinks he has more than exploded by saying that *the idea we have of God does not, more than the concept of any other thing, transcend our proper powers of thinking*[3]. If by these words he only means that the concept which we have of God without the aid of supernatural grace is no less natural than all the concepts we have of other things, he is at one with me; but on that basis nothing can be concluded against me. If, however, he thinks that that concept does not involve more objective perfections than all the others taken together, he is obviously wrong. I myself, on the other hand, have founded my argument entirely on this preponderance of perfections, in which our concept of God transcends other concepts.

In the six remaining articles[4] there is nothing worthy of note except the fact that, when he wishes to distinguish the properties of the soul, he speaks of them confusedly and inappropriately. I have said[5] that these are all to be subordinated to two predominant properties, one of which is the perception of the understanding, the other the determination of the will. These two *our friend* calls

---

[1] p. 433. [2] 'Medit.' Vol. I, p. 157. [3] p. 433. [4] p. 434. [5] p. 434.

'*understanding*' and '*will*[1].' Then he subdivides what he calls '*understanding*' into '*perception*' and '*judgment*.' In this point he differs from me, for when I saw that, over and above perception, which is required as a basis for judgment, there must needs be affirmation, or negation, to constitute the form of the judgment, and that it is frequently open to us to withhold our assent, even if we perceive a thing, I referred the act of judging, which consists in nothing but *assent*, i.e. affirmation or negation, not to the perception of the understanding, but to the determination of the will. Thereafter he enumerates, among the species of perception, nothing but *sense, memory*, and *imagination*[2]; from which one may gather that he admits no *pure intellection* (i.e. intellection which deals with no corporeal images), and, accordingly, that he himself believes that no cognition is possessed of God, or of the human mind, or of other immaterial things. Of this I can imagine but one cause, namely, that the thoughts he has concerning these things are so confused that he never observes in himself a pure thought, different from every corporeal image.

Finally, in closing[3], he adds these words, taken from some portion of my writings: '*No men more easily attain a great reputation for piety, than the superstitious and the hypocrites.*' What he means by these words I fail to see, unless perhaps he ascribes to hypocrisy the use he has made of irony, in many places, but I do not think that by that means he can attain a great reputation for piety.

For the rest, I am constrained to admit here, that I am covered with shame to think that in time past I lauded *this author* as a man of most penetrative genius, and wrote somewhere or other that 'I did not think he taught any doctrines which I should be unwilling to acknowledge as my own[4].' But in truth when I wrote these words I had as yet seen no specimen of his work in which he was not a faithful copyist, except only on one occasion in one little phrase[5], which brought such ill results to him, that I hoped he would make no further venture in that line; and, as I saw him in other matters embrace with a great show of zeal the opinions that I deemed nearest the truth, I attributed this to his genius and penetration. But now a manifold experience compels me to conclude that he is swayed not so much by love of truth as by love of novelty. As he holds all he has learned from others to be old-world and out-worn, thinking nothing sufficiently novel except what

---

[1] p. 434. [2] p. 434. [3] p. 434.
[4] Letter to Voetius. [5] Hominem esse ens per accidens.

he has hammered out of his own brain; and, at the same time, is so unhappy in his inventions, that I have never noted a single word in his writings (excluding what he transcribed from other men), which I did not condemn as containing some error, I must therefore warn all those who are convinced that he is a champion of my opinions, that of these opinions—I speak, not only of those in the *Metaphysics*, on which he openly opposes me, but also of those in the *Physics*, for he treats of this subject somewhere in his writings —there is none which he does not state awry and distort. Hence it causes me more indignation that such a Doctor should handle my writings and undertake to interpret, or in other words, to falsify them, than that other men should attack them with the utmost bitterness.

For I never yet saw one of these bitter critics who did not father on me opinions different from mine by a whole heaven, and so maundering and preposterous, that I had no fear that any man of intelligence could be persuaded that they were mine. Thus, even as I write these words, two new pamphlets are brought me—productions of an adversary of this type[1]. In the first of these it is stated that '*There are some Neoterics who deny all credibility to the senses, who contend that the Philosophers deny God, and dare to doubt His existence, and who, meantime, admit that there are implanted by Nature in the human mind actual notions, species, and ideas of God.*' In the second it is said that '*these Neoterics barefacedly proclaim that God is, not only negatively, but positively, the efficient cause of Himself.*' In either pamphlet the only thing effected is the conglomeration of numerous arguments to prove, first, that we have no *actual* knowledge (*cognitio*) of God in our mother's womb, and accordingly that '*no actual species or idea of God is inborn in our mind*'; secondly, that '*we must not deny God*' and that '*they are atheists and punishable by law who deny Him*'; and thirdly and finally that '*God is not the efficient* cause of Himself.*'

I might well suppose that all these *dicta* were not directed against me, because my name is not mentioned in the pamphlets, and of the opinions attacked in them there is none which I do not think absurd and erroneous. Nevertheless, as they are not dissimilar to those which have often ere now been slanderously imputed to me by men of that kidney, and as there are no other

[1] Pamphlets by Jacques de Rives (Jacobus Revius).

persons recognizable to whom these opinions could be attributed; as, finally, there are many who do not doubt that I am the object of attack in these pamphlets, I take this occasion to admonish their author to this effect:

First:—By innate ideas I never understood anything other than that which he himself, on page 6 of his second pamphlet, affirms in so many words to be true, viz. that '*there is innate in us by nature a potentiality whereby we know God*'; but that these ideas are *actual*, or that they are some kind of species different from the faculty of thought I never wrote nor concluded. On the contrary, I, more than any other man, am utterly averse to that empty stock of scholastic entities—so much so, that I cannot refrain from laughter when I see that mighty heap which our hero—a very inoffensive fellow no doubt—has laboriously brought together to prove that *infants have no notion of God so long as they are in their mother's womb*—as though in this fashion he was bringing a magnificent charge against me.

Secondly:—I have never taught that *God is to be denied, or that He can deceive us, or that one must doubt about everything, or that all credibility is to be denied to the senses, or that sleep cannot be distinguished from waking,* or the like—doctrines which are sometimes thrown in my teeth by ignorant detractors. I have repudiated all these doctrines expressly and with the strongest arguments—stronger, I make bold to say, than any that have by any man before me been brought to the refutation of these doctrines. That I might the more fittingly and effectively compass this end, I proposed, at the beginning of my Meditations, to regard as doubtful all the doctrines which did not owe their original discovery to me, but had been for long denounced by the sceptics[1]. What could be more unjust than to attribute to a writer opinions which he states only to the end that he may refute them? What more foolish than to imagine that, at least for the time being, while these false opinions are being propounded previous to their refutation, the author commits himself to them, and that, accordingly, the man who states the arguments of the Atheists *is an Atheist for the time*? What more childish than to say that, if he were to die meantime, before writing or evolving the *hoped for refutation* he would die an Atheist—that he taught pernicious doctrine merely as a preliminary, but that '*evil should not be done that good may*

[1] Vol. I, pp. 144—149.

come of it' and so forth? Some one will say, perhaps, that I related these false opinions, not as the opinions of others, but as my own. But what of that? In the self-same book in which I related them I refuted them all. From the very title of the book it might be understood that I was altogether hostile to these beliefs, for it purports to give *'proofs of the existence of God.'* Is there anyone obtuse enough to think that the man who compiled such a book was ignorant, so long as he was penning its first pages, of what he had undertaken to prove in the following? I enunciated the objections as though they were my own, to suit the exigencies of the style of 'meditations,' which I judged the style best fitted for unfolding arguments. If this explanation does not satisfy our captious critics, I should like to know what they say of Holy Scripture—with which no human documents are to be compared—when they see in it some things that cannot be rightly understood unless they be supposed to be the utterance of impious men, or, at least, of others than the Holy Ghost and the Prophets? Such are Ecclesiastes, chap. ii., these words *'There is nothing better for a man than that he should eat and drink, and that he should make his soul enjoy good in his labour. This also I saw that it was from the hand of God. For who can eat or who else can hasten thereunto more than I?'* and, in the following chapter, *'I said in mine heart concerning the estate of the sons of men, that God might manifest them, and that they might see that they themselves are beasts; for that which befalleth the sons of men befalleth beasts; even one thing befalleth them: as the one dieth so dieth the other: yea they have all one breath: so that a man hath no pre-eminence above a beast,'* etc. Do they believe that here the Holy Spirit teaches us that we should indulge the belly, and have abundance of delights, and that our souls are no more immortal than the souls of beasts? I do not think they are so mad. Neither should they calumniate me because in writing I have not made use of the precautions which are observed by some other writers, but not by the Holy Spirit.

In the third place, and finally, I warn the author of these pamphlets that I never wrote that *'God should be said to be, not only negatively, but positively, the efficient cause of Himself,'* as he affirms in a very rash and ill-considered manner in page 8 of his second pamphlet. Let him turn over, read, and thoroughly search my writings, he will find in them nothing like this, but the very reverse. The fact that I am far indeed from accepting such monstrous opinions is well known to all who have read my writings, or have any knowledge of myself, or, at any rate, do not think me utterly fatuous. On this account I am only moved to wonder what is the aim of these detractors; for if they wish to convince any one that I wrote things of which the very contrary is found in my writings, they should have taken the preliminary precaution of suppressing all my publications, and should even have wiped out the memory of them from the minds of those who had already read them; for so long as they fail to effect this they do themselves more harm than me. Moreover, I marvel that they should inveigh with such bitterness and such zeal against me, who have never troubled them, nor done them any hurt, though, perhaps, possessing the power to hurt them if they provoked me; and meantime should take no action against many other men who devote whole books to the refutation of their doctrine, and ridicule them as simpletons and blindfold gladiators[1]. But I am unwilling to add any word here that might make them renounce their habit of impugning me in their pamphlets. I am glad to see that they think me of so much importance. Meantime I pray Heaven to grant them sanity.

Written at Egmond, in Holland,
    towards the end of December 1647.

---

[1] 'Simplicios et Andabatas.' Andabatae were Roman gladiators whose masks had no opening for the eyes and who fought blind in order to amuse the spectators.

INDEX TO VOLUME I

OTHER DOVER BOOKS ON PHILOSOPHY

AND SCIENCE

Abbott, Edwin A. FLATLAND. Introduction by Banesh Hoffman. 128pp. 5 3/8 x 8.   **Paperbound $1.00**

Abro, A. d'. THE EVOLUTION OF SCIENTIFIC THOUGHT: FROM NEWTON TO EINSTEIN. Second revised and enlarged edition. 21 diagrams. 15 portraits. xx + 481pp. 5 3/8 x 8.   **Clothbound $3.95**

Abro, A. d'. THE RISE OF THE NEW PHYSICS. Second revised edition. Two volume set. 994pp. 38 portraits. 5 3/8 x 8.
The Set: **Paperbound $3.90**

Adams, F. D. THE BIRTH AND DEVELOPMENT OF THE GEOLOGICAL SCIENCES. 79 illustrations. 15 full page plates. v + 506pp. 5 3/8 x 8.   **Clothbound $3.95**
Paperbound $1.95

Archimedes. WORKS (including 'The Method of Archimedes'). Edited by T. L. Heath. 506pp. 5 3/8 x 8.   **Clothbound $4.95**
Paperbound $1.95

Ayer, Alfred Jules. LANGUAGE, TRUTH AND LOGIC. Second revised edition. Index. 160pp. 5 3/8 x 8.   **Clothbound $2.50**
Paperbound $1.25

Bonola, Robert. NON-EUCLIDEAN GEOMETRY. Authorized English translation with additional appendices by H. S. Carslaw and an introduction by Federigo Enriques. This new edition contains an appendix of the G. B. Halsted translations of Lobachevski's "The Theory of Parallels" and Bolyai's "The Science of Absolute Space." 431pp. 5 3/8 x 8.   Clothbound $3.95
Paperbound $1.90

Boole, George. LAWS OF THOUGHT. 448pp. 5 3/8 x 8.
Clothbound $4.50
Paperbound $1.90

Born, Max. THE RESTLESS UNIVERSE. Second revised edition. 120 drawings and figures. 12 plates. 3 tables. 315pp. 6 1/8 x 9¼.
Clothbound $3.95

Bragg, William, CONCERNING THE NATURE OF THINGS. 57 figures 32 plates. 264pp. 5 3/8 x 8.   Clothbound $2.75
Paperbound $1.25

Bridgman, P. W. THE NATURE OF PHYSICAL THEORY. Index. xi + 138pp. 5 3/8 x 8.   Clothbound $2.50
Paperbound $1.25

Butcher, S. H. ARISTOTLE'S THEORY OF POETRY AND FINE ART. Fourth revised edition. New introduction by John Gassner. lxxvi + 421pp. 6 1/8 x 9¼.   Clothbound $3.95
Paperbound $1.95

Campbell, Norman. WHAT IS SCIENCE? Index. 186pp. 5 3/8 x 8.
Paperbound $1.25

Cantor, Georg. CONTRIBUTIONS TO THE FOUNDING OF THE THEORY OF TRANSFINITE NUMBERS. Translated from German and with introduction and notes by Philip E. B. Jourdain. Bibliography. Index. ix + 211pp. 5 3/8 x 8.   Clothbound $2.75
Paperbound $1.25

Cassirer, Ernst. SUBSTANCE AND FUNCTION AND EINSTEIN'S THEORY OF RELATIVITY. Two books bound as one. Bibliography. Index. 465pp. 5 3/8 x 8.   Clothbound $3.95
Paperbound $1.95

Cassirer, Ernst. LANGUAGE AND MYTH. Translated by Susanne K. Langer. Index. x + 103pp. 5 3/8 x 8.　　　**Clothbound $2.50**
　　　Paperbound $1.25

De Morgan, Augustus. A BUDGET OF PARADOXES. Unabridged republication of the second edition, edited by D. E. Smith. New introduction by Prof. Ernest Nagel, Columbia University. Two volumes bound as one. Vol. I: viii + 407pp. Vol. II: 387pp. 5 3/8 x 8.
　　　Clothbound $4.95

Descartes, Rene. THE GEOMETRY. The complete French text in facsimile plus the complete translation by D. E. Smith and M. L. Latham. vii + 248pp. 5 3/8 x 8.　　　**Clothbound $2.95**
　　　Paperbound $1.50

Descartes, Rene. THE PHILOSOPHICAL WORKS OF DESCARTES. Translated by E. S. Haldane and G. R. T. Ross. An unabridged republication of the last corrected edition. Two volumes. Vol. I: vi + 452pp. Vol. II: viii + 300pp. 5 3/8 x 8.　　**The Set: Clothbound $7.90**
　　　The Set: Paperbound $3.90

Dewey, John. ESSAYS IN EXPERIMENTAL LOGIC. vii + 444pp. 5 3/8 x 8.　　　**Clothbound $3.50**
　　　Paperbound $1.75

Dreyer, J. L. E. A HISTORY OF ASTRONOMY FROM THALES TO KEPLER. (Formerly titled "History of Planetary Systems from Thales to Kepler.") 448pp. 5 3/8 x 8.　　　**Paperbound $1.95**

Einstein, Lorentz, Minkowski, and Weyl. THE PRINCIPLE OF REL-ATIVITY.. An English translation of eleven of the most important original papers on the general and special theories of relativity. Notes by Sommerfeld. Translation by Perrett and Jeffrey. viii + 216pp. 5 3/8 x 8.　　　**Clothbound $3.50**
　　　Paperbound $1.50

Hadamard, Jacques. THE PSYCHOLOGY OF INVENTION IN THE MATHEMATICAL FIELD. xiii + 145pp. 5 3/8 x 8.　**Clothbound $2.50**
　　　Paperbound $1.25

Struik, Dirk J. A CONCISE HISTORY OF MATHEMATICS. Second revised edition. Bibliography. Index. 47 illustrations. xix + 299pp. 5 x 7 3/8. **Paperbound $1.60**

Unamuno, Miguel de. THE TRAGIC SENSE OF LIFE. Translated by J. E. Crawford Flitch. Index. xxxv + 332pp. 5 3/8 x 8.

Clothbound $3.95
Paperbound $1.90

Wölfflin, Heinrich. PRINCIPLES OF ART HISTORY. The Problem of the Development of Style in Later Art. Translated from the seventh revised edition by M. D. Hottinger. 150 illustrations. xvi + 237pp. 6 1/8 x 9¼. **Clothbound $4.50**

Wulf, Maurice de. PHILOSOPHY AND CIVILIZATION IN THE MIDDLE AGES. 320pp. 5 3/8 x 8. **Clothbound $3.50**
Paperbound $1.50

Wulf, Maurice de. HISTORY OF MEDIAEVAL PHILOSOPHY. Translated by Ernest C. Messenger. (In three volumes.) 5 3/8 x 8. Vol. I: From the Beginnings to the End of the Twelfth Century. Bibliography. Index. 41pp. Introduction. xviii + 317pp. **Clothbound $4.00**
Vol. II: PHILOSOPHY IN THE THIRTEENTH CENTURY.

Clothbound $4.00
Vol. III: MEDIAEVAL PHILOSOPHY AFTER THE THIRTEENTH CENTURY. **Clothbound $4.00**

Available at your dealer or write Dover Publications, Inc., Dept. PH, 920 Broadway, New York 10, New York. Send for free catalog of Dover books on Philosophy.

Minnaert, M. THE NATURE OF LIGHT AND COLOUR IN THE OPEN AIR. Trans. by H. M. Kremer-Priest and K. E. Brian Jay. Index. 202 ill. including 42 photographs. xvi + 362pp. 5⅜ x 8.   **Clothbound $3.95**
    Paperbound $1.95

Newton, Isaac. OPTICKS. Preface by Professor I. B. Cohen. Foreword by Professor Albert Einstein. Intro. by E. T. Whittaker. cxv + 406pp. 4½ x 7.   **Paperbound $1.90**

Oparin, A. I. THE ORIGIN OF LIFE. New introduction by Dr. S. Morgulis. xxv + 270pp. 5⅜ x 8.
    Paperbound $1.70

Poincaré, Henri. SCIENCE AND HYPOTHESIS. Index. xxvii + 244pp. 5⅜ x 8.   **Clothbound $2.50**
    Paperbound $1.25

Poincaré, Henri. SCIENCE AND METHOD. Trans. by Francis Maitland. 288pp. 5⅜ x 8.   Clothbound $2.50
    Paperbound $1.25

Russell, Bertrand. ANALYSIS OF MATTER. With a new introduction by L. E. Denonn. viii + 408pp. 5⅜ x 8. (T)
    Clothbound $3.95
    Paperbound $1.95

Spinoza, Benedict de. THE CHIEF WORKS. Translated from the Latin with an Introduction by R. H. M. Elwes. Includes unabridged: Ethics, Political Treatise, Theologico-Political Treatise, and selected letters. Two volumes of the Bohn edition in one. 5⅜ x 8.   Clothbound $2.95

Spitta, Philipp. JOHANN SEBASTIAN BACH. Unabridged. Three volumes bound as two. 1840pp. 5⅜ x 8. (T)
    The Set: Clothbound $10.00

Struik, Dirk J. A CONCISE HISTORY OF MATHEMATICS. revised edition. Bibliog. Index. 47 ill. xix + 299pp. 5⅜ x 7⅜.   Paperbound $1.60

Unamuno, Miguel de. THE TRAGIC SENSE OF LIFE. Translated by J. E. Crawford Flitch. Index. xxxv + 332pp. 5⅜ x 8.   **Clothbound $3.95**
    Paperbound $1.90

THE GEOMETRY OF RENÉ DESCARTES

This is the only book on mathematics that Descartes wrote, and is of interest as an example of his principles in their purest form. First published in 1637, the book laid the groundwork for analytical geometry. Although classical mathematicians had combined geometry and algebra, Descartes was the first to use this technique systematically and fruitfully. "Not only did this new method make possible a systematic investigation of known curves," E. T. Bell has pointed out, "but what is of infinitely deeper significance, it potentially created a whole universe of geometric forms beyond conception by the synthetic method."

The Geometry had many important consequences. It led to the geometric interpretation of negative quantities. It established the idea of continuity, which in turn led to the theory of functions and the theory of limits. Descartes also made several valuable contributions to the theory of equations in this book, and introduced the letters a, b, and c to designate known quantities, and x, y, and z, unknown ones.

Now republished in an unabridged edition containing both the original French text (in facsimile) and the distinguished English translation of David Eugene Smith and Marcie L. Latham, *The Geometry* is a book that will be enjoyed by philosophers, mathematicians, and those concerned with the evolution of the deductive sciences. Notes. xii + 246pp. 5 3/8 x 8. Illustrated. Clothbound, $2.95. Paperbound, $1.50.